Guitar Masters

Guitar
Masters
INTIMATE PORTRAITS

ALAN DI PERNA

Hal Leonard Books
An Imprint of Hal Leonard Corporation

For Mom and Dad

Published in 2012 by Hal Leonard Books
An Imprint of Hal Leonard Corporation
7777 West Bluemound Road
Milwaukee, WI 53213

Trade Book Division Editorial Offices
33 Plymouth St., Montclair, NJ 07042

Printed in the United States of America

Book design by Damien Castaneda

Library of Congress Cataloging-in-Publication Data is available upon request.

ISBN 978-1-4234-8988-7

www.halleonardbooks.com

CONTENTS

Meeting the Masters

IT WAS THE WINTER OF 1966. Folk rock was coming on strong as the British Invasion's rightful successor. Psychedelia was just a rosy glow on the horizon. And I'd just gotten my first electric guitar. The instrument itself wasn't much, a Tiesco Del Rey thinline hollow body with a commensurately crappy amp. But could there have been a better time in all of history to take up the electric guitar?

There was so much to explore. Dylan and the Byrds had flung wide open the door to folk music with its rich fingerpicked and flatpicked legacy. The Stones, the Animals, and others had opened that Pandora's box called the blues, another treasure trove of arcane guitar lore. The Beatles, the Yardbirds, and others were soon to shine a light on ragas from India. Guitar music was everywhere. The crystalline jangle of electric twelve-strings, the sprung reverb poetry of surf music, the primordial raunch of garage rock . . .

Ah, yes, garage rock. Suburban garage bands were the outsider art medium through which all of these guitar influences were being interpreted, deciphered, and, quite often, mutilated during the crucial years of the mid-sixties. Armed with a cheap Japanese guitar, spotted mod shirt, and Beatles boots, I eagerly joined the garage band army at about age fourteen.

One's first experience of what multiple electric guitars sound like when played live, and more or less in tune, together is a profoundly powerful, life-changing thing. In early garage band epiphanies, I remember being struck by how unlike records the whole thing sounded. A billion times worse in one regard, but undeniably more exciting. There was something in the buzzy, crackling rawness coming out of the amps. The thuggish thud of the drums. I was hooked.

At that very same moment in history, hundreds of thousands, perhaps even millions, of adolescents all over the globe were plugging into the same mystical experience. The Holy Communion of the electric guitar. The supreme brotherhood of garage rock. Just a few years later, Jimi Hendrix would call it something similar, the Electric Sky Church.

Much has been written—a good deal of it by me—about how the electric guitar changed the sound and essential nature of popular music in the middle years of the twentieth century, launching a counterculture youth revolution as a sideline. And much of this cultural history has focused on the tremendous advances in electric guitar technology that took place from roughly the 1930s to the 1970s, and the work of pioneers like Leo Fender, Ted McCarty, Paul Bigsby, Jim Marshall, Roger Mayer, and others. All of this is undeniably true. But none of it would mean a damn thing had it not been for the visionary guitar players who adopted this fledgling technology and, each in his own way, made glorious, game-changing, populist, heart-wrenchingly beautiful art out of the stuff.

It is to these supremely gifted individuals that the present volume is devoted. The guitar masters profiled here have all played key roles in shaping the way we all think about the electric guitar and how we all go about playing the thing. Chronologically, this book places special emphasis on players whose greatest contributions fall into the years between the birth of rock and roll, circa 1955, and the music's eventual, inevitable enshrinement as something called classic rock somewhere in the mid- to late seventies.

It's not that there haven't been innovations after that. There have been plenty. But the first two or three decades of the rock-and-roll era were the crucible. The solid-body electric guitar was just coming into its own at that time. The field was wide open. There was no rule book. There were no guitar magazines until the end of the period in question. Nor were there any instruction books that seriously addressed techniques used in the "barbaric" triumvirate of rock, blues, and country. And there was certainly no Google.

So popular music provided a forum for guitar experimentation free of any orthodoxy or burden of tradition. For a long time, the music was considered, quite frankly, garbage—which gave innovators like the ones profiled here *carte blanche* to do whatever the hell they wanted, to go wherever their hearts, imaginations, and keen ears led them. Sure there were antecedents in earlier manifestations of blues, country, and even jazz. But what one did with those antecedents was entirely a matter of one's own instincts, proclivities, and individual genius.

This unique creative opportunity tended to bring quite a cast of characters out of the woodwork. And in this book you will meet some of these characters, up close and personal, as it were. The other magnificent thing about the vacuum tube transduction magic that made the electric guitar possible is that it also gave rise to television and radio—the great social equalizers of the mid-twentieth century. So the significant guitar innovators came to us from all walks of life. The electric guitar has always been an equal opportunity instrument.

In my work as a music journalist over the past thirty-two years, it has been my immense privilege, crazy good karma, and profound pleasure to spend quite a bit of time in the company of many of the world's great guitar masters. Imagine getting to sit around for hours on end with someone like Jeff Beck or Buddy Guy and ask, "How did you do that? Where did *that* come from?" And to be answered graciously and patiently in most cases. And then to have the opportunity to share that wealth of info with guitar fiends everywhere.

But what any experienced and capable interviewer sooner or later realizes is that celebrated musicians—celebrities of any variety—are people just like anyone else. They're exceptionally good at one thing—playing the guitar in this case—but otherwise subject to the same foibles, follies, and calamities that beset the rest of us. Musical genius doesn't exempt one from accidents, addictions, afflictions, divorce, estrangements, feuds, fights, financial setbacks, incarceration, litigation, rip-offs, and all the other nasty stuff that life throws our way. Nor, fortunately, does the music gift cancel out life's other enduring blessings: love, friendship, family, financial security, and a sense of purpose.

All of these things have been woven into the profiles of the guitar masters collected in this volume—not in a sensationalist way, hopefully, but with an attentive awareness of the many ways in which art and life are connected. When you combine the artistry and personal life passages of these great players with the ways in which they responded to and impacted the music and culture of their times, you begin to arrive at a complete sense of what makes each one of these individuals so unique.

Some of the material in this book is derived from feature and cover story interviews I've done over the years, a good deal of them for the pages of *GuitarWorld* magazine. However, I conducted a substantial amount of brand-new interviews for the present work as well. As much as possible, I've endeavored to let the artists speak for themselves, but in some cases I've selectively added observations from bandmates, girlfriends, managers, and other key eyewitnesses, who all add valuable perspective.

It has also been a key concern of mine to provide the necessary historical and critical contexts—a sense of the tremendous excitement generated by the work of these guitar masters, and how this incredible music sounded and *felt* at the time it was first released. Although only a few scant decades separate our present time from the events in these chapters, recent rapid advances in digital technology have rendered even the recent past as remote as ancient times in many ways. From this somewhat abruptly telescoped perspective, it seems clear that what we are a looking back on is a golden age of guitar playing. We may never see its like again.

Alan di Perna, 2012

Guitar Masters

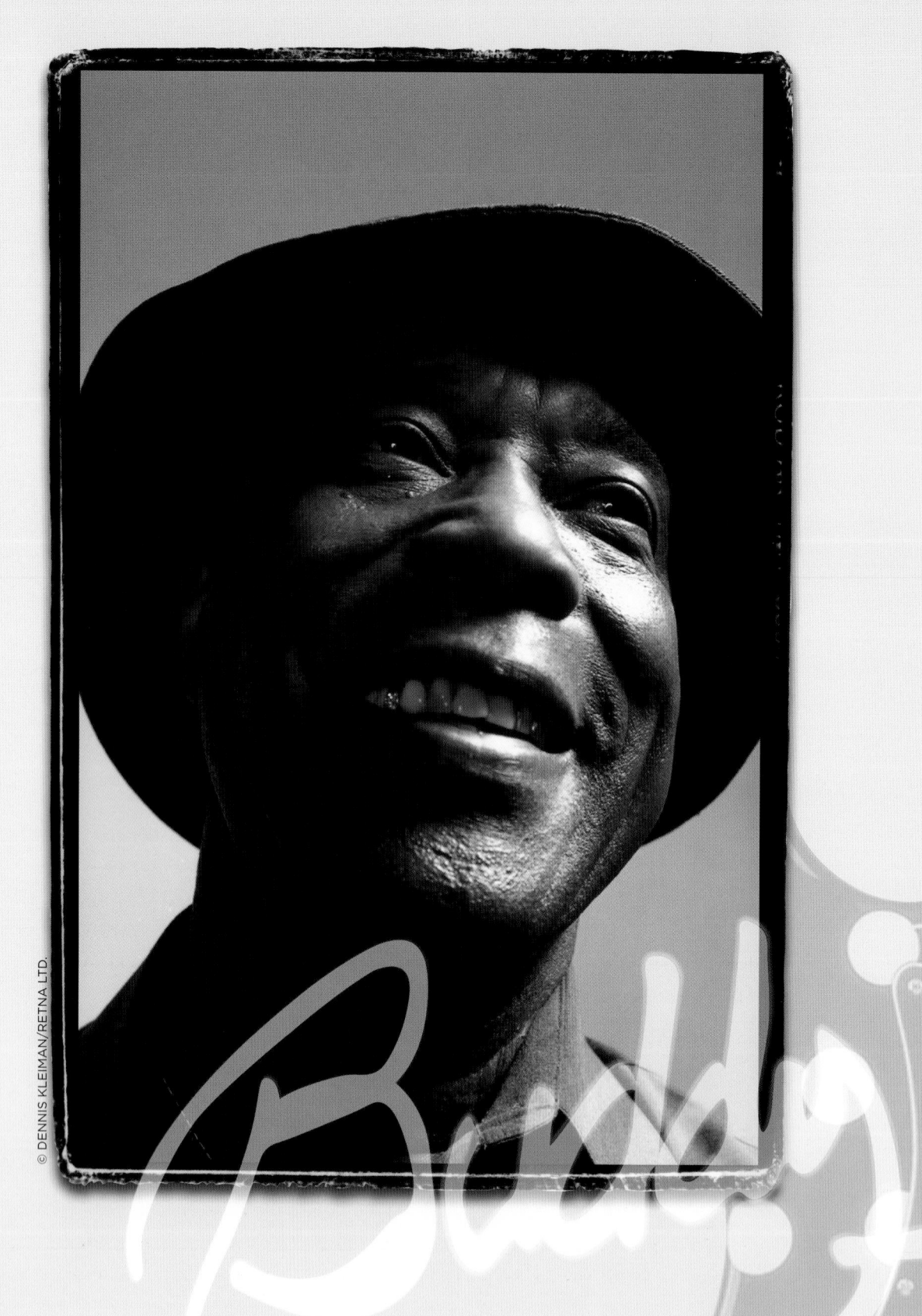

Buddy

Buddy Guy

A LIFETIME IN THE BLUES

WHEN BUDDY GUY WAS JUST A BOY, he was so crazy to hear his family's 78-rpm recording of John Lee Hooker's "Boogie Chillin'" that he'd take a necktie stick pin, place it between his teeth, and use it as a stylus to ride the grooves while the disc rotated so he could hear the song. "You could take a straw outta a broom and do the same thing," he adds.

The aspiring guitarist's skull served as the resonating amplifier for Hooker's music—a direct transmission from the master. The profound depth and unswerving fidelity of Buddy Guy's devotion to the blues is both the key to his extraordinary power as a performer and the inspiration he provides for all who would dedicate their lives to this music. "I Can't Quit the Blues" was the title of a seminal Buddy Guy track from 1968, which later lent its name to a box set compendium of landmark tracks from the man's half-century-plus life's work.

Can't quit the blues? The blues is like a drug. The blues is like whiskey. The blues is like that street corner gal that you know you shouldn't go near, yet you can't help yourself. The blues is like life: sweet to the taste yet filled with pain. This is the essential truth of Buddy

Guy and his music. The blues is something he just can't quit. Because to do so would be to give up on life itself.

"Blues has got a part in this world, as far as music is concerned," Buddy once said. "If I quit, who's gonna be playing it? I don't think you're gonna look up one day and see me gone away. You'll say, 'He did it till he died.' That's how I feel about it.

Buddy Guy's lifelong passion for the blues is one of America's cultural treasures. He is our greatest living link between the blues' storied past and its vital present. This is a man who sat and played with immortals like Muddy Waters, Howlin' Wolf, Willie Dixon, Little Walter, and Otis Spann, and who still climbs up onstage at events like the Crossroads Guitar Festival to jam with greats like Eric Clapton and Jeff Beck. He's heavily invested in recording and performing with next-generation bluesmen as well, guys like John Mayer, Jimbo Mathus, Derek Trucks, and Robert Randolph. These days, it just isn't a guitar or blues festival without Buddy Guy and his iconic polka-dot Fender Stratocaster. When you see that man and that guitar, you know you're about to encounter the timeless truth of the living blues.

There would have been no Jimi Hendrix without Buddy Guy. Eric Clapton is another major acolyte and has repeatedly called Buddy "the greatest living guitarist." Stevie Ray Vaughan would never have picked up a Fender Stratocaster without Buddy's inspiration. As blues guitarists go, they just don't come any better. His sense of phrasing is utterly unique. Terse bursts of staccato notes that seem hardwired to the emotional logic of choked-back tears. Languorous legato passages that plead and seduce. Buddy's peerless guitar tone and style seem an extension of his emotive, gospel-inflected vocal delivery. He can make those steel strings wail and growl in all the right places. Astoundingly agile, he can make a Stratocaster sing the proud exuberance of human joy and sorrow transmuted to pure beauty.

Buddy's secret? He combines an authentic, old-school blues feel with an accomplished technique that places him on a par with other rock guitar legends. No one else has quite that blend. He's as fast as any young gun. Yet he can also break your heart with just one yearning note in the middle of a cavernous twelve-bar void. In the grand scheme of blues/rock history, you might say that Buddy Guy came along at just the right time, born in rural Lettsworth, Louisiana, on July 30, 1936—a good two decades later than Howlin' Wolf, but a decade or so sooner than Clapton or Hendrix.

"I come from a poor family but God has been good to me," he says. "My family used to sharecrop a farm and there was five of us. Neither one of my parents had a third grade education. I sometimes wonder how the family got along. But it did."

Buddy took to the guitar at an early age, along with his younger brother Phil. "My dad had this old guitar with two strings," Buddy recalls, "and Phil and I would scuffle for it. If the strings would break, I'd use hairpins to fix them."

Buddy's early guitar influences were eclectic—another factor in his uncanny mastery of the instrument. He absorbed blues tradition like a sponge. But he didn't stop there.

"When I grew up in Louisiana, you would hear music outta Texas," he says. "When we finally got a radio, it was mostly country and western. A lot of people called it hillbilly music back then. And I listened to that. I didn't gave a damn what you called it. I just wanted to hear the guitar. I was in love with the guitar. And I would listen to Eddy Arnold, Tex Ritter on a horse with the acoustic guitar, Roy Rogers, and Dale Evans. I figured I would learn one or two country-and-western licks and put it with the blues. 'Cause I listened to everybody to try to improve my playing."

Another great leap forward came in Buddy's teens, when he moved to Louisiana's capitol city of Baton Rouge. It was there that he acquired his first proper guitar—one with all six strings in place.

"I'm the oldest boy in my family and I went to Baton Rouge to live with my sister to try to go to high school. We had just one room and a little kitchen with a rollaway bed inside. She was single and tryin' to help me go to school. I went and bought her three cars later on. I tell her I owe my success to her runnin' me out of the house 'cause I couldn't play. So I'd go sit on the front step with my little homework and my guitar with two strings. And one evening a real dark-skinned black guy passed by. He said, 'Son, I bet if you had a better guitar you would learn how to play it.' I said I probably would. He said, 'You be out here Friday evening?' I said yeah.

"My dad had this old guitar with two strings . . . . If the strings would break, I'd use hairpins to fix them."

"And when that Friday evening come, he walk by and say, 'You ready?' Ready for what? He say, 'I'm gonna buy you a guitar!' We went to downtown Baton Rouge and he bought me this Harmony guitar. I think it was fifty-nine dollars and some cents. We come back on the bus, sit on the steps; I got a brand-new guitar. No case, just a guitar. My sister come home from work and say, 'What the hell is this? Country boy with a guitar and a country man?' But the man say, 'Let's get some beer, girl!' He got a quart of beer. She drank some out of a glass. Another ol' friend come up. Ol' raggedy-ass Chrysler. Said, 'Let's get another quart of beer.' My sister said, 'Well, shit, we got a whole car. Let's go out to see my mom and dad.' We gets in the car. They throw me in the back with this Harmony. Just hummin', singin', drinkin' beer. They drove me sixty miles out to Lettsworth, Louisiana. Walks in the door, I'm like, 'Look, I got a new guitar!' I couldn't play shit. Sits down and this guy and my dad talked for ten minutes. And you know what? They had played together as little boys. Before my dad died in 1967, I tried to find that guy so I could pay him back. My dad said that guy that come here was a preacher. I never did find him. His last name was Mitchell."

A true story? Legend is where history meets mystery. And the enigmatic, beer-drinking Preacher Mitchell certainly qualifies as a stand-in for the Biblical Good Samaritan, the wayfaring stranger, the one on whose kindness Tennessee Williams's sad angel heroine Blanche Dubois so desperately depended. Buddy Guy's next encounter with his six-string destiny came in the better historically documented form of bluesman and showman Guitar Slim (born Eddie Jones). It was in his hands that Buddy first laid eyes on his ultimate instrument of choice, the Fender Stratocaster.

"Guitar Slim had this hit record called 'Things I Used to Do,' and a record called 'I Done Got Old.' Ray Charles was the arranger. Man, he was killing me. The first time I saw [Guitar Slim] was in Baton Rouge, and I didn't even know what a Strat was. I must have been sixteen. Back then, the band would start to play before the main guy come on. B.B. and Bobby Bland always did it that way. As long as B.B. isn't on, people still buyin' drinks. So I'm standing at the bandstand watchin' these horn players. The band is just cookin', and this guitar is just wailin'. And I'm sayin', 'Shit, I spent my money for them to come and fake me out like this. I hear that guitar, but that guitar player ain't here.' Then, all of a sudden, this heavyset guy comes out with Guitar Slim on his shoulders. Like if you was walkin' in the park and you hold a little baby with his legs 'round your neck. Well, this guy had Slim on his back with this Strat and this red suit on, man, and white shoes! Whippin' the fuck out of this guitar. This guy brings him to the stage and he walks off. I was saying, 'Oh shit. I wanna play like B. B. King, but if I ever get on a stage, I wanna act like this son 'bitch.' He didn't even have a strap on the guitar. He had a fishline. He had wore the strap out. He was wild. And this Strat was *scratched*, man."

By his late teens, Buddy was blasting Baton Rouge nightspots with a few different bands. But his eyes were on an even greater prize. He arranged to cut a demo in a Baton Rouge radio station with a plan to bring it north to Chicago, which was then coalescing as a burgeoning post-WWII African American community and all around center for the blues.

"The disc jockey's name was Dinky Dolin," Buddy recalls. "I went up to his radio station in Baton Rouge, WXOK-AM, and made a tape. 'Cause I told him I was going to Chicago looking for a job. He say, 'Take this and go to Chess Records and I think they'll sign you and let you make a record.'"

By the late fifties, Chess Records had become a major outlet for the music of Afro American culture on its journey from the rural South up to the industrialized North. Through seminal recordings by Muddy Waters, Howlin' Wolf, Little Walter, and others, Chess had pioneered a new kind of blues sound: electrified, strident and pulsing with the urgent, urban buzz of mass transit and mass culture. Buddy arrived in Chicago on September 25, 1957, and shortly thereafter landed on Chess's doorstep at 2120 South Michigan Avenue. He got inside, but not all the way.

"I went there with my guitar and amplifier and gave them a little demo," he recounts. "When they saw my stuff, they wanted to use it. They take my guitar and gave it to [guitarist] Wayne Bennett, who I think was cutting a doo-wop group that day. That's how I met him. I'm like, 'Okay, I met this guitar player making a session and I'm gonna get a chance to meet the musicians.' I wanted to know them. But it didn't work."

Chess passed on Buddy Guy at that time. He found himself out on the streets of Chicago roundabout 47th and Lake Park, homeless and hungry, on his third day without food. Only water. Until another wayfaring stranger brought him around to the 708 Club at 708 E. 47th. It as there that he met the legendary left-handed blues guitarist and singer Otis Rush, who had scored a hit on another Chicago label, Cobra Records, with his recording of 'I Can't Quit You Baby.' Through Rush, Buddy met another stellar Chicago-based blues guitarist, Magic Sam. These newfound friends and mentors brought Buddy onto the stage at the 708 Club. By this point, he'd fully absorbed the lessons of Guitar Slim and procured for himself a 100-foot guitar patch chord. This he used to leave the stage and mount the bar at the 708 Club, throwing off killer licks all along his path, like a farmer chucking corn to his hungry brood of chickens.

"Most of the blues cats at that time was sittin' down playing the blues," Buddy remembers. "Even harmonica players—Little Walter and all of them—play sitting down. But word got out and Magic Sam say, 'We gotta learn how to stand up, man. 'Cause this cat here is getting attention.' Then they started having guitar jams."

It was Magic Sam who advised Buddy to try his luck at Cobra Records. Still a newcomer to Chicago, the country boy from Lettsworth, Louisiana, wasn't sure how to get to the address he'd been given: 12th Street and Coleman. "I didn't know how to catch a bus and go there," he says. "But I met this young lady and she say, 'I'll come get you and show you how to get the bus.' We went over to Cobra Records and [pianist] Harold Burrage and Magic Sam were there. They called in Willie Dixon. They say, 'Well, let us hear what the fuck you got.' Everybody was cursin'. I say, 'Shit, they don't like me if they talk like that.' They took me in the back. I got my guitar and amp and started singing 'Sweet Little Angel' by B. B. King. Hal Burrage hollered at the president of Cobra Records, Eli Toscano, and say, 'Sign that motherfucker, man!' They come out with this paper. His hand was shaking. I didn't know what the hell I was signing. I just wanted to make a record. They said, 'Get here tomorrow, motherfucker. We got some songs we gonna make.'"

At the time, the great blues songwriter, producer, and upright bassist Willie Dixon was on hiatus from Chess and working for Cobra. He would become a key figure and creative partner in the life and career of Buddy Guy, although their working relationship wasn't always amicable. After signing the Cobra contract, Dixon took Guy out to a celebratory dinner at a barbecue joint. The Lettsworth country boy was still a little uncertain about big city table manners, but soon learned quite a lesson from Dixon.

"I say to myself, 'Okay, I'm from Louisiana. Be cool, Buddy. Just watch and learn.' 'Cause I don't have an education. [Dixon] told me he was gonna take me to this barbecue joint and we gonna sit down and eat and talk about these songs. Now you know he was a huge man. He walks in the joint and orders a whole fuckin' chicken. So I'm figuring he's ordering this chicken, we gon' take a fork and knife and carve it up and me and him would eat it. But he pulls this whole fuckin' chicken in front of him and look at me like, 'What you want?' I just wanted a little drum stick or breast and I was gonna carve that and eat it. But he picks the whole chicken up with his two hands, breaks it in half, and eats it. That was the beginning of that."

The very next day, Guy turned up at Cobra, ready to cut what would become his first commercial release, a solid performance of Dixon's composition "Sit and Cry the Blues." Buddy can still recall the funky setup at Cobra:

"They had a little record store out front: 45s and 78s. You walk in and it was an old garage in the back. That's where you would record. It was just a car garage, but that's where I was getting that real sound you hear on there."

Released in 1958 on Cobra's subsidiary label, Artistic, "Sit and Cry the Blues" wasn't a major success, but it did launch what would be one of the greatest careers in all of blues history. It was followed later that year by a second Artist single, "This Is the End," penned by Ike Turner. Not long after, Cobra went belly-up following the somewhat mysterious death of Eli Toscano. "I think Eli got killed or drowned or something," Buddy recalls. "I heard a lot of stories about that."

The demise of Toscano and his record label wasn't the only setback that Buddy suffered at the time. The Les Paul guitar he'd brought with him from Louisiana got stolen off a bandstand sometime in '58. Buddy had to scramble to get a new ax. The theft of his old one proved to be a blessing in disguise, however. Buddy was able to replace it with a '57 sunburst Fender Stratocaster, the same kind of guitar that his hero, Guitar Slim, played. The Strat would become integral to Buddy Guy's unmistakable tone and style—a legacy that he would soon pass on to Jimi Hendrix. But acquiring the instrument was a financial hardship at the time.

"I had to get on my knees and beg this lady at this famous blues club called Theresa's Lounge at 48th and Indiana," Buddy recalls. "And she finally lent me the money for that Strat. I think it was $149 or $159. I was making six dollars a night playing the clubs. I don't know how I paid her back for that guitar, but I did."

With his new Strat in hand, Buddy was finally taken on by Chess Records in 1960. Some three years after arriving in Chicago, he had realized the dream that had first brought him to the Windy City. Headquartered in a former auto parts factory, Chess was headed up by the brothers Phil and Leonard Chess, Polish immigrants and former liquor salesmen who had built the Chess and Checker labels into a blues empire, releasing classic discs by Muddy Waters, Howlin' Wolf, Little Walter, Sonny Boy Williamson, Elmore James, and Jimmie Rodgers, not to mention seminal early rock-and-roll sides by Chuck Berry and Bo Diddley. Willie Dixon was back at Chess by this time, and it was he who put Buddy together with the first song he recorded for the label, pianist Eurreal "Little Brother" Montgomery's 1936 composition "The First Time I Met the Blues."

"That was when I kinda got a little more familiar with Willie Dixon," Buddy relates. "He had a one-room kitchenette apartment at 4625 Lake Park. I came over there and he showed me how to fix this big steak with onions on it. And that's when I met Little Brother Montgomery, who wrote 'The First Time I Met the Blues.' He had made a hit out of it before he left Vicksburg for Chicago."

While not written by Buddy, "The First Time I Met the Blues" would become one of his signature tracks: central to the mythology of Buddy Guy's lifelong entanglement with the blues, come hell or high water. A chilling allegory, the song recounts a fateful crossroads encounter with the blues itself, here personified as an ominous manifestation of all life's sufferings. Buddy wrests maximum drama from the song by singing in the emotive, high-pitched voice that would also become a stylistic hallmark of his—the eerie wail of a soul in torment, in this case crying, "Please, blues, don't murder me." In this bold vocal style, he was encouraged by his new producers, Phil and Leonard Chess.

"They told me I could do it with a higher voice," he says. "They were trying to lead me kind of in the direction of B. B. King. There ain't but one of him, but they wanted me to sing it kind of high. It's one of the most talked about songs I ever did at Chess."

The track gains further emotional impact from its stark opening.

There's no intro whatsoever. Buddy and his backing band slam straight into the first verse vocal. "It originally had an intro," Buddy reveals, "but the Chess brothers cut it out with a razor blade. 'Cause back then a record had to be less than three minutes. And I had a bad habit. I had to get into a song first before I could sing it. But some of my intros were too long and they would cut it. But I could never have started in like I did on 'First Time I Met the Blues' without an intro."

REDFERNS/GETTY IMAGES

Buddy Guy and the Chess brothers would often come into conflict over Buddy's desire to crank his amp up to the max and foreground his guitar playing. "When I went into Chess I used to turn the guitar up to get the extortion [sic] and feedback," he notes. "And they would tell me, 'Get the fuck out of here. Turn that noise down.'"

But conflicting musical visions didn't prevent Buddy from recording some of his finest work ever at Chess, a brilliant string of sixties singles, many of which are still in Buddy's repertoire today: "Ten Years Ago," "Let Me Love You Baby," "Stone Crazy," and "When My Left Eye Jumps." On nearly all of these he was supported by the solid rhythm section of Jack Meyers on electric bass and Fred Below on drums. The first commercially available electric bass, the Fender Precision, had been introduced in 1951, so it was still a fairly new instrument at the time.

"All of a sudden, it's 1966, '67. I woke up one day and someone says, 'Hey, man, the college kids are protesting this Vietnamese War and a lot of white people are listening to the blues.'"

"When the Fender bass first came along I remember seeing this kid Jack Meyers play it with [guitarist] Earl Hooker's band," Buddy recounts. "Hooker actually owned the bass, so the only time that boy could play he had to work with Earl Hooker. But I found out that Willie Dixon had a Fender bass that he'd pawned at a place on 47th and State. So I told that boy, 'If you wanna play with me, I'll go get that Fender out of pawn from Dixon.' And I gave it to Jack because he was a good little bass player."

As for Below, Guy says, "Fred could play music on the drums. He had a wrist he could snap. Could no one play that shuffle like Below." Apparently the drummer was also a bit of a cutup in the studio. "They finally had to build a pen around him, like a cardboard box," Buddy recalls, "so he couldn't mess with anybody."

Another key player on Buddy Guy's Chess recordings was Otis Spann, one of the greatest blues pianists ever and Muddy Waters's half brother. "Every session I made after I met Otis Spann I wanted him on keyboards," Buddy says, "'Cause he could make you *play*, man."

Like many in Chess's extended family of musicians, Buddy had a dual role. While recording and releasing his own singles, he also served as a session guitarist on legendary sides by Muddy Waters, Howlin' Wolf, and other great Chess artists. He became part of the great Chess gestalt—that magical combination of the right people coming together at the right time and in the right place.

"Leonard Chess used to hum the parts he wanted," Buddy recounts. "When Howlin' Wolf cut 'Killing Floor' I wasn't on the session, and the guitar player they had couldn't hear what Leonard was talking about. So somebody said, 'Call that motherfuckin' Buddy. He know how to play by ear.' I got out of bed and come down. Leonard Chess says, 'Can you play this?' and he sings the part. I tuned my guitar, one, two, three, four. . . . I think it was two cuts and we had it. They said, 'The motherfucker know how to listen *and* play.'"

Buddy is fond of citing the favored mode of address at Chess. "By then I'd learned that I'm not Buddy Guy no more. I'm motherfucker, called that by Leonard Chess, Phil Chess, Willie Dixon. . . . Was nobody Willie Dixon. Was nobody Leonard Chess. Everyone was a motherfucker."

The name might have troubled Buddy a little, but not the money. "You'd get $30 for making a session with them, and that was the best money you could make in Chicago," he says. "The highest money I was making when I first come here in the clubs was three or four dollars a night. Muddy was making $12 a night when I come in the blues clubs."

Phil and Leonard Chess were businessmen. They weren't necessarily out to create fine art. But in the process of discovering and consistently producing a sound that sold well on the R&B market, they created some of the greatest music ever committed to vinyl disc or any other medium. Music with a universal appeal that would soon extend far beyond the African American neighborhoods of Chicago and other U.S. cities.

Ultimately, of course, there's no quantifying the magic of the Chess sound—those rolling, loose-limbed rhythms and the fuzzy glow of distortion enveloping the guitar and harmonica tonalities.

One can cite Buddy's '57 Fender Strat and famous '59 Fender Bassman amp, Chess's analog tube recording gear, or the room itself, designed by engineer Jack S. Weiner to have no parallel walls. But somehow the end result is so much greater than the sum of its component parts.

"When I come in the studio with Muddy and them, we used to drink wine, beer, and whisky and set it on the amps," Buddy recalls. "And all the control knobs on my amp had frozen from the dirt, cigarette butts, and all that got spilled in there. All I had that worked on that Fender Bassman was the on and off switch."

Buddy was on acoustic guitar—an archtop borrowed from Muddy Waters—for one particularly significant Chess date: the sessions for Waters's 1963 *Folk Singer* album. "Chess heard about college kids buying folk music," says Buddy of the disc's origin. "So they called Muddy in and wanted to rush one of those records out on him. They gave him a train ticket and told him to go down south and find some of those older guys who play that kind of [acoustic folk blues] stuff. And Muddy said, 'Set the motherfuckin' session up for tomorrow.' I got it. They thought Muddy was gonna call some old-time guy and put him on a train. When Leonard Chess came in that morning and saw me sitting there, that guy called me a motherfucker so many times I almost cried and left the studio. But Muddy told him, 'Shut the fuck up and listen.' After we got done playing, they stood there with their mouths open. All they could say to me was, 'Motherfucker, how'd you know that?' I know how to back Muddy up on that shit, man."

The album represented Chess's bid to become part of a cultural groundswell gaining momentum at that time. Young white listeners, primarily college students, were becoming fascinated with American folk idioms, including the blues. While attention was initially focused on acoustic bluesmen like Josh White, Mississippi John Hurt, and Brownie McGhee, this new audience would soon embrace the electric blues of Muddy Waters, Howlin' Wolf, Buddy Guy, and others as British Invasion bands like the Rolling Stones, the Yardbirds, and the Animals became outspoken in their admiration for these artists. This expanded the new blues audience beyond college students, bringing in the teenage and even preteen fans of the new British groups then enjoying worldwide prominence.

MICHAEL OCHS ARCHIVES/GETTY IMAGES

The Stones wielded enough power to bring Howlin' Wolf onto the teen-oriented national rock-and-roll TV program *Shindig*. It gave many a young white rock-and-roll fan his or her first glimpse at the real blues. Wolf was no teenage idol. All of sudden a mature, 300-pound black man was shakin' his thing on mainstream network U.S. television, while blond-haired Rolling Stone Brian Jones sat at Wolf's feet gazing up at him like a devotee admiring his guru.

"The Stones will tell you about the time I talked to them when they came to America on their first trip," Buddy recounts. "They couldn't believe that people in America didn't know who Muddy Waters was. They said, 'And we named ourselves after one of his records, 'Rollin' Stone.'"

The Rolling Stones visited Chess Records in 1964, and the Yardbirds soon followed suit. Buddy guy got his chance to return the favor and make his first trip to Europe in 1965. He came over as part of the American Folk Blues Festival, a package tour organized by German promoters Horst Lippmann and Fritz Rau and featuring greats like Mississippi Fred McDowell, Big Mama Thornton, John Lee Hooker, and Roosevelt Sykes. Willie Dixon spearheaded the project on the American side, and had been bringing the foremost American blues performers over to Europe ever since 1962. So the road was relatively well paved by the time Buddy got there in '65.

"I wasn't traveling much at the time, 'cause my wife had recently had a baby," he says. "But I took a break and went over just to do the two weeks there. 'Cause it looked like the blues was at a standstill so far as Chicago."

For Buddy, it was a chance to meet blues artists outside of the Chess stable. The Folk Blues Festival tour provided him with his first encounters with Big Mama Thornton and his longtime hero John Lee Hooker. Suddenly Buddy found himself face to face with the man whose record he'd played over and over as a boy, with that stickpin between his teeth for a stylus.

"Everybody was heavy drinkers back then,' Buddy narrates. "I went down to breakfast in the morning and they had whiskey eggs, whiskey eggs. . . . I sat in the corner with an acoustic guitar and started playing John Lee Hooker's 'Boogie Chillin', which was the first thing I learned how to play by myself. And this guy comes up and taps me on the shoulder. He was drinkin' and stutterin' bad. 'Y-y-y-you t-t-t-tryin' to play J-J-Johnny.' I say, 'Yeah I guess so. I'm just tryin' to figure out who the fuck you are, stutterin' so.' Finally Fred Below said, 'That's John Lee Hooker right there!' And Hooker just started to laugh. He laughed so hard he was crying. I didn't know it was him because I didn't realized you could stammer when you talk, but not when you sing. We became best friends till the day he died. I was at his funeral."

As part of the '65 European trek, Buddy played in London for the first time. His performance was attended by the future superstars of British rock, Jeff Beck and Eric Clapton. Clapton famously slept in a van out in front of the venue along with other members of the Yardbirds in order to be one of the first ones in. He was intrigued by Buddy's performance, particularly the "out of phase" tones he wrested from his Strat by setting the guitar's original three-position pickup selector between two of its notched resting points, thus bringing two pickups at once into the circuit.

"Eric Clapton said to me, 'I didn't know you could make a Strat sound like that,'" Buddy later recounted. "I said, 'I didn't either.'"

It was a time of incredibly rapid change in both music and society. "All of a sudden, it's 1966, '67," Buddy recalls. "I woke up one day and someone says, 'Hey, man, the college kids are protesting this Vietnamese War and a lot of white people are listening to the blues.' And now I looks around and there wasn't anymore blacks in the clubs I was playing at. I said, 'This is a complete turnaround.' And it's still that way today. The blues business is still 95 percent white."

With the ascendancy of Clapton, Beck, Jimmy Page, and Jimi Hendrix, Buddy's wild guitar histrionics came to be viewed in a different light by the Chess brothers. The "extortion" sound that they'd been suppressing for years was suddenly cool . . . and commercial. Leonard Chess's act of contrition is perhaps one of the best-known Buddy Guy stories, recounted so many times that it almost doesn't matter whether it actually happened or not.

"Some time around '66 or '67, Leonard Chess sent Willie Dixon to my house," Buddy relates. "And Dixon said, 'Put your suit on. Leonard wants to talk to you.' I thought, 'Oh God, they probably don't want me to make another session.' I thought they're tired of my noise. I walks in the office and there was no one there except Leonard and me. He says, 'Come on in here, motherfucker.' He bends over and says, 'I want you to kick me in my ass.' He was trying to put the needle on this record. I think it was Cream or Hendrix or something. He pulls his coat up. He had his suit on. He says, 'I want you to kick me in the ass. Motherfucker, you been tryin' to bring this shit to us ever since you came here. And we was too fuckin' dumb to listen. And this here is sellin' millions of records. And this is your shit!'"

Despite Leonard Chess's mea culpa, Buddy Guy's days at Chess were already numbered. In the mid-sixties he'd become tight with the great harmonica player and vocalist Junior Wells (Amos Blackmore). Wells had replaced Little Walter in Muddy Waters's band back in the fifties, but by the mid-'60 was somewhat adrift.

"Junior and I had the same manager, Dick Waterman," Buddy explains. "I told him to put us together because Junior had a band problem. And I had a good rhythm that Junior could play with."

Soon to become one of the most famous duos in blues history, Buddy Guy and Junior Wells first recorded together in '65 for Junior's *Hoodoo Man Blues* disc on Delmark Records. Because he was working for another label, Buddy performed under the unlikely sobriquet, "Friendly Chap." Ultimately Buddy ended up leaving Chess and following Junior over to Vanguard Records, making his solo debut for the label, *A Man and His Blues*, in 1968. At the time Vanguard was one of the premier labels of the folk music boom, home to such leading folkies as the Weavers, Joan Baez, Buffy Saint-Marie, Ian & Sylvia, and Richard and Mimi Fariña. In the mid-fifties the label had enlisted blues historian Sam Charters to create a series of blues recordings. It was Charters who now became Buddy Guy's producer.

While Buddy did some fine work for the label, both on his own and in tandem with Junior Wells, his 1968–'72 Vanguard period doesn't quite hold up to his best work with Chess. In the final analysis, Charters's respectful academic approach wasn't as effective as the Chess brothers' roughshod "motherfucker" aesthetic. But with a catalog that also included rock, jazz, and classical, Vanguard was a less "ghettoized" label than Chess, and therefore perhaps better able to bring Buddy Guy to a growing international audience crossing over for rock and eager to hear and learn about the blues.

Buddy Guy and Junior Wells became one of the hottest live acts of the late sixties and early seventies, playing blues joints, colleges, and rock palaces like the Avalon Ballroom in San Francisco. It was on the road that Buddy got to meet Jimi Hendrix. Someone had played the elder bluesman an early British recording of Hendrix's "Red House." "When I heard it, I said, 'That's Buddy?'," he relates. "They said, 'No, man, it's Jimi.' 'Jimi who?' 'Jimi Hendrix.' 'Whoa.' So Jimi give birth to something that came from Buddy Guy. And I know if Jimi was here he would be the first one to tell you that."

Hendrix's admiration for Guy has been well documented and Buddy's influence can clearly be heard all over Hendrix's lead work. The two guitar icons met for the first time in 1968. "It was the night of the death of Martin Luther King [April 4]," Buddy remembers. "I was playing at a place and my manager at the time, Dick Waterman, he used to stutter like John Lee Hooker. And he kept yelling, 'Dat-dat-dat's Hendrix.' I say, 'So what? Who the hell that?' And everybody started laughing and looking at Hendrix. So Jimi came up and said, 'Pay that no mind. Can I tape what you're playing?' And I said yeah. Somebody had a tape [recorder] on 'em and Jimi got down on his knees and he just stayed there at the corner of the stage. We got a chance to jam a lot together after that, and I got to sit and talk with him—as much as he did talk, which wasn't much. Guys like Hendrix and John Coltrane were just so creative. Years ahead of their time. Guitar Slim made a comment in a magazine once. Somebody told him he was living too fast, and he said, 'Every time you live one day, I live two.' That's what Hendrix was like."

Rock stars lined up to pay tribute to Buddy Guy during this period. The Rolling Stones selected Buddy and Junior to open up for them on their 1970 tour, bringing them to perhaps a wider audience than they'd ever reached before. That same year Buddy made his first of many recordings with Eric Clapton. At the time Clapton was moving in a new direction himself. With Cream and Blind Faith behind him, he was in Miami to make his first recording with an American backing band, a project that would become Derek and the Dominos' classic *Layla and Other Assorted Love Songs*. Clapton was also in the early stages of a debilitating heroin addiction at that point. But that didn't make him forget his friend and mentor. It was at the tail end of the *Layla* sessions that Clapton mentioned Buddy Guy to Atlantic Records label chief Ahmet Ertegun.

"At this time Aretha Franklin was poppin' and everything Ertegun touched was turning to gold," Buddy explains. "Clapton told him, 'I don't know why you want to record me. The best guitar player in the world is touring with the Rolling Stones right now.' So they grabbed a plane and flew to Paris and watched me and Junior Wells open the show for the Stones that night. Afterwards [Ertegun] just walks up and says, 'I'll make a fuckin' hit record on you. When you get off this tour with the Stones, come straight to Miami and record an album for Atlantic Records.' We went down there

and Eric told me later on he hardly even remembers making that record. He was high all the time."

The song they cut was Buddy's composition "Man of Many Words." It didn't surface until 1972, when it became the lead track on the 1972 album *Buddy Guy and Junior Wells Play the Blues*. The track typifies the funk-soul direction that Guy took in the seventies, particularly in his work with Wells.

The year 1975 found Buddy in Africa, where he was touring as part of a State Department cultural exchange program as his divorce from his first wife was being finalized. "When I was traveling in Africa, they had a station wagon and I had my guitar strapped to the top," he recollects. "The guy was driving about ninety miles an hour and my Strat blew off and popped out of the case. Naturally, it went bouncing down the street. The guy stopped and I ran out of the car. To keep the guy from running my guitar over from behind I was gonna lay down on the street and say, 'Hey, don't hit me!' I picked up my Strat and the E string was out of tune. One head got hit and it was bent, but not broke. I looked at that guitar and said, 'You lived through that, you'll be my favorite guitar for the rest of my life. If it would have been any other kind of guitar, I'm sure it would have been totaled."

Buddy remembers the ill omen he received on returning from that trip in 1976. "When I got off the plane, I found out Howlin' Wolf had passed away," he says. That same year, Buddy's beloved

'57 Strat was stolen from his home. It was the start of a rough period for the bluesman. For one, his partnership with Junior Wells had gone south.

"I thought the both of us might make it together," he says. "But it never worked. They had us playing in small places and sometimes we only had an hour to play. Junior would get to drinking sometimes, and so would I. And by the time we both soloed on one song, the hour would gone and the people were saying, 'They through? They don't play no more?' And it was only $300 they were giving us and the band. So we had to break that up. We tried as long as we could."

Like the Biblical prophet without honor in his own home, Buddy Guy spent the late seventies and most of the eighties without an American recording contract. He was able to scrape by, just barely, by reprising his past triumphs for various European labels. While the rock audience had flirted with Buddy Guy in the late sixties and early seventies, he'd always remained very much a blues player. Young white rock fans had embraced Buddy's acolyte Jimi Hendrix more readily. But then Hendrix was younger than Buddy and he presented himself as a rock musician—in psychedelic attire and a wild Afro. In contrast Buddy had always performed like a bluesman, in sharply tailored suits and with relatively close-cropped hair. So he got left behind as much of the rock audience and the younger African American audience abandoned the blues for new genres such as prog rock, metal, disco, New Wave, and hip-hop.

Buddy's luck improved dramatically, however, when Eric Clapton invited him to take part in the all-star 24 Nights concerts that Clapton staged at London's Royal Albert Hall in 1990 and '91. This led to a contract with Silvertone Records and a major comeback.

"This British guy comes up to me backstage and says, 'I wanna sign you and do this album.' I'm sayin', 'Okay, Buddy, this is British guys now. Here's your Johnny-come-later Jimi Hendrix chance. You can do your own thing now. I went to Battery Studios in England, cut *Damn Right I Got the Blues*, and that was the biggest record I ever had."

Released in 1991, the disc benefited from John Porter's crisp yet unobtrusive production, an adequate budget (for a change), and first-rate backing worthy to back an artist of Buddy Guy's stature and experience. *Damn Right I Got the Blues* was a triumph—and a vindication. After wandering in obscurity for most of the eighties, Buddy was back in action, like an exiled king from an ancient Greek drama, returned to claim his kingdom. As if to reassert Buddy's right to the throne, the album includes confident rereadings of the Buddy Guy classics "Five Long Years" and "Let Me Love You Baby," along with a strong selection of new material. The title track is the statement of a man who has fully paid his dues. The tag line, "I can't win, 'cause I ain't got a thing to lose," encapsulates the desertion that Buddy must have felt during his down years. But now all that was behind him.

The album includes outstanding guest appearances by Jeff Beck, Eric Clapton, and Mark Knophler, affirming Buddy's place of honor among the legion of guitar heroes. And the disc closes with "Rememberin' Stevie," Buddy's tribute to fellow blues guitar icon Stevie Ray Vaughan, who had died the previous year. Acknowledging Buddy's immense contribution in establishing the Stratocaster as one of the premier instruments of blues and rock, Fender created the first Buddy Guy signature model Strat, with its distinctive polka-dot design, in 1994.

Throughout the eighties a new market and audience for the blues had been slowly but surely developing, bubbling under the mainstream for the most part, but spearheaded by labels like Alligator and the work of new artists like Stevie Ray Vaughan, the Fabulous Thunderbirds, and Robert Cray. Buddy Guy was eagerly received by this new audience and quickly recognized as an elder statesman of the blues with credentials as peerless as his talent. Buddy quickly found his own style and voice in this new blues idiom—completely contemporary, yet classic as well.

In the years since *Damn Right I've Got the Blues*, Buddy has cultivated this mature latter-day style, and taken it in some surprising new directions. In 2001 he traveled down to Oxford, Mississippi, to record the album *Sweet Tea* with producer Dennis Herring and a select group of players from the alternative rock world, including bassist Davey Faragher and drummer Pete Thomas from Elvis Costello's band, and guitarist Jimbo Mathus of Squirrel Nut Zippers/Knockdown Society fame. Also on the dates were bluesmen Junior Kimbrough and T-Model Ford, both of whom record for Fat Possum Records, the maverick raw blues imprint distributed by LA punk rock label Epitaph. It was a major and significant meeting of musical cultures, connecting the primal truth of the blues with the barefisted urgency of the punk/post-punk/alternative legacy. This potent combination also triggered some of the grittiest and most expansive guitar playing that Buddy Guy has ever committed to disc.

"When I first came to Chicago, I found Wolf, Otis Rush, Otis Spann, and all those guys," he said. "I thought I done dug up everything there is. But when I went down there to Oxford, Dennis Herring started bringing up the Junior Kimbrough stuff. He's a guy never did leave Mississippi. I said, 'Wow, man, I didn't dig deep enough.' It just goes to show, you never get too old to learn."

"Every man got to do his thing. Even if you are talked about, you still got to be proven."

Buddy dug even deeper into his roots on the 2003 disc, *Blues Singer*, a primarily acoustic blues outing. The title riffs on the Muddy Waters *Folk Singer* record that Buddy played on back in '63. "But that was me playing behind Muddy," he says. "This one was me out front."

Blues Singer brought forth a more introspective side of Buddy Guy while also demonstrating his mastery of the acoustic blues idiom. This time Eric Clapton and B. B. King joined Jimbo Mathus in backing Buddy on acoustic workings of songs by old friends and colleagues, including Willie Dixon and John Lee Hooker, who had passed in 2001 and to whom the disc is dedicated.

The most recent Buddy Guy album, at the time of this writing, is *Skin Deep*, another cross-generational effort that includes contributions from Eric Clapton, Derek Trucks, Susan Tedeschi, and gospel pedal-steel phenomenon Robert Randolph. With consummate generosity and effortless grace, Buddy Guy continues to encourage and inspire each rising new generation of blues and roots music players, while also continuing to grow and innovate at age seventy-one. Perhaps he consorts with younger players because his own outlook remains so youthful.

"Every man got to do his thing," Buddy Guy reasons. "Even if you are talked about, you still got to be proven. And that's what I still have got to do now: prove myself to the ones who don't know about me yet."

©MARTY TEMME ARCHIVES

Jeff Beck

THE LONELINESS OF THE LONG-DISTANCE GENIUS

IN JEFF BECK'S CONVERSATION, you can sometimes catch little echoes and glimmers of the fiercely original guitar style that has made him one of the most influential and revered guitarists of all time. His speech, like his playing, is peppered with witty turns of phrase, unexpected transitions, graceful offhand nonchalance, and sly, often self-deprecating humor. One senses a keen, restless intelligence bristling beneath the surface, and also a profound honesty. All of which makes him a great interview subject. It's always a pleasure to hear that clipped, suburban London accent and easy laugh coming from across a phone line, bar, or dinner table.

Unlike other rock icons, Beck is rarely evasive. He tackles even thorny questions in an unflinching, head-on manner, although with plenty of the aforementioned humor—often, as stated, at his own expense. He's far less inclined than many of his sixties peers to embroider, invent, or outright lie about the facts of his amazing life and times. His memory seems relatively unclouded by either drug abuse or ego. It was with some justice that his first solo album was named *Truth*. Because in the end, that's what really grabs you about Jeff Beck's guitar playing. Its emotional truth. Yes, his technique is astounding and arguably the most innovative ever to be applied to the electric guitar. But at the end of the day, none of that would mean a thing if his playing didn't resonate on some more elemental and deep level. You don't have to be a guitar geek to be moved by the expansive psychedelic freedom of "Shapes of Things," the yearning majesty of "Goodbye Pork Pie Hat," or the postmodern frenzy of a latter-day Beck gem like "Trouble Man."

For all his accomplishment, there's a poignant sense of struggle in Beck's playing. Amid the triumphs of his career, there have been dramatic setbacks, formidable health challenges, and an ongoing creative struggle to find and define a fiercely original vision in a world all too often limited by commercial constraints and status quo values. You can hear all of this in Beck's profoundly soulful guitar work. It's as if all that blinding technique were being marshaled in a heroic effort to express what is ultimately beyond expression. Maybe that's why they call him a guitar hero.

"It's proved to be as evolutionary as the wheel," says Beck of his chosen instrument. "You can't make the wheel rounder than round and you can't make the guitar any better than it is. It's just a facility which is infinite. There's no lengths to which you can't go. It's unlimited what you can do with it."

Among the infinite universe of guitar possibilities, Jeff Beck has certainly boldly ventured where no man has gone before. And while his playing appeals to a wide range of listeners, he holds a special importance and place of highest esteem among guitarists. In 1998, Brian May of Queen—no crap guitarist himself—created a tour de force solo track titled "The Guv'nor" and invited Jeff Beck to play lead on it. May and Beck are old friends and close neighbors in the upscale London suburb of Surrey. But had Beck taken up residence in Timbuktu, there still would have been no other guitarist for May's track.

"Well, he is the guv'nor, isn't he?" May said of Beck at the time. "Jeff is the standard by which many of us measure ourselves as guitarists."

Every so often, a prodigious talent arrives on earth at an ideally opportune cultural moment, finding just the right artistic medium to express his or her genius. William Shakespeare rose to prominence in late-sixteenth-century London during the reign of Queen Elizabeth I, a fertile period in the development of the English language and poetry, and a time when the English theater was just coming into its own as an art form that would impact the whole world. Some four centuries later—on June 24, 1944, to be precise—Geoffrey Arnold Beck entered this life in a place just outside London called Wallington, Surrey, at a similarly pivotal time in cultural history.

"It's extraordinary that Eric Clapton, Jimmy Page, and I were from the same county in England," Beck muses. "We were all born within about a twelve-mile distance from one another. I don't know what it was. Maybe that part of the planet has some kind of energetic vibe about it."

Jeff Beck came of age in the fifties, during the first wave of a rebellious and infectiously rhythmic new style of music called rock and roll. He emerged as an electric guitarist during the sixties' Swinging London era, becoming one of the most important guitar players of that wildly creative period in which rock music evolved at an astonishing rate, emerging as one of the most influential art forms and social phenomena of the twentieth century.

And of course Beck found his *métier*, his expressive medium, in the electric guitar. The solid-body electric guitar was still a relatively new instrument, its full potential as yet untapped, when Beck first took it up circa 1957 as a twelve-year-old boy. Beck belongs to a distinguished generation of guitarists—including Page, Clapton, Pete Townshend, and Jimi Hendrix—who revolutionized the instrument in radical ways during the sixties and beyond. But even in this company of giants, Beck's approach to the guitar is remarkable for its dazzling originality. He is one of the few rock guitarists who picks with his fingers rather than a plectrum. All the fingers of his right hand come into play not only to pluck the strings but also to manipulate the vibrato arm and volume control of the Fender Stratocaster, which has been his main ax since the mid-seventies.

An uncanny combination of vibrato-arm technique and left-hand string bends have made Beck a master of legato phrasing and microtonality, the pitches "between the notes" of a tempered Western scale. This makes him better able than most rock guitarists to evoke the sounds of Indian, Bulgarian, and other forms of world music that have captivated his restless imagination at various times, also lending a certain *je ne sais quoi* to his straight-up rock playing. Beck's quantum sense of tonality is astoundingly fluid and supple. Close encounters with it mystify even virtuoso players like Beck's colleague Steve Lukather.

"You can't make the wheel rounder than round and you can't make the guitar any better than it is."

"He hits a harmonic, pulls up the bar, and then goes above the nut and pulls the note up some more," Lukather marvels. "I go, 'How do you think of stuff like this? You're an alien!'"

So perhaps it's fitting that one of Beck's earliest guitar influences was a wizard, the Wizard of Waukesha, that is, Les Paul. At about age seven or eight, young Geoffrey became besotted with Paul's seminal recording "How High the Moon," keying in on the humor in the playing and the wild, slap-back echo sound and other sonic innovations of Paul's late-forties/early-fifties work. In the true spirit of Les Paul, Beck set about to build his own guitar. He made several during his teen years, actually. But with only photos to guide him, he had no real idea about neck length or fret spacing. Who knows? Maybe his experiences playing those early handmade instruments lie at the root of the beguilingly open-ended approach to tonality and phrasing that would distinguish the playing style he went on to develop.

With the mid-fifties arrival of rock and roll in the UK, Beck joined the legions of British youth who went hog wild for this bold and brash new kind of music from America. He went through a Buddy Holly phase, which is when he first became captivated by the Fender Stratocaster. But he became absolutely obsessive about Cliff Gallup, the lead guitarist in Gene Vincent's band. Studying the country-flavored work of Gallup and Chet Atkins provided Beck with the rudiments of the unique fingerpicking style he would soon develop.

"I was fascinated with how Chet Atkins played a bass part and the melody simultaneously," Beck recalls. "I had to learn that. It helps the brain with coordination to keep a rhythm going with claw-hammer style [picking]. It all comes from folk banjo, and God knows where else."

Like most guitar-playing kids, Beck absorbed influences from records at first, only later venturing out to connect with other guitar players. By far the most important of these to enter his early life—and indeed become a lifelong friend—was Jimmy Page. He owes that introduction to his sister, four years his elder and a student a Ewell Technical College, which Page was also attending at the time.

"My sister came home and said, 'There's a guy with a goofy-looking guitar like yours at college.' And I went, 'Where is he? Take me to him!' 'Cause there was nobody else on my block or even in my town who even knew what a Fender Strat was. So it was great to find Jimmy, like meeting your long-lost brother. And we've got on well ever since."

It was with Page that Beck started to explore the blues, the African American musical form that had spawned rock and roll. Blues music became the focal point for a coterie of up-and-coming young London musicians who would go on to play in groundbreaking bands like the Rolling Stones, the Yardbirds, John Mayall's Bluesbreakers, Fleetwood Mac, and others. Beck had begun his own passage through a succession of journeyman groups, starting with the Deltones—an outfit that gave him his first encounter with a Fender Telecaster—and moving on to Nightshift and the Tridents. It was with the latter group, in particular, that the young Jeff Beck began to spread his wings sonically. By this point he'd acquired his first Strat, a sunburst job, which he put together with an obscure German echo unit, a Klempt Echolette. Denizens of London's top R&B venue, Eel Pie Island, had never heard anything like it.

"Eel Pie Island, which was the spawning ground for all that, is where I started these noises." Beck remembers. "Using tape echo to the point where it could play itself by itself. Just put the guitar up on the amp and it would make these amazing sounds, just make people go crazy. Anything was good. You could play twenty-minute solos just messing around with noises like that. It was like somebody going crazy with a paintbrush or just smacking color on the wall and watching people enjoy it. They were half out of their heads anyway. Staggering about. I had a great time."

By this point Beck had already begun to explore the musical possibilities of guitar feedback, hitherto considered an unwanted and ugly byproduct of guitar amplification. Beck claims to have started discovering that feedback could be much more than that as early as 1960.

"Because I had a terrible amp that fed back anyway," he laughs. "And when we started playing big ballrooms, you'd turn up the volume and wheeeee. And everybody would start looking at me, thinking I wanted to be dead 'cause I'd made this mistake. So I had to turn a horrible sound into a tune to make them think I meant it. That's where it all came from. The inability of sound systems to cope with the needed volume. We had no real PA. The singer would use the house PA with a terrible microphone. One of those little square things that was all bass and nothing else."

In another place and time, Beck's new take on electric guitar playing might have been dismissed as insanity or worse. But he happens to have come along just as the London blues/R&B scene was reaching critical mass and on the verge of moving at warp speed beyond the twelve-bar idiom that had been its first catalyst.

"That was the heady days of '63, maybe up to '64," says Beck. "There was all this great interest in the Rolling Stones and Muddy Waters. There was great expectation in the air. I suppose kids still get that now. But to us it was really special. The music business was a tiny little island compared to what it is now. The Rolling Stones were outrageous hooligans, considered aliens, unwashed. We thought it was great. It always felt weird watching people with fairly long hair and maracas against the back end of the rockabilly thing. That would not have been acceptable."

While Beck was swept along in the era's brisk tide of sonic adventurousness—often leading the pack, in fact—a part of him never let go of the rockabilly era. Where some guitarists might have sought to conceal their fondness for a bygone, no longer fashionable music, Beck flaunted his.

"I remember having an insulting criticism from Eric Clapton saying, 'You gotta get rid of that folk style of country picking,'" Beck recalls. "Probably because he couldn't do it. I know it used to annoy him. I'd be out in the middle of some simple groove and then out would come this claw-hammer picking. I felt like doing it, so I did."

While Beck worked the clubs with the Tridents, his old friend Jimmy Page had begun to carve out a lucrative career as a session player. Page also turned Beck on to some session work. Notably Beck backed Brit wild man Screaming Lord Sutch on a few recordings. But arguably the greatest favor that Jimmy Page ever did for Beck was to recommend him for the job of playing lead guitar for the Yardbirds.

In 1965 the Yardbirds were on the cusp of worldwide success and an enduring place in rock history as the band that originated the very idea of the extended rock guitar jam. They'd taken over from the Rolling Stones as house band at London's Crawdaddy Club in 1963 and quickly established a reputation as a hard-hitting blues-based outfit fronted by blond singer Keith Relf, who blew a mean blues harp and bore an uncanny resemblance to Rolling Stones guitarist Brian Jones.

The rhythm section, consisting of drummer Jim McCarty, bassist Paul Samwell-Smith, and rhythm guitarist Chris Dreja, was both tight and supple in support of original lead guitarist Andrew "Top" Topham and his successor, a young guy named Eric Clapton, who had already begun to amass a reputation as one of London's hottest guitarists.

Blazing through long, action-packed sets at the Crawdaddy, the Yardbirds had pioneered a new mode of extending the middle section of a song to feature wild guitar improvisation. They'd create excitement by changing up the tempo and building to orgasmic crescendos. "Rave Up" was the catchphrase that the band's manager Giorgio Gomelsky coined for this vivacious new musical style.

A goateed Euro-beatnik whose passion for art often outstripped his business acumen, Gomelsky had managed the Stones early on and, as the Yardbirds manager, had hooked them up with the song that would become their first big hit, "For Your Love," by the talented tunesmith Graham Gouldman. Gomelsky had also fostered the idea of featuring a harpsichord and bongo drums on the track—very unique instrumentation for a rock recording at the time. The combination paid off in spades. "For Your Love" was a worldwide success. Everyone was happy—except for Eric Clapton, who didn't like the group's move away from the blues to play the pop singles game. (An interesting position for a man who would later score big with pop ballads like "Wonderful Tonight" and "Tears in Heaven.")

And so Clapton quit the Yardbirds in '65. Gomelsky asked Jimmy Page to replace him, but Page was making better money as a session guitarist and also leading an easier life in town, far from the rigors of the road, rock touring being quite a hard road to travel in the mid-sixties. And so Page recommended Beck for the gig. Within a year or so, ironically enough, Page would also join the Yardbirds. But for now, it was Jeff Beck's moment.

Beck agonized over leaving the Tridents, but ultimately found the Yardbirds' offer impossible to refuse. He was married at the time, to dressmaker Patricia Brown, whom he'd wed in '63, and the prospect of joining a pop group with a hit record offered financial stability, among other perks. But more than that, the Yardbirds offered him a tremendous opportunity to grow phenomenally as a guitarist, and do so before an appreciative worldwide audience. Unlike Clapton, the core Yardbirds members weren't

JEFFREY MAYER/WIREIMAGE/GETTY IMAGES

blues purists. Urged on by Gomelsky, they wanted to experiment, to explore new musical styles. So they nurtured Beck's growth as Beck, in turn, pushed them to new creative plateaus.

"Of the three original guitar players—Clapton, Beck, and Page—I think Jeff brought the most to the table," says Chris Dreja. He's absolutely remarkable."

Beck was given a very short time to learn the band's entire Clapton repertoire, including the songs from the influential *Five Live Yardbirds* album, in order to meet the Yardbirds' concert commitments. He was still fairly new to the group early in '65, when he turned up at London's Advision Studios to record the Yardbirds' next single, the much anticipated follow-up to "For Your Love." Gomelsky had chosen another darkly minor-key Graham Gouldman composition, "Heart Full of Soul," cut from the same cloth as "For Your Love."

Figuring that novel instrumentation had helped make "For Your Love" a hit, Gomelsky had arranged for an Indian sitar player and tabla accompanist to perform on "Heart Full of Soul." This was several months before the Beatles would popularize the sitar with their film *Help* and its accompanying soundtrack album. "If you look at the dates for a lot of things," Dreja remarks, "it appears the Yardbirds did them first."

Indian music is based on a complex system of rhythmic cycles called tals. The problem on the "Heart Full of Soul" session was that these rhythm patterns didn't sit well with the song's rock beat.

"The sitar player just couldn't play in 4/4 time," Beck recalls. "What he was doing was totally magical, but it just didn't have any groove to it. So I showed him on guitar what I thought would be a good idea, which was an open D string with this little riff an octave above. Everybody in the room said, 'That sounds great! Let's just leave that.' And we sent the little Indian man on his way."

In his usual offhand manner, Beck had happened on something brilliant that would dramatically influence the course of rock music in the late sixties. He'd discovered that the harmonic overtones of an overdriven electric guitar (which was a '58 Telecaster through a Sola Sound Tone Bender fuzz box and Vox AC 30 amp, in this instance) could be employed to emulate the rich droning of Indian string instruments such as sitar and tamboura. The fuzztone was a brand-new innovation in guitar gear at the time. But it is Beck's unique playing technique that really enabled "Heart Full of Soul"'s now-legendary guitar riff. By picking with his fingers rather than a plectrum, he could sound the open D string as a drone while executing the main riff an octave higher, starting on the B string at the third fret. Beck's subtle but effective microtonal string bending also enabled him to emulate the sitar's unique tonality and timbre.

It was the start of a revolution in guitar playing. Once the Beatles did popularize the sitar and all things Indian, circa 1966–'67, electric guitarists everywhere were droning away and bending notes in mixolydian intervals that approximated the mystical sounds of Indian music. Psychedelic music—specifically the psychedelic subgenre known as "raga rock"—had been born, ushered into existence by Jeff Beck's guitar playing on "Heart Full of Soul."

On tour with the Yardbirds, Beck acquired the instrument that would become his signature guitar during the Yardbirds period, a 1954 Fender Esquire. He had been playing a '59 Tele left over from his Tridents days. But after the instrument went missing at a Paris gig supporting the Beatles, Beck began searching for a replacement. For a while he used a red Telecaster that the Yardbirds had formerly leased to Clapton. But Beck soon purchased a well-worn '54 Esquire for £75 from John Walker of pop group the Walker Brothers, with whom the Yardbirds were touring at the time.

The single-pickup Esquire was originally conceived as a more affordable version of the dual-pickup Telecaster. But what really attracted Beck to Walker's guitar was its maple neck. This was a time when Fender, newly acquired by CBS, had started featuring rosewood necks on Telecasters. But Beck knew he wanted a maple neck, the traditional Telecaster fingerboard wood. So a used instrument was definitely the way to go. The Esquire he purchased was already visibly worn and Walker had planed contours into the original slab body to make it more like a Stratocaster body. But that battered instrument was soon to become one of the most iconic guitars in all of rock history, especially as depicted on the American release *Having a Rave Up with the Yardbirds*. With his Esquire stripped to bare wood, well-cut black suit, desert boots, and Beatle-esque hair style, Beck was the consummate mid-sixties lead guitar man—the first great guitar hero of the rock era.

The Jeff Beck lineup was the first Yardbirds incarnation to make it over to the United States for a tour in 1965. Rock tours in the sixties were hardly the well-organized, highly professional ventures they are today. And Yardbirds tours seem to have been particularly disorganized, chaotic, and grueling, even by sixties standards. But the band did manage to make two momentous stops at historic American recording studios, committing some of their greatest recordings to tape in a few hurried sessions.

Down in Memphis, they wangled a session with Sam Phillips at his legendary Sun Studios. A decade earlier, Phillips had put rock and roll on the map by discovering and recording Elvis Presley and cutting some incredibly rip-roaring rockabilly records with Jerry Lee Lewis, Carl Perkins, Johnny Cash, Roy Orbison, and others. Reluctantly, the legend goes, Phillips agreed to cancel a fishing trip he'd planned to unlock Sun Studios and record the Yardbirds. For rockabilly fanatic Jeff Beck, it was an unforgettable day:

"We actually bashed on his door on a Sunday morning, and said, 'We're coming to record. Is that okay with you?' He didn't want to do it. But Giorgio was totally persistent and we got in there. And it was great. I was on air that day—meeting Sam Phillips and standing exactly where Elvis and Scotty Moore must have stood."

The band cut two songs with Phillips, the slow-burn protest number "Mister You're a Better Man Than I" and a radically retooled arrangement of the rockabilly rouser "Train Kept A-Rollin.'" For most of the latter song, they replaced the I, IV, V chord progression of the Tiny Bradshaw original with a driving, low-string guitar figure that is quite arguably the mother of all metal riffs.

It was something of a tense day. Keith Relf got drunk and couldn't perform well. (He overdubbed his vocals later on in New York.) Phillips embarrassed Beck by loudly denigrating Relf within the singer's hearing and acting the curmudgeon in general.

"I was so disappointed when we went to hear the playback because he played it so soft," Beck recalls of Phillips. "And I said, 'Can you turn it up?' He said, 'I'm gonna make you an acetate. You can take it back to your hotel and blast your heads off. I'm not blowing my speakers up for you.' No one had told [Phillips] that there was a whole new era coming. D'you know what I mean? He was still puffing his chest out from the Elvis days and not receptive to the Rolling Stones. He probably hated them, hated us. It's just that we were really into the rock-and-roll trios—Elvis and Scotty Moore and all that stuff—that made him interested in us."

Shortly after the Sun Sessions, the Yardbirds found themselves in the hallowed halls of Chicago's Chess Studios—site of landmark recordings by Muddy Waters, Howlin' Wolf, Chuck Berry,

Bo Diddley, Little Walter, and other legends of blues and early rock and roll. Here too the Yardbirds were following in the wake of the Rolling Stones—the first English rock-and-roll band to record at Chess. The studio staff was still a little bemused at this influx of young white guys with strange accents, according to Beck:

"The engineer at Chess couldn't understand why we wanted to go there. It was just a lowly, kind of ill-equipped studio. But that was the reason why we went, to get the crude, open sound that we wanted. We heard the playbacks and we were just over the moon. That big, powerful bass drum."

"They had an old drum kit set up," Jim McCarty recalls. "I remember that had a big bag of sand in the bass drum. I thought, 'This is a funny old kit. We'll have to try this out.' But it really sounded great. In England you never really got such a good drum sound in those days. You had to go to the States."

The Chess sessions yielded the definitive Yardbirds recording of "I'm a Man," which features some stellar interplay between Beck's guitar and Relf's harmonica, culminating in a hailstorm of chicken-scratch guitar noises. With its terse rhythmic changeups and big bass crescendos, the track exemplifies the rave-up vibe that had rocked the Crawdaddy club during the Yardbirds' formative years.

While at Chess, the band also cut another song destined to become a Yardbirds classic: "Shapes of Things." By this point, the Yardbirds had begun to write their own material. Penned by Relf, McCarty, and Samwell-Smith, "Shapes" combines an antiwar lyric—the hugely unpopular Vietnam conflict was then raging—with the band's trademark raga-rock guitar stylings and stop-and-go dynamics.

"I remember working that song out when we were rehearsing at some club in Chicago, before we got to Chess," says McCarty. "It really happened when we hit on that double-tempo feel for the guitar solo in the middle."

The latter is easily one of the greatest guitar solos that Jeff Beck—or anyone else for that matter—has ever committed to tape: an exotic rush of melody that bathes the cranium in Day-Glo colors as it whooshes past the listener's skull. "There was mass hysteria in the studio when I did that solo," Beck recalls. "They weren't expecting it, and it was just some weird mist coming from the East out of an amp. Giorgio was freaking out and dancing about like some tribal witch doctor."

Even in this early phase of his creative journey, Beck's guitar solos already possessed the manic, nonlinear, almost schizophrenic quality that sets his work apart from that of all other guitarists. A frantic burst of notes high up on the fret board would be followed by an unexpected and vertiginous swoop down to the low strings, like an aircraft suddenly losing cabin pressure.

"Obviously the brain acts in certain ways when you're soloing," Beck explains. "It thinks, 'I'm not impressing anybody. Hurry. Quick. Get the good stuff out!' Constant searching is what it is. The discomfort of being in the wrong register, or perhaps dissatisfaction with a solo that is headed toward disaster."

It's that sense of danger that makes his playing so poignant. Much of Beck's genius is born of an intensely self-critical nature. He can be hard on himself, which has led him at times to place almost impossible demands on his fellow musicians. But even on relatively minor Yardbirds tracks, it's a delight to hear Beck's mature style in embryo: the moody volume-knob swells on "Still I'm Sad," the way he can stretch and strain the parameters of a twelve-bar, like in "I'm Not Talking," while remaining almost magically within the pentatonic blues idiom.

While not major pop hits, Yardbirds records like these were eagerly taken up by the aspiring guitarists and other rock-and-roll obsessives who were forming garage bands at that time. This growing coterie of fanatics would soon blossom into a genuine rock underground. A whole new sensibility was growing up around a handful of Yardbirds tracks, the Stones' eleven-minute opus "Goin' Home" from their *Aftermath* album, Bob Dylan's *Highway 61 Revisited*, and the Byrds' *Fifth Dimension*. While all these artists enjoyed Top 40 hits, the music's more reflective fans began to look to album tracks by Dylan, the Stones, the Byrds, and the Yardbirds for a deeper musical experience, something edgier, something with a little more heft and danger.

In one of the most unlikely developments in cultural history, teenage pop music was becoming a valid art form. In bringing instrumental improvisation to rock music, the Yardbirds and their peers gave the music a level of credibility somewhat akin to jazz—although without jazz's inherent musical snobbery, at least not during the fertile '65–'66 period. Rock was a joyously participatory and inclusive thing. Garage bands were springing up everywhere. Little or no formal musical education was required. In fact, it was usually a hindrance.

For these incipient rock bands, hastily cobbled-together American LPs like *For Your Love* and *Having a Rave-Up with the Yardbirds* were sacred artifacts. Not too challenging vocally, chordally simple, yet full of intriguing guitar passages, the Yardbirds music made ideal garage-band fare. Garagey Yardbirds sound-alikes, like Count V's "Psychotic Reaction," began to make inroads on the charts, and every cover band covered the Yardbirds.

"We'd do a lot of gigs where the opening band would play all our songs," McCarty recalls.

Among all the elements of what would become rock culture that were falling into place in the mid-sixties, the venerable institution of groupiedom was also coming into its own—albeit still in somewhat rudimentary form. "Some of them were pretty memorably horrible," Beck recalls. "I think they were going in for a huge arse contest or something. Badly camouflaged."

Beck fared better in Southern California, a sun-kissed place famous for two of the things Beck loves most: beautiful cars and beautiful women. During the Yardbirds' '65 sojourn in LA, Beck began to immerse himself in SoCal hot-rod culture while simultaneously starting up a liaison with actress-model Mary Huges. Beck's obsession with fast and sexy cars dates back to an early day job at an automotive paint shop. And where the female gender is concerned, Beck is one of rock's consummate ladies men, a notorious groupie magnet. His entire demeanor changes when a woman enters the room. Even if he's not actively "on the make," he becomes more animated, more "on." It's like an unconscious reflex with him. It also seems part and parcel of the exhibitionist side of his art, something which has always existed in delicate counterbalance with Beck's penchant for acerbic self-criticism.

For all their delights, musical and otherwise, those mid-sixties tours with the Yardbirds took a serious toll on Beck's health, both physically and emotionally. In mid-'66 he collapsed after a gig in Marseilles, fell down three flights of stairs, and spent several days in the hospital. His condition was exacerbated by a severe throat infection and the emotional strain of touring and maintaining his status as rock's most adventurous guitarist.

"Oh, I collapsed everywhere back then, didn't I?" he scoffs. "It was terrible. I collapsed in Marseilles with food poisoning. That took care of me big-time. I couldn't get my strength back. I think it was a lot more serious than it was diagnosed. It was more like a meningitis type of headache. Terrible. So silly was the pain I just felt, 'Somebody must be able to hear it.' It was that bad."

With his health declining and nerves stretched to the breaking point, Beck became ill-tempered and his behavior erratic on the road. He'd storm offstage in the middle of a set. Guitar gear got flung, kicked, and otherwise conscripted as a punching bag for his pent-up rage, frustration, and pain.

Added to these health and psychological challenges were business woes stemming from the group's growing dissatisfaction with Gomelsky's management. "We fell out over a number of things," Gomelsky recalls. "I was driving them too hard, I guess. I saw a great possibility for the Yardbirds to take over in terms of innovation. And I said, 'Guys, I know it's hard work but you gotta put in another three years and stop all this beer drinking and shit going on.'"

At one point, Gomelsky even suggested firing Beck and taking on a keyboard player in his place, "I said, 'Fellows, that Beck is freaking out too much,'" Gomelsky recollects. "I even had a keyboard player in mind, a kid of eighteen that I'd heard play with Brubeck in a pub in Brighton. In the end, they were against it, so we just parted company then."

The Yardbirds' management was taken over by Simon Napier-Bell, whose girlfriend was a friend of Paul Samwell-Smith's, who, in turn, began to move out of his bass-playing role with the Yardbirds, shifting toward what would become a very successful career in record production. Which is how Jeff Beck ended up playing bass as well as lead guitar on the Yardbirds' next hit, "Over Under Sideways Down."

"It was really inspired by 'Rock Around the Clock' by Bill Haley and the Comets," says McCarty of the song. "Jeff and I just played through a boogie—the two of us—doing all the breaks in the middle. Everyone else just sort of played on top of that. Then Jeff came up with that riff in the beginning, which was like dynamite."

Rather than playing anything that sounded remotely like rockabilly guitar, Beck devised a whirling dervish Middle Eastern line that became the song's hook. The result was another addition to the lexicon of all-time great rock riffs, and another prime example of the romantic exoticism and international scope of Beck's six-string sensibility.

In the States "Over Under Sideways Down" was the title track of what is really the Yardbirds' only proper studio album, conceived and recorded as a whole—albeit in just about a week's time. In England it was simply titled *The Yardbirds*, although it has affectionately come to be known as "Roger the Engineer," in honor of the cartoon drawing of session engineer Roger Cameron that Chris Dreja drew for the album cover.

By the time the LP was released, however, Paul Samwell-Smith had quit the Yardbirds. The last straw for Samwell-Smith came when the Yardbirds played at the Oxford May Ball in 1966. Once again Keith Relf had overindulged at the bar, blown raspberries at the upper-crust audience, and fallen over the drum kit. "Paul Samwell-Smith was always a bit of a snob and he got really uptight," says McCarty. "After that, he decided to leave the band."

"It was quite a blow having Paul Samwell-Smith leave," says Beck, "which was realized more fully after he'd gone, because we didn't have that huge bass sound anymore. He pioneered those four-string bass chords."

In one of the strangest moves in rock history, the Yardbirds hired Jimmy Page to be their

new bassist. "Jim was not a bass player, as we all know," Beck says. "But the only way I could get him involved was by insisting that it would be okay for him to take over on bass in order for the Yardbirds to continue. And gradually, within a week I think, we were talking about doing dual-guitar leads. So we switched Chris Dreja onto bass to get Jimmy on guitar."

And so for a brief while, there was a rock band with both Jimmy Page and Jeff Beck on guitar. This dynamic duo only made a few recordings with the Yardbirds, the greatest of which is unquestionably "Happenings Ten Years Time Ago." The track also features John Paul Jones on bass, making it a key Led Zeppelin precursor.

"I remember Keith and I getting this fairly simple tune together," McCarty recalls. "We were basically talking about déjà vu and being reborn and all that stuff, and we put it down as a simple, Indian type of tune. And then Jeff and Jimmy came in with all these mad ideas for it."

Page played the rhythm guitar on "Happenings Ten Years Time Ago," leaving the leads to Beck. The solo section is a true tour de force. An ominous European-style police siren—courtesy of Beck's guitar—leads the way into a full-on six-string apocalypse with atomic bomb blasts and shards of scarified riffing. Beck's voice is heard, heavily processed and doing a frenetic spoken bit: "Pop group are ya? Got that long hair . . ." It sounds rather ominous, but it is actually Jeff Beck's spot-on impersonation of a doctor at a VD clinic in Hammersmith that the pop groups would frequent when they'd caught a dose of the clap. Meanwhile, the cataclysmic bomb blasts and siren wails that Jeff Beck coaxed from his guitar and amp on "Happening Ten Years Time Ago," clearly paved the way for Jimi Hendrix's similarly bellicose rendition of "The Star-Spangled Banner" at Woodstock some three years later.

The B side to "Happenings" was "Psycho Daisies," a fairly disposable, and brief, Chuck Berry-ish twelve-bar, notable for some stinging guitar leads. The only other Yardbirds studio recording that Beck and Page made together was for a film titled Blow Up, by Italian art-house film director Michelangelo Antonioni. Set in Swinging London, the film's script included a nightclub scene in which a beat group smashes their equipment. Antonioni had wanted to film the Who, whose climactic gear-smashing set finales were creating a huge buzz at the time. But when the Who weren't available, the director settled for the Yardbirds, requesting Beck to smash a guitar in the film sequence, even though this wasn't a usual part of the Yardbirds' act. While Beck was no stranger to abusing his gear onstage in this time period, it was awkward and vexing for him to fake it, particularly time after time in obedience to Antonioni's frequent calls for retakes.

A few different music tracks were under discussion for the scene, but Antonioni was really keen on having the Yardbirds perform an earlier hit of theirs, "The Train Kept A-Rollin'." When copyright issues prevented this, however, the band went in the studio and knocked out a slightly different version of the song with altered lyrics, entitling it "Stroll On." It is generally inferior to their original recording of "The Train Kept A-Rollin'," but it does contain a few tantalizing seconds of dual-lead-guitar interplay between Beck and Page, a beguiling hint of what might have been. And the Yardbirds segment of the Antonioni film is essential viewing for any rock fan.

Looking back on these three recordings, Page says, "It's only 'Happenings Ten Years Time Ago' that means anything, as far as that went. And then 'Psycho Daisies.' The 'Stroll On' thing is a bit chaotic, really. 'Cause I was playing guitar on the track and doing bass on the film; 'cause Chris Dreja hadn't got the bass together yet. It was bizarre, really. But it was a good time. I enjoyed that, playing with Jeff."

The Beck–Page Yardbirds lineup only lasted for a handful of live dates. There was a twelve-date English tour with the Rolling Stones and Ike and Tina Turner. There is no recorded document of these performances, but those who were there report amazing feats of harmonized and unison guitar leads, not to mention tandem soloing. One senses, however, that the two guitar titans were just starting to find a way to operate together and hadn't quite perfected a collective approach. "It could be brilliant with Jeff and Jimmy," recalls McCarty, "but it got a bit messy sometimes. A bit too much going on."

"Obviously the two-guitar thing with Jimmy was a great idea," says Beck. "But it was also fraught with disaster, because sooner or later one of us would have been cramped, style-wise."

As it turned out, things never reached that point. In October 1966, following their English tour with the Stones and Ike and Tina Turner, the Yardbirds were slated to tour America as part of the Caravan of Stars Tour organized by American pop-music TV host Dick Clark. They shared the bill with a number of relatively lightweight pop acts, including singer Brian Hyland (famous for the novelty hit "Itsy Bitsy Teenie Weenie Yellow Polka Dot Bikini"), Gary Lewis and the Playboys (led by the son of comedian Jerry Lewis), and Sam the Sham and the Pharaohs (best known for the hits "Wooly Bully" and "Little Red Riding Hood").

This was just the sort of inappropriate billing that Jeff Beck had come to loathe. "The touring was rigorous and I was tired of being misrepresented," he says. "Being put on Dick Clark road shows was not where I wanted to go."

According to Jimmy Page, "The conditions on the bus for the Caravan of Stars tour were really appalling. There were no bathrooms. And there were even ladies—background singers for Sam the Sham—that we had to share the bus with. It was horrifying. Jeff decided that he had had enough of that."

Beck lasted for just two dates on the tour. After that, he simply got off the bus and went back to England. He describes his decision to leave as "traumatic. I walked out on the one thing that gave me life, gave me recognition. I didn't feel proud about dumping [the Yardbirds] in the shit. I got home and just faced a bleak winter in England with nothing to do. I must have been desperately unhappy to walk off the tour bus like that."

⌒ THE JEFF BECK GROUP MARK I ⌒

The period immediately following his departure from the Yardbirds was a grim one for Jeff Beck. At several times in his career he has hit what has seemed to him an impasse with no clear direction forward. What he didn't realize at the time was that the seeds of a triumphant new phase of his career had already begun. Right at the tail end of the Beck–Page incarnation of the Yardbirds, the two guitar titans had collaborated on what would become the first Jeff Beck solo track, "Beck's Bolero." It is one of the great rock instrumentals, epic in scope, harmonically and rhythmically ambitious yet infused with primal energy. It set the stage for the era of heavy, powerful rock with progressive ambitions that were soon to come.

Jimmy Page, who is also credited with writing the song, played rhythm guitar on a twelve-string. On bass, once again, was John Paul Jones, another top London studio musician (and of course Led Zeppelin's future bassist), whom Page had met on the session circuit. The drummer for the date was none other than Keith Moon of the Who, rock's most accomplished drummer at the time and a bona fide wild man. Completing the lineup was rock pianist extraordinaire Nicky Hopkins, another top sessioneer of the day, who would contribute immensely to recordings by the Rolling Stones, the Who, and others.

"It was my melody over Jimmy's rhythm," says Beck of the track. "Jimmy came up with that bolero rhythm on the twelve-string, but it's my riff in the middle. I'd decided that the Yardbirds trademark was to stop, break up the rhythm, and come into another complete thing. So we used that as the signature, to continue that kind of raw break."

In Keith Moon, Beck had found a drummer who could match his own manic intensity. The two men formed a particularly close bond. "I couldn't get enough of him," says Beck of the late drummer. "A day would go by in half an hour when you were with Moonie. Just complete lunacy, and genuine organic humor. Your jaw would ache from laughing. How [the Who] put up with him for as long as they did, I'll never know."

For a few crazy moments there was talk of making the "Beck's Bolero" lineup a permanent band, which surely would have been the first (and perhaps the all-time greatest) rock supergroup. Keith Moon and John Entwistle were reportedly weary of working with Pete Townshend and Roger Daltrey. They were supposed to quit the Who and join forces with Page, Beck, and Hopkins.

But rock music's evolution was fated to unfold along other lines. What could have become one of rock's greatest supergroups instead formed the basis for Jeff Beck's debut as a solo artist.

The whole thing actually grew out of a business deal. With the Yardbirds rapidly unraveling, Simon Napier-Bell also jumped ship, selling his managerial interest in the group to Peter Grant in January 1967. An imposing figure of a man, 6' 6" tall and heavyset, Grant was partnered with producer Mickey Most in an organization called RAK Management and Production. Jeff Beck has vivid memories of the duo's cramped business office.

"Mickie Most's sidekick at the time was Peter Grant. All I ever saw of him was this huge chair on the opposite side of the office, with this huge jacket that was big enough to make three suits for me out of it. 'Cause Peter weighed about 350 pounds."

And so it was arranged that Grant and Most would take on the Yardbirds and also launch a career for Jeff Beck as a solo artist.

Chronologically, it was the perfect moment for Beck to emerge in this new context. By 1967 the rock underground that had started to coalesce circa '65–'66 had blossomed into a vibrant music culture.

The emergent hippie scene, with its joyous philosophy of free love and consciousness expansion, formed the backdrop for landmark albums like the Beatles' *Sgt. Peppers Lonely Hearts Club Band* and the debut of guitar-heavy acts like the Jimi Hendrix Experience and Eric Clapton's Cream, who took electric guitar experimentation and virtuosity to new heights of artistry.

Unfortunately, Jeff Beck's new producer was completely oblivious to all of this. Not that Mickie Most was totally clueless. He'd produced a brilliant string of mid-sixties singles for the *Animals*, including the classics "House of the Rising Sun," "It's My Life," and "We Gotta Get Out of This Place."

Most would also go on to do an excellent job at helping Scottish balladeer Donovan transform from Dylan-esque folksinger to major flower power pop idol. But Most was an old-school guy. To him the producer's role was to "manufacture" a sound and even an image for the artist. So he proceeded to mold Jeff Beck—arguably the greatest rock guitarist of all time—as England's newest pop vocal sensation.

"Mickie was a forward-looking pop producer and he had good, quality acts who were annoyingly good at selling records," says Beck. "But he also couldn't see a market in America for underground, sort of hooliganistic rock. In '67 and '68, when I was in big trouble with my musical career and wondering what direction to take, he explicitly said to me, 'Oh, that Jimi Hendrix and all that twang twanging and feedback nonsense, it's finished.'"

"Obviously the two-guitar thing with Jimmy was a great idea, but it was also fraught with disaster, because sooner or later one of us would have been cramped, style-wise."

Which is how "Beck's Bolero" came to be the B side of Jeff Beck's debut single, "Hi Ho Silver Lining," a jaunty pop ditty sung with great reluctance by Jeff Beck. The track is one of Beck's enduring career embarrassments. The fact that it was a substantial commercial success only makes matters worse.

Two more embarrassing Most-masterminded singles followed: "Tallyman"—written by Graham Gouldman, who'd penned the early Yardbirds hits—and a cover of the French light-orchestral instrumental hit "Love Is Blue." All were fairly painful for the intensely self-critical Beck, who often disdains even his best work. But his contract with Most left him with little or no veto power. And as testimony to Most's pop savvy, the singles did chart substantially, bringing in an income to keep Beck going during this somewhat difficult and awkward period of transition and self-discovery.

But on the B sides of "Tallyman" and "Love Is Blue," he'd begun to lay the groundwork for the next Jeff Beck career high point, and assert his own vision of what the Jeff Beck Group might ideally sound like. The B sides to the two singles mentioned previously feature a singer relatively unknown at the time: Rod Stewart, a stalwart blues/R&B belter with a sweet Sam Cooke side who'd seen service with Long John Baldry & His Hoochie Koochie Men, the Giorgio Gomelsky managed Steampacket featuring organist Brian Auger (who'd played the harpsichord on the Yardbirds' "For Your Love"), and the Shotgun Express with guitar ace Peter Green and drummer Mick Fleetwood.

Beck was more than happy to cede the microphone to Stewart. But Most wasn't down with the idea. And so Stewart wound up harmonizing with Beck on "Hi Ho Silver Lining." Only on the B side, "Rock My Plimsoul," was Stewart allowed to come into his own. In hindsight, "Plimsoul" is generally regarded as the first significant recording by the Jeff Beck Group. Stewart also took up the mike on "I've Been Drinking," the B side to "Love Is Blue." But his presence was barely tolerated by Mickie Most.

"Where Rod was concerned, Mickie told me, 'You don't want that poof on your record,'" Beck recalls. "And that's when I started to hate him. I said, 'You, in your infinite pop wisdom, can't see that this guy's gonna rule big-time?'"

This awkward impasse was brought to an end when Most agreed to transfer management of Beck over to his partner, Peter Grant. "Mickie couldn't see that the guitar was what I should be doing," Beck reflects. "But Peter Grant did. And it was just that thread of lifeline that got us to America with Rod. Peter Grant believed in the act."

Grant arranged for the Jeff Beck Group to perform at the Fillmore East, ground zero for the emergent New York hippie scene and one of the most influential rock venues at the time. A converted movie theater in Manhattan's counterculture East Village neighborhood, the Fillmore East had first opened its doors in March 1968. And on the 14th and 15th of June that same year, the Jeff Beck Group opened for the Grateful Dead onstage at the Fillmore.

By this point, the lineup for Beck's backing group had solidified . . . sort of. After coming and going a few times, Ron Wood had settled in as the group's bassist. He'd previously seen action as guitarist with London R&B group the Birds (not to be confused with the American group, the Byrds). Beck had persuaded him to switch to bass. And on drums was Mickey Waller, a veteran of the Cyril Davies All Stars who had also played with Rod Stewart in Long John Baldry's band. The Jeff Beck Group galvanized the New York audience who'd turned out for a trippy evening with the Dead but found themselves going berserk for some of the hardest-hitting, dead-on-the-money power rock anyone at that time had ever heard.

"I damned and confounded New York when I came back with that band," says Beck. "All the bad reviews about me being a bad boy leaving the Yardbirds in the shit were all just washed away when we played the Fillmore East. Don't get me wrong. We were shitting our pants. Rod wouldn't come and sing to the audience direct. He was hiding behind some curtains. I finally had to say, halfway through the set, "There is a human actually making those noises in this building.'"

On the strength of the Fillmore gigs and the successful American tour that followed in their wake, the Jeff Beck Group, augmented by Nicky Hopkins, were able to go in the studio and produce their first proper album, the now-classic *Truth*. The timing turned out to be ideal. The hippie dream of '67 had given way to a more angry, militant mood in youth culture with an attendant appetite for a heavier, nastier form of rock music. The long-playing album had succeeded the 45-rpm single as rock's prime medium of expression. So Beck's previous misguided singles ended up not counting for much, particularly in the United States. Meanwhile, Cream and Hendrix, aided by the advent of massive 100-watt Marshal amp stacks, had established a new guitar-heavy take on blues-based rock.

So it was a perfect moment for Beck to weigh in with his unique interpretation of this exciting new rock genre. Anyone who'd been following rock music seriously for the past four or five years knew that Beck was the original exponent of extreme, adventurous rock guitar playing. So the rock audience was primed to hear Beck's new group.

They certainly delivered the goods. *Truth* opens with a high-powered reworking of the Yardbirds' "Shapes of Things." Reprising the '65 hit was a bold declaration, as if Beck were saying, "Forget the past. Here's where I'm at *now*." The tempo is slowed to a menacing lurch, propelled by Waller's fluid drumming. Wood's crazed bass lines climb all around the 4/4 structure like some chemically altered spider as Stewart kicks Keith Relf's original vocal into a higher register, straining even his own impressive voice to the limits.

But the real revelation is Beck's guitar. Grainy single-note leads weave around a gutsy slide-guitar track in a left-right stereo ballet that manages to be both graceful and brazen. By this point

Beck had moved on to a Les Paul through a Marshall, the de rigueur rig circa '68. The guitar solo section isn't as melodic, or coherent, as the Yardbirds' original, but that seems to be the point. Beck seems to be gleefully embracing the chaos of the cultural moment.

"Rod loved that song," Beck notes. "He thought it would be a great idea to do another angle on it. And it became the precursor to a lot of power rock and roll—that plodding sort of rhythm that we nailed. That's what I wanted to do. And I supposed whenever I get named as a heavy metal innovator, that's probably one of the best examples of heavy metal in embryo."

Like many rock albums of the period, *Truth*'s ten tracks rely heavily on the blues. Beck and company offer up an inspired version of Willie Dixon's "You Shook Me" that predates the Led Zeppelin recording of that song by several months. (In fact, the tune became something of a sore point between Beck and Page, straining their long friendship.) But the real standout among the disc's blues numbers is the group's reading of Dixon's "I Ain't Superstitious," originally recorded by the immortal Howlin' Wolf.

Where most bands of the day were a bit over-reverent in their approach to the blues, Beck's take on Dixon's classic twelve-bar is deliciously slapdash. Not content to shuffle along in semiauthentic Chicago blues mode, the Beck version of "I Ain't Superstitious" stutters and stumbles about in a radical update of the Yardbirds' start-and-stop dynamics. Even in playing the blues, Beck refuses to let the listener settle into anything comfortable or familiar. The groove grinds to a halt at the top of nearly every twelve-bar cycle for Beck to restate his own perverse interpretation of Dixon's mighty pentatonic riff.

"I Ain't Superstitious" is also Beck's wah-wah pedal tour de force on *Truth*. A relatively new device at the time, the wah-wah had been put to creative use by Clapton, Hendrix, and others. But Beck was the first guitarist to fully exploit the contraption's potential as both an implement of sonic punishment and a source of rude humor.

But for all its swagger, *Truth* also showcases Beck's lyrical side, another key element in his playing throughout his career. This comes out most notably in his rendering of the English ballad "Greensleeves," performed on Mickie Most's Gibson J-200 acoustic, "which by the way is the same as Elvis's" Beck's liner notes proudly state. His arrangement of Tim Rose's "Morning Dew," something of a hippie-era standard, is more up-tempo than most, taking on an almost Motown feel, but nonetheless contains some passages of dreamy guitar work that even Hendrix would be proud to own.

The *Truth* era marked a high point in Beck's life in many ways. In 1968 his marriage to Patricia Brown was laid to rest after a long period of discord and difficulty. He'd found a new muse and lover in the British model Celia Hammond. Their liaison would prove to be one of the most lasting and deeply influential in the guitarist's life. Hammond's winsomely beautiful facial features even provided the model for the painting that adorns *Truth*'s front cover art.

All told, *Truth* was a triumphant assertion that while the styles and sounds of rock music had shifted and many new talents come along, Jeff Beck was still well at the head of the class. Further confirming Beck's status as the guitarist of the moment in '68 were high-profile session dates like Beck's brilliant turn on Donovan's hit single "Barabajagal" and his work on the Frank Zappa–produced LP by prominent LA scensters/groupies the GTOs, *Permanent Damage*, the latter engagement also enhancing Beck's reputation as one of rock's great ladies' men.

But Beck, of course, constantly agonized over his standing in the rock pantheon. Like all of the British guitar gods at the time, he felt threatened by the ascendancy of Jimi Hendrix.

"We just didn't realize that someone was going to come along and whip the carpet out from under us in quite such a radical way," Beck says of Hendrix. "And there wasn't any turning back after that. You can't unpull the carpet. You just do something else. That was the most ponderous time in my life: 'What to do now that this guy's done what he's done?' And when I found out that people still wanted to hear what I had to say, I carried on. But it was pretty rough, I must say. A pretty grim time."

Hendrix and Beck became good friends, however. Hendrix always acknowledged Beck's profound influence, and offered encouragement to his British forerunner. And for a magical period of several weeks in 1969, during a Jeff Beck Group residency at Manhattan hot spot the Steve Paul Scene, audiences were treated to the spectacle of Jeff Beck and Jimi Hendrix trading guitar riffs in nightly jams.

"Jimi would come in just about encore time and everyone would freak out," Beck recalls. "He'd come onstage and completely overshadow and undermine what we'd done. But nobody cared. It was so great. And to have Rod singing as well, two guitars blazing away . . . forget it. I thought, if he's not afraid to stand onstage with me, I'm not ashamed to go anywhere. The place was just crammed to capacity every night.

"There was such a contrast between the way Jimi was onstage and the way he was offstage. He spoke in whispers. He would never raise his voice above a whisper. It was all in his expressions, in the hands. Unbelievable comedy and profound statements just by the raising of an eyebrow. He did burn the candle, though. I couldn't keep up. We went out one night, from the Scene. We'd already played two hours of raving rock and roll with him coming on for the encore. Then we went to the New York Brasserie to have something to eat, and somewhere after that. At four o'clock he said, 'Let's go back to the hotel.' I thought, 'Thank God. He'll fall asleep and I'll go off home.' But instead he'd start playing stuff and we'd go out somewhere else at five o'clock. This was just an everyday occurrence. I'd be history for two days afterwards, and he'd be still at it. The guy was on a big-time roll. It was as if he'd been commissioned to be Chief Motherfucker in charge of everything. Suddenly this guy comes along and upturns the whole apple cart. Playing with his teeth, behind his head. He made the rest of us look like a bunch of librarians standing up there."

Librarians or not, the Jeff Beck Group became a major touring attraction in Europe and the US throughout 1969. Beck notably passed, however, on an offer to play at the Woodstock festival. Truth be told, Beck had little use for the whole hippie phenomenon. The "hippie chick" look did not appeal to him, nor did the psychedelic drugs so prevalent then.

"Pretty girls were a rarity at that time," he gripes. "You look back at those photos from Woodstock and there's one girl who looks good in a crowd of five million. They all had face paint. I don't know what went wrong then. I'm not totally antidrug, but I never took anything. I was constantly faced with thousands of people all drugged out of their heads and thinking I was too. Wrong! Looking at the behavioral changes of people that are drunk or drugged, I tried to give them what they wanted and stay ahead of them even though I hadn't had anything at all. Very strange. Obviously there was some extraneous pot smoke drifting onto the stage, which would probably have had some effect, especially at the Fillmore West. Forget it. The whole place was thick with blue smoke."

Despite the success that the Jeff Beck Group was enjoying, the internal tensions that would soon shatter the band had exacerbated to a critical stage by 1969. As lead singer, Stewart harbored a long-standing resentment that the group bore Beck's name. It particularly irked Stewart to be told on leaving the stage, "Great show, Jeff," something that happened on more than one occasion.

"Well, I was the name, you know," Beck counters, "because of the Yardbirds and all. I couldn't really hide behind Rod and expect anyone to book us. Rod didn't like that at all. There was sour hatred and resentment for having my name on the tickets, yet he was singing."

Beck had also bounced Mick Waller out of the band. "Mickey was a great drummer," he says. "Unfortunately, having seen Keith Moon, I just couldn't be happy unless I had someone who had that amount of charisma of power. Mickey didn't have the charisma. He had great dexterity and fantastic Motown chops. He'd been flatmates with Motown's drummer Benny Benjamin for a long time. A great opportunity was missed by not having somebody say to us, 'Look, you bastards, stop dicking about. This is a great opportunity to make another great album and carrying on like that.' But things were so nuts then."

Ron Wood had also left the group in a huff, but returned just as Beck and the band converged on London's Kingsway Recorders in mid-'69 to record the follow-up album to *Truth*. At the time, the band was well into its second American tour behind *Truth*, and audiences were growing hungry for some new material. Many bands agonize for months, if not years, over their sophomore effort. Beck and his band merely canceled a batch of US tour dates, flew back to London, and knocked out *Beck-Ola* in less than two weeks: four days for tracks and a week for overdubs and mixing.

In Waller's absence, Tony Newman had taken over the drum throne. Nicky Hopkins, who'd become a full-time member of the Jeff Beck Group, turning down an offer to join Led Zeppelin to do so, was also on the sessions.

"That album was pretty much dreamt up on the spot," Beck admits. "I didn't know what I was going to do in the morning at breakfast. It was made in desperation to get product out. We just got vicious on it, because we were all in bad moods and it came out wild."

It sure did. Wood's bass work is especially ferocious. The scrappy musical setting seems to have inspired Beck to great guitaristic heights. The slapdash way in which the record was assembled may account for the fact that there are two Elvis Presley covers on the disc, although "All Shook Up" got so heavily Beck-ified that the only recognizable elements left from the original are a few lyric lines. The closing track, "Rice Pudding," became a big favorite among Beck fans. Originally titled "Mother's Old Rice Pudding," the extended instrumental had been a mainstay of the Jeff Beck Group's live set before being committed to tape.

For some of the album sessions, Beck laid aside his Les Paul and reverted to a '54 Stratocaster. "I suppose seeing Jimi Hendrix with my old guitar strapped around his neck had something to do with it," Beck laughs. "Because a Strat is where I came from. Sounding the way it did, it made me interested to go back to that again." For the next few years, Beck would alternate between Les Pauls and Strats, finally emerging as a confirmed Strat man in the mid-seventies.

As it turned out, *Beck-Ola* was the last album ever to be recorded by the Stewart–Wood incarnation of the Jeff Beck Group. They split up shortly afterward. Stewart and Wood went on to join the Faces. Today, Wood is a Rolling Stone, and Rod Stewart is an international pop icon whom no one ever calls Jeff.

"Unfortunately, we didn't have enough material to keep the Stewart band going," says Beck in retrospect. "Rod was writing ghastly lyrics—just thrown together. It didn't have the attention it deserved, that band. We should have had a writer or producer come in and take over. If Rod and I could have chatted over the name thing, maybe we could have sorted it out, found another name. But we couldn't talk. The whole situation needed more tolerance from him and more artistic input from everybody, management included. We were pretty much left to fend [for] ourselves."

Beck's reservations aside, *Beck-Ola* was well received upon its release in 1969. Many of the tracks became FM album-rock staples and the album is still highly regarded today among Beckophiles and fans of great guitar playing.

↶ SEARCHING FOR A NEW DIRECTION ↷ (1969–1975)

By now, a pattern had become abundantly clear. For all of Jeff Beck's prowess as a guitar stylist, innovator, and all-around titan, he is no songwriter. He once described the songwriting process as "bloody murder. It's the blank sheet of paper syndrome, you know? I need fun, laughter, and girls or whatever to take away the dullness of songwriting. It shouldn't be an effort. If it is an effort, then something's wrong. It should be a heartfelt desire that just makes you do something really good. I imagine a comedy writer having the worst job in the world: on a rainy Monday morning when you've gotta make people laugh on Tuesday and you're not feeling funny. If the ideas don't come, I just don't do it."

This would prove to be his major challenge moving into the seventies and beyond. Hendrix and Clapton had been able to evolve into competent and even inspired tunesmiths, which in turn proved a major factor in the success of each. Jimmy Page found an ideal writing partner in Robert Plant. But Jeff Beck's mercurial and utterly unique talent was destined to take a different road. And it would take several years, numerous false starts, and a few creative blind alleys before he was able to find that road.

And as had happened once before, the creative and career dead end that Beck hit after the group with Stewart split up was rendered dramatically worse by a severe health challenge. On the evening of November 2, 1969, Beck was involved in a serious car accident. He was thrown from his 1923 Ford Bucket-T onto the road. He suffered a four-inch fracture to his skull, a broken nose, dental damage, and injuries to his spine. The skull fracture exacerbated a similar injury he'd sustained as a child. The recovery process was a long and difficult one for Beck. He was on and off painkillers, suffered frequent, blinding headaches, and complained of an inability to concentrate. In effect he was back where he'd been after leaving the Yardbirds, sick and lost for a direction forward, another legendary band now behind him.

It was around this time, encouraged by Celia Hammond, that he became a vegetarian. He found it not only helped improve his physical health, but also made him less moody and prone to fits of anger. A love of animals was something the couple came to share, their cottage in the English countryside becoming a virtual menagerie.

But just outside this bucolic retreat lay a rapidly changing rock landscape, not to mention a public eager to hear Jeff Beck's next creative venture. The early seventies were an uncertain time in rock. The Beatles had split up. In the space of a few short years, the music would lose many major icons—Brian Jones, Jimi Hendrix, Janis Joplin, and Jim Morrison—to early and drug-related deaths.

In the absence of unifying figureheads to point the way forward, rock had started to segment into subgenres such as glam, prog, art rock, Southern boogie, and heavy metal. Each latched on to one or two aspects of what had made rock great, but none had the complete picture. Of the sixties old guard, the Stones, the Who, and the Kinks were doing some of their best ever, career-defining work. But where these artists once held center stage, they now had to vie for attention with a whole slew of new artists and genres—everyone from David Bowie to Black Sabbath.

Many people in this uncertain period—both artists and fans—tried getting back to some earlier musical roots and/or musical influences outside rock. Beck was no different. Only he'd already exploited his rockabilly and blues influences through his sixties work. So now he turned to Motown for inspiration. He'd always loved the music coming form Berry Gordy's Detroit empire, which had also provided the soundtrack for the mid-'60 mod movement in Britain. So Beck, in tandem with drummer Cozy Powell, flew to Detroit for a series of sessions at Motown with legendary bassist James Jamerson and other stalwarts of the label's renowned studio band. It was an interesting experiment; Motown had never been a vehicle for virtuoso guitar playing. But the sessions ended up going nowhere and were shelved.

It was on the rebound from this failed experiment that Beck and Powell got together with bassist Clive Chaman, keyboardist Max Middleton and vocalist Bobby Tench to form a new incarnation of the Jeff Beck Group. With this lineup, Beck cut the *Rough and Ready* album, released in late 1971.

"I feel like I wasn't there for that one really," says Beck in retrospect. "It's a post–car crash album. Rod wasn't there. It was like, 'What do we do?'"

Still the album has its moments, and some of the musical relationships forged during the sessions would prove to be enduring. Keyboardist Max Middleton, in particular, would have a significant influence on Beck's overall musical approach. Nicky Hopkins had been somewhat peripheral to Beck's music, an overdub, in essence. And Hopkins, while classically trained, was a pianist who flourished within the confines of three-chord, blues based guitar rock—the unsurpassed master of playing with guitar bands like the Stones, the Who, and the Kinks.

Middleton, on the other hand, was more of a jazz-based keyboard player, possessed of the typical keyboardist's obsession with big, dense, harmonically complex, ten-fingered chords and less inclined than Hopkins to fit himself into the basic root-fifth voicings of guitar rock. In a way, the ability to play dense, ten-note tonal clusters spread out over several octaves is one advantage that keyboardists have over guitarists, who can only play six notes at once, all in a somewhat limited range. And for Beck, this posed an intriguing challenge and indeed a hint at the way forward he'd so long been seeking.

The Middleton–Tench–Powell–Chaman lineup reunited with Beck to cut a second album together, 1972's *Jeff Beck Group*, often called the "Orange Album" in honor of the ripe citrus fruit that figures on the front and back cover art, itself perhaps a back reference to the Magritte-inspired apple that graces the cover of *Beck-Ola*. Reprising the Yardbirds' strategy for recording "Train Kept A-Rollin'" and "Mister, You're a Better Man Than I," Beck returned to Memphis to record, this time with Stax session guitarist extraordinaire Steve Cropper at the production helm.

The results, alas, were somewhat less stellar than the Yardbirds' historic Memphis session. Bob Tench, for all his virtues, was no Rod Stewart, and the *Orange* album, like its predecessor, comes off as a halting attempt to walk in the giant footsteps of *Truth*. Still the disc, like *Rough and Ready*, is not without its virtues. Beckophiles, in the early seventies, learned to find their diamonds in the rough. Beck's wildly chromatic soloing on the twelve-bar blues-jam classic "Going Down," seems terse, tense, and angry, somewhat akin to Miles Davis's furiously muted trumpet passages, as if Beck were pissed off at the twelve-bar format but still not quite able to transcend it. The same conflicted guitar aesthetics redeem the lyrically challenged "Ice Cream Cakes."

Meanwhile, the group's reading of Bob Dylan's "Tonight I'll Be Staying Here with You" offers up the beatific dose of Jeff Beck guitar lyricism that devoted fans were now coming to expect, if not outright slavishly crave.

But the *Orange* album would prove the last gasp for the Jeff Beck Group's second incarnation. The ever restless Beck was already moving on. But he still hadn't exhausted his Motown preoccupation. His new Motown focus was the label's blind seer, Stevie Wonder, then in the process of evolving from the prepubescent hit-making sensation "Little" Stevie Wonder into a timeless and visionary artist.

"Hearing [Wonder's album] *Music of My Mind* really just moved my spirit," says Beck. "I really took to that. I was at someone's house; I picked up that record and played it. I couldn't hear what the people in the room were saying for the next hour. I was just completely mesmerized by the sounds coming off that record. And I thought, 'There he goes. There's a genius reinventing himself.' The thought that I'd be standing next to him in the studio was way beyond my dreams. But having raved about the record, it must have reached somebody at Epic. Out of the blue, they said, 'Stevie would be interested in having you go over.' And I sort of went 'ulp.'"

So Beck journeyed to Electric Lady Studios in New York, where Wonder was at work on what would become his landmark 1972 album, *Talking Book*. "It was a most memorable time," Beck says of his sessions with Wonder. "It was frustrating at first, because you know he can't see you. There's a barrier right there. But within a couple of days, that was gone. It was really uplifting just to be around and watch him put together a song so quickly and perfectly that nothing could be improved. He'd do a rough tryout of something that was better than anything I could ever come up with. He was someone with songwriting skills unknown to me before. I thought, 'I just better stick around here for a couple of hours.' And he put me on one of his songs on the *Talking Book* album ['Lookin' for Another Pure Love']. I couldn't care less if the solo stank. Just the way he said, 'Do it, Jeff,' on the record, that meant a million quid to me. No one could talk to me for six months afterwards.

"There was another song he wanted me to go on, but I was so out of it on that occasion. Some friends and I dropped by the studio. But we'd really been out on the, uh, cold drinks, so I declined the offer to play. I couldn't bear to disgrace myself in that state. We could really put it away. I never did take drugs, but we did lube up occasionally."

Wonder and Beck did co-write another tune together, however, the smash hit "Superstition." Beck actually played drums during the songwriting session. The original plan was for Beck to record the tune, but once Motown heard the track, they insisted that Wonder put it out, although Beck did record his own version later on. It became perhaps the most well-known song by his next group, Beck, Bogert & Appice.

Ever since the dissolution of the original Jeff Beck Group, the guitarist had been talking to bassist Tim Bogert and drummer Carmine Appice, formerly of the Long Island, New York, "spaghetti rock" group Vanilla Fudge, who had scored big with a heavied-up version of the Supremes' "You Keep Me Hanging On." A solid yet supple rhythmic foundation had always been essential to Beck's playing. His frenetic style, with its dizzying twists and turns, wry fillips, and abrupt, unexpected transitions demands a rhythm section that can keep pace. And Beck felt that he'd hit the jackpot in the Vanilla Fudge duo, although many fans at the time were puzzled at his selection of these two American players.

"I suppose seeing Jimi Hendrix with my old guitar strapped around his neck had something to do with it, because a Strat is where I came from. Sounding the way it did, it made me interested to go back to that again."

"I was always trying to get a drummer like Moonie that seriously kicked ass," Beck explains. "And Carmine did it. He was really devastatingly good. Carmine and Tim could entertain on their own, do a shuffle boogie. Carmine was probably the last of the forties-style big-band, fuck-off drummers. Yet he still had that forward-thinking Billy Cobham–type feel."

Beck, Bogert & Appice, or BBA, was Jeff Beck's power trio, albeit a few years down the road from rock's great era of power trios.

The group did a self-titled studio album and a live disc to follow up. Bogert and Appice handled vocals in a game, "go for it" manner not likely to induce fits of jealousy in Rod Stewart, although BBA enjoyed success as an arena boogie-band attraction.

It was also during Beck's tenure with BBA that he began to employ the so-called mouth bag—a small speaker driver mounted in a small receptacle connected to the end of a plastic tube. By holding the end of the tube in his mouth and silently forming words, the player could filter his electric guitar signal in a way that mimicked human speech.

"There was a guy named Mike Pinera who had one," Beck recalls, "and he used to do just bass riff noises with it. Just guitar lines. Then he said, 'You can speak. You can actually use the voice cavity with injection through this plastic tube to the guitar.' It took me about three or four days to get the vowel sounds. Amplified through a mike, it gives you even more flexibility. Because the mike reads certain frequencies more accurately. The guitar becomes the voice. It would floor people. They'd go, 'What the hell's that?' Then they'd see this sort of colostomy bag stuck to me. In fact, there was a review where one guy thought it was a bladder."

Re-introduced years later as the Heil Talk Box, the device is no doubt of creative use to some guitarist somewhere. But it seemed a bit beneath Beck's dignity. BBA was brought down by the same factors that had scuppered Beck's previous two bands: a paucity of good material, personal differences (notably Bogert's tendency to overplay and step on Beck's turf), and business issues.

"We had more power than we needed, but not enough of a story line, so to speak," Beck philosophizes. "Not enough good songs. Great actors but no story line—although that seems to sell millions of dollars worth of films these days. Also the Anglo American management was never destined to be great success. The left hand didn't know who the right hand was diddling, as they say."

✧ YEARS OF TRIUMPH ✧

Finally, in 1975, the pieces started to come together for Jeff Beck. One major cue and inspiration came from the jazz fusion movement of the early to mid-seventies. It was spearheaded by British jazz guitarist John McLaughlin and his Mahavishnu Orchestra. McLaughlin had earlier played on Miles Davis's landmark *Bitches Brew* album and was a notable disciple of the Indian spiritual master Sri Chinmoy. With the Mahavishnu Orchestra, he pioneered a guitar style that combined the intensity and punishing volume levels of rock music with the harmonic and rhythmic complexity of jazz.

"When I first heard the Mahavishnu Orchestra playing in Central Park, I just began to develop wings because of that," Beck recalls. "They were hugely popular at that time. And it seemed to me that everyone was getting so involved in, and so in love with, playing music. It was a vital thing for me to have that."

McLaughlin and his band, moreover, had pulled off a rare feat indeed. They'd scored a huge commercial success with their instrumental 1972 album *Birds of Fire*. This also provided a crucial spark of inspiration for Beck: he could abandon the endless, frustrating struggle to find the right singer to match his six-string prowess. He could go all instrumental, making his guitar playing the main attraction, the lead voice, as it were.

Another piece of the puzzle fell into place when Beck hooked up with former Beatles record producer George Martin. Beck says he was "tremendously encouraged by the fact that George Martin showed interest at a point where I was really kind of wondering whether I should continue in the business. Having him on board was almost sort of like a rescue father."

Like Mickie Most, George Martin certainly knew how to produce hit records. In fact, his track record in that regard far surpasses Most's. But unlike Most, Martin was also a highly accomplished, classically trained musician. As such, he could understand the new direction that Beck wanted to take with his music, and help him to make real progress down that new road.

"George Martin certainly didn't know what he was getting involved in!" Beck laughs. "I put some tapes on his desk one day. He saw through the mist and said there might be something there." The sessions took place at Martin's AIR studios in London, his post–Abbey Road enclave. Beck had assembled an exceptionally capable and sympatico ensemble of supporting players. On keyboards once again was Max Middleton, the man who'd begun pushing Beck in a jazz direction during the second incarnation of the Jeff Beck Group. The rhythm section was made up of two guys that Middleton had been playing with in a group called Gonzales, bassist Phil Chen and drummer Richard Bailey. Gonzales had been exploring another key aspect of the mid-seventies musical landscape, the funk and disco rhythms coming from African American culture. This influence can be heard on *Blow by Blow* tracks like "Constipated Duck" and "AIR Blower."

That album was just one of those things that was so easy," says Beck. "They were great players, willing to play, and decent material. And in four days, we'd tracked all the songs. Of course, the overdubs then took much longer! But the tracking was really quick. For one, we didn't have a lot of dough."

While the work went fairly easily, George Martin was no pushover.

Tall and imposing with the commanding air of a patrician English headmaster, Martin had kept the Fab Four in line all throughout their wild ride through unprecedented fame. He certainly wasn't going to accept any less from Geoffrey Arnold Beck than the very best he had to give. For once, Beck was matched with a producer as musically savvy and as critically demanding as he was.

"Some of my favorite solos got trashed because George thought they were hideous—not musical," Beck remembers. "He'd say, 'That's really the most dreadful noise I've ever heard.' And I'd say, 'That's what I want!' But I'd usually come round to his way of thinking. George is almost like a dad: relaxed, very focused on the sound. I was looking to him sort of as a parental figure: someone to help me present some of my more outrageous visions in a way that would be acceptable to the general public. And he did it quite well. George Martin was probably the best producer I've had. The guy who could framework what I do without interfering."

Blow by Blow is crammed with tracks destined to become Jeff Beck classics. Middleton's composition "Freeway Jam" became a concert staple, although playing it so many times has left Beck a bit sour on the song. "I hate that tune," he once complained. "It's pretty awful. I could care less if people still like it. It felt like a slowed-down Irish reel to me."

The mouth bag makes its swan-song appearance on "She's a Woman." Covering a Beatles tune was a fond tribute to Martin, although Beck took the Lennon–McCartney composition in a markedly different direction by setting it to a reggae beat. It was Middleton who initially suggested playing the song.

"Max was playing in a band for Linda Lewis," Beck explains. "She was the wife of Jim Cregan, who is Rod Stewart's guitar player. And she started making waves, playing Ronnie Scott's jazz club [one of London's main jazz venues]. And Max said, 'She does this song, "She's a Woman" and people go crazy.' They loved her version. And I turned it into reggae, and that really seemed to make it take off."

Reggae was another vital element of the mid-seventies musical zeitgeist, the one form of music loved and respected by punk rockers like the Clash, just coming into their own at the time, and old guard rockers like Beck. While there are many great reggae artists, the music owed its seventies ascendancy to the worldwide popularity of the Jamaican superstar Bob Marley.

"What a sad loss," says Beck of Marley's 1981 passing. "It taught me to cherish more the friendship of people who mean something to you in life. Because in two fifths of a second, they're gone." To this day the guitarist treasures fond memories of his one meeting with the reggae icon, at London's Speakeasy Club.

"He had rasta hair out for days and it was actually steeped with the smell of pot. He'd look left or right and the air displacement would blow the pot smell in your face, even though he wasn't smoking. Fantastic. I lost the phone book in which he wrote his own phone number for me. It was my most cherished possession at one point."

The influence of black music is all over *Blow by Blow*—pervasive yet subtle—another factor in the album's tremendous success. The disc contains Beck-ified versions of not one, but two Stevie Wonder tunes, "Thelonius" and the poignant ballad "'Cause We've Ended as Lovers." The latter has become another Jeff Beck standard and favorite.

The album closes with "Diamond Dust," an inspired pairing of Jeff Beck's guitar mastery and George Martin's orchestral majesty. Orchestral settings are another musical context that Beck would return to and explore throughout his subsequent career. *On Blow by Blow*, the guitarist finally had all the things he'd been trying to put together ever since the end of the Yardbirds: great songs, great players, and a great producer who really understood what Beck was after.

The disc became Beck's biggest commercial success, giving him his first gold record. He exchanged his country cottage for a grand and historic Tudor manor house dating back to 1591, the reign of Queen Elizabeth I, situated on eighty acres in the Sussex countryside. There he and Celia Hammond would add to their growing family of domesticated animals, and Beck would establish a fully outfitted garage for working on his beloved hot rods. Life was good indeed. *Blow by Blow* has become an enduring classic, a clear forerunner and inspiration for the virtuoso guitar instrumental ascendancy of artists like Steve Vai and Joe Satriani in the eighties and beyond.

"A lot of people liked *Blow by Blow* because it simplified McLaughlin and it complicated rock and roll," Beck asserts.

Or to phrase it slightly differently, Jeff Beck put the rock back in jazz-rock fusion. For all their finesse, most of the fusion players didn't really get the rock aesthetic. They were jazz guys experimenting with a new form, perhaps even going for the gold, glory, and groupies that accompany success in rock. But they hadn't lived, breathed, sweated, and imbibed rock and roll the way Beck had.

Many excellent rock guitarists who get into jazz succeed only in becoming second-rate jazz players. Not Beck. He possessed both the chops and strong sense of identity to embrace jazz fusion without losing the rock feel. He never succumbed to the snobbery inherent in much of jazz culture—the tacit assumption that it is somehow "superior" to rock or other forms of pop music. Even though Beck won jazz guitar awards, he always made it clear in interviews: "I'm a rock guitarist!"

But what Beck did appropriate from the jazz tradition was the role of the featured instrumental soloist. *Blow by Blow* liberated Beck from the standard expectation that a rock guitarist should perform alongside a lead vocalist or function as some kind of pop star. From that point forward, Beck's career and standing in the world would be more akin to that of a great jazzman like Miles Davis or John Coltrane. He would record and perform primarily instrumental music with an ever-revolving cast of sidemen. What people crave from great instrumentalists like these is to hear them in different and intriguing musical settings, and to hear their unique interpretation of a musical composition. It doesn't matter whether or not the performer wrote the composition in question.

Nor is the instrumental soloing meant to offset a vocal performance. Great instrumental soloists can work with a singer from time to time, as Beck would. But with *Blow by Blow* he'd established a precedent whereby rock guitar, if played well enough, could stand on its own as an object of beauty, fascination, and fervent fan devotion. In the years to come, Beck would work hard to make his lead guitar as expressive as a human voice—a very demanding task.

"It's difficult without a vocalist," he says. "It's really rotten without some kind of vocal input to make people listen. To have them fascinated enough to stay and listen to a song without words, lyrics, and stuff. Guitar hooks can sound crummy as hell if you don't watch it."

Even for Jeff Beck, following up on the success of *Blow by Blow* was a tall order—especially since he could easily have sidestepped the whole issue by joining the Rolling Stones. He was one of several leading guitarists who received an offer to take the place that Mick Taylor left vacant when he

© MARTY TEMME ARCHIVES

left the Stones late in 1974. On one level, it might have made a lot of sense. Beck came out of the same London blues/R&B scene as the Stones, they'd both been managed by Giorgio Gomelsky, played the same clubs, and Stones pianist Ian Stewart was an old friend of Beck's.

But Beck never could have become another cog in the well-oiled machine that is the Rolling Stones. His obsessively driven nature would have rubbed against Jagger and company's leisurely approach to laying tracks. The drug-free Beck wouldn't have made much of a pal or partner for Keith Richards. But most of all, searing single-note guitar leads aren't really part of the Stones aesthetic. Brian Jones was never that kind of a guitarist, nor is Keef. Even Mick Taylor—a fine guitarist, but no Jeff Beck—stood out at times as being a little too "widdley widdley woo" for the Rolling Stones. So the band actually did much better in taking on Beck's former bass player, Ron Wood, as their guitarist.

But still, imagine the temptation for Beck. If he'd still been struggling to find himself, and success, he might have succumbed. But with the triumph that was *Blow by Blow*, he was clearly on a roll. And as he girded himself to create a worthy successor to that album, he formed another musical partnership that would prove pivotal to both his career and guitar style.

The classically trained Czech keyboardist Jan Hammer had ridden to fame as a member of the Mahavishnu Orchestra. He'd established himself as the undisputed master of the Mini Moog synthesizer. Like most synths at the time, it was a monophonic instrument, meaning you could only play one note at a time. Which confined players of synthesizers like the Mini Moog to single-note melodies—or the improvisational, single-note solos that had long been the domain of lead guitarists.

Hammer was the first synth player to truly master the Mini Moog's pitch and modulation wheels and panel of control knobs for filter and amplitude parameters. Generally operated by the player's left hand, the use of these controls has just as vital a musical role—perhaps even more of one—than the notes played by the right hand on the keyboard. Mastery of these knobs, wheels, and switches gave the player a degree of expressive control comparable to that of an electric guitarist with his amp, effects, and infinite gradations of fretboard touch. Indeed Hammer's dueling leads with McLaughlin had been one of the main attractions of the Mahavishnu Orchestra.

In a way, working with Jeff Beck was a logical progression for Hammer. They profoundly influenced one another. The origins of the stunning techniques Beck subsequently developed for manipulating the Stratocaster's vibrato arm and tone/volume controls may well lie in Hammer's way with a synth pitch wheel and bank of knobs. Beck has often acknowledged as much, but adds that Hammer "was influenced by the Indian quarter-tone scales. All the bends and stuff. So it's just a recycling of that."

And indeed, it was around the time Beck began working with Hammer that he laid aside his Les Pauls and made a full-time commitment to the Strat: "I thought, 'I can't be dicking around with a lot of different guitars,'" he says. "'Cause it was a totally different feel from one to the other. I wanted to be absolutely comfortable. And the Strat is what I started on. I became interested in going back to that again."

And so Jeff Beck's *Wired* album, the follow-up to *Blow by Blow*, is energized by Beck's re-engagement with the Strat, and his new creative partnership with Jan Hammer. Added to the equation was the stalwart Max Middleton, rocking the clavinet and Fender Rhoads electric piano for most of the disc, providing funky syncopations and jazzy chordal stylings to underpin Hammer and Beck's single-note solo frenzy.

While Richard Bailey returned to play drums on a couple of tracks, the bulk of the drumming duties on *Wired* was assumed by another Mahavishnu protégée, Narada Michael Walden. Soon to emerge as a gifted record producer and tunesmith in his own right, Walden also contributed several compositions to *Wired*. Rounding out the lineup was the quintessentially funky Wilbur Bascomb, a veteran of James Brown's band.

As if all that weren't enough, George Martin was once again at the production helm, at least for the initial stages of the project. For *Wired* soon took on a life of its own, taking off from whence *Blow by Blow* left off. Indeed, heard in retrospect, *Blow by Blow* seems almost a warm-up for *Wired*. The latter disc is edgier, more frenetic, quite arguably the best Jeff Beck album ever. It kicks off in high gear with the swaggering "Led Boots," a title taken by many to be a reference to Beck's old friend Jimmy Page and his most famous band. On this track Beck and his band certainly equal, if not outstrip, Zeppelin's vaunted ability to play tricky time signatures and still rock hard.

Bascomb's presence on the sessions brings the funk to the fore on tracks like "Come Dancing." Another *Wired* highlight is the kinetic "Blue Wind," a Beck–Hammer duet (they're the only players on the track), which finds the two instrumental giants trading riffs and solos, goading one another to ever-escalating levels of fury and frenzy. But at the other end of the spectrum, Beck's interpretation of jazzman Charlie Mingus's bluesy ballad "Goodbye Pork Pie Hat" offers some of his most lyrical and heart-wrenching solo guitar work of his entire career.

While not quite as successful as *Blow by Blow* commercially, *Wired* nevertheless sold briskly and is a much loved disc. By the time he came to record *Wired*, Beck had deleted the mouth bag from his effects arsenal. In the mid-seventies, the contraption became too closely associated with ex–Humble Pie guitarist Peter Frampton, who found huge success as a solo artist at the time.

"I checked into a hotel and the radio had been left on in the room," Beck recalls. "And I heard the bag being used and it was *Frampton Comes Alive* they were playing. I thought, 'Wait a minute, someone's bootlegged my album.' 'Cause no one else was using that thing at that time. But it was Peter Frampton. And that was the abrupt end to my use of the bag. From that night on, I never used it."

"For most of the eighties, the [music] business just went to a place where I didn't want to go. The clothes were more important than the music at one point, I think."

Beck would continue to ride the fusion train till the end of the eighties. He did a live album with the Jan Hammer Group and made guest appearances on discs by fusion luminaries like Stanley Clarke and Narada Michael Walden. It's intriguing how Beck could run with jazz players highly schooled in music theory without being much of a theoretical guitarist himself. His profound musical intuition and keen ear for melody and harmony were more than adequate to carry him through. Stanley Clarke remembers Beck's mysterious and mercurial way of coming to terms with a piece of music in a session:

"He'll go off in a corner by himself and fiddle around on the guitar. After a while, you'll say, 'You got it, Jeff?' He'll mumble something and fiddle some more. 'Jeff? Jeff!' But when it's time to do the take, he comes out and nails it."

"It's probably to my best advantage not to know what's going on," Beck laughs. "Like Jimmy Page was telling me about working with Puff Daddy on a remake of 'Kashmir.' Jimmy said, 'I want to have the tune moved up. We could do it in D or E.' And Puff Daddy said, 'I don't know nothing about no D or E.'"

But by the end of the seventies, fusion had definitely outworn its welcome. The advent of punk rock and New Wave had substantially reduced the rock audience's appetite for extended instrumental "wanking." Overexposure also contributed to fusion's demise. Too many albums appeared by sideman and sidemen of sidemen, with the inevitable resultant decline in originality and interest. Or as Stanley Clarke once put it, "Everybody and Maha-fuckin'-vishnu's cousin started putting out albums."

Beck's own fond farewell to the fusion era came in the pivotal year of 1980. On his appropriately titled *There and Back* album, about half the tracks were done with Jan Hammer. But the other half were done with two musicians who would play a big role in Beck's future: drummer Simon Phillips and keyboardist Tony Hymas. Both players had joined a touring band that Beck and Stanley Clarke had put together the year before. Hymas, in particular, would become an important Beck collaborator, taking up the keyboard role formerly played by Middleton and Hammer. The *There and Back* gem "El Becko" is one of Beck's notable early collaborations with Hymas. But the dynamic between two musicians is sometimes a volatile one, the classically trained keyboardist rubbing up against a profoundly intuitive rock guitarist.

"Obviously we're both total lunatics and never the twain shall meet," says Beck. "But perhaps that's our best thing. We disagree so violently that maybe something good will come out. If we were both in the same ballpark, it would turn into uninteresting schmaltz. What's fish to one person is fowl to another. Literally foul."

✌ COASTING THROUGH THE EIGHTIES ✌

As rock approached its fourth decade in the eighties, a few interesting phenomena began to develop. Enough time had elapsed that the period between roughly 1965 and 1977 had clearly emerged as rock's classic era—a golden age the likes of which will most likely never be seen again. And of course Jeff Beck had taken his place alongside the great guitar heroes of this golden age, iconic players like Jimi Hendrix, Eric Clapton, Jimmy Page, Pete Townshend, and David Gilmour. The musicians and music of the classic rock era became somehow serenely detached from the steady onward march of time, as it were, seemingly impervious to the vicissitudes of changing musical fashions and virtually guaranteed a loyal audience among not only their original baby boomer fan base but among each rising new rock generation.

And speaking of rising new generations, the dawn of the eighties witnessed a new breed of guitar hero. The pyrotechnic Eddie Van Halen and neo-classical Yngwie Malmsteen and Randy Rhoads had taken rock guitar in a new direction, far less blues based than the great sixties and seventies guitar innovators. But the new shred guitar gods of the eighties were universal in their love and admiration for Jeff Beck— the sixties rock player who'd arguably done the most to blaze a trail leading outside the blues box.

Furthermore, with Beck, Page, and Clapton all well established as classic-rock guitar legends, they were no longer competitors. Each had long since proven his mettle and secured his place in history. So the time was ripe for them to become collaborators. In 1981 Clapton invited Beck to participate in a charity concert called The Secret Policeman's Other Ball held at the Theatre Royal in London's Drury Lane to benefit Amnesty International. The highlight of the evening came when Beck and Clapton took the stage together, jamming on several songs.

The two guitar titans got together for another charity event in '83, the ARMS concerts at London's Albert Hall benefiting ex-Faces bassist Ronnie Lane's multiple sclerosis organization and the Prince's Trust. This time the event's organizers upped the ante by adding Jimmy Page to the bill. The monumental end-of-show jam featuring Beck, Clapton, and Page marked the first time that all three Yardbirds guitar alumni had shared the same stage. The eighties were also the period when rock videos first came to the fore, and the ARMs concerts became a successful home video release.

Historic reunions and pairings with fellow classic-rock icons were thick on the ground for Jeff Beck throughout the eighties. He got back together with Rod Stewart for a hit recording of the Curtis Mayfield gospel standard "People Get Ready" and a few other singles. He rejoined his fellow former Yardbirds Paul Samwell-Smith, Chris Dreja, and Jim McCarty for a few recordings under the band name Box of Frogs. Beck teamed with Jimmy Page and Robert Plant to cut some sides with their ad hoc group the Honeydrippers, and he contributed substantially to two Mick Jagger solo albums, *She's the Boss* in '85 and *Primitive Cool* in '87. And outside the British Invasion old boys' club, Beck guested on eighties discs by everyone from Tina Turner and Diana Ross to former Sex Pistols manager Malcolm McLaren.

But nostalgic reunions and session work could never fully satisfy Beck's relentless need to move forward with his own music. The decline of the fusion era led to another difficult period of creative soul searching, exacerbated—as always—by Beck's ongoing struggle with the expectations of the music marketplace. A power shift at Beck's longtime label, Epic, led to a revival of Mickie Most's idea that Beck should step forward as a vocalist as well as guitarist, or at least put out another predominately vocal album.

That's what led to the 1985 release of *Flash*, generally regarded as the least satisfying album in the entire Beck cannon. The guitarist reluctantly sang a few numbers and then ceded the mike to vocalist Jimmy Hall of the seventies album-rock band Wet Willie. Production of the album was handled by Nile Rodgers. A fine guitarist in his own right who'd forged an innovative and much-sampled rhythmic sensibility with his funk-disco group Chic, Rodgers had become the producer du jour in the mid-eighties, scoring monster hits for artists as diverse as Madonna, David Bowie, Duran Duran, and Mick Jagger.

As an instrumentalist rather than a vocalist, Beck didn't have much in common with any of the previously named artists. But he nonetheless ended up getting processed through Rodgers's hit-making machine. The producer called on the standard eighties go-to guys, drum machine programmer Jimmy Bralower and remix master Arthur Baker to affix their highly marketable stamps to Beck's project. In the past Beck had done some wonderful work with funk rhythms and black musical idioms. In the future he'd do some killer stuff with programmed beats. But none of these elements seemed to work as well for him on *Flash*. Ditto for the vocals. Significantly, the *Flash* track that won a Grammy was the instrumental "Escape."

"For most of the eighties, the [music] business just went to a place where I didn't want to go," Beck later said. "The clothes were more important than the music at one point, I think. And the video prerequisite was something I wasn't interested in. And the domination of synthesizers in the eighties made me very depressed—to think that they could possibly overshadow real playing. But for a while they did."

In between high-visibility guest shots and celebrity jams, Beck became a somewhat reclusive figure in the eighties, spending longer periods of time on his estate in Surrey, working on his hot rods, and spending quality time with the sheep, pigs, dogs, and cats on the premises. His longtime relationship with Celia Hammond petered out toward the end of the eighties, although the two remained friendly. Beck also spent some tax exile time in the United States.

It may have seemed like he was drifting, but in 1989 he reemerged with another career-defining album, *Jeff Beck's Guitar Shop* with Terry Bozzio and Tony Hymas. A versatile and accomplished drummer, Bozzio had led synth-pop hit makers Missing Persons and played with Frank Zappa before coming to Beck. The drummer brought something new to the well-established dynamic between Beck and Hymas. *Guitar Shop* offered a new slant on the power trio concept, with keyboards taking the place occupied by bass guitar back in the day. Of course keyboards have a wider dynamic range and far more polyphony than a bass, leaving less space for the lead guitar. But this didn't seem to challenge or bother Beck. Guitar Shop went on to cop the '89 Grammy for Best Rock Instrumental Performance.

During sessions for the album, Tony Hymas had turned Beck on to *Le Mystere des Voix Bulgares*, an album of traditional Bulgarian choral music performed by a female choir. The disc had emerged in the US and UK as part of the world music boom, becoming a minor hit among hipsters and world beatniks. Beck had always been fascinated by world music and the microtonal mysteries of non-Western scales. But there was something in that choral record that touched him profoundly. "That is the deepest music I ever heard pass my ears," he says.

Beck became obsessed with the delicate, ethereal vocal sound on that disc and set about trying to emulate it on the guitar. He developed an elaborate technique that made its debut on the song "Where Were You" from *Guitar Shop*, and has since become one of his sonic trademarks. Basically he'll play a melody entirely in harmonics, using the Strat's vibrato arm to modulate pitch microtonally and the volume knob to emulate the natural attack and decay characteristics of the human voice:

"It's not easy. Especially when the harmonic isn't in the right notes. You know, when it's a semitone sharp [i.e., from a natural, open string harmonic.] So rather than tune the guitar down, I'll just bend the string down before I hit the harmonic and just guess at it. Or I'll hit it and bend it up. Whatever it takes. There are no rules in that."

Beck had discovered a device, the Trev Wilkinson roller nut, that proved useful in facilitating the radical pitch-bend maneuvers that he was starting to explore. It also went a long way toward alleviating the age-old tuning problems associated with extreme string bending and wang bar use on a Strat. The Wilkinson nut became a stock feature of the Fender Strat Plus in the late eighties, which in turn became the basis for Fender's first Jeff Beck signature model guitar, introduced in 1990:

"I would have had a 1954 Strat with cigarette burns and wear and tear on it and been just as happy," Beck says. "But if they're going to sell a signature model, they're going to have to have some of your input on it. And those are the only alterations I would have made, improvement-wise. One thing you don't want is bad tuning. Hendrix went all over the place with a Strat and he had tuning problems galore. In the end, it didn't seem to matter. But the white kid from Surrey has big problems with tuning."

One of the first prototypes for the Beck signature model was a surf green guitar that Beck used on "Where Were You." Autographed for Beck by the rock and roll legend Little Richard, it has become another one of Jeff Beck's iconic guitars.

THE DIVERSIFIED NINETIES

But as the nineties dawned, Beck went through another period of retrenchment. It was as if he were avoiding the issue of making a follow-up to *Guitar Shop*. "I'm not a studio rat like people like Jan Hammer," Beck once said. "He coined that phrase, a studio rat, I think. He never comes out. I wish it were me. But I don't like to be tied to any kind of musical routine. There's gotta be a genuine desire to go and do it. The sad thing is that bands are so different and insular now. There's no more, 'Oh well, see you at the studio and we'll get something done.' That's gone. Way back in the seventies gone. Everybody writes stuff that's so finished now. Fifteen-hundred bucks will get you a good home setup that you can record on. And that makes it very difficult to get that camaraderie thing to continue. We used to just go in some crappy pub and rehearse in the room above and it would be a great blast. No obligations. No tape recorder. Just having a good old go at it. Those days are long gone now."

But Beck found other types of projects that afforded an element of old-time camaraderie while also giving him a convenient excuse to get to work on his next major album statement. First, he

dabbled in TV and film work, writing a score for the TV mini series *Frankie's House* with keyboardist-composer Jed Leiber (son of Jerry Leiber of the hit songwriting duo Leiber and Stoller). He even did a few minor cameo appearances in films and Britcoms.

Then Beck went back to his roots with a CD tribute to his boyhood hero, guitarist Cliff Gallup of Gene Vincent's Blue Caps: *Crazy Legs: Jeff Beck and the Big Town Playboys*. Teaming with the Playboys, a London rockabilly purist outfit, brought Beck some of the musical camaraderie he'd been missing. It also gave him an opportunity to revisit and reassess some of the foundations of his own playing style. As an adolescent guitarist struggling to find his own way forward, Beck had been heavily influenced by Gallup's fingerpicking technique. But he soon went his own wild way with it. For the *Crazy Legs* project, Beck was after historical accuracy:

"I was heartbroken that I had to use finger picks!" he says. "Cliff Gallup and Chet Atkins in the fifties used to use finger picks, and you can't possibly get that crispness and clarity without finger picks. And for the Blue Caps tribute, I had to learn to play with finger picks. It was ghastly. They kept falling off and springing across the room. But to get that sharpness, you need them."

As usual, however, the intensely self-critical Beck is selling himself short. Armed with a period-authentic Gretsch, he was able to approximate his mentor's sound and style with eerie accuracy. But you'll never convince him of that:

"I thought at one stage I was getting close," he says. "But when I listen to the original, tonally I'm nowhere near it. It does have the spirit and sometimes the notation is perfect. But you put that old Gene Vincent and the Blue Caps album on and it's just one of the minor miracles of our time."

In the final analysis, *Crazy Legs* was a fun and intriguing project for Beck and his fans, but clearly not the new direction that Beck found himself seeking in the early nineties:

"As much as I still dearly love rockabilly, I don't think that there's much to be gained by pursuing that any further," he said at the time. "One can't progress by going back too far. I still use some of the [rockabilly] gimmickry. Slap echo is always going to be one of the best inventions ever. But there the similarity ends, really."

By this stage of his career, Beck was also paying a heavy price experienced by many rock musicians, particularly those who came up in the era when 100- and 200-watt amps were a brand-new invention and nobody understood the damage they could do to one's hearing. Beck suffers from tinnitus—a constant ringing sound in the ears—and the high-frequency hearing loss that generally accompanies tinnitus. The condition is particularly acute in his left ear. He has described it as "terrible, wicked. The damage is done, you know."

At one point, Beck wore headphones connected to a CD player almost continually, playing music constantly to mask the ringing in his ears. He has also explored the possibility that the condition may be exacerbated by the two head fractures he suffered from his '69 automobile accident and the '66 tumble down a staircase in Marseilles.

"When I told one specialist that," Beck recalls, "he said, 'Well, what are you wondering about then? A four-inch crack in the back of your head and you're wondering why you've got a ringing noise?'"

Fortunately the advent of in-ear monitors has enabled Beck to continue performing live while reducing the risk of further auditory nerve damage from loud volume levels. And in the studio, volume levels can also be managed. But when the news of Beck's hearing difficulties became widespread, fans began to wonder if they'd ever hear new music from the master. As if to confirm those fears, Beck's film work and retro rockabilly romp were bracketed by a slew of retrospective "best of" reissue releases, most notably the wonderful three-disc *Beckology* box set. But there was an end-game feel to these releases. The big box set usually comes when an artist's career, or life, is over, or nearly so. And for Beck, there were longer and more frequent periods of retreat into his garage to be alone with his hot rods:

"It helps me forget about music or the nasty things in life," he says of his automotive work. "Or, actually, it's not true that I forget about music. The sounds in the garage like the air line and the compressor—that's all rhythmic stuff. There are so many sounds in a shop. Bang, crash . . . it's a musical place to be. Subliminally, I'm picking up on that."

⌁ BECK'S TECHNO TRILOGY ⌁

Beck's next album release, 1999's *Who Else!*, would certainly capture the relentless clangor of mechanical sounds, while also dispelling any fears that the game was up for the legendary guitarist or that his best work all lay behind him. Once again Beck managed to surprise and delight the world with a bold new musical direction, this time by embracing the frenetic, digitized beats and textures of electronica, one of the predominant musical styles of the nineties and beyond, but not one usually associated with rock guitar.

This futuristic new mode of dance music had emerged out of the Detroit techno scene of the mid-eighties and the UK/European rave scene of the late eighties. Young people were converging in massive, euphoric gatherings fueled by the then-new drug ecstasy and the heavy electronic beats. By the nineties, the movement had gone mainstream with the ascendancy of new DJ heroes like the Chemical Brothers, Orbital, and Paul Oakenfold. The music was characterized by frantic BPMs (beats per minute) far beyond the capacity or endurance of any human drummer and a brisk cut-and-paste aesthetic full of wild segues and abrupt transitions made possible by emergent music software technologies.

In short, electronic music had arrived at the frenzied non-linearity and unfettered sonic adventurousness that had characterized Jeff Beck's guitar work from the start. And by the late nineties, the original techno-rave sounds had morphed into a dazzling array of spinoffs and subgenres: the jerky fractal rhythms of drum and bass, jungle, breakbeat, and IDM (intelligent dance music), and the blissfully chilled-out textures of downtempo, ambient, acid jazz, trip hop, and scores of other microstyles all constantly evolving and changing at a dizzying pace, driven by the insatiable hunger of club kids for another new sound, beat, or vibe.

Of course most guitar aficionados hated the stuff, deeming it "artificial" and totally missing the fact that much electronica foregrounds the two things that guitar fiends love most: a blurry, super-fast succession of notes and interesting sonic textures. It took a genius of Jeff Beck's magnitude to make the inspired connection. Where other guitarists felt threatened, Beck dove right in.

It was no instant epiphany, however. *Who Else!* evolved by means of a convoluted, tortuous, and typically Beckian process. In the mid-nineties Beck started on an album project with fellow guitar hero Steve Lukather as producer. But like many other Beck projects, that ended up being shelved and for all too familiar reasons. "Steve's probably a really great producer," says Beck, "but we never found how the thing could be 'cause we were so sorely lacking material."

The next step was a series of live recordings built around some Tony Hymas compositions. But when Beck reviewed these tracks, he was disappointed. "Good playing," he says, "but no electricity coming off. So I dismembered all those takes on the multitrack and got down to some serious surgery. I retained all the solos and drum parts that were good."

Beck called on programmer-producer Mel Wesson to perform some radical editing and reshaping on the Tony Hymas composition that became the album's opening track, "What Mama Said." "It's completely a rebuild," says Beck. "There's barely anything left of Tony's original composition there. We had all these bits and pieces and I turned that into the main thing. I just felt it was far more exciting to use these things that were peripheral to the main theme. It jumps straight to the goodies, like the jungle groove and the guitar solo. It seemed to work more for me than something that starts with a verse and then goes to a bridge and has a nice, persnickety chordal structure. I thought, 'Two plays of that and people are gonna start to skip over it. It's too long and there's not enough events.' I wanted a mega opening track. A sonic explosion of sound."

With the advent of Pro Tools technology and the post-techno production aesthetic, Beck finally had a way of working that could keep pace with his restless imagination and even challenge him. Another programmer-producer, Donal Hodgson, was called in to work on another track, "Space for Papa."

"They're a younger set of guys who I think are going to be vitally important," said Beck of Wesson and Hodgson. "They've got this great chop-it-up attitude. They'll slice a tune in half and make me think again. Whether they have an affinity for the music or not, you're gonna get chopped—like it or not. And that's great. 'Cause I can see what they're reading into the music."

Another new ingredient on *Who Else!* was American guitar virtuoso Jennifer Batten. Beck had first seen her perform on Michael Jackson's 1993 Dangerous tour and was instantly captivated. He vividly recalls his first sight of "this animal coming onstage with her hair blown up six feet high. It was a great foil for her to be onstage with the biggest pop star in the world. And she's just so nonplused about it. She's the coolest creature in the world. I was talking to her four or five years ago about doing something."

Beck had been contemplating adding Batten to his band for quite some time, but the idea didn't come to fruition until Beck was mired in the creative process that would eventually yield *Who Else!* "Right out of the blue, she walked into the studio with this big spray of flowers she'd brought me. I went, 'Someone cares. [Laughs.] All is not lost.' And I knew she was a demon guitar player. She could shred most guys. I knew she'd be a great player to have in the band."

Batten's role on the disc was mainly MIDI guitar, acting almost as another keyboard player to provide textures and chordal contexts. Beck felt that this would be a better use of her talents than a dueling lead-guitar scenario. "I don't want this to be a big shootout at the OK Coral with guitars," Beck said at the time. "That's a silly thing to do. It entices trouble."

When all is said and done, *Who Else!* is a satisfyingly diverse record, bringing together many of Beck's traditional strengths while exploring some exciting new directions. About half the tracks are in Beck's newfound techno mode. But then "Brush with the Blues" is a fine, jazzy-bluesy ballad in the mode of "Goodbye Pork Pie Hat." Elsewhere on the disc, "Blast from the East" touches on Beck's long-term love affair with world music, while "Angel (Footsteps)" is a lovely slide guitar exercise played on one of Beck's Telecasters. The guitarist's fusion-era comrade Jan Hammer even makes an appearance, contributing keyboards and drums to "Even Odds."

The approach that Beck found on *Who Else!* served him so well that he employed it on two more albums. For 2000's *You Had It Coming*, he brought in producer-programmer Andy Wright, who'd worked with the seminal trip-hop group Massive Attack. Jennifer Batten came into a larger role on that disc as well, writing one of the compositions, "Earthquake," and co-writing another, "Loose Cannon." But once again, Beck mixes things up, throwing in a shot of pure blues with a rollicking rendition of the Muddy Waters classic "Rollin' and Tumblin'," with a guest vocal from Imogen Heap, who would become another frequent collaborator.

The third and final installment in Beck's techno trilogy arrived in 2003. Simply titled *Jeff*, it is the most fully realized, and most radical, embodiment of the "Beck goes techno" concept. It's as if he'd finally managed to morph his guitar completely into the circuitry. The album is filled with glorious head-rush moments wherein the distinction between foreground and background is blurred as Beck's guitar becomes just one more gleaming whoosh in a hypersonic pinball game darting from speaker to speaker.

"I didn't want the guitar's role to be thrust in people's faces, with just a little bit of backing," he says. "I wanted it to be integrated. I wanted it to weave in and out and let other sounds be heard. Otherwise, the music is less rich for it. I mean, when it's time to shred, then shred. But otherwise, let the rhythm do something."

When shred time does arrive, Beck's soloing reaches new heights of abstract expressionism on *Jeff*. His intro riffing on the track "Trouble Man" is the aural equivalent of a Jackson Pollock action painting. Distressed guitar timbres fly everywhere, landing far outside all known coordinates of melody and harmony. His solo on the song "My Thing" also ranks among his most frenzied and furious guitar work.

"Half of the solo was done live in the studio with about thirty people in the control room, falling over drunk," Beck confides. "I like to go berserk, but with other people around. Because they actually do make me play slightly more energetically and frantically. So we were lucky to get that solo. We morphed the track into something completely different, but we kept that guitar solo."

Age fifty-nine at the time of the album's release, Beck's choice of co-producers for the disc show that he'd kept his finger on the pulse of cutting-edge contemporary music. While bringing Andy Wright and Tony Hymas back into the studio to share production duties on *Jeff*, Beck also called in the electronic duo Apollo 440 (aka Noko Fisher-Jones, Howard, and Trevor Gray), Dean Garcia (formerly of the seminal noise pop-shoegaze band Curve), and guitarist-producer David Torn, a David Bowie collaborator who'd also recorded several edgy albums under the nom de disque Splattercell.

As on *Who Else!* and *You Had It Coming*, however, *Jeff* also touches on Beck's other long-standing musical interests and strengths. His obsession with *Le Mystere des Voix Bulgares* emerges on the track "Bulgaria," an arrangement of a traditional Bulgarian tune gloriously realized with a full orchestral arrangement and some of Beck's most lyrical playing:

"It's just a traditional hillside folksong from Bulgaria," says Beck. "Those girls, I mean, they sing . . . I think there's four parts. Four voices. And it's very difficult sometimes to pick out the lead melody, because the vocal lines are so tightly woven together. But in this particular song, there is a strong melody that sticks out. So I sort of adapted it, and instead of four voices, I used a thirty-seven-piece orchestra.

Another track, the atmospheric "Pork-U-Pine," contains hints and echoes of another long-standing favorite world music for Beck. He employs the vibrato arm of his Strat—as only Jeff Beck can—to emulate the tricky vocal trills found in Indian music:

"One more element that helps me play is the way the Eastern Indian girls sing, when they do that amazing scale," he says. "It's almost unwritable. You can't even tell what's going on unless you slow it down. And it's great—a bit of oxygen for my playing style. I don't like to rip off complete phrases. But some of the quick vibratos I do help me to form my own style, so I adapt it to the blues. Indian blues is really the way I describe it."

Even Beck's guitar for the album reflects an Indian musical influence. His principal ax was a Strat named Anoushka in honor of the sitar player Anoushka Shankar, the daughter of Indian music patriarch Ravi Shankar, who autographed Beck's Strat for him at a Rainforest benefit concert at which both instrumentalists had performed.

"She's divine," says Beck of the youthful sitar virtuoso. "She's rock and roll, innit? She laughs and jokes. She's more of a good-time player rather than 'Oh, I'm tradition. You're no good and I'm fabulous.' I said to her, 'Just please sign this.' And she signed my guitar. She couldn't believe I asked her. So now that Strat is Anoushka."

Another key Indian musical influence for Beck is the Indian slide guitar player Vishwa Mohan Bhatt. "It's almost too exquisite for words, the way he can control the bottleneck and make it sound like Ravi Shankar," says Beck. "If you don't see him play, you might not even guess it's a bottleneck. It's hard to believe it's not a guy who's bending a string from the same position as a sitar would."

All told, the moody atmospheres of contemporary electronic music fused with the timeless cadences of world music and blues proved to be an ideal setting for showcasing Jeff Beck's many moods and far-reaching musical tastes. The song "Plan B" from *Jeff* garnered him his fourth Grammy Award. But shortly after the release of *Jeff*, the guitarist announced that the disc "will probably by my last record made with a computer screen and mouse." He was feeling the urge to get back with live musicians once again.

In the early years of the twenty-first century, for perhaps the first time in his life, Beck began showing signs of becoming comfortable with his formidable past and rich musical legacy. Always his own harshest critic, he'd spent much of his career downgrading and sometimes blatantly denigrating his own landmark recordings. But in September 2002 he was persuaded to take part in series of concerts at London's Festival Hall, celebrating the wondrous and vertiginous trajectory of Jeff Beck's music and career. The evening found him sharing the stage with many of his musical contemporaries and peers, from John McLaughlin to Roger Waters, whose 1992 solo album *Amused to Death* had been greatly enhanced by Beck's guitar stylings. But as if to confirm Beck's consummate hipness and vital connection with contemporary music, the guest performers also included the White Stripes, who joined Beck in stripped-down performances of several Yardbirds classics. The event served to confirm

Beck's towering status as the only guitar hero equally revered by virtuoso shred geeks and garage band primitivists.

One can only marvel at Beck's perpetual youthfulness. Not only does he move with the times musically, he never seems to age much physically. While his guitar hero contemporaries have grown visibly gray and paunchy, or taken to sporting facial hair and wire-rim specs worthy of some suburban anesthesiologist, Beck still looks much as he did in 1966—slender and agile, his British Invasion haystack hairdo mysteriously intact. His secret?

"I don't go to parties," he said in '03. "I don't get drunk all the time. I mean, I do get drunk, but only on special occasions. I live in the country where just going up to my shop, my garage, is about a hundred yards. I do that about ten times a day without even thinking about it. And then there's the animals [to care for]. I do about four miles a day, walking and running. And then physical lifting of things. So it does keep me in good shape."

Beck was in sufficiently good shape in 2005 to marry blond beauty Sandra Cash, some twenty or so years his junior and dishily described by the tabloid press as "wife number six." It was Cash—along with Leo and Sally Green, principals of London's fabled jazz club Ronnie Scott's—who helped persuade Beck to play a week-long residence at the venue in November 2007. Beck says his original response on being asked by Leo Green, "Hey, why don't you play Ronnie's?" was "Hey, why don't you f**k off?"

So the world owes a huge debt to Cash and all those who talked Beck into doing the gig. The performances the guitarist and his band at the intimate venue were captured on camera, and the best moments were released on the superb '08 DVD *Jeff Beck Performing This Week . . . Live at Ronnie Scott's*. The top-drawer production offers loving close-ups of Beck's hands in action, giving guitar fiends an unprecedented opportunity to study the master's technique in detail. The DVD also helped introduce another new and outstanding Beck backing band, consisting this time of drummer Vinnie Colaiuta, keyboardist Jason Rebello, and Beck's latest discovery, the uncannily youthful Australian bassist Tal Wilkenfeld, with her abundant Pre-Raphaelite tresses and formidable musical savvy. Twenty years of age at the time of the Ronnie Scott residency, she looked more like fourteen.

"After forty odd years, it's nice to be recognized. It's nice to know there's someone there ringing the bell for me."

In fitting recognition of his towering contribution to rock, Beck was inducted into the Rock and Roll Hall of Fame in 2009. He'd earlier been inducted as a member of the Yardbirds, but this more recent honor acknowledged Beck's entire body of work and was fittingly bestowed by the guitarist's old friend Jimmy Page.

"Largely, I disapprove of overblown ceremony," Beck commented at the time. "But it's difficult to say no to something like that. After forty odd years, it's nice to be recognized. It's nice to know there's someone there ringing the bell for me."

The closing years of the new century's first decade have seen Beck moving into high gear. Now under the management of Harvey Goldsmith, who took over from Beck's longtime manager Ralph Baker, the guitarist released the elegiac *Emotion and Commotion* album in 2010, featuring some singularly expressive guitar work from Beck in lavish orchestral settings that take up where *Blow by Blow* and *Jeff*'s "Bulgaria" left off. That same year has witnessed the release of another DVD paying tribute to Beck's roots, *Jeff Beck's Rock and Roll Party to Honor Les Paul*.

Back when he first became intrigued by Les Paul's records as a boy, Jeff Beck had no idea that his fascination with the guitar would take him on a lifelong journey of musical discovery, a strange and wondrous trip that has profoundly enriched the art of guitar playing for all time to come. Although his road has not always been an easy one, Jeff Beck has triumphed by remaining faithful to his own unique musical truth.

"I would never sit and write or record something that's going to slippery-eel its way into the business," he says. "I think it's better to write music for yourself and then say, 'Hey, I think people will like this.' I just figure if I have people out there wanting to hear from me, then I'd better get on with it, hadn't I? Make an account of myself."

Steve Cropper

SOUL MAN TO THE RESCUE

THE MAGIC OF MEMPHIS SOUL MUSIC from the mid-sixties is readily felt, but hard to quantify. It's an amalgam of many immeasurably miraculous elements. First and foremost, there are unbeatable songs like "In the Midnight Hour," "Respect," "I've Been Loving You Too Long," and "Knock on Wood." And phenomenal singers like Otis Redding, Wilson Pickett, Eddie Floyd, Carla Thomas, Sam Moore, and Dave Prater. Underpinning it all is superb musicianship—tight and succinct, always tastefully understated, yet generating an intense level of heat.

But beyond and beneath all of these obvious factors, there's something else—a deliciously indescribable *texture*, a distinctive *crunchiness* to the grooves and sounds. Soul music is like soul food in that regard—a deeply satisfying concoction that's more than the sum total of its ingredients. It nourishes your entire being and makes you feel good.

The amazing texture of this music also derives, in no small part, from the unique acoustic properties of the room where it was born. The Stax recording studio was a former movie theater converted into a palace of sound at 926 East McLemore Avenue in Memphis. Stax nurtured the collective soul—to coin a phrase—of a rare and gifted group of individuals whose life paths brought them together in that repurposed cinema in the middle years of the sixties, at a time of dramatic social change and cultural innovation.

One of the finest talents drawn into that creative vortex was a Missouri-born guitar man with a deep, easygoing drawl and even easier laugh. As house producer, A&R man, session guitarist, and one of the principal songwriters at Stax, Steve Cropper was a major architect of the Memphis soul sound, and he remains an icon for guitar players and music lovers. Large of stature and great of heart, his unmistakably graceful, evocative guitar playing is instantly recognized and reverently treasured worldwide. It is integral to our musical heritage. Crisp, clean, and wondrously fluid— baptized and sanctified in the trifold rivers of blues, country, and R&B—Cropper's Telecaster styling functions almost as another human voice on classics like Sam & Dave's "Soul Man" or Otis Redding's "I've Been Loving You Too Long."

"With music, most people listen to what's on the top, but what's magic about music is what's underneath."

Not unlike a Greek chorus, it enhances the drama. It curls around the lead vocal like pungent smoke, wordlessly answering and commenting on what the singer has to say, but never stealing the scene. In the dense landscape of a Stax arrangement, rife with two-fisted keyboard work, big horn charts, and powerful vocals, Cropper's guitar always rings through plangently and beautifully.

"With music, most people listen to what's on the top," Cropper explains. "But what's magic about music is what's underneath. It's the energy that's involved into the music. It's not the notes as much as the way those notes are played. And the energy. If you sell energy, you will be a lot more successful than you will be trying to sell notes."

Cropper's multifaceted artistry as a guitarist, songwriter, producer, arranger, and A&R man has been integral not only to the Stax artists but to the work of musical giants ranging from Jeff Beck to John Lennon. Cropper has always been the guy who gets the job done, who gets the hits made— from penning a lyric or setting up mikes to driving the finished master around town to tastemaker DJs. His razor-sharp musical instincts are matched by a relentless work ethic.

"I've always been a band member, a team player," he humbly states, "and that's the way I like to do it. If I'm missing out by not being a front man, I'll just have to miss out."

Cropper got a chance to reflect on his long and eventful musical journey recently, when the very first guitar that he ever played—an old Gibson F1 flattop acoustic originally belonging to his uncle—came back into his life. "My dad gave it to me for Christmas last year," he says, "I'd been trying for years to get it from my aunt when my uncle passed away."

Cropper first started to mess around with that guitar at around age ten. When he was nine, his family had moved to Memphis, Tennessee, from Missouri—where Steve had been born on October 21, 1941, in the town of Dora. He was an only child, and even after the move to Memphis, young Steve would go back to Missouri to visit his aunt and uncle.

GUITAR PLAYER ARCHIVES

"I used to go and spend a week or so with them up on their farm in Missouri," he says. "My uncle played piano and fiddle. He didn't really play guitar, but he kept one in the closet for other people to play. Because they used to have music jams after church on Sunday. People would come over and there was always someone who played guitar but didn't have one. So my uncle bought a guitar for those events. And I used to get that guitar out, with their permission, and just sort of pluck the strings. Basically just the big sixth E string . . . just to hear that sound like a rubber band, you know? I didn't know what I was doing. But that kind of got me fascinated with guitars.

"From that time on, I was interested in the guitar, and definitely interested in music. My mother wanted me to play piano, but I didn't want to take piano lessons. I was one of those kids who thought that taking piano was a Little Lord Fauntleroy, sissy thing. I guess because a lot of girls played piano. Now I'm kicking my butt, because I sure could use the knowledge of music you get from studying the piano."

But young Steve found other ways to amass musical knowledge. His family's move to Memphis had brought him to a city with an exceptionally rich musical heritage. Not only the proverbial home of the blues, Memphis was the cradle of American musical civilization, where the strains of down-home country music crossbred with African American musical forms like gospel and blues. The air around Memphis was filled with great music—and so were the airwaves. Memphis was the home of the first African American radio station, WDIA, where musical giants like B. B. King and Howlin' Wolf served turns as DJs. Once Cropper honed in on WDIA's signal, his life was never the same.

"I didn't seriously start listening to anything until we moved to Memphis in 1951," he recalls. "We got a radio. I turned it on one night and started listening to gospel music. There was a big station called WDIA. I later became friends with them. And they were playing gospel music. I went, 'Wow, what is that!?' I was just taken by the feel of it, the sound of it. I went to church too, but all our church music was a cappella—very poor a cappella, if I remember correctly. My granddad actually led the singing. My family belonged to a church that didn't believe in musical instruments. That was taboo and Devil's music, so we had to listen to all this a cappella stuff. But when I first heard gospel music, it really turned me around."

Memphis in the early fifties was where all those gospel, blues, and country roots would mutate into a wild and rebellious new musical strain called rock and roll. Sam Phillips's Memphis studio and label, Sun Records, became ground zero for this musical explosion, releasing history-making discs by Elvis Presley, Carl Perkins, and Jerry Lee Lewis. And by the time the rock-and-roll revolution got underway, Steve Cropper had equipped himself with a guitar all his own.

"When I was around 14, I asked my dad if he would buy me my own guitar. And he said, 'Well, son, I'd love to, but I can't afford to buy you one.' So I literally just found odd jobs, from mowin' other people's yards to shinin' shoes. I got a little job as a pin boy at a local bowling alley that was within walking distance—settin' pins before they had automatic pin setters. I used to get ten cents a game for that. I'd work all day to make just a few bucks. I saved and saved that money up. There was one guitar I looked at in a Sears and Roebuck catalog: a Silvertone flattop country guitar that looked very much like the one that my uncle had. And I think it was seventeen dollars. So I saved seventeen dollars and I had my mom help me order the guitar. Then we waited. They said they would deliver it on a Saturday. I think I sat on the front porch for about three or four hours, waiting to see that truck turn the corner.

GUITAR PLAYER ARCHIVES

"They come up with the guitar. It was in a box. I couldn't wait to see it, but they said, 'That'll be a twenty-five cent delivery charge.' Well, they'd never mentioned anything about that. I did not have 25 cents. A quarter was a lot of money in those days. So my mom lent me the quarter. She always tells the story and says if she had not lent me twenty-five cents, it probably would have changed my whole career.

"So I get the guitar, figure how to put the bridge on, string it, and tune it. My dad, bless his heart, looked at me and said, 'Son, you learn how to play that and I'll buy you a good guitar.' And he kept his word; he sure did."

The Cropper family was not affluent. Steve's dad had been a farmer, then a teacher, then a policeman. But once the boy demonstrated the requisite proficiency on the humble Sears instrument, Mr. Cropper found a way to procure a very nice Gibson archtop electric for his gifted son.

"He bought me a used electric," Steve narrates. "He found some guy. I think he was a sergeant on a police force, or a policeman, who was selling a guitar. So Dad and I went over and looked at it. I played it a little bit and Dad said, 'Okay, thanks for showing it to us.' The guy had an amp and all that. Of course Dad said, 'Aw, son, that's just too much; we can't afford that.'

"That evening, my mom says, 'Better go in the living room.' This was around Christmastime.

And lo and behold, there was that guitar with the case open laying on the floor. Dad went back and got it. He liked to surprise people. And I've got a picture of me holding that guitar. I think it's in the Rock and Roll Hall of Fame in Cleveland. It was a Gibson cutaway, thin body, sunburst, single pickup with a trapeze bridge. I think it was an ES-175. It was a pretty cool guitar."

By this time Cropper had befriended a young guy who would eventually accompany him on a mutual ride to fame as his bassist and closest friend: Donald "Duck" Dunn. To the best of Crop's recollection, he and Dunn were in the same homeroom in the fifth grade at the Sherwood school in Memphis. From there they went on to high school together.

"When we were teenagers," Cropper recollects, "Duck looked at his mom and said, 'When I grow up I want to be a musician.' She looked at him and said, 'Son, you can't do both.' And I do think Duck and I sort of refused to grow up. We always liked to play music and hang out and have a good time. I think that kept us young through the years. At least in feeling. Music is energy. It keeps you up."

Cropper and Dunn bonded over a mutual, and what would become a lifelong, passion: golf. "We grew up playing golf and fell in love with the game," says Cropper. But what really brought them together was an all-consuming fascination was the brand-new rock-and-roll sounds of the day.

"Like everybody else, we listened to Elvis Presley, Chuck Berry, and Little Richard," says Cropper. "As a guitar player, I listened to people like Chet Atkins and Duane Eddy, who later became my good buddy. And of course Scotty Moore, who also became a good friend of mine later on when I got into the recording business. I love what Scotty played on 'Mystery Train' with Elvis. That was one of my favorite records. I still have the old 78 [rpm vinyl disc] upstairs. It still has my name scribbled on it. 'Cause when we'd do sock hops—little parties at somebody's house—we all brought our records. But we'd write our names on them so we could take our records back home at the end of the night. Otherwise, they'd get mixed up and nobody would remember whose records were whose."

More obscure but equally compelling influences were Lowman Pauling, guitarist for the North Carolina vocal group the 5 Royales, and Billy Butler, who played guitar with R&B keyboard great Bill Doggett. Even the name of Cropper's first professional band, the Royal Spades, seems an homage to the 5 Royales. But by the time their first single, "Last Night," was released, the Royal Spades had rechristened themselves the Mar-Keys, a reference to the theater marquee out at the front of the former movie house that was home to the band's new record label, Satellite Records. And in 1961, the same year "Last Night" was released, Satellite changed its name to Stax Records.

The label was started in 1957 by Jim Stewart in conjunction with his sister, Estelle Axton. Satellite initially focused on country and pop releases before finding its niche in the burgeoning R&B genre. "Last Night" was one of the first records released under a distribution and partnership deal that Satellite inked with the major label Atlantic/Atco Records. While the Atlantic deal was a good thing for the small Memphis label, more widespread distribution brought Satellite Records to the attention of a California label that had been operating on the same name for a longer period of time. Faced with the threat of legal action, the Memphis Satellite changed its name to Stax, a combination of the first two letters from Stewart's and Axton's surnames. Soon Stax would become one of most revered names in American musical history.

A funky, organ-driven instrumental track, "Last Night" didn't even have a guitar on it. But

Cropper was on the session, playing a one-note continuo to underpin the main organ part. He also helped with the arrangement, including the track's distinctive drum intro. But his guitar playing had a role in other material by the group and their live performances. By this point he'd traded his earlier Gibson archtop for a more upmarket Gibson Byrdland. Not long thereafter, however, Cropper moved on to the solid-body Fender electric guitars that would become a mainstay for him. He bought an Esquire that would soon be joined by a series of Telecasters.

"I traded the Byrdland for an Esquire," he says, "so that I could play more sessions. The producers were really diggin' the Fender Telecaster and Esquire sounds."

One of the producers who was happy to give Cropper work was Chips Moman, head of A&R at Satellite/Stax. Cropper credits Moman as another significant influence on his guitar style:

"Chips was a great songwriter, guitar player, and producer. He gave me my first session at Stax. And he showed me the trick of using a B string in the place of a G string. In those days when you bought a set of guitar strings, buying different gauges was not as easy as it is today. They came out of the box the way they came. And most of the string sets had a wound G string. You couldn't bend one of those very well. So Chips Moman taught me that if you take a B string and put it on as a G string, you can bend notes more easily. He said, 'You gotta learn how to play with it and mute it a little bit, because it's too wobbly because the gauge is too small.' Now I'm playing a 17 or something like that, which is unwound. I play Gibson Sonomatics. But those B strings were probably closer to a 13. Chips taught me how to bend that string. A lot of country players embellished that idea. They even built guitars where they could push on the neck and it would raise and lower the string and get that pedal steel sound. But I learned to bend them together, bend the G string against the B string and things like that."

The more limber G string may have also facilitated one of Cropper's trademark moves. He calls them "hammer licks." The intro to Sam and Dave's "Soul Man" is a prime example. Cropper became a master of building fluid glissando riffs and melodic lines phrased in inverted thirds played on the G and high E string. Countless guitar players subsequently picked up on Crop's "hammer licks." Like much of his playing, it's a sound and style that has one foot in country and one foot in the blues. Combined with a supple sense of rhythmic comping, it adds up to one of the most distinctive guitar styles in popular music, and an essential part of the electric guitar vocabulary.

"Another influential figure for me was a guy named Clarence Nelson," Cropper adds. "I think he played in [saxophonist] Ben Branch's band. Duck had played in that band too. And Clarence Nelson was a phenomenal Telecaster player. I picked up on him, and so did Reggie Young, who became the guitar player over at American Recording where Chips had gone."

When Moman left Stax to accept an A&R and production post at American Recording in Memphis, Cropper was appointed as Moman's successor at Stax. He was still quite young, but Stax chief Jim Stewart sensed he was ready to graduate from some of the more menial tasks he was performing in the studio and in the record store that Stewart's sister, Estelle Axton, ran out in front of the studio, in what once had once been the former movie theater's ticket booth.

"It was kind of a gradual transition," Cropper says of his elevation to producer and A&R man at Stax. "I was still sweeping floors and logging tapes, and still trying to work up front in the record shop. So one day Miss Axton went to Jim and said, 'You're going to have to start paying Steve, because he don't spend any time in the record shop anymore. He's always in the studio.' So I started getting paid through the studio rather than through the record shop. Same amount of money, but the checks came out of a different checkbook."

Of course Cropper's role included playing guitar in the Stax house band, the nucleus of which consisted of keyboardist/multi-instrumentalist Booker T. Jones, drummer Al Jackson Jr., and bassist Lewie Steinberg, who was succeeded by Duck Dunn in 1965. The band's main role was to back Stax vocalists in the studio, but they became a hit-making instrumental ensemble in their own right—Booker T. and the MG's. Officially the initials MG stood for "Memphis Group," but the British MG sports car carried a tremendous cachet of cool in the early and mid-sixties, so the name worked on that level as well.

"So I just started playin' and [Otis Redding] he started singing, 'These arms of mine . . .' I'm telling you, true story, the hair stood up on my arms. I had never heard a voice that good. Just magic."

The advent of Booker T. and the MG's as featured Stax recording artists grew out of a jam that took place while the group was waiting for singer Billy Lee Riley (of "Flyin' Saucers Rock 'n' Roll" fame) to turn up at the studio for a recording session. That jam led to another, as tends to happen with jams. And the day's second jam became one of the most often-covered and influential instrumental hits of all time, "Green Onions."

"Billy never did show," Cropper recounts. "But we were just jamming on this blues stuff while we were waiting on him. Jim Stewart had the tape on the machine and everything ready to go in the control room. He just reached over an punched 'record.' So we get through this blues and we're just kind of laughing and still settin' there. Jim said, 'Hey, guys, why don't you come in [to the control room] and listen to this.' We said, 'What? You put that down?' He said, 'Yeah, it's pretty good.'

"So we listened to the playback, and it was a pretty good blues.

But we were still kinda laughing about it. Then Jim said, 'Have you guys got anything that you could put on the B side, if we decided to put this out?' We thought he was kidding us. We did not take him seriously at the moment. But after a bit we realized, 'Jim's real serious about this.' We were dumbfounded. We didn't have any material. The stuff I had been writing was vocal stuff, not instrumentals. But I remembered a riff that Booker had played me about two weeks before, which turned out to be the main lick of 'Green Onions.'

"So I asked him if he remembered that riff. He said, 'Yeah, I think I do.' 'Well, let's go down to the organ and see.' He started playing that lick and everybody said, 'Man, that's great.' So Lewie sat down on the bass, Al Jackson sat down on the drums and started playing. I just started playing the bass line with Lewie, and we went on and did the song. In the middle, I started doing these little chink things on guitar, you know? So we put it down like that.

"Jim said, 'Steve, that thing you're doing in the middle, why don't you put that on the intro

and play it. Then when the third verse comes, why don't you just play a regular solo?' I said okay. And I'm pretty sure that 'Green Onions,' as we know 'Green Onions,' was the third take of the day."

The next morning, Cropper took the recordings of the two jams over to Sun Records in Memphis, where the legendary Elvis lead guitarist Scotty Moore was working as a mastering engineer. "Jim Stewart, in his mind, was still going with the blues thing as the A side," Cropper narrates. "But I just knew that 'Green Onions' had the perfect dance beat for what was going on at that time. So I called Scotty Moore over at Sun. I said, 'Scotty, have you got time to cut a dub for me?' He said, 'Yeah, I got time.' So I went over there and cut a dub on 'Green Onions.' Scotty said, 'Yeah, that's pretty cool.' I said, 'I know. Jim likes this other one, a blues. But I like this one.' So I took it home with me, and the next day I got up and went to see a friend of mine called Ruben Washington. I used to come down on his radio show from time to time and hang out with him and drink coffee with him while he was on the air. He was on drive time.

"I said, 'Ruben, we cut something on Sunday. I think it's a hit. I want you to listen to it and tell me what you think.' So he puts it on the turntable. He plays the intro, and about two or three bars into the verse, stops, backs it up and plays it again. I thought he wanted to hear the intro again. But what he did was flip a switch and put it out on the air. He then proceeded to play it three more times and the phones lit up. 'What's the name of the song? Who's the artist?' And all of that. He was kind of teasing the audience. He said, 'Well, you people will just have to call in and find out.'

"That was about seven-thirty, eight o'clock in the morning. I hung around a little and I went over to the record shop by about a quarter to nine. I usually went to work at nine o'clock. Miss Axton was there early that day and she said, 'What have you done? The phones are ringing off the wall. They want to know what you were playing on the radio this morning.' I said, 'Well, it's something we cut this weekend. Something with the guys.' I had it with me. She said, 'Let me hear it.'

"So she calls Jim Stewart—he was working over at the bank at the time—and says, 'Jim, I think on your lunch break you need to get over here. We got something happening.' He didn't even know what was going on. So he shows up. He goes, 'What is it?' She said, 'This thing you cut with Steve, Booker, and them on Sunday—Ruben played it on the radio and the phones are lighting up. Everybody wants this record.' He said, 'You're kidding me. Well, call the guys in.' We got hold of Al, Booker, and Lewie. Came in and had a meeting. I told them what was going on. And Jim just went with it. I think at first he thought it was the blues causing all the excitement. But it wasn't. It was the other one.

"Jim said, 'We gotta get this out. We gotta come up with a title. So Lewie Steinberg says, 'I got the title for you. Number one, that's the stinkin'est music I ever heard. We need to call it "Onions."' I said, 'That's pretty good, but it's kind of negative.' But in those days, when you said some music was stinky that meant it was really good. It was funky. That was an early word for funky. So I said, 'What if we call it "Green Onions?"' 'Cause green onions . . . you know, Sunday dinner, you go over anybody's house and they've got green onions on the plate.' They said, 'Yeah, that's a good idea.' So that's what we went with.

"I called Scotty and said, 'Can you cut me some parts on the dub you made me yesterday?' So we cut the parts for 'Green Onions.' We picked up the finished records on Friday and I took off with Bill Biggs, who worked with Music Sales record distributors. I said, 'Can I go with you this weekend?' He always took Friday afternoon and the weekend to call on jukebox operators. He said, 'Yeah, come on.' So I took two boxes of records and put them in the trunk of his car. And while he'd call on the jukebox operators, I'd go call on the local radio stations. They were glad to see anybody, out there in Arkansas. We went to Helena, Fort Smith, Little Rock, all the way to Texarkana. And the following week I went down to Jackson, Tennessee; down to Jackson, Mississippi; Tupelo; and round. I think I even went to Oxford somewhere down by the college, came back up to Memphis, where the record had been taken over to WDIA. All this happened within a two-week period.

"The record was on Volt 102. [Volt was a Stax subsidiary label.] And Jerry Wexler, the vice president of Atlantic, called up Jim and he said, 'What is going on with this record down there?' And Jim said, 'Man, we got a local hit. I mean, local all over: Arkansas, Mississippi, Tennessee . . . everybody's goin' crazy over this record.' And Wexler said, 'It's on Volt? You gotta get it off Volt. We ain't got time to promote a new label. Get that thing on Stax!'"

"I started the song in the shower that night. I was still goin' that morning with it. I got dressed, went down to pick up Otis. I said, 'Otis, I got a good idea for you.' 'What is it?' I said, 'They call me Mr. Pitiful everywhere I go. . . .'"

Cropper's anecdote attests to his ability not only to make major musical contributions in the recording studio but also to see the big picture—a profound understanding of how music affects listeners and how that affect, in turn, impacts the marketplace at large. After "Green Onions" became a massive hit, Booker T. and the MG's began to crank out singles for Stax on a regular basis in the early sixties, along with key Stax artists like William Bell of "You Don't Miss Your Water" fame, Rufus "Walkin' the Dog" Thomas, his daughter, Carla Thomas, and a host of others.

Working at Stax became a full-time job for Cropper. "The hours were extremely long," he says. "I can tell you I worked more than nine hours every day. And that stretched into fourteen and fifteen almost religiously, about six days a week. Even though we only recorded five, I would come in on Saturdays and hold auditions. And then the rest of Saturday afternoon into the evenings we'd either be writing or I'd be logging tapes of the stuff we did that week. I would go and do mastering if there was something to be mastered that we wanted to think about putting out. I'd go get Scotty Moore or somebody to cut me dubs on it, so we could have a meeting on Monday morning and play it.

"Sometimes I'd even work seven days a week. I'd go in on Sunday too and work all day long. But I loved it. To me, it was like going to church every day. I felt secure, safe, excited, and glad to be there. Once you went through the doors, that was it. Everything outside was left outside. You didn't bring your home problems and all that stuff to work with you. You took care of them before you got there or took off and took care of them later. But you didn't bring them to work.

"Everybody there—musicians and employees—all had the same drive and the same attitude.

Whether it was musicians, typists, secretaries, whatever any of us were doing, it was all about trying to get the company going and get hit records. A big team effort on everybody's part."

The workload kept Cropper away from home a lot of the time, putting a strain on his first marriage, which would eventually dissolve.

"The only thing that probably saved the marriage at that time," he says, "was the fact that Booker wanted to go to college, which meant that Booker T. and the MG's couldn't really tour. And that really opened Duck and I up to do more sessions. Had we been on the road all the time, my career might have turned out different—probably not as well. But the fact that we would work in the studio all week meant there were more releases and more hits. Often, we'd have sessions Monday through Thursday. On Friday, we'd be flying out of there midday to do a show that night, then go to the next show on Saturday, fly home on Sunday, and be back to work on Monday. So there was very little home life going on."

While Cropper denies the legend that all the equipment was nailed to the studio floor at Stax in order to discourage robberies, it is true that the mikes, amps, instruments, and other gear never moved from their sweet spots. This, along with the unique acoustic properties of the studio's sloped theater floor and other peculiarities of the room, accounts for both the consistency and groovy beauty of the Stax sound. Everything was dialed in to the max.

"Nothing left its place," Cropper confirms. "The piano, organ, drums, baffles, and all of the mikes—not that there were that many—all stayed the same. In other words, you didn't tear down at the end of a session then put it back up for the next session. So all the horns were done on the same mike. All the drums were done on the same two mikes. The bass had a mike. The guitar had a mike, the piano, the vocals. . . . That was it. It never moved. That sound didn't change. If anything about the sound changed, it was on the mixing board, by equalizers or whatever. Once we found the right mike for the right thing, that's what we stuck with."

Cropper's amp for the earlier, 1962–'64, portion of his Stax tenure was a small but mighty tweed Fender Harvard through which he played first his Esquire and later a Telecaster—the first of many in his life—that he recalls as being of 1961 or '62 vintage. These served him well in his work with a stunning series of soul superstars, the first of whom was Otis Redding. The soon-to-be legendary singer first made his way into Stax in 1962, as part of singer Johnny Jenkins's entourage. Cropper can vividly recall Redding's arrival at the start of a Jenkins session:

"We had been in the studio a little bit and somebody said, 'Hey, let's go outside and smoke a cigarette.' So we were standing out on the sidewalk smoking a cigarette and this Cadillac pulls up. This big, tall guy gets out, gets the keys, and unlocks the trunk. He starts tearing amps, cords, and all of that out of the trunk. I wasn't going to say anything at first, but I saw these microphones and said, 'Hey, yeah, you know, we got mikes in the studio. You don't need to bring in mikes.' He was bringing [it] in like he was settin' up for a gig. 'Thanks, but this is a recording studio!' That's when I said my mind. He said, 'Well, I gotta bring this stuff in anyway.' I said, 'Well, you bring it in. We're not gonna use it. You can leave the mikes in the trunk.'

"I just assumed—since he drove the car, got out, unlocked the trunk, and started carrying amps and stuff in for Johnny—that he was his road guy. Like his valet or driver, roadie, whatever. So we set up and started recording a session, songs that Johnny had come up with and some ideas we had. We were

listening to a playback when Al Jackson came to me and said, 'You know that guy who came here with Johnny, you know gettin' out of the car, who drove up here? He says he's a singer. He wants you to hear him sing.' He wanted me to listen to him and I told him, 'Well, you're the A&R guy.' And Al asked me, 'You got time to listen to this guy?' I said, 'Al, not now. Maybe later after the session, if there's time.'

"I'd forgotten all about it by the end of the day. We finished the session and Al says, 'Hey, Cropper, you got a minute? This guy's still buggin' me to death about listening to him sing.' And I said, 'Oh, okay, I'll take time. Tell him to come down to the piano.' So we went and got him; he came down in. And I said, 'Okay, play something. Sing something.' He said, 'I don't play piano. I play a little gut-tar.' I said, 'Well, I don't really play piano either. I just play a little bit to write with.' And he said, 'Well, can you play some of them church chords?' What he was talkin' about, I guess, was 6/8 triplets, by technical standards. So I just started playin' and he started singing, 'These arms of mine . . .' I'm telling you, true story, the hair stood up on my arms. I had never heard a voice that good. Just magic.

"So I said, 'Hold it right there.' I left the piano and said to Jim Stewart, 'You got to get out here right now. You gotta hear this guy sing.' So I start playing again, he starts singing 'These Arms of Mine.' Jim said, 'Oh man, we gotta get that on tape.' The band had already broken down and they were going home. Duck later reminded me that I ran out of the studio to bring him back in. He was putting his bass in the trunk of my car. 'Cause he was gonna go home and eat and go to his gig. All these guys had night gigs. They played till one or two o'clock in the morning.

"So I went and got Duck. Al was still there. Johnny Jenkins was still there. So I played piano, Al played drums, Johnny Jenkins played guitar, and Duck played bass on 'These Arms of Mine.' For the next day's session, we were cutting a B side for 'These Arms of Mine' instead of cutting Johnny Jenkins, which is what we were hired to do. I truly do not know what happened to Johnny Jenkins. I do know what happened to Otis Redding. From 'These Arms of Mine,' he had something like seventeen hit singles in a row. He never had anything that we would call a flop, or something that didn't make it. Every song he ever released sold a lot of records."

Tall and handsome, a gifted singer and dynamic performer, Redding would take the Stax sound beyond the R&B ghetto and into the mainstream pop music market of the mid-sixties. In this regard, he is successor and heir to great soul singers like Ray Charles and Sam Cooke, who also crossed over to broader audiences. Redding hits like "Respect," "I've Been Loving You Too Long," and "(Sittin' On) The Dock of the Bay" are among the most iconic songs of the sixties. And Steve Cropper's guitar style and overall musicality were a key ingredient in creating Otis's sound. The singer and guitarist became good friends and songwriting partners:

"The thing about Otis was he always had ideas for songs," says Cropper. "He carried around with him—and I'm not making this up—ten to fifteen unfinished song ideas in his head and on his guitar all the time. Anytime you saw Otis you could say, 'Hey, Otis, what you got?' And he'd have all these different ideas. All I did was just kinda help him finish them. Lyrically speaking I just basically used to write about him. He was bigger than life and very easy to write about."

Such was the case with Redding's 1964 song "Mr. Pitiful."

"I heard a disc jockey call Otis Redding 'Mr. Pitiful' And I thought, 'What a great idea for a song!' I heard the phrase on the way home from the studio one night about midnight. A disc jockey on WDIA named Moola said, 'Here's another one from the great Otis Redding; Mr. Pitiful, Otis Redding!' I went, 'Wow, he just called Otis Mr. Pitiful.' And he called him that 'cause he was so sad when he sang a ballad. Just the way he crooned, just beggin' and pleadin'.

"I started the song in the shower that night. I was still goin' that morning with it. I got dressed, went down to pick up Otis. I said, 'Otis, I got a good idea for you.' 'What is it?' I said, 'They call me Mr. Pitiful everywhere I go. . . .' He and I finished the song in the car. I said, 'I'll tell you what, Otis. When the band gets here, you go work with the horns on it, and I'll go teach Duck and them the bass line and the chord changes.' We did and cut it. I think we made about two takes on it, and that was it."

Otis's 1966 single "Fa-Fa-Fa-Fa-Fa (Sad Song)" was one of several Redding/Cropper songs to emerge from hotel room writing sessions. "We were at the Holiday Inn on 3rd," Cropper recollects. We'd already written one and we were starting on another. And he was humming me a horn line he heard in his head. He said, 'I want the horns to go fa-fa, fa-fa-haa, fa-faa.' He was makin' a saxophone sound. I said, 'Fa-fa-fa-fa-fa-fa. That's it! We just started there and wrote that song in about ten minutes."

Cropper and Redding would often both play guitar on writing and recording sessions. "On the original songs we wrote, there are really no minors," says Cropper, "because Otis played tuned to an

E-major chord, which the old blues guys called "'bastapool." [I.e., Sebastopol tuning, which can be open E or D.] They used to tune to a chord and play slide. That's the way Otis played too, so I adopted that."

To play live shows with Redding, Cropper even acquired a second Telecaster—a '63, as he recalls—which he kept in open tuning. "So I could just switch for the Otis songs and play the same licks that I played on the record without having to modify," he explains.

But Redding was just one of many soul giants who passed through the front door of Stax and onto stardom and legendary status, benefiting significantly from Steve Cropper's talents as guitarist, songwriter, producer, and A&R man. Many of these artists came through Stax's distribution deal with Atlantic records. Several Atlantic R&B singers were sent down to Memphis for the full "Stax treatment." One of these was Wilson Pickett, nicknamed "the Wicked Pickett" allegedly for his frisky ways with the Atlantic secretaries. But the name applies equally to the relentless way Pickett could tear up a stage and wring every last drop of soul from a song. In the mid-sixties, his fame rivaled Redding's.

Cropper didn't know much about the young singer when he first came down to Stax in 1965. But someone told Cropper that Pickett had been a gospel singer in the past, which led to the creation of what is arguably Pickett's biggest hit, "In the Midnight Hour." In the Stax record shop Cropper found a gospel disc with the lyric "I'm gon' see my Jesus in the midnight hour." "I said, 'What a great idea for a song!'" Cropper recounts, "'I'm gon' be with *my baby* in the midnight hour.' I came in with that idea and Wilson came in with the idea for 'Don't Fight It,' a song with a great lyric about a wallflower. I helped him finish it a bit and it became his second single after 'Midnight Hour.'

"Jim Stewart and Jerry Wexler had set us up in a hotel. They went and had dinner and a meeting, then came back to see how we were doing. We played them 'Midnight Hour' and 'Don't Fight It' and I thought they were gonna die. They went crazy. They said, 'My God, this is great! This is great! Just keep writing.'

"So next I just started this kind of church groove, 'cause I knew he'd been into gospel. We came up with 'I've been lovin' you baby a long, long time and I'm not tired.' And he'd scream. Oh man, he was something else. And that was 'I'm Not Tired,' which became the flip side of 'Midnight Hour.' We went in the studio the next day and cut all three songs."

The relentlessly driving groove behind "In the Midnight Hour" is said to have originated during the session at Stax, when Atlantic exec Jerry Wexler demonstrated a new dance step the kids were doing, suggesting that the band pick up on that. Cropper responded with the rhythm comp that nearly every guitarist knows today—single-note leading tones on the low strings setting up downstroked D7 and G chords sharply accenting the two and four beats along with the snare drum. Put together with a killer chord chart, the song became a massive hit.

Eddie Floyd was another former gospel singer who'd come out of the same group as Pickett, the Falcons. Floyd first came to Stax as a songwriter, teaming with Cropper to write many of Wilson Pickett's most successful tracks. When Floyd became a recording artist for Stax as well, his second single and breakthrough hit was a song that he and Cropper had originally written for Otis Redding, 1966's "Knock on Wood."

The vocal duo of Sam Moore and Dave Prater also came to Stax through the Atlantic conduit, churning out a string of soul hits that includes "Hold On, I'm Coming," "Soul Man," and "I Thank You," many of them penned by another legendary Stax songwriting team, Isaac Hayes and David Porter. Cropper made his own indelible contribution to these iconic Sam & Dave tracks. In particular, his inverted third "hammer lick" guitar intro to "Soul Man" merits a high place on anyone's list of great guitar hooks.

By this point, Cropper had moved on from his miniscule Harvard amp to a more powerful Fender amp, a Super Reverb. "It had four 10s in it and a lot of wattage, especially compared with the little Harvard," says Cropper. "And it got a great sound. That's the amp I used on 'Soul Man.' I think I used it on 'In the Midnight Hour' too. It's on some of the stuff we did with Don Covay, like 'Sooki Sooki,' plus a lot of the Sam & Dave recordings and a lot of the later Otis stuff as well."

Stax classics like "In the Midnight Hour," "Respect," and "Knock on Wood" became garage band staples in the mid-sixties and to this day remain standard bar band repertoire. Virtually every group of sixties basement rockers took on at least one of those numbers, which means that Cropper's guitar style got deeply engrained in the hearts and minds of many players, becoming a key element of the electric guitar heritage. Playing those covers also gave many white suburban kids their first taste of soul music.

In many regards, the Stax sound was the soundtrack for the breakdown of racial barriers in the sixties, in the wake of the civil rights movement. Songs like "Soul Man" and "Respect" were anthems for black pride. And the Stax operating model, particularly the biracial lineup of Booker T. and the MG's, offered a sterling example of blacks and whites working in together in harmony.

"We were working in harmony, but there was no such thing as black and white," says Cropper. "There wasn't any colors. Never was. Period. It was just a bunch of guys working together, like a basketball team. Everybody was there for the same purpose."

But once they walked out of Stax's front doors, Cropper and his comrades were still in the racially divided Deep South. "Memphis was totally segregated," he says. "It's amazing how segregated it was. I don't know what my compadres thought about it. I didn't really think about it much. It was just a way of life and something we dealt with. I'd go over to Booker's house and hang out with him. His mom would open the door and welcome me. There was nobody following me around saying, 'Hey, you can't do that.' Otis Redding and Eddie Floyd would come over my house. We'd hang out, party, have a big time, write songs, and do whatever we wanted to do. Or we'd go over Al Jackson's. Al had a big house with a big swimming pool. We'd go over there on a Sunday, swim in the pool, barbecue, and have a good time with our families. Nobody thought one thing about that. We created our own way of life."

Touring the segregated South with a biracial band presented its own set of challenges, but even these were met with good grace. "There were certain things we could and could not do," says Cropper. "Sometimes we'd do a gig at a college and we'd wind up staying in a dorm, which was fine. And often there was no way we could go downtown and get a hotel room. We tried it a couple of times. It just wasn't gonna happen. So we had to stay out on the highway at a motel that needed the money. They didn't care who stayed there. The good part about that was we were already halfway outta town, so it worked to our advantage.

"But we never had problems getting on and off airplanes or sitting together. Nobody looked at us or said anything. Having a hit record and being in demand, going up north to play, we noticed that things were definitely different. Because you didn't have that segregation up north, in Detroit, Chicago, and places like that."

The big-time chart success of the Stax artists created an increasing demand for the great Stax singers to hit the road—accompanied, of course, by the studio's legendary house band. This tore Cropper and his fellow MG's away from the studio and Stax's busy production schedule, but by '67 the demand for their skills as a live band reached critical mass.

"Otis Redding said, 'Okay, that's it. I gotta have you guys on the road with me,'" Cropper recalls. The soul sound was hitting big overseas as well. "Otis had already been over there without us," says Cropper, "And they said, 'You gotta take the band over there now, because Otis Redding is one of the biggest artists in Europe right now.'"

And so Cropper hit the road with Booker T. and the MG's, along with the Mar-Keys horn section, as backing band for the Stax/Volt Soul Revue of 1967. Redding headlined a bill that also included Sam & Dave, Eddie Floyd, Carla Thomas, and Arthur "Sweet Soul Music" Conley. The revue electrified audiences throughout Europe. One of the few down moments was the theft, in Copenhagen, of Cropper's second Telecaster, the one he kept in open tuning. He had to finish the tour with just one guitar.

In a sense, the Stax/Volt Revue tour of Europe was the warm-up for Redding's triumphant appearance at the Monterey Pop Festival in June 1967. The first large-scale rock festival, Monterey was also the coming-out party for the burgeoning hippie scene. The broadening of the rock audience's musical tastes in the wake of psychedelia and the dawning of a generation's socio/political/spiritual consciousness brought with it a new appreciation for African American genres like blues, jazz, and soul.

Jerry Wexler got Redding on the bill at Monterey. Backed by the MG's, Redding's electrifying performance won him the admiration of a whole new audience. This was no mean feat at a festival that also included breakthrough performances by Jimi Hendrix, the Who, Janis Joplin, the Jefferson Airplane, and Ravi Shankar. On the flight to Monterey with his band, Cropper was accompanied by fellow guitar legend Mike Bloomfield and his band at the time, the Electric Flag, with drummer Buddy Miles. Bloomfield's former bandmate, the pioneering white bluesman Paul Butterfield, was also on hand.

"We knew all those guys and we were just hanging around," says Cropper. "We were all just buddies. Nobody was in awe of anybody. We were just glad to be there."

For a group of Southern boys, soon to take the stage in matching suits to perform choreographed stage moves, the colorful, fanciful garb and free-loving ways of the nascent hippies were a mystification—albeit a pleasant one:

"Duck and I went out and walked around a little," Cropper recalls. "They had all these art tents set up, with people selling their art wares. We were impressed by that. We checked out all sorts of stuff. We were just fascinated by the way people were dressed. We'd never seen anything like that. It was pretty interesting. The air was a little thick too [i.e., with marijuana smoke]. That was another experience we hadn't been around either, something we didn't cater to and didn't do. But there we were. I still remember the aroma."

Monterey kicked Redding's career into overdrive. He was entering a new creative phase as well. Not long after Monterey, Cropper was in the studio when he got a phone call from the singer. "Otis called me from the airport and wanted to know if I was in the studio," Cropper remembers. "He said, 'I've got a hit, Crop! Got a great idea. Gotta show it to you right now.' So he left the airport—it was about fifteen minutes away—and came down to Stax. He said, 'Get your gut-tar, get your gut-tar.' So I got it out and he started singing, 'Sitting on the dock of the bay . . .' Just strumming. I went, 'Oh man!' And then I helped him finish the rest of it. Wrote the bridge with him and all that."

Cropper attributes the unique flavor of the song's bridge ("Looks like nothin's gonna change. . . .") to Redding's preference for open-E-major guitar tuning. "The bridge goes to the VI chord," he explains. "And most times, you'd go to a minor VI for a bridge. But instead, 'Dock of the Bay' goes to the VI major, 'cause Otis was tuned to a major chord. Which gives it a different kind of sound. And when you build on top of that with the horns and everything else, it just becomes this big, giant, fat chord and creates its own sound."

"(Sittin' On) The Dock of the Bay" was recorded the day after Redding and Cropper finished writing it. "As soon as we cut 'Dock of the Bay' we knew we had a hit," says Cropper. "Without question. We said, 'This is it, this is our number one record. Anything from here on will be album cuts or saved for next time. So we recorded for about two weeks, and we cut a lot of songs. And [Stax engineer] Ronnie Capone said to me, 'Steve, do you notice how well Otis is singing?' Otis had a throat operation and was just kind of recovering. Getting back to singing again. He hadn't really sang much since probably the Monterey Pop Festival, and went into this operation. And I said, 'You're right, man. His voice sounds better than it's ever sounded.'

"So at night, after the band would leave, we'd go back to the studio with Otis and start getting out old tracks. We had Otis resing three, four, or five songs that we had in the can. And then Otis and I started coming up with these ideas. And Ronnie said, 'Well, let's put it down.' Now Ronnie Capone, a lot of people don't know, was a great drummer, as well as a great engineer. So we set up the sound. I'd get the sound on the drums and go back out into the studio, and Ronnie got the sound on the guitar. We already had the vocal mike open. And Otis would sing and sometimes play a little tambourine. We cut four songs—'Ton of Joy,' 'Lovin' by the Pound,' 'Champagne and Wine,' and 'Direct Me'— with just the three of us playing. Then I had to overdub other stuff. I had Booker play on some of it. Overdubbed the horns on some of it and stuff like that."

Cropper's unforgettable "hammer lick" leads for "Dock of the Bay" were also overdubbed after the fact. "I got out my old Harvard tweed amp and set it up in a microphone in the control room so I could sit there, play, and mike it at the same time," he says. "We had a four-track machine by then, so I could do overdubs."

Regrettably all of those tracks, including "Dock of the Bay," were doomed to become posthumous releases. Otis Redding never got to hear the lead guitar overdubs that Cropper had put on his iconic song. Not in this world, anyway. He died on December 10, 1967, when his small private plane went down in a storm over Wisconsin. Cropper and some bandmates were at the Indianapolis airport when they received news of the accident.

"We were stuck in the same weather storm Otis was stuck in," Cropper relates. "We were at the airport waiting on a connection to go to Memphis. All flights had been cancelled and everything had backed up. So David Porter said, 'We better call home and let them know we're not going to be on that other flight we missed. Tell 'em when we're coming in. Tell the wives when to pick us up.' So one guy said, 'Well, hey, rather than spend four or five dimes, David, just have your wife call everybody and tell 'em what's goin' on.' So he goes to make that phone call. He comes back and David Porter's white as a sheet. We said, 'David's what's wrong? You sick, man?' He said, 'My wife just said that Otis Redding's plane went down. They can't find him. As far as they know now, there's no survivors.' Well, that was about the worst news you could ever get."

Redding's death seemed to usher in Stax's period of decline. Jim Stewart's ill-advised late-1966 decision to bar all outside sessions from Stax had weakened the business. And in '67, Stax's advantageous distribution deal with Atlantic ended, and Stax lost the ownership of their back catalog. Cropper soldiered on with Stax for a few more yeas, but doesn't have too much good to say about his first solo album for the label in 1969, *With a Little Help from My Friends*:

"So now we've got this whole new generation. Their grandparents grew up with Stax music. I never knew I'd live long enough to be my own cover band."

"It's a pretty good record and we had a lot of fun doing it. The problem was they wanted to rush this thing out as part of some 'Let's hit the world with a whole bunch of albums' campaign they had going. And I said, 'I'm not through with it yet!' They said, 'No, we gotta have it ready this week.' 'But I'm not through!' I said, 'Guys, if you make me put this out, I'll never do another one.'"

While Cropper hasn't carried out that threat to the letter, solo discs from him have been very few and far between. "I'm just not big on solo records," he says.

The end of the sixties was a time of uncertainty and dissatisfaction for Cropper. "My close friends knew that I was unhappy," he says. "In my private moments, they could tell that I just wasn't myself and I wasn't very happy. A lot of it could have stemmed from Otis's passing. But there were a lot of other artists and things going on at Stax. I was just unhappy with the whole situation. The whole atmosphere of the studio had changed. The workload was becoming ridiculous and there were some bad business decisions."

Cropper finally broke with Stax in 1970, moving on to start TMI Studios in Memphis with some old Stax cohorts. Crop's role in this new venture began late one evening when he got a mysterious phone call. "I was already in bed," he says. "I'm pretty sure it was past midnight. I answered the phone and it was a buddy of mine, who said, 'Just want to know if you're there, 'cause we're on our way over.' 'What?' About twenty minutes later, there's a knock on the door. It's two friends of mine. They said, 'Come on, you're going with us.' 'What the hell? Where we goin'?' 'We'll tell you later. You goin' with us. Everything's fine. We just wanna show you something.'

"So we headed downtown. We park in the back of this building and we walk in and they said, 'This is yours.' It was a pretty phenomenal recording studio. They said, 'You'll be a partner in this. Whatever you can make of it.' I spent several hours there looking at the place. And I said, 'Well, guys, this is impressive. But I can't make a decision on this now.' And so I go back home and I can't sleep and the next day I'm thinking about it all day long. 'What am I gonna do here?' It was a real good opportunity.

And I'd already had other big labels call me and talk to me about coming to work for them either in an A&R position or a vice president. I had so many opportunities to go so many different ways. There was an offer to go to Atlanta. One to go to Nashville, another to go to New York. Those kind of things.

"So I milled it around in my mind for two or three days. I woke up one morning and said, 'Damn it, I'm gonna do it.' So I went in, had a meeting with Jim Stewart, and said, 'I want out of my contract. I'm leaving.' He said, 'You can't leave.' I said, 'Oh yes, I can. I'm gone. I've had it and I'm not gonna put up with this anymore. I've got things I wanna do.' Lawyers got involved. I had to make pretty serious decisions moneywise. All the main players at Stax had a contract with a promissory amount they would get for signing the contract. I made a decision to forfeit all of that. I've never looked back."

On leaving Stax, Cropper assured Stewart that he wasn't going to set up a new shop to compete directly with his former label. Instead he wanted to try his hand at producing other styles of music, which were proliferating in the early seventies. At TMI, Cropper handled album productions for Rod Stewart, Ringo Starr, Tower of Power, John Prine, Jose Feliciano, and many others. One of his most notable productions during this period was his work with fellow guitar legend Jeff Beck on the latter's 1972 album, *Jeff Beck Group*. This is the disc that contains Beck's recording of the jam night perennial "Going Down" and a track that Beck and Cropper wrote together, titled "Sugar Cane."

"Oh, it was great," Cropper says of the project. "I'd be settin' there and Jeff would be playing. I'm looking at his hands going, 'You know, I play guitar too and you can't do that! You can't make that sound and those notes in that position!' Well, he did. He is phenomenal. And he throws the guitar in the corner like I do and goes to work on cars. Only I fix screen doors, light bulbs, whatever. Just whatever odd job I can do."

By 1975 Cropper had relocated to Los Angeles, where he became a highly valued session player. Plans to reform Booker T. and the MG's came to a halt with the murder of Al Jackson in '75. Cropper had lost another dear friend and close musical ally. But there were plenty of other projects to claim his attention.

Another one of his highly notable mid-seventies projects was session work for John Lennon's *Rock and Roll* album. Lennon's collection of fifties rock-and-roll covers was the somewhat infamous product of his boozy "Lost Weekend" period when the former Beatle was separated from Yoko Ono and living wild in LA. But Cropper has only good memories of the sessions. Lennon's and Cropper's paths had almost crossed back in 1966, when the Beatles were contemplating doing some recording at Stax. Brian Epstein vetoed that idea, but Lennon remained a huge fan of the group he fondly called Booker Table and the Maitre'Ds.

"He was just an awesome guy," says Cropper of Lennon. "I had met him before at the Bag o' Nails [club] in London in 1967 and he remembered that. And he was always a big fan of Booker T. and the MG's. We were at A&M Studios in LA. working on *Rock and Roll*. He said, 'Cropper, can you stay over after the session? I got a little something I want to show you.' I said, 'Well, yeah.' So it was just him and me in the studio, and he showed me this riff. He said, 'I wrote this riff years ago and I always thought it would be good for Booker T. and the MG's.' That was pretty cool. We just hung out a bit at the studio then and I left, and that was the end of that. They later went on to New York to finish the album."

The late seventies brought Cropper into a multifaceted project that would prove to have

uncanny longevity. Crop and Duck Dunn were drafted to play in the Blues Brothers, the R&B/blues ensemble fronted by comedic actors Dan Aykroyd and John Belushi, who were then in the cast of television's phenomenally successful *Saturday Night Live* program. Born of a long-abiding love of the blues on the part of Aykroyd, who'd played in blues bands in his native Canada, and a neophyte's passion for the music on Belushi's part, the Blues Brothers had begun as a 1978 *Saturday Night Live* sketch. But it quickly morphed into a full-blown pop culture phenomenon, spawning a series of albums, starting with 1978's *Briefcase Full of Blues*, and a series of feature films that commenced with 1980's *The Blues Brothers*.

Adopting the stage personae of Jake and Elwood Blues, Belushi and Aykroyd played their roles for laughs, but the underlying reverence for the music was deep and sincere. Cropper and Dunn had been brought into the band at the suggestion of *Saturday Night Live* keyboard player and musical director Paul Shaffer, and many of the other band members were key *SNL* players. The Blues Brothers hit a nerve in dawn-of-the-eighties culture. The band's vintage blues and soul repertoire was a fresh new sound to younger ears and a welcome nostalgia trip for the baby boomer demographic.

Cropper became close friends with both Aykroyd and Belushi. He vividly recalls being read the script for the first Blues Brothers move by Aykroyd. "I know the passion behind Danny," Cropper says. "He's a great writer and he was so proud of that script. He called me up one day and says, 'How soon can you get down here?' So I show up at Danny's house out in LA and he puts me on the couch. He gets a little ottoman and sits on that and he's got the script inside the covers of a Yellow Pages phone directory. I guess he'd ripped the pages out of an LA telephone book and put the script in it. That's how thick it was. So he starts acting out these scenes, and I'm belly-rolling on the couch. He's puttin' me on the floor. He's killin' me. I couldn't believe it. And that was the Blues Brothers script."

And while Cropper had no inclination to share in Belushi's notorious drug and booze binges, he was well aware of his friend's weakness. "John's whole reputation was based on that he'd party for two or three days and then he'd crash on somebody's couch somewhere. And that would be the end of that. He'd get up, go take a sauna, and get back to feeling good, get rid of the booze, sweat it all out, and take care of himself."

But Belushi went a little too far on the evening of March 4, 1982. The following morning, he was found dead of a heroin and cocaine overdose in a bungalow at the Chateau Marmont, LA's upscale celebrity hotel on the Sunset Strip.

"He'd left New York to come out and read for or have meetings about a new movie," says Cropper. "I got a call from a friend of his, who wanted to know if I'd seen John. I said no. They said, 'Well, did you know he was in town?' I said, 'No. He always calls me when he comes to town. I'm one of the first people he calls.' And they said, 'Yeah, well he's been here since Sunday.' I think this was on a Wednesday. And the guy said, 'Looks like it's gonna be a long week.' Boy, we didn't know how long that week was gonna be.

"I kept waiting for a call. When John was in town he always called me. He always came by the house. Even if he and I didn't hang out, he always came by the house a little bit. He'd come by, and he and I would go to some of the places that he was last seen going to. We'd hang out, have a drink. It was just a good time. It wasn't anything overboard or that kind of stuff. But that week he just got hung up with the wrong people, who supplied him with his demands, and he just went overboard with it. He just got too far to come back."

Cropper had lost another close friend and creative collaborator. But the Blues Brothers survived Belushi's passing, and Cropper still tours with an ever-shifting Blues Brothers lineup. "Over in Europe we've developed a whole new audience," he says. "So now we've got this whole new generation. Their grandparents grew up with Stax music. I never knew I'd live long enough to be my own cover band."

These days Cropper lives in Nashville with his second wife, Angel.

Their children, Cameron and Andrea, are growing up fast. Steve is especially proud that his daughter recently won a golf scholarship to the University of Mississippi. "My back's out and I can't play much now, but I think you're gonna see her in the PGA. She was a championship player in high school. Her mom was a scratch golfer when I met her. And still is basically. Her grandparents and great-grandparents all play golf on her mom's side."

There's a fishing boat out in Cropper's driveway. He's fond of fishing for bass. "But the boat's been just sitting there for two years," he says. "I used to go all the time, but all of a sudden I started working."

Up until the time of Duck Dunn's death on May 13, 2012, at age seventy, while on tour in Tokyo, he and Cropper toured with the Stax Show, fronted by the legendary Eddie Floyd. Cropper lends his talents to charity shows as well. And in 2011 he released *Dedicated: A Salute to the 5 Royales*. This CD tribute to the R&B act that profoundly influenced the teenage Cropper during the mid- to late fifties paired his unmistakable guitar work with the sounds of great singers and players like Steve Winwood, B. B. King, Brian May, Lucinda Williams, Bettye LaVette, Buddy Miller, Dan Penn, and others. Going back to one's roots is always a learning experience, and *Dedicated* was no exception.

"I didn't know until I got into this project that most of the songs I was listening to were written prior to 1953," Cropper states. "Some of them back in the late forties, early fifties. When King Records signed the 5 Royales to their label, they also bought up their old masters from previous labels and re-released some of the old hits. We just thought they were brand-new songs when we were kids, 'cause we'd never heard them before. We didn't know they'd actually been out before."

As is the case with many classic artists, Cropper's music is also kept in the zeitgeist through licensing deals. The Stax sound has recently graced ads for brands ranging from Macy's to Viagra to Depend adult diapers. "I never ever thought my music would be used to sell diapers," Cropper marvels.

Still, the guitarist doesn't seem to mind the commercialization of his music, which once served as a soundtrack for a generation's coming-of-age. Given the hard life of roadwork and rip-offs that many musicians endure, Cropper counts himself one of the lucky ones. Although he modestly tends to downplay the role his own prodigious talents have played in making that luck. He says he'd most like to be remembered "just for the fact that I was a good guy trying to help people out. I'd like to be known as a fair, honest, and good guy. I never took one nickel or any credit for anything I didn't actually do. If my name is on it, then I had something to do with creating it."

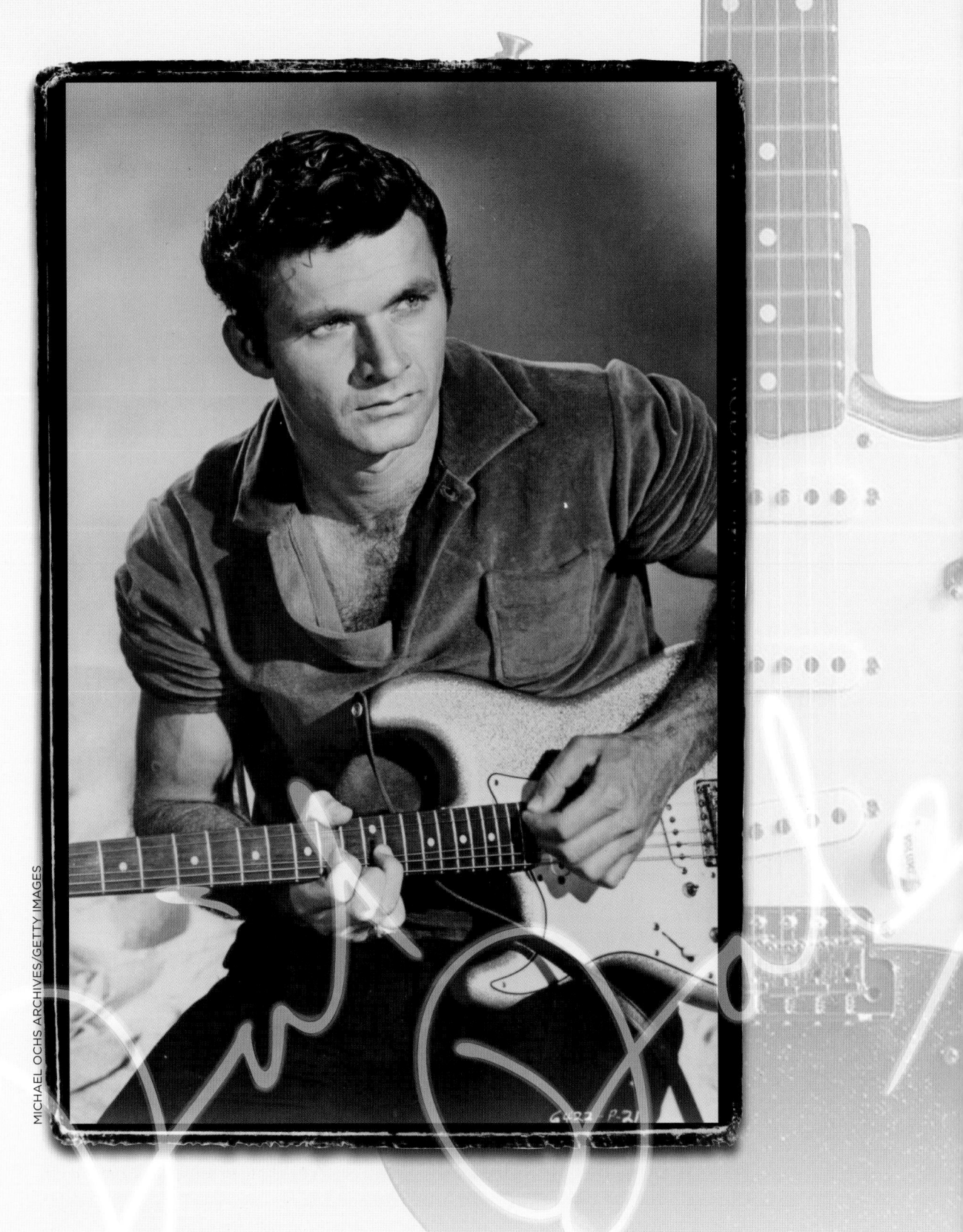

Dick *Dale*

THE OUTSIDER KING

IF ONLY DICK DALE'S BATTERED, gold-sparkle Stratocaster could talk. It would have quite a tale to tell. But even sitting mutely on a stand, the instrument is remarkably eloquent. Its worn surfaces tell of long service in the hands of one of the world's most distinctive guitarists, an American maverick who is hailed as the King of the Surf Guitar but whose accomplishments and passions extend far beyond the fun-in-the-sun music of Southern California's coastline.

Dale's Strat is a left-handed instrument, but strung for right-handed playing, which points out a defining factor in his fiercely original technique. He belongs to the small but select group of "upside-down lefties," left-handed guitarists who play conventional right-hand stringing, adapting their finger positioning and picking technique accordingly. Other notable upside-down lefties include Albert King, Otis Rush, Elizabeth Cotton, Coco Montoya, Jimmy Cliff, and Doyle Bramhall II. But even in this exalted company Dale stands out. His lightning-fast double-picked runs, reverby timbre, and evocative Middle Eastern tonalities revolutionized rock guitar playing in the early sixties and indeed for all time.

"I'm not a guitar player," Dale emphatically states. "I'm just a manipulator of the instrument. I either get pain or pleasure out of it. I don't know how to play a goddamned scale. I don't know what a thirteenth is, or an augmented ninth. I could give a shit. All I do is make the guitar scream with pain or pleasure."

A battle-scarred slab of musical history, Dick's Strat has been heavily modified over the years, reflecting its owner's restlessly inventive mind. The upper-bout strap peg has been replaced by a big old eyebolt, the kind you can buy at any hardware store—an eminently pragmatic solution to the problem of keeping the strap in place during Dale's frenetic, high-energy live performances. The tone and volume knobs have long since been pulled off, a vestige of the days when Dale had to flip right-handed guitars upside down and try not to knock into the volume and tone controls with his forearm while playing, thus altering the settings inadvertently. A series of small toggle switches provide a handy alternative to the Fender five-position pickup selector. And a clip for holding extra picks is mounted on the pick guard.

"I'm not a guitar player. I'm just a manipulator of the instrument."

Dale goes through picks at an alarming pace, owing to his fast and furious double-picking and fondness for super-heavy-gauge strings. Legend has it that he's been known to melt picks with his playing. But also, ever since slicing off the tip of his finger with a paper cutter in 2008, he has a harder time than ever hanging on to a plectrum.

A number of peeling, fading stickers on the Strat speak of Dale's extra-musical loves and fascinations. There's a photo of his son, Jimmy, an up-and-coming guitarist in his own right, as well as an American flag and the insignia of the Kenpo school of martial arts. Dale has been an avid student of the martial arts, and their underlying Taoist/Buddhist-influenced philosophy, since the mid-sixties. And indeed his playing is not unlike a black belt karate demonstration—highly disciplined, supremely focused, blindingly fast, yet serenely graceful, a beautiful example of mind over matter.

In recent years, Dale has become a sort of guru figure for fledgling guitarists, surf punks, and sundry other soul searchers. He lives way out in the desert, near Twentynine Palms, California, but journeys to towns and cities for gigs and workshops, a ninja rock-and-roll patriarch in a black leather motorcycle jacket and black headband. He says he has never smoked, drank alcohol, or used drugs. A longtime vegetarian and animal rights activist, he advocates clean living and traditional values such as respect for elders. He has triumphed over cancer and numerous other physical afflictions on multiple occasions. It's a minor miracle that he's alive at all, let alone still actively gigging in his seventies. Dick Dale is indeed a force of nature.

"When kids come to me and say, 'I wanna play like you. How do you get that sound?' I say, 'Sit down, son, and let me cleanse your soul,'" Dale declares. "They don't realize that everything we do in this life comes from within. Your body follows your mind. If you feed your mind shit, your body's gonna act like shit."

MICHAEL OCHS ARCHIVES/GETTY IMAGES

Although he would come to be associated with the sunny culture of Southern California, the man the world knows as Dick Dale was born on the opposite coast, in South Boston, on May 4, 1937. Of mixed Lebanese, Polish, and Belarusian descent, his birth name is Richard Anthony Monsour.

"In Lebanese and Middle Eastern cultures, the suffix '-our' signifies royalty," he says, "whereas just '-or' doesn't. Even today when I go over there, they say, 'Monsour? -our? Not '-or'? I tell 'em, 'That's right.'"

Dick took to music at an early age. His father, Jim, was a big-band enthusiast, and one of Dick's most profound musical influences was big-band drummer Gene Krupa. "I would bang on Mom and Dad's flour pans and sugar pans, those little containers," he recalls, "listening to Gene Krupa on the big albums [i.e., 12" 78-rpm phonograph records]."

An ad for a cowboy-themed ukulele in the back of a Superman comic book caught Dick's eye at a tender age. "It had a horse on it, and a rider with a lariat and it was green," he remembers. "You know, green was my favorite color at the time and I'm going, 'Wow! I can be a cowboy singer.'" Scraping up money by selling Noxzema skin cream door to door, Dick sent away for the instrument, but was disappointed when it arrived.

"I waited for three months before it ever came, and when it did come it was just compressed cardboard or something. The tuning pegs would fall out. I was so disenchanted and disheartened that I just smashed that thing into the garbage can."

Never a quitter, Dale raised a little more cash and got a better uke. "It was brown and cream plastic," he recalls. "And the tuning pegs had screws in them, so they actually worked!" Dale learned his basic ukulele chords from a magazine. The fingering puzzled him at first because he was holding the instrument upside down, but—characteristically for him—he soon forged his own path.

"From playing along to those Gene Krupa records on pots and pans, I had all the rhythm in my left hand," he says. "So I grabbed the ukulele left-handed, and I'm going, 'Wait a minute now, how do I play this?' But the first song I learned was the 'Tennessee Waltz.' And when school let out for summer recess, I'd go to my grandma and grandpa's place. They were farmers and came from Poland. They would want me to help them with the plowing, but I would say, 'Grandpa, I gotta play my ukulele.'"

Dale insists on using the traditional Hawaiian pronunciation, "oo-ke-lay-le," as opposed to the more popular "you-ke-lay-le." Employing the more common pronunciation in his presence will merit a correction and a lecture. In a sense, his early adoption of the instrument was prophetic as he would spend quite a bit of time in Hawaii later on in life.

The next stage in Dale's early musical evolution came a little bit after he began playing the uke. He procured his first guitar on a ramble through the woods near his grandparents' place. "My buddy and I would walk out into the swamps, 'cause it was all wilderness and we were picking blueberries for my grandma," Dick recalls. "She was making blueberry turnovers. All of a sudden, we hear this strumming. It sounded like four or five guitars. So we walked and found this old shack where the sound was coming from. It was a bit scary, kind of like the film *Deliverance*. But we walked into the shack and these guys were strumming away on flattop guitars. One guy had a pack of cigarettes rolled up in the sleeve of his T-shirt like a real tough guy. He says, 'My guitar's for sale.' I say, 'How much?'

and he says, 'Eight bucks.' And I say, 'Whoa!' That was a lot of money. That's when I was working in a bakery for, like, five cents an hour. In those days, gasoline was like eleven cents a gallon. But I gave the guy fifty cents down, and the deal was I was going to pay him another fifty cents every week until the eight bucks was paid off. I tried to give him a quarter down, but he wouldn't go for it.

"So what happened was, I said, 'Wow, look at all those strings.' And the guy said, 'Just play the top four strings, like on a ukulele.' The ukulele chords worked for the first four strings, but I'd listen to the other two strings and it didn't make sense. He says, 'Don't play those strings. Just muffle them.' So I was strumming away and nobody knew the difference. Everyone thought I could play the guitar and I was just playing ukulele chords and singing Hank Williams songs with a ruck-a-tuck beat."

Starting out by learning ukulele chords on guitar is something Dale shares with John Lennon. Lennon didn't learn conventional guitar chords until he hooked up with Paul McCartney. And Dale's guitar evolution took a big leap forward when his family moved to Southern California in 1954.

"I graduated from the eleventh grade in 1954," he recalls. "And that's when my daddy was hired by Hughes Aircraft, so we all went to California. I said good-bye to all my friends in Massachusetts: 'I won't be seeing you in the twelfth grade.'"

With thriving aerospace and entertainment industries, Southern California was a fast-growing and prosperous place in the mid-twentieth century. Middle- and working-class people could attain a standard of living that seemed quite luxurious compared to what their parents had known. Average families could afford a little ranch house in one of the many beach towns along the Pacific coastline, enjoying newly accessible consumer goods such as the television sets that were quickly becoming a standard item in American homes. And a whole youth culture of surf boards and hot rods took shape on the sunny beaches. As an adolescent, Dick found his place in this culture, first as one of the crowd but soon as a leader.

Young Richard Monsour got his first electric guitar shortly after arriving in Southern California. "I found a pawn shop and got this thick solid-body guitar," he recounts. "To this day, we don't know what it is. It was purple, but I painted it white to make it look country and I started strumming on that."

Along the way, Dale also learned to play keyboards, drums, sax, trumpet, and harmonica. But the guitar would always be his destiny. And while he would go down in history as the King of the Surf Guitar, he makes no secret of the fact that country music is his first love. He cites Ernest Tubb, Tex Ritter, and Johnny Cash as particular favorites. And as Dick was taking his first steps on electric guitar, country music was sprouting an exciting new offshoot called rockabilly—a uniquely countrified strain of the rock-and-roll craze that swept the world in the mid-fifties. And it was essentially rockabilly that Dale was performing when he started to play gigs, first at the Rinky Dink Ice Cream Parlor in Newport Beach, and later in large tent shows organized by Los Angeles disc jockey and promoter Art Laboe.

"In the late fifties it was said that anyone who played guitar was playing the Devil's music and evil music," Dale remembers. "That's why you couldn't get a permit to throw a dance for teenagers if you were playing guitars. And that's why Art Laboe was throwing his concerts with Johnny Otis, Black

Sonny Knight, Little Julian Herrera and the Tigers, and those guys in tents out on muddy marshes and hilltops. I was the only white guy playing with them."

By this point, Dick's father had taken his son's musical career in hand. Together they arranged a residency for Dick and his band, the Del-Tones, at the Rendezvous Ballroom in Balboa, a neighborhood in Newport Beach, California. Built in 1928, the hall had been a top venue for the big bands of the thirties and forties but had fallen into disuse.

"My dad and I spoke with the owners of the ballroom and asked if we could open it up. And they said, 'No, you can't get a permit. The only things we can rent it to is the high school and junior high school dances when they're throwing their graduation parties. And they use horn bands—trumpets, trombones, saxes, drums, and stuff like that.'

So what happened was we went to the city. We had secret meetings. They didn't want anybody to know we were meeting. And we met with the police, the fire department, the PTA . . . all those people. And I said to them, 'Would you rather have your children out on the street drinking T-Bird—that's Thunderbird wine—and you've got no control, or would you rather have them in one building where you know where in the hell they're at and you can control them?' And they said, 'Well, okay, but they gotta wear ties.'

"So whoever heard of surfers wearing ties? Well, my father bought a box of ties that we could hand out at the door. And they gave us the permit. On the opening night all we had were seventeen people in a huge building. Seventeen surfers—the ones I was surfing with in Huntington Beach. I said, 'I'm playing tonight; come on down.' Those are the ones who first called me the King of the Surf Guitar. And that's how it all started. We ended up packing 3,000 people a night, all by word of mouth. We didn't have money to create what you call PR or anything."

The Rendezvous Ballroom is where Dale forged his distinctive sound and style, honing it night after night on the bandstand, pushing his showmanship and decibel level to greater and greater extremes. One key ally in this effort was Leo Fender, who was at the time still very much at the start of building his own legend. Riding on the success of his pioneering solid-body electric guitar, the Telecaster, he'd introduced a sleek new model in '54, the Stratocaster. And Dick Dale would become one of the earliest guitarists to take that iconic instrument to international fame. Dick often speaks of his first meeting with Leo at Fender HQ in Fullerton, California.

"I said, 'Mr. Fender, I'm Dick Dale. I'm a surfer and I have no money. Can you help me?' He looked at me and said, 'Here, try this guitar.' He handed me a Stratocaster and said, 'Play it.' I grab it and when I turned it around, held it upside-down backwards, and started playing ukulele chords, Leo almost fell off his chair laughing. And Leo never laughed. He was like Einstein—very stern."

Dale forged a close relationship with Leo Fender and his right-hand man, Freddie Tavares. "Leo was really into boats, and that's one thing we bonded over," Dick notes. "And then there was country music, which we both loved. We used to sit together in his living room listening to Marty Robbins on a little ten-inch Jensen speaker."

Dale worked closely with Fender on amplifier design, goading him to create guitar amps with more and more power. "Leo took a liking to me because I was blowing up everything he was making," Dale laughs. He was going, 'How are you doing that?' Eventually he came up with

the saying, 'Anything that can stand up to Dick Dale's barrage of punishment is fit for human consumption.'"

Output transformer design became a mutual obsession for Dale and Fender. "An output transformer usually only favors highs, mids, or lows," Dick explains. "It doesn't favor all three. And I wanted all three. Where there were only seventeen people in the Rendezvous Ballroom, my guitar sounded okay. But when it became two hundred people and more, now the bass was being sucked up by their bodies. So now it was sounding really tinny and thin. So I'd go back to Fender and we'd sit in Leo's tiny cubbyhole. And nobody would come in except for [Fender factory manager] Forrest White, who'd stop in to say hi to me. But things didn't really start happening until Leo went to watch me play. Freddie was the one who dragged him there. Because he would always call me into the factory to test stuff, but it just wouldn't happen in there. The amp was loud there and it sounded fine. But we got to the stage, with the crowd, we lost it. And I couldn't explain it to him. I said, 'You gotta be there, Leo.' So Freddie dragged Leo down, and Leo said, 'Now I know what Dick's trying to tell me. Back to the drawing board!'

"I said, 'Mr. Fender, I'm Dick Dale. I'm a surfer and I have no money. Can you help me?' He looked at me and said, 'Here, try this guitar.' He handed me a Stratocaster and said, 'Play it.'"

"Then he called me at three o'clock one morning. 'Cause he used to work around the clock. And he said, 'Dick, get down here quick. I got it! I got an eighty-five-watt output transformer peaking at one hundred watts.' So then we needed a speaker. I'd fried every Jensen he ever had. So we went to JB Lansing and said, 'We want a fifteen-inch speaker with a birdcage enclosure around an eleven- or twelve-pound magnet.' And I wanted an aluminum dust cover on the front so I could hear the click of the pick. They thought we were nuts. 'What are you gonna do with that?' they said. 'You gonna put it on a tugboat?' Leo just looked at them and very quietly said, 'You want my business? Make it.' So they made it. It became the fifteen-inch JBL D130.

"Next we built a three-foot-high cabinet for it, two feet wide and twelve inches deep with no port holes, and we packed it with fiberglass. We wanted the speaker to push itself outward and inward. And what happened was all of a sudden the speaker would freeze. Freddie would take out the speaker, put his fingers on the cone, and move it back and forth. It was supposed to move silently, but it was creaking. He said, 'Dick, what are you doing to these speakers?' We figured it out. The machine-gun style of picking I was doing was confusing the speaker as it was pumping in and out. So we went back to Lansing and said, 'We want you to put a rubberized coating all around the ridge of the speaker so it will flex more smoothly and catch every vibration. They did, and I never blew up another speaker after that. It became the JBL D130F speaker. 'F' means 'Fender specifications.'

"There's nothing on the planet that sounds like those speakers in a three-foot cabinet. When I plugged that into the amp that Leo had created, the world of pansy-ass electronics came to an end.

It was like Einstein had split the atom. Onstage, I wired up six amps behind me and when I struck my sixty-gauge low-E string, my feet came off of the stage. The thing just lifted me up. But eventually I just went to one amp on each side of the stage."

Extremely heavy-gauge strings [low to high 60, 49, 39, 20, 18, 16] are another key ingredient in Dale's monstrous tone. "When I started playing those heavy strings the girls at a school dance started gyrating," Dale says. "And they were gyrating so sexually that the woman principal who was overseeing the whole dancing concert made them all sit down on the floor and cross their legs. This was the late fifties. That's why rock and roll scared people. Music is sex. It always has been. It has a sexual, sensual drive that makes you want to move your body. Undulate. I got that word from a fourteen-year-old girl who came up to me at one of my concerts and said, 'Please, Mr. Dale, would you sign my arm? Because your music makes my body undulate.' Well, I had to go look that word up to find out what it meant. But the point is that there's a lot of sensuality in music."

Dale is one of those rare musicians who can switch readily between abstract philosophizing on the nature of music and life to geeking out obsessively over the mechanics of wattage and voltage. The electronic discoveries that Leo Fender made with Dale's help became the basis for the Fender Showman and Dual Showman amps. Dick says he inspired the name for the legendary amp as well.

"The Showman was named after me. At the end of a song I used to jump off the five-foot-high stage and slide across the floor on my knees underneath the girls who were dancing the lindy. They had a about twenty-five petticoats on. I used to point at them at the end of a song with a big fanfare. Mr. Showbiz. My dad would yell and swear at me, 'Goddamnit, you're never gonna walk right when you're older. Your hips are gonna disintegrate, and your knees . . .' And Leo used to say, 'God, you're a showman!' And that's where the name came from."

Jim Monsour soon realized that his son's talent was too big even for the spacious Rendezvous Ballroom. So he launched Deltone Records, largely as a vehicle for bringing Dick's music to the world. Dick Dale's first single was "Ooh-Whee Marie," released in 1959. But the first disc that really caught on was Dale's fourth Deltone release, 1961's "Let's Go Trippin'." A contagious I, IV, V rock song, front-loaded with a guitar riff built around muted arpeggiated barré chords, the track is generally considered the first-ever surf instrumental and is clearly the template for later surf classics like the Surfaris' "Wipe Out" and "Surfer Joe," not to mention "Surfin' Bird" by the Trashmen. The title, "Let's Go Trippin'," incidentally, is a reference to SoCal car culture—trippin', as in taking a ride. LSD trips wouldn't impinge on pop culture consciousness until a good five or six years later.

But the track that really put Dale on the map was his sixth Deltone single, "Misirlou." To this day it remains his signature song and one that exemplifies what we think of as the Dick Dale guitar style and sound. All the ingredients are in place, thunderous double-picked low-string runs and exotic melodic moves based on the Middle Eastern *Hijaz Kar*, or double harmonic scale (E, F, G♯, A, B, C, D♯), which plays a flat second against the major third and seventh. Dale's recording is based on a folk song known throughout the Middle East. The song is Greek in origin and the title "Misirlou" translates as "Egyptian girl," or more literally, "Non-Christian Girl," carrying a suggestive hint of exotic romance and moral lassitude. (Other commentators claim Egyptian origin, and translate the title as "Christian Girl." But the connotation of alluring otherness remains the same.)

Dale's choice and performance of this song as his sixth recording clearly reflects his own Middle Eastern family background. In the great melting pot of American music, this is one of Dale's unique contributions. Many subsequent rock guitarists and other musicians picked up on the mysterious vibe of the *Hijaz Kar* scale. Adaptations of it peaked in the psychedelic late sixties with tracks like the Jefferson Airplane's "White Rabbit."

The chromatically descending double-picked guitar runs Dale plays on "Misirlou" are generally regarded as evoking the sound of the crashing surf. A skilled surfer, Dale was certainly familiar with this sound. But he has always insisted that this element of his style came from a desire to translate Gene Krupa's furiously rhythmic drum rolls onto the guitar. And while the surf guitar sound is commonly described as "reverb drenched," Dale insists that he did not use any kind of electronic reverberation on his original recording of "Misirlou."

"'Misirlou' was not cut with reverb. It was just done hardcore. I recorded it ninety-five times because the guy who was engineering couldn't control it. It was a little teeny room, a hallway that wasn't six feet across and about thirty feet long."

To the best of Dale's recollection, he didn't add spring reverb to his guitar sound until after 'Misirlou,' and was first attracted to the technology as a vocal effect. "My voice doesn't have any natural vibrato, and I wanted to extend my voice, like you hear on a piano with a sustain pedal. So I went and pulled the spring reverb unit out of a Hammond organ, brought it to Leo, and said, 'This is what I want.' He made the box. I plugged my [vocal] microphone into it and I sounded like Dean Martin and Frank Sinatra. Then after a couple of weeks I plugged my Stratocaster into it and it sounded kinda neat."

Dale's steady stream of Deltone singles eventually led to his first album, *Surfer's Choice*, released on Deltone in 1962. The front cover bore a photo of Dick himself riding a wave on his surf board. Surf music was one teen-pop trend that wasn't cooked up by forty-year-old guys in New York's Brill Building. The music's originator was an actual surfer, one key to the authenticity and enduring appeal of Dick's music from this era.

That appeal grew exponentially when Capitol picked up *Surfer's Choice* for distribution. It was the start of an extended contract with the influential label, negotiated by Jim Monsour. It's interesting to compare Dale's career with that of Brian, Carl, and Dennis Wilson of the Beach Boys, the other key exponent of surf music and also Capitol recording artists. Like Dale, the Wilsons were managed by their father, a domineering figure who could be quite demanding and harsh in his criticisms.

"It's an interesting parallel," says Dale's more recent manager and biographer, Matt Marshall. "But Jim Monsour was no Murray Wilson. I don't think he was anywhere near as hard on Dick as Murray was on Brian and his brothers."

But Dick does remember being goaded onto a stage for the first time—a seventh grade talent show—by his dad, and not really wanting to do it initially. "Some people have parents from the old country, like me," Dick says. "If I hugged my dad, his arms would just be hanging down. He didn't know how to say he loved me. A lot of parents don't know how to say they love you. But they do."

Dick Dale's first full-on Capitol release was *King of the Surf Guitar* in 1963. The disc helped transform Dale from a regional SoCal hit maker to a national, and indeed international, star. Dick and the Del-Tones appeared on the popular TV variety program *The Ed Sullivan Show* and youth-cult beach movies like 1963's *Beach Party* and '64's *Muscle Beach Party*. It was part of a worldwide media fascination with the sunny, carefree Southern California lifestyle; and surf guitar instrumental music was very much the soundtrack to this pop culture dream.

Garage bands were springing up in every suburb in America and elsewhere, and surf instrumentals formed the backbone of their repertoire. Good singers have always been in far shorter supply than competent guitarists, but fledgling groups could sidestep the issue by working up a set of surf instrumentals. There was plenty of material to choose from: "Pipeline" by the Chantays, "Walk Don't Run" by the Ventures, "Penetration" by the Pyramids, "Outer Limits" by Jerry Cole and His Spacemen, and the aforementioned classic "Wipe Out" by the Safaris.

Garage bands continued to assay these nuggets even after the vocal-driven style of the Beatles, Rolling Stones, and other British Invaders came into vogue in the mid-sixties. But when it comes to surf instrumentals all roads lead back to Dick Dale.

Dick cranked out two albums a year for Capitol in 1963 and '64.

However, the advent of the Beatles and their British rock colleagues effectively curtailed the careers of many American rock and R&B performers, including Dick Dale. The Beatles were also on Capitol in the U.S. and they became a priority. But Marshall feels that Dale had been poorly handled by the label all along.

"Do you know who produced *King of the Surf Guitar?*" Marshall demands. "It was Voyle Gilmour, the same guy who reinvented Frank Sinatra on Capitol and then produced the Kingston Trio. And then here comes Dick Dale. For all his talent, Voyle Gilmour had no business producing Dick Dale. Dick himself didn't like the stuff he did for Capitol and a lot of it was just ridiculous. I mean, why would he want to record 'Never on Sunday'? [The theme song from a popular movie of the day.] And that's not an attack on Dick at all. He was told to be in the studio the next day and be ready to record an album. And his dad was a big band–era guy. That's not rock and roll."

Moreover, Dale has always been an outsider. He had no interest in playing the showbiz or Hollywood game. He just wanted to go on living as he always had, surfing with his pals, hanging out and listening to country music with Leo Fender and tending to his growing menagerie of tropical fish, birds, and cats out in Balboa. So when the British Invaders changed the music game, there was no real plan B for Dale. He wasn't the kind of guy to segue into acting or hosting a TV variety show.

"Dick just sort of never wanted to be in the business," Marshall states. "He says it point blank, 'I didn't like what my dad was doing. I didn't like to go into Hollywood. I never hung around with those people. I had no interest in the business whatsoever.'"

It was Jim Monsour who got Dick out of his deal with Capitol. "Dick still had another seven years to go on his contract," Marshall explains. "But his career wasn't going anywhere at Capitol, and the Beatles certainly weren't helping. So Jim negotiated directly with [Capitol chief] Alan Livingston to get Dick off and take the master tapes with him, which is mind-boggling."

Those master tapes would fuel a career renaissance for Dale a few decades down the line. But the mid-sixties found him in a very low place indeed. In 1966, he was diagnosed with rectal cancer and given very slim odds of surviving. Dale describes the surgical treatment he received at the

GUITAR PLAYER ARCHIVES

time as "Neanderthal. Fuck, they cut fourteen inches out of my rectal tract. Six tumors and seven cysts later, I went down to ninety-eight pounds."

To exacerbate matters, Dale had a falling out with his father, which caused him a great deal of anxiety. Weakened and despondent, he retreated to Hawaii, half expecting to die there. Instead he found a new way of life. He hooked up with Ed Parker, founder of the American Kenpo school of the martial arts and a personal trainer to Elvis Presley. Dale became fascinated with Kenpo, which has its roots in Chinese and Japanese martial arts traditions and philosophies.

"I went to the islands and met people in the martial arts—grand masters, underground people," Dick recalls. "They took me in because they said I had the eagle in my eye. They called me *hapa hoele*—half white and half something else. So that became my lifestyle."

The Kenpo breathing exercises and physical discipline helped nurse Dale back to health. And the discipline's underlying philosophy gave Dale a fresh outlook on life and on his art. In Hawaii and California he spent time studying with monks from the Shaolin Temple in China, an ancient seat of Chan Buddhism—the Chinese antecedent to Japanese Zen Buddhism—and the Shaolin school of kung fu. From the monks, he absorbed the central Buddhist doctrine of egolessness and service to others.

"Ego is what causes all the problems in life," he says. "To know oneself is to empty oneself. When you empty yourself of ego . . . that's how I defeated cancer."

Dale even discovered that he could apply monastic discipline to his music. "At Shaolin Temple, they never let you touch the skin of a drum for five years, until you can tongue [i.e., sing] what you want to play. That way you learn to project from your brain into your arms, hands, and muscle memory."

Hawaii is also where Dale met his first wife, Jeanie, a Polynesian dancer. They got married in the United States in 1967, and soon Dick was back onstage with Jeanie as part of the act. "She would do some Polynesian dancing," says Marshall. "And Dick taught her how to play the trumpet. She would sing as well."

It was the start of a new phase in Dale's career, playing the casinos and nightclubs of Las Vegas, Reno, and Lake Tahoe. "The Golden Nugget [in Las Vegas] was the big place that he played," says Marshall. "He got to know [Vegas entrepreneur] Steve Wynn and his family very well. There are photographs of marquees at the Golden Nugget with Dick Dale's name alongside Ray Charles, Merle Haggard, and Conway Twitty. Very cool."

Vegas is of course where Elvis Presley made his comeback in 1969. Still, working the casinos might have seemed like a step down for a man who'd been a teen idol and crowned King of the Surf Guitar. But Dale took it in stride, selflessly priding himself on his ability to read an audience and give them anything they wanted, whether it was 'Misirlou' or 'Won't You Come Home Bill Bailey." This is something he now teaches in his workshops.

"I always say, find the beauty in every type of music there is," he advises. "Do not play to other musicians, play to other people. Learn to be an entertainer, because entertainers get paid more than sidemen."

While he wasn't recording or in the national spotlight during the seventies, it was a good decade for Dale in other ways. Investing his Vegas/Reno/Tahoe earnings in real estate, he met with considerable financial success. He and Jeanie moved into the Gillette mansion in Balboa, the palatial former home of the razor blade magnate. The guitarist opened a string of successful Southern California nightclubs, including the Rendezvous I and II, named in tribute to his early-sixties glory days at the original Rendezvous Ballroom.

Adjacent to one of his venues, he established a two-and-a-half-acre wild animal menagerie, where he kept lions, tigers, elephants, hawks, cheetahs, and mountain lions, among other exotic species. Dick's passion for wildlife had began back in the sixties, when he lived near a pet store in Balboa and began to collect tropical fish, birds, and domestic cats. But now his interest had blossomed into full-scale animal activism.

"Ego is what causes all the problems in life. To know oneself is to empty oneself. When you empty yourself of ego . . . that's how I defeated cancer."

"I wanted to make my guitar sound really big like the lions, tigers, and elephants I was raising to preserve these animals so they wouldn't get killed off by poachers. I would imitate those animal sounds. So they could have called me Dick Dale, the King of the Jungle, instead of the King of the Surf Guitar."

In his love for animals, Dale stopped eating meat, embracing a vegetarian diet. "I'm a veggie guy," he says. "I eat veggie burgers. On the road, I go to Burger King and say 'Double me on tomatoes, onions, pickles, etc. and leave off the meat.' And it looks like it's six inches thick. I eat kidney beans. Put mushrooms, peppers, onions, etc. in spaghetti sauce and you swear you're eating meat."

In a way, Dale's seventies period echoed the late-fifties/early-sixties pre–Capitol Records age of innocence, when he could rock the clubs, surf, and enjoy his friends and hobbies without the pressure of a major label recording career. He studied to be a pilot and started collecting airplanes. He designed a luxe home for his parents. And, as in the early days, he continued to hang out with Leo Fender and Freddie Tavares, frequently dropping by the Fender factory.

"When I brought my Rolls-Royce around, Leo would sit in the backseat and just keep opening and closing the picnic tray, looking at the hinge," recalls Dale. "He'd say, 'Freddie, Freddie, come here and look at this! Look how the hinge activates itself.' He was interested in how everything is built. That's something we had in common. He would spend the whole afternoon drawing the interior of boats. He had a Matthews and Stevens and I had a cabin cruiser."

Fender and Dale never stopped tinkering with Dick's guitar and amps. Early on Dale had been one of the first guitarists to discover the "out of phase" tones that a Stratocaster could produce if one slid the original three-position pickup selector between settings. This is one factor that led to the five-position pickup selector that has long since become standard equipment on Strats.

"But I hated it," Dale confesses. "'Cause there were too many positions and it just confused

me. So I took it out and put my three-position selector back in. And then I put in separate toggle switches. If my pickup selector was on pickup one or two, the toggle switch would automatically put them both together. It would not affect the third one, which is closest to the saddles. That's the way I still play."

But as the seventies drew to a close Dale was brought low once again, first by illness. While surfing off Newport Beach, he sustained what seemed at first to be a minor puncture wound. But the water was so polluted that the wound became infected and Dale came perilously close to having his leg amputated. As a result, he became an environmental activist as well as an animal rights advocate. Having barely recovered from the complications of his swimming injury, Dale suffered third-degree burns to his left hand in 1984, after accidentally spilling a pot of boiling cooking oil on himself. For a while it wasn't at all certain if he'd ever be able to play the guitar again. But he pulled through the injury with characteristic resolve.

Dale saved his hand and leg only to lose his fortune in 1986, after a long and difficult divorce from Jeanie and a slew of legal complications. "Dick lost his house and pretty much everything," says Marshall. "He always says that he watched nine million dollars go out the window. 'Jeanie and I could have split it,' he says. 'She would have gotten $4 million and change, but it just didn't go that way.' Because of the huge court battles that went on for years. It was a huge fall for him—going from being a really successful club owner, realtor, and musician all the way down to zero. Living in your parent's driveway in a motor home. It's a sad but essential part of his story."

A setback of these tragic proportions would send many people into a deep depression or worse. But not Dick Dale. "Dick's chemical makeup just doesn't include depression," says Marshall. "A lot of people deal with depression. It's a very common situation. But he's never, to my knowledge, had to deal with clinical depression. He's just an unstoppable force at times. There is no bottom of the heap in the life cycle for him. When he's on a high, he can enjoy it, but he doesn't let it go to his head. And when he's on a low, he can still have a great time. A lot of people like to portray him as a superhuman being, with his drive and philosophy. And that's true to some degree. But I think we're all capable of doing what he's done, if we had the right sort of chemistry. Part of that is what's going on in your brain."

Dale lost no time in fighting his way back to success. He reconnected with producer Gary Usher (the Beach Boys, the Byrds, the Hondells, and Brian Wilson), with whom he'd worked back in '63. Usher paired Dale with blues guitar legend Stevie Ray Vaughan to cut a version of the Chantays' surf hit "Pipeline" for the soundtrack to the 1987 film *Back to the Beach*. Fittingly enough, the film was a fond parody of the mid-sixties beach party movies that had featured the music of Dick Dale and the Del-Tones. The Dale/Vaughan recording of "Pipeline" garnered a Grammy nomination for Best Rock Instrumental, effectively putting Dale on track for a new career high.

The guitarist's personal life was also looking up as the nineties dawned. December 13, 1992, saw the birth of Jimmy Dale, son of Dick Dale and his new wife, Jill. "Dick always says that thirteen is his lucky number," Marshall observes. The proud new father soon set about training his progeny to be his successor—a guitar-slinging kung-fu warrior. "I trained my son in karate from when he was five years old," Dick proudly recounts. "When he was seven years old, weighing just fifty pounds, he was penetrating a one-inch board with two knuckles, because I taught him the breathing, the speed, and stuff like that."

As a result of the Grammy nomination for "Pipeline" and Dale's increased visibility in the early nineties, he won a recording contract with HighTone Records, the roots Americana label that was home to blues greats like Robert Cray, Joe Lewis Walker, and R. L. Burnside, and alt-country pioneers like Jimmy Dale Gilmour, Joe Ely and Buddy Miller.

Dale's first release for HighTone was 1993's *Tribal Thunder*. The disc is a glorious restatement of the classic Dick Dale sound, the bright sparkle and ominous roar of his Strats and Showman amps.

"The albums Dick did with HighTone are important because they put him on the map with the *CMJ (College Music Journal)* radio stations, which connected him with a whole new audience," says Marshall. "For the first time Dick was reviewed in *Rolling Stone*, which wouldn't happen again until we reissued *Surfer's Choice* in 2006."

"I wanted to make my guitar sound really big like the lions, tigers, and elephants I was raising to preserve these animals so they wouldn't get killed off by poachers. I would imitate those animal sounds. So they could have called me Dick Dale, the King of the Jungle, instead of the King of the Surf Guitar."

Dale hit another peak in 1994, when director Quentin Tarantino chose "Misirlou" as a key soundtrack song for his hugely influential film *Pulp Fiction*. Tarantino's fast-cut editing and casually stylized violence encapsulated the edgy transience and dark undertows of Southern Californian culture as it lurched toward the twenty-first century like a speeding car with dodgy brakes. And the frenetic, sun-baked urgency of Dale's music provided the perfect aural analogue for Tarantino's vision.

During Dale's long absence from the limelight, a new Southern California youth culture had sprung up. The skate punk and surf punk scene came to life in the same Orange County beach towns that had nurtured the original surf music explosion in the early sixties. This new generation of restless outsiders embraced Dick Dale as a precursor and patriarch. The guitarist even performed on the punk-fest Warped Tour in 1996, in support of his *Calling Up Spirits* album on the hip Beggar's Banquet label.

Meanwhile, the Dales had taken up residence in a new home out in the California desert town of Twentynine Palms. It's called Dick Dale's Sky Ranch, and boasts its own airstrip where the guitarist maintains several personal aircraft. But once again, dark clouds were looming on the horizon. Dick and Jill divorced in 2008. Shortly thereafter, Dale suffered a serious cancer relapse. Now in his seventies, his chances for survival seemed grim. But he endured a tortuous round of surgical procedures and chemotherapy and came up cancer free.

GUITAR PLAYER ARCHIVES

"They don't call me the King of the Surf Guitar anymore," he jokes grimly. "They call me the cancer warrior. I was getting over a thousand e-mails a day when I was in the hospital. Even with the best of surgeons—three of them—they all thought it was going to be a two-hour operation. It was eight hours I was on the operating table."

Along with his lifelong struggle with cancer, Dale is also diabetic and said to be a near candidate for kidney dialysis. Yet he still tours whenever possible, often performing in tandem with Jimmy. And although Leo is long gone, Dick is still collaborating with Fender on guitar and amp designs and has recently introduced the Malibu line of signature electro-acoustic guitars. His current companion is Lana Parnell, a trim blonde some years younger than Dick, but not entirely age inappropriate. She appears to function as both girlfriend and caregiver. Her fondness for Dale is both obvious and touching.

"The chemotherapy turned his insides to cement," she recently commented to me, her eyes filling with tears.

And Dick Dale continues to rock on—for how long, no one knows. But awareness of his age and health challenges makes each day precious, for him and his fans. With the latter, he continues to share the wisdom he's acquired in the course of his long and eventful life. He often quotes the Buddhist sayings he learned from the Shaolin monks. One of his favorites goes as follows:

"Thoughts become words. Words become actions. Actions become habits. Habits become character. And your character becomes your destiny."

To break it down in simpler terms, I once asked Dick Dale what he'd most like to be remembered for. His response was swift and direct:

"An attitude."

REDFERNS/GETTY IMAGES

Pete Townshend

THE SEEKER

THE PROFOUND BLUENESS of Pete Townshend's eyes is a little unsettling at close range. They're the eyes of a lifelong seeker. Eyes that have witnessed post—WWII British austerity, Swinging London's mid-sixties mod explosion, art school, the hippie scene, spiritual awakening, drug and alcoholic blur, mass Woodstock adulation, deep disillusionment, the edge of insanity, literary and theatrical accomplishment, and troubled maturity. They're the eyes of the man who wrote "Behind Blue Eyes." The one who wrote "I Can See for Miles." But who also wrote "Deaf, Dumb and Blind Boy."

When those eyes engage yours in conversation, it's a little like a spell. Pete counts on that. Perhaps too much. He's one of the great rock interviews—fascinating in his ability to weave colorful threads of ideas and memories in endlessly surprising and inventive ways. But he shares with many novelists and creative types a constitutional inability to distinguish fiction from fact in every particular.

This isn't out of an intent to deceive. Nor is it necessarily the result of a drug-addled memory. It's just the nature of an artist who has spent his life probing his own emotions and those of his audience, and recognizing that, in the realm of emotions, truth is complex and certainties nonexistent. In a 1996 interview, Townshend came out and admitted as much to me.

"Often when I'm doing interviews," he said, "talking about my career, trying to explain things that I don't really understand, I'm hoping to draw conclusions to some extent. Saying things and looking into the eyes of the interviewer and thinking, 'Am I on the right track? Could I be right about this, or am I wrong? I don't really know!'"

The hyperactive Townshend imagination can make him a tricky interview subject. But that same imagination has given the world artistic innovations like the rock opera, masterworks like *Tommy* and *Quadrophenia*, and a full portfolio of brilliant, concise, and witty pop songs that still serve as the benchmark for just how great a three-minute slab of vinyl, or digital nothingness, can be. As guitarist and chief songwriter for the Who, and as a solo artist, Townshend elevated rock music to the stature and grandeur of fine art in the sixties and seventies, all without losing his sense of humor and irreverence about the whole thing.

"I've been perceived as someone who is very serious about rock and roll and perhaps sometimes even serious about myself," he laughs. "And that's been something of a black ticket for the Who. But looking back on it, rock is very, very important and very, very ridiculous."

Townshend is such a great songwriter that people sometimes overlook what an accomplished and imaginative guitarist he is. Much of what we think of as rock guitar playing originates with him—slashing power chords, the Marshall stack, the creative deployment of feedback, and a hyper-aggressive, belligerently theatrical approach to the instrument that completely reconceptualized the way people perceive and play the guitar. No one can say for sure who invented the electric guitar in the thirties. But it's certain that Pete Townshend *reinvented* the electric guitar in the sixties, paving the way for Jimi Hendrix, Jeff, Beck, Jimmy Page, Eric Clapton, and the whole pantheon of rock guitar heroes. In that regard, Pete is the godfather of rock guitar, the thinking person's guitar hero, a man who riffs on ideas as deftly as he riffs on notes and chords.

"I've got two strains to me," he says. "There's one side that loves music and is very musical. Then there's this other side that got into the idea of rock and roll as something that had music in it, but what was more important was its function."

Peter Dennis Blandford Townshend was born into a musical family on May 19, 1945, in the London district of Chiswick. His father, Cliff, was a successful big-band sax player, and his mother, Betty, a professional singer. Musically Pete grew up somewhat in his father's shadow. He speaks of feeling intimidated by Cliff's prowess as a sight reader and player. When Pete started playing guitar, at around age twelve, Cliff provided some early tutelage and encouragement.

"To me, the guitar was always a second instrument," Pete confides. "I wanted to be like my father, and my father was a saxophone player. But when I couldn't get a note out of a reed, he suggested that I try what was then his second instrument—guitar. So I always felt like I was playing a second instrument, not a very important instrument, but one that had been appropriated by rock and roll because it was sexy, and by the blues because it was cheap. You could make one yourself! In fact, the first guitar I ever played had been made for my best friend by his father. And the very fact that I was able to get a tune out of this thing, which was strung with piano wire, made my father decide to help me progress on the guitar. Because I think up to that point, he felt that I had no hope in music. Because I'm not actually very musical. So I kind of drifted into the guitar as an aficionado of music. As a musicologist. I loved all kinds of music, and still do."

Like many other British youths of his generation, Townshend fell deeply in love with rock and roll when the music first burst out of America in the mid-fifties. He was captivated by the songcraft of artists like the Everly Brothers and Ricky Nelson. "You heard the first truly great pop songs and you were hooked," he recalls. "'Cathy's Clown,' 'Hello Mary Lou,' 'Three Steps to Heaven'—songs of that quality. A lot of that came out of a Nashville-based tradition that I suppose was started by somebody like Hank Williams and developed into a more elegant style of . . . not so much storytelling, but with what I call vignetting. Creating little vignettes, little views, sushi-like slices of life. And I loved that stuff. I just loved the music, the way the guitars were used as an orchestral instrument. So from the time I was ten or eleven or twelve and first started to hear that kind of great American pop music, I was hooked into it. There was Buddy Holly, who actually created characters, you know, like 'Peggy Sue.'"

"I've been perceived as someone who is very serious about rock and roll and perhaps sometimes even serious about myself . . . . But looking back on it, rock is very, very important and very, very ridiculous."

Townshend would become one of rock's great narrative songwriters, pioneering musical forms that crossbred rock with fiction, drama, and, of course, opera. But even when he was very young, his listening and musical influences extended beyond rock and roll.

"I also listened to Wes Montgomery, Johnny Smith, and Barney Kessel," he says, "the guitar players of my father's era, really. That kind of stylish lounge jazz player. And the first guitar players I listened to were the country and pop players. People like James Burton playing with Ricky Nelson—probably the most important guitar player in American music in some ways. And still very, very undervalued in that respect, but only because he was with Rick Nelson, who is also completely undervalued as an artist, tragically so. Burton used to use two second strings instead of a second and a third. So the second was usually very, very, very slack. Usually much too loud because it resonated too much and was tuned low. So the string balance would be bad. But there was a style which came out of that which was a fingerpicking style, which I used a lot when I was training myself as a guitar player. I studied Chet Atkins too, who is another country player and I'm very good at that stuff. It might probably surprise people, but I can do all that stuff."

Pete started out on a very cheap acoustic he'd received from his grandmother, moving on from there to a slightly better £3 guitar from Czechoslovakia. But when he joined his first band in 1959, at age fourteen, he was on banjo. The Confederates were a trad jazz band that Townshend formed with John Entwistle, a close friend and gifted multi-instrumentalist who would become Pete's most intimate musical collaborator for decades to come. Entwistle was on trumpet in the Confederates. Trad, or traditional Dixieland jazz, was popular in Britain in the fifties and sixties. But Entwistle was soon lured away to play bass guitar in the Detours, led by a tough street kid from nearby Shepherd's Bush named Roger Daltrey. Townshend soon followed Entwistle into Daltrey's band—enticed, it is said, by the Detours' possession of a real Vox amp.

Thus began one of rock's great love-hate relationships; Townshend and Daltrey, a dynamic that would define the explosive sound of the Who, and indeed the trajectory of rock music in the sixties and beyond. Daltrey was top man in the Detours, a legacy that would engender a momentous power struggle as that group morphed into the one the world knows as the Who. Singers are typically the focal point of bands, but Townshend possessed a strong personality, an eloquent way with words, and he would soon develop into the group's chief songwriter. So who was to call the shots, then, the belligerent, bellicose Daltrey or the cerebral, pensive Townshend? Would fists carry the day, or words?

"I didn't have Roger's courage, but I had audacity," Pete commented years later. "I was a cynic; I was acerbic and full of ideas and quite spunky, but I certainly didn't know what to do in a street fight. But together Roger and I make a good combination."

Playing in a band satisfied a deeply ingrained need on Townshend's part. "One of my psychological quirks was that I loved to belong," he says. "I was starting to feel like I belonged to this neighborhood group. We were making a bit of money and playing pubs long before we got our first record deal. I was only sixteen. Roger Daltrey, John Entwistle, and our then drummer, Doug Sandom . . . they made me feel part of the gang. I wasn't special then. I wasn't the writer then. I was just the rhythm player. But I loved that feeling of belonging."

Daltrey was the Detours' lead guitarist at first, but ultimately decided to concentrate solely on vocals. A series of lineup changes eventually left Townshend as the group's sole guitarist, a development that would have a momentous impact on the style he would eventually develop, the muscular, chordal guitar aesthetic of a power rock trio.

By around 1962 the Detours had discovered the American R&B and blues sounds that were coming into vogue in London. The blues idiom also expanded Townshend's guitar vocabulary.

"It must be hard for guitar players today even to understand the difficulty of bending a string in 1962," he says. "First, you had to go out and buy a set of guitar strings, of which there were only one type available in the corner store—one weight. Put them on your guitar and frig around with the strings to get the effect you wanted."

By this point, Pete had already begun attending Ealing Art School, where he eagerly absorbed bohemianism, marijuana, pop art, and avant-garde music, along with blues, R&B, and jazz sounds from America. Pete would soon start incorporating concepts he learned at Ealing into his band, which had been rechristened the Who by Pete and his art school friend and roommate Richard Barnes. Both were high on, among other things, the aesthetic of the pop art movement, then ascendant in the visual arts, and its embrace of pop culture disposability.

"The name the Who was supposed to be a name that was forgotten," says Townshend. "Like, 'You remember the Who, don't you?' And you go, 'The who?' And we were already forgotten. That was written into the manifesto for the group, which was readopted by punk twenty years later. And it was a brilliant manifesto, rooted in the highest ideas of New York pop art. I used to look at these guys like Andy Warhol, Larry Rivers, Jasper Johns, and Roy Lichtenstein, but also Rothko, de Kooning, and all those people. Rothko's thing about just being a painter who decorated. All those things were real radical for me when I was in my first year of art school."

A final piece of the puzzle fell into place in 1964, when an (often literally) explosive young drummer named Keith Moon joined the Who. A natural-born anarchist and iconoclast, Moon certainly didn't need an art school education to teach him how to upset the apple cart. His freewheeling mastery of the drum kit was an art statement in and of itself, and just the rhythmic dynamite needed to ignite the sound that Townshend, Entwistle, and Daltrey were starting to foment. The band became the favorites of London's fast-paced, fashion-obsessed mod movement, playing the current R&B and Tamla/Motown sounds that, along with Jamaican ska, formed the musical backdrop for the mod scene. The Who forged their own unique and high-energy approach to this repertoire, which came to be known as "maximum R&B."

A recently restored film clip of the young group in action at the Railway Hotel in April 1964 conveys a sense of just how exciting and powerful they were, even at this early stage. Their approach to the standard R&B numbers "Ooh Poo Pah Doo" and "I Gotta Dance to Keep from Crying" is remarkably fluid, with Moon's drums clattering all over the place yet always landing squarely on the beat, and Entwistle's effortless yet supple bass fills imparting a tremendous sense of freedom and spontaneity. Townshend's rhythm comping is like a freehand sketch by a great master, offhand yet incisive, deftly stating the song's harmonic structure with a few terse strokes and lines. And Daltrey's gravelly singing is laced with equal measures of menace and abandon. As defined by nights like these, before crowds of ecstatic mod kids, maximum R&B was a completely fresh, distinctly British take on the American musical idiom. Townshend would also argue that it was a decisively British working-class phenomenon.

"When British kids that were in bands discovered R&B," he says, "what they discovered was a way to write pop songs which was purely British. And I think that's possibly because it came from a bleaker lifestyle. You know, America in the fifties was a very, very affluent country, from our point of view in Britain anyway. Growing up, you know, I'd never seen chewing gum, never had a glass of cold milk. I'd never seen frozen peas. I'd never ridden in a car. So for us, we responded to the message of the underclass that blues created. Because we felt like an underclass."

In that context, mod was all about working-class empowerment. It was the look and sound of a new generation, giddy on the first glimmer of economic recovery from the grim years that had followed in the wake of WWII, and expressing that elation in a fervent obsession with fashion—a sharply defined and rapidly evolving code of sartorial splendor and fine-cut detail. Conspicuous consumption, certainly, but marked by a strong sense of generational bonding around music. Townshend, Daltrey, Entwistle, and Moon became poster boys for the nascent mod scene, decked out in the latest finery and rocking London's clubs and pubs with their maximum R&B sound.

As such they were taken up by entrepreneur Pete Meaden, who rechristened them the High Numbers, a term from mod parlance denoting a trendsetter, a leader, but also perhaps a mod scenester high on amphetamines, the movement's drug of choice. Under Meaden's aegis, the newly renamed group recorded their first single, "Zoot Suit," backed with "I'm the Face," the latter being a rewrite of bluesman Slim Harpo's song "Got Love If You Want It." With lyrics consisting almost solely of mod fashion buzzwords, the two recordings were competent and credible, but didn't have much of a commercial impact. Meaden didn't last much longer after that, and the band eventually reverted to calling themselves the Who.

They had already started to acquire a reputation as the loudest band on the scene. At first, Townshend was playing Rickenbacker model-360 twelve-string guitars through a Fender Pro amp, although he also played the export model Rickenbackers distributed by Rose Morris and Company in the UK, including the model-1993 electric twelve and models 1997 and 1998. Pete accentuated the Who's aural assault by literally attacking his guitar quite aggressively, whirling it around over his head, slamming it into speaker cabinets, and otherwise heaping what at the time (and by some, even now) would be considered abuse. The normative attitude was for musicians to love and cherish their instruments, keeping them well polished and protected. But here was this guy bashing his guitar about.

"You know, America in the fifties was a very, very affluent country, from our point of view in Britain anyway. Growing up, you know, I'd never seen chewing gum, never had a glass of cold milk. I'd never seen frozen peas. I'd never ridden in a car. So for us, we responded to the message of the underclass that blues created. Because we felt like an underclass."

"It was all a part of that art school tradition I'd got of breaking the rules," says Townshend. "I was at an art school where the course was dedicated to breaking the rules, and I just drafted that into my work as a guitar player. Most of the techniques that I used were very virulent, violent, and aggressively expressive. Because I was in this kind of mode where the guitar was a weapon. And wonderful though my Fender Pro amp was, and wonderful though it sounded, it wasn't loud enough. So I went out and bought a Fender Bassman as well and plugged into both. And wonderful though that was, that wasn't loud enough either. So I went to Jim Marshall's, stomped down my Fender Bassman, and said, 'Here, I want that—twice as loud!' And from that came the Marshall stack and the big amplifiers of the sixties."

Marshall's was one of the premier music shops in London. It was actually Entwistle who had started the movement toward bigger and louder amplification gear by purchasing one of the then-new 4 x 12, closed-back speaker cabinets that Jim Marshall had started to manufacture. The cabinet gave him such a substantial volume boost that Townshend felt compelled to get his own Marshall gear to keep up.

Townshend's genius was to turn his attention toward what might lie beyond the amplifier's front panel, and how the circuitry there might be manipulated to produce not only more volume but also different tonal effects than anything that had been heard from an electric guitar before. Goaded by Townshend, Marshall came up with his soon to be legendary 100-watt head and speaker cabinets.

Townshend's guitar at the time, as mentioned, was a Rickenbacker 360 twelve-string, a

hollow-body instrument that had been popularized by the Beatles' George Harrison and the Byrds' Jim McGuinn. But by coupling the guitar with a Marshall stack, Townshend achieved a markedly different tone than the famous jingle-jangle chime of Harrison and McGuinn. Townshend's guitar work in this period retained some of the glassy Rickenbacker clarity, but coupled it with a gritty undercurrent of distortion. Increased wattage, combined with the Rick's hollow body, also brought Townshend to discover new dimensions of tonality within feedback. Hitherto, feedback had mainly been regarded as an unwanted byproduct of amplification—a nuisance, a noise. But in true art school fashion, Townshend found the music in the noise.

"When I bought my first Rickenbacker, I packed [the body] with paper," he recalls, "and found I could produce feedback on harmonics, which is quite extraordinary. By moving the guitar in relation to the speakers, I could get different harmonics. That was an extraordinary thing to do live. As long as I kept that guitar—which was briefly—I could do it."

"A lot of the quite violent punky kind of stuff that the Who drew out of the mod movement denied, to a great extent, that there was a strong, peacock, feminine expression running through it."

Guitarists have long taken this kind of thing for granted, so it's hard to convey how revolutionary all of this was in 1964–'65. Townshend's violent mode of performing combined with Marshall's high wattage to produce a variety of sonic effects. He would scrape the slotted surface of the old-style mike stand clutch across the strings, producing a grinding sound. And he'd flick the toggle switch up and down in rapid-fire sequence. "You know," he says, "the toggle switch thing was literally to make the guitar sound like a machine gun—dih, dih, dih—while it was feeding back."

The sounds engendered now-legendary stage moves like the "windmill," in which Townshend would vigorously rotate his left arm full circle, rhythmically strumming chords, and the "birdman," which found Townshend standing stock still onstage, legs splayed wide, arms straight out in crucifixion position, allowing his Rick 12 to feedback wildly and randomly, just grooving in the chaos and cacophony of the sound.

But the belligerent nature of Townshend's approach to guitar performance reached its perhaps inevitable conclusion for the first time in public during a gig at the Railway Hotel in the summer of '64. The room had quite a low ceiling, and when Townshend accidentally sent the neck of his guitar crashing through that ceiling, cracking the neck, he instantaneously decided to make the accident look deliberate by smashing the rest of instrument, quite theatrically, repeatedly slamming the guitar down on the stage and into the speaker cabinets until it had splintered. A new rock ritual had been born.

"He knew the guitar was going to die, because the neck was cracked," Entwistle recalled in a 1994 interview. "Pete used to do this thing where he used to put his guitar up in the air, play a chord, spin round, and get tangled up in the lead and then spin back. So he did that and the head went through the roof. We knew the roof at the Railway Tavern was too low."

Guitar smashing would become a burden for Townshend, both financially and artistically. But at first it was an incredibly powerful statement, a sacrament almost, a ritual sacrifice, acting out the pent-up frustration and rage against the machine felt by sixties youth, and indeed the youth of all time. Controversial as well, it certainly got the Who noticed.

"Four hundred thousand dollars later and we were still in debt," Entwistle said in '94. "But that just happened to be the first night that Kit Lambert, our future manager, saw us."

Kit Lambert and Chris Stamp (brother of actor Terrence Stamp) were filmmakers out to document London's mod scene. They promptly took on management of the Who and landed the group a deal on Brunswick Records, the UK subsidiary of the American Decca imprint.

And so in November 1964 the quartet loaded into London's Pye Studios to record their first single as the Who, A-sided by an early Townshend composition, "I Can't Explain," which has since become a revered part of the rock canon.

In charge of the session was the American producer Shel Talmy, known for his work with artists like Manfred Mann, the Easybeats, Creation, and David Jones (later to achieve fame as David Bowie). But Talmy was perhaps best known for the string of hard-edged hits he'd produced for the Kinks, pioneering a powerhouse guitar sound on tracks like "You Really Got Me" and "All Day and All of the Night." Townshend has admitted to modeling "I Can't Explain"'s slashing chordal guitar riff after the aforementioned Kinks hits. Legend has it that the Kinks' Dave Davies achieved his gnarly guitar tone on those tracks by slashing the speakers on a small El Pedo practice amp with a razor blade and using it to preamp a Vox AC 30. Townshend's amp rig on "I Can't Explain" was considerably beefier, if slightly more prosaic.

"It was probably a Fender Pro with the internal speaker disconnected and the amp routed into a 4 x 12 cabinet," he recalls. "A Fender Pro or Fender Bassman. I might have had a Marshall by then, but I don't remember that I used them in the studio. You know, I never liked them. I liked the cabinets. But Marshall didn't exactly copy the Fender Bassman [circuitry]. They found they couldn't do it because of the way the power rail was constructed, so the treble was overweighed by the bass when you went into heavy distortion."

Also lending punch to the track's guitar chords is second guitarist Jimmy Page, a London session ace at the time, who'd frequently worked with Talmy on records by the Kinks and others. The use of session musicians was pretty common on rock sessions at the time and was standard procedure for Talmy.

"There was a [session] drummer there too," Townshend recollects. "I can't remember his name. Keith Moon threw his drums out the door. But Jimmy Page was a friend of mine."

The two guitarists bonded over a woman, Anya Butler, with whom they'd both been romantically involved. Then they got down to the business at hand. "I said to Jimmy, 'Well, what are you doing here?'" Townshend narrates. "He said, 'I'm here to give some weight to the rhythm guitar. I'm going to do the guitar on the overdubs.' And I said, 'Oh great.' And he said, 'What are you going to play?' 'A Rick 12,' I told him. And he said, 'I'll play a . . .' whatever it was. It was all very friendly. It was all very congenial. But Keith was over telling the drummer, 'Get out of the fucking studio or I'll kill ya! On a Who record, only Keith Moon plays the drums.'"

"I Can't Explain" went a long way toward establishing Townshend's early brief as a songwriter—to give voice to the turbulent, conflicted, and often confused emotions of youth. Classic early singles like "Anyway Anyhow Anywhere" and "My Generation" also caught the mood of youthful rebellion, not only with words that sputtered defiance but with instrumental sections that unleashed all the virulent chaos of the guitar techniques that Townshend had pioneered in the London clubs—toggle-switch machine-gun fire, the menacing crackle and siren wail of guitar feedback. In concert the guitar-noise rave-up at the conclusion of "My Generation" would serve for years as the sonic backdrop to Townshend's guitar smashing and Moon's nightly devastation of his double-bass Premier drum kit. This auto-destructive orgy was like a suicidal acting out of the song's most devastatingly polarized lyric line, "I hope I die before I get old."

"It was very much a vengeful, angry, punky, bitter kind of thing to say," Townshend admits. "But I was only twenty. I really was just twenty when I wrote 'My Generation.' I was writing a bunch of songs for the Who's first album, and 'My Generation' just happened to be one of the bunch that I pulled out. If fact, it wasn't very distinguished in its first version. It was like a blues shuffle. It took Chris Stamp, one of our managers, to realize that it was special."

Townshend's songcraft took a psychological narrative direction very early on as well. "I'm a Boy" deals with a young lad whose parents can't accept his gender and dress him as a girl. "Pictures of Lily" recounts another young man's masturbatory love affair with photographs of a turn-of-the-century pinup girl, given to him by his father. Pretty adventurous stuff for the 1965–'66 pop market. Bob Dylan was starting to open the way toward more ambitious lyrical content. But Townshend had a lighter touch than Dylan. While thoughtful and reflective, his material also always worked as lighthearted, highly infectious pop. And pop never takes itself too seriously. It was only decades later that Pete began to disclose that songs like the above-mentioned grew out of some of his own childhood issues.

As Townshend's lyrical gift blossomed in the mid-sixties, his guitar vocabulary expanded rapidly in tandem. He forged a sonorous style of chordal playing that places triads or other clusters against an open droning string. The 1966 song "Substitute" is a classic example, an inventive D-major deployment of I, IV, and V chords along a droning open D string. The origins of this style have been partially attributed to the close string spacing on the Rickenbacker twelve-string fingerboard, which encourages broad chord voicings and finger stretches that would be daunting on another guitar. Equally important, however, is the eclectic nature of Townshend's listening at the time. He cites everything from Appalachian bluegrass to European baroque as influences on his unique way of chord voicings. He's long maintained that the mordant, stately bridge in "I'm a Boy" was inspired by the English baroque composer Henry Purcell.

"Purcell did this one very short piece which is called *Symphony Upon One Note*," Pete explains. "And it's a very plaintive piece. It's almost like the Samuel Barber piece, *Adagio for Strings*. It's a sad, wistful piece, but it was written in 1600 or something and it tends to be recorded with viols, an instrument that has no vibrato. And through that whole piece runs a single bowed note. I found that a stunning thing to call upon when I was in the process of writing. I analyzed every single chord in the piece and found ways to play them. And I used a group of those chords in 'I'm a Boy.'"

Quotes like that soon distinguished Townshend as one of the most fascinating interview subjects in the then-nascent field of rock journalism. His verbal wit and sophistication set him apart from many of his pop peers, many of whom could barely mumble predictable rejoinders to queries about their favorite color or beverage. And Townshend could be absolutely devastating in critiquing rival groups or tunesmiths, never hesitating even to savage sacred cows like the Beatles or the Stones. The Who's initial run of singles and debut album, *My Generation*, made them the toast of Swinging London. Despite his art school ambitions, Townshend found himself seduced by *la dolce vita*.

"I'd grown up surrounded by a fairly wild bunch of people," he says, "a very cosmopolitan bunch of people, particularly Kit Lambert, Chris Stamp, his brother Terrence, and [fashion model] Jean Shrimpton. Some of the real hot-shot glitterati of the Kings Road sixties scene, on the one hand, and the mods on the other."

Sexual or gender ambivalence has always been a key theme in Townshend's work. In later life, he would admit to having had a few tentative homosexual affairs during the swinging sixties. The precise nature of his close bond with Kit Lambert has often been a topic for speculation.

"A lot of the quite violent punky kind of stuff that the Who drew out of the mod movement denied, to a great extent, that there was a strong, peacock, feminine expression running through it," Pete says. "The idea that boys cared about fashion at all. That just didn't exist before mod."

But while the Who ruled Britannia's airwaves in the mid-sixties, the group's US popularity lagged behind, owing in no small measure to parent record company Decca's utter cluelessness as to how to market recent trends in pop music to a Stateside audience. The American version of their debut album, mawkishly retitled *The Who Sings My Generation*, contained an edited version of what is arguably the albums greatest track, "The Kids Are Alright," and mid-sixties American youth were more likely to be familiar with a cover version of "My Generation" by Seattle quintet Paul Revere & the Raiders than the original. In the absence of US tour support from the label, there was little the group could do about it.

Meanwhile, relations with Shel Talmy had begun to disintegrate. Talmy later put it down to a conflict between himself and Kit Lambert over who could, or should, best mentor young Peter Townshend. There were legal difficulties as well. As an upshot, the Who's second album was produced by Kit Lambert, with Chris Stamp credited as executive producer. Titled *A Quick One* in the UK, the disc was rechristened *Happy Jack* in the States, a nod to the album's transcontinental hit single, added to the US release at the last minute, but also most likely an instance of puritanical American reticence over the potentially erotic (or perhaps alcoholic) overtones of the phrase "a quick one."

Cut loose from Talmy's crisp professionalism, the Who and their manager/producers proceeded to run delightfully—but also highly creatively—amok. As a result, Townshend would, years later, pronounce the disc the most fun of all the Who albums to make.

"Basically that record was a scream from start to finish. Running around the studios banging bass drums, playing pennywhistles, going out in the street and coming back in, with the poor engineer trying to follow us with a microphone. It was a good, good period for the Who. Everybody in the band wrote a couple of songs for the record, including Roger. That album was when we realized that studios were the *greatest places*."

So many harbingers of great things to come are nestled in this often overlooked rock album classic. First off, as Townshend indicates, it was one of the first discs where artists—young people

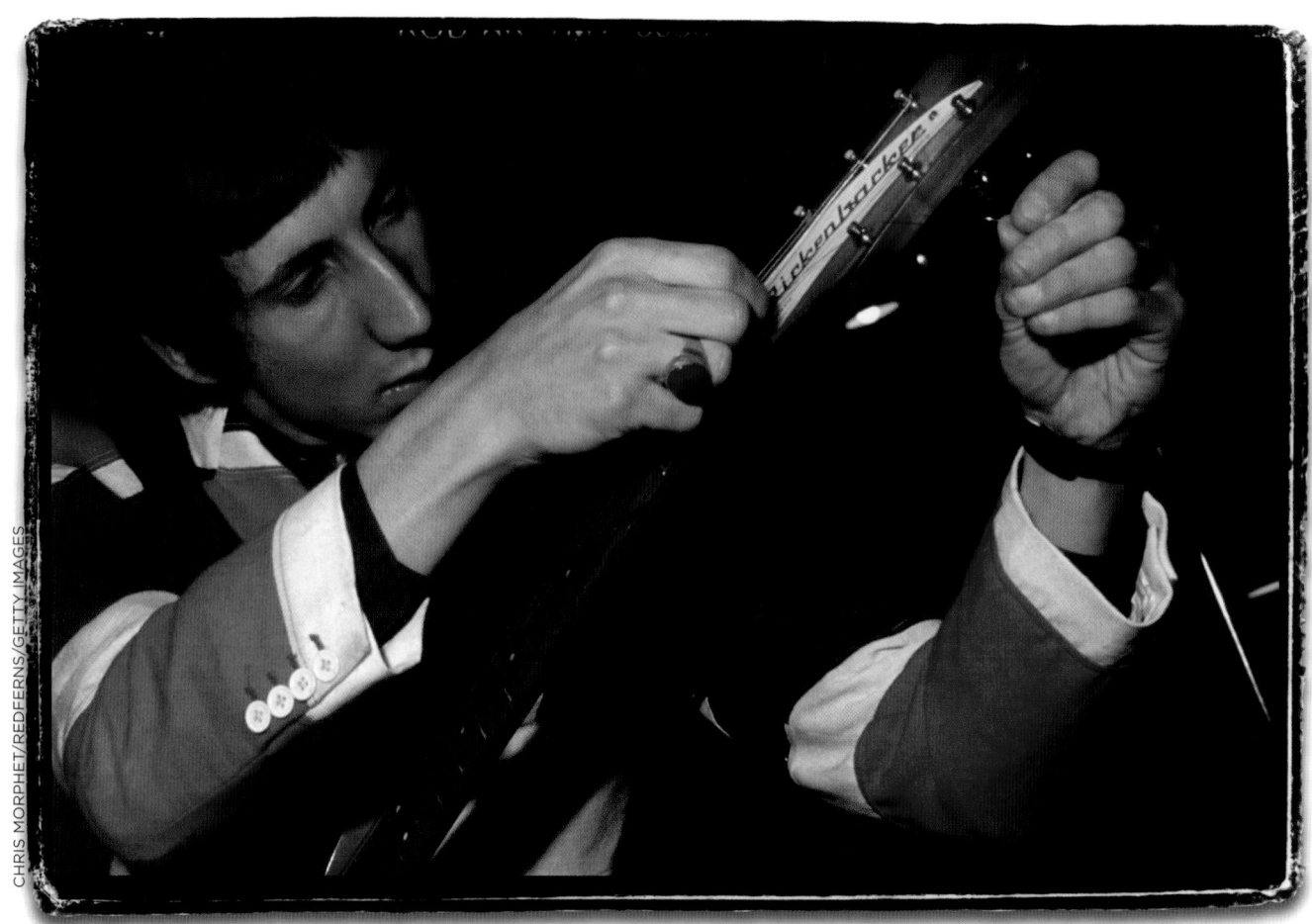

CHRIS MORPHET/REDFERNS/GETTY IMAGES

generally—seized control of the recording studio, the means of production. This would have a momentous impact on the trajectory of rock music in the next two decades. Once the Beatles gave up touring in '66 and released *Sgt. Pepper's Lonely Hearts Club Band* in '67, the recording studio would become the new ground zero where innovations in rock took place. In the late sixties and early seventies, the recording studio became the rock star's atelier, brothel, tavern, and opium den. This produced some of rock's greatest artistic achievements, and also some of its worst excesses. And *A Quick One/Happy Jack* set the stage for all this.

But Townshend was even a few steps ahead of this game. One of Lambert and Stamp's first moves upon assuming management of the Who was to purchase a tape recorder for the band's budding tunesmith, encouraging him to experiment. This was also quite a new development. Before this, singers and musicians were regarded strictly as the "talent," relegated to the "other side" of the control room window. They had no knowledge of the recording studio's sonic resources, nor were they expected to. But having innovated the technology that electric guitarists used onstage, Pete soon became engaged with the technological resources at the disposal of the recording guitarist.

"On our first album, I was the only one allowed into the control room to hear playbacks, because [engineer] Glynn Johns told Shel Talmy I was interested in recording. John, Roger, and Keith didn't get in. Bands didn't go and listen to playbacks."

Townshend would change all that. The tape machine in which his management had invested, would soon grow into one of the world's first artist-owned multi-track recording studios. Superstars like Paul McCartney and Mick Jagger would later follow suit.

"I was certainly the first person I knew of, outside of jazz and after Les Paul, to have a fully equipped, multi-track recording studio at home," Pete asserts. "I think I helped break the ground for the idea that the artist's technical understanding of the medium that they're working in is important. That it's like, for example, a painter knowing that there are certain acids, oils, or pigments in the paints they use that will make the paint lay on in a particular way."

Thirdly, *A Quick One/Happy Jack* is the first Who album where the distinct and individual personalities of all four band members begin to manifest themselves. As such, it is a clear forerunner of the Who's 1973 classic album *Quadrophenia*, in which Townshend would develop and overlap musical themes based on each member of the Who. Brief band member bios on the *Quick One/Happy Jack* back cover delineate four distinctively different personalities, albeit in the light, fan magazine style of the period. Townshend's bio points out his interest in [electronic music composer] "Stockhausen, brandy and painting." A brief essay by Nick Jones of leading UK music paper the *Melody Maker* hails the Who as "The World's Most Sensational Group." Furthermore, *A Quick One/Happy Jack* is the only Who album to which all four band members made songwriting contributions. This is the disc where Entwistle's dark, macabre sensibility first asserts itself with the grotesquely comedic "Boris the Spider" and an all-too-prophetic tale of alcoholic insanity, "Whiskey Man." Keith Moon's loopiness manifests itself in the carnivalesque "Cobwebs and Strange," but also the pensive, harpsichord-driven "I Need You." Daltrey, the helpless dancer pop idol, manages just one composition, the Buddy Holly influenced "See My Way."

Not surprisingly, Townshend takes on the lion's share of the writing, with five compositions to his credit, all awash in plangent Townshend guitar chords, open strings ringing out like clarion bells. The album's closing selection is perhaps the most significant of these. It is none other than Townshend's first recorded "mini-opera," "A Quick One While He's Away." The roots of *Tommy* and *Quadrophenia* lie right here. "Mini" was a major buzzword of the mid-sixties. Miniskirts. Minicars. Mini everything. So why not a mini-opera? It was entirely within Townshend's pop art brief, and beyond even that, an irreverent clash of pop culture and high culture.

"A Quick One" is really just a compendium of pop song fragments, tuneful bits of verses and choruses, each of which could easily have formed the basis of yet another Pete-penned hit single. Yet here these snippets of brilliance are crammed together, one after the other, in a rapid-fire sequence reflecting the amphetamine-fueled pace of mid-sixties pop culture. The whole thing's over in some ten minute's time. And yet there's an overarching narrative, one of romantic infidelity, then betrayal, then forgiveness.

It was all very lightweight and disposable in the context of the times. Yet Townshend would later speak of how the plot was rooted in his own conflicted feelings about his mother's purported infidelities during his childhood, while his father was out on the road. Betrayal and belonging are the keys to Townshend's lifetime opus.

Somewhere within the pivotal years of 1966–'67, Townshend traded frail Rickenbackers for the more hardy, workingman's heft of Fender Telecasters and Stratocasters. These guitars took longer to smash to bits than Ricks. What's more, their bolt-on necks made them easier to reassemble after a cataclysmic performance, enabling the still-struggling quartet to move on to the next gig.

It was right at this critical nexus in Townshend's development that a bold new guitarist arrived in London, a guy who'd just recently styled himself Jimi Hendrix. Townshend was already a rock star when Hendrix got off the plane in London in 1966. And Hendrix had clearly studied Townshend's work, basing much of his approach to amped-up guitar playing and stagecraft on Townshend's pioneering strides in this field. Hendrix would become both a colleague and competitor for Townshend. Their destinies seemed inextricably linked.

"The first time I saw Hendrix was in a club behind Piccadilly," Pete recalls. "I can't remember the name. I think it was called 21. It was the site of an Arab nightclub. Then I saw him at Blazes, which was another club in Soho. And on that occasion, everybody was there. Mick Jagger was there, and Paul McCartney. I was with Eric Clapton . . . again! We used to go around back then, kind of hanging on to one another like children, wondering what [Hendrix] was going to come up with next."

Townshend became a supporter. The Jimi Hendrix Experience was signed to the Who's label, Track Records, in the UK. The two men met for the first time when Hendrix stopped by a Who recording session at London's IBC studio.

"We were in the studio," Townshend recalls, "and Chas Chandler brought Jimi in to meet me. Jimi was covered from head to foot in dust. He looked like he had just come out of what we call a skip in England, which is where you put builders' rubbish. He was very, very scruffy and his military jacket had obviously seen better days. His skin was bad. He was very pale and he was immediately nervous and shy and couldn't speak. I just put out my hand and said, 'I've heard a lot about you.' And Chas said, 'Jimi wants to know what kind of rig to buy.' I said, 'Well, you catch me at a strange time, 'cause I'm just shifting from Marshall amps to Sound City. And Chas said, 'Well, that's what we'll do too.'

"And a couple of days later he appeared with them at the Saville Theater, which was owned by Brian Epstein, the Beatles' manager. I believe the Who and the Jimi Hendrix Experience were the first rock concert to play there. Jimi opened for us, and he had the exact same rig as me, with his amplifiers in the same kind of arrangement. And I actually felt like I'd given too much away. It was like giving your enemy your weapons. Because, to me, these were weapons. It was always me who went in to people like Jim Marshall and Dave Reeves—who started Sound City, which became Hiwatt amps—asking them to make bigger, better, and cleaner-distorting big amplifiers. I was always pushing, pushing, pushing. And the answer at first was always, 'No. No, it's not possible to have four big valves on the power rail.' And I'd say, 'Give it a try. Find some fucking way of doing it. We need more power!' And eventually we started getting into multiple amplifiers and stuff like that. So I handed all that to Jimi. I've never really recovered from that.

"I foolishly got involved in comparing myself to him. 'Cause it seemed to me at the time that I was the only competition he had. Possibly me and Eric [Clapton]. There was a kind of conceit—a vanity—in that. I could only see me and Jimi; there wasn't anybody else. I shared with Eric that, fucking hell, when I first saw Jimi play I wanted to go and kill myself. And he said, 'Well, I did too. But I didn't think that affected you. I mean, he wasn't in your arena.' But he *was*. He was someone who was working with showmanship, which is one of the directions where rock and roll was inevitably going to go. Rock and roll was inevitably going to get bigger, and Jimi was one of the people who showed there was something you could do in the curve of an arm or the movement of the tongue, the stance of the body or a hairdo, where you combined showmanship and stagecraft. It was the beginnings of a great genius that unfortunately had nowhere to go. But at that time, I decided to concentrate on not being a guitar hero. I did get away with it. I'd already established a whole modus operandi and stylistic stage stuff. I never felt very comfortably with it, though."

"I could play anything and John would follow me. Absolutely anything—even atonal stuff—and he could follow me."

The Who finally broke in America in 1967. "Happy Jack" garnered fairly substantial airplay on US radio and the group finally managed to tour the States. By far the most significant date in this initial year of US touring was the closing night of the Monterey International Pop Festival on June 18. A milestone event in rock history, Monterey was very much the coming-out party for a hippie scene that enthralled youth and rock culture in '67. Attracting one of the largest rock concert audiences at that time, the festival showcased the diversity of musical styles that fell within the love embrace of what would soon be known as the hippie counterculture—from the gentle folk stylings of Simon and Garfunkel to the NYC grit of the Blues Project to the international sounds of Ravi Shankar and Hugh Masekela. Monterey played a key role in launching the careers of three superstars who would have a tremendous impact on the sound and style of rock in the years to come: Janis Joplin, Jimi Hendrix, and the Who.

Once again Townshend was saddled with his guitar-abusing doppelganger, a man he loved and admired yet also feared. Worse yet, the Who and the Jimi Hendrix Experience were slated to go onstage back to back, performing their sets one right after the other. The only thing to be decided at the actual gig was who would go on first, and who would follow. As both groups had a similar guitar approach, and both were planning to destroy a guitar at the conclusion of their set, whoever got the second slot ran the risk of coming off as a tremendous anticlimax. And so a scene between Townshend and Hendrix took place backstage in the presence of the Rolling Stones' Brian Jones, who was there to announce some of the acts, as well as Cass Elliot and John Phillips of pop vocal group the Mamas and Papas. Phillips was co-producing the festival as well.

"Jimi was on acid, and he stood on a chair," Townshend recounts. "I was trying to get him to talk to me about the fact that I didn't want the Who to follow him onto the stage. I was saying, 'For fuck's sake, Jimi, listen to me. I don't want to go on after you. It's bad enough that you're here. It's bad enough that you're gonna fuck up my life. I'm not gonna have you steal my act. That's the only thing we've got. You're a great genius. They'll appreciate that. But what do I do? I wear a Union Jack jacket and smash my guitar. Give me a break. Let us go on first.' And he was kind of . . . I thought . . . teasing me. You know, playing the guitar and ignoring me. But Brian Jones later told me that Jimi was just fucking *completely* whacked on acid. So John Phillips flipped a coin and it came down in my favor and I said, 'Right! We go on first.' And that has become apocryphally told as a story where I was arguing with Jimi. I was shouting at Jimi, yes, because he was ignoring me. But I wasn't angry with him. I loved him very, very much."

Despite having to go on with a rented backline (American-made Vox Super Beatle amps), the Who left a profound impression on the nascent flower children and incipient hipsters assembled that day. And when, at the conclusion of "My Generation," Townshend slipped his sunburst Fender Stratocaster from his shoulder, gripping the neck in both hands and slamming the body down on the stage, the repeated, squealing blows sent shock waves through the rock universe that are still reverberating today. The Jimi Hendrix Experience had to work very hard indeed to match the Who's performance, but also acquitted themselves quite brilliantly. Both groups would go on to become rock legends.

And indeed comparisons between the Who and the Jimi Hendrix Experience—or between Townshend and Hendrix, for that matter—are of limited usefulness. Despite a similar approach toward guitar pyrotechnics, the two groups were markedly different. Hendrix's work was much more rooted in blues-based, single-note riffing. The Who offered quite a different style of musical experience, one rooted in Townshend's unique and inspired chordal and harmonic sensibility. They were unique in combining the hard-hitting approach of power trios like Cream and the Jimi Hendrix Experience with a Beatle-esque gift for memorable vocal melodies and well-executed three-part harmonies. No one else in the late sixties offered quite that combination.

Plus the Who were somewhat reluctant to embrace the flower power hippie aesthetic of the late sixties. While they'd taken to sporting frilly, ruff shirt fronts, parti-colored shawls, floral-print blazers, and other psychedelic peacock plumage straight off the King's Road, they remained at heart a bunch of boozy, belligerent Shepherd's Bush mods. In a way, this was their red badge of courage. In the late sixties the Who appealed tremendously to the sort of rock fan who tended to look askance at hippiedom's more egregious excesses of self-important posturing. The Who appealed tremendously to the proto-punk rock fan, one might say.

And the Who's apparent indifference to the codes of hippiedom seem to be confirmed by the band's next album, which appeared in early '68, *The Who Sell Out*. "Sell out" was a term of ultimate vilification in the resolutely anti-commercial hippie context. So for a group to label itself a "sell out," albeit ironically and with tongue firmly planted in cheek, was a provocative move indeed. But Townshend wasn't quite ready to trade his Warholian pop art fixation for Bay Area sanctimony.

The Who Sell Out is a concept album inspired, in part, by the recent demise of pirate radio in England—the maverick, and illegal, offshore broadcasters who had been beaming the latest cutting-edge rock sounds into London, in defiance of BBC regulations. The album takes the form of a broadcast by pirate station Radio London, with advertising jingles and station IDs interspersed among the songs. In the wake of the Beatles' *Sgt. Pepper's Lonely Hearts Club Band* and its paradigm shifting impact, rock music had gone mad for concept albums. And conceptualizing is what ad people do all day long.

Once again adumbrating *Quadrophenia*, the cover art and song sequence of *The Who Sell Out* is based around a four-part structure rooted in the image and likeness of the four band members. Splitting the front and back covers in half are four mock ads, each featuring one member in a product endorsement. These pictorial cover ads are supported by musical spots, composed by Townshend or Entwistle, for the products seen on the cover. The musical pieces range from throwaway jingles, like Entwistle's marching-band spot for Heinz Baked Beans, to Townshend's beautifully realized composition "Odorono," a skillfully developed narrative with what seems a deliberately crass punch line: an aspiring singer misses her chance at success and romance because "her deodorant had let her down; she should have used Odorono."

Much like *Sgt. Pepper's*, the overarching concept behind *The Who Sell Out* doesn't hold for the entire disc. The songs tend to veer away from, and upstage, the conceptual frame. And also like the Beatles' masterwork, the Who's third album stands the test of time because of its abundance of great songs. Townshend's trademark deployment of inventive chord progressions based around open strings hits a new height on the wistfully ironic "Tattoo," which uses an open high E string as the common note in a B-flat verse progression. The acoustic guitar ballad "Sunrise" contains some of the jazziest chordal work Townshend has ever committed to disc.

"There's kind of a [session guitar ace] Mickey Baker influence there, really," Pete notes. "He's another guy I used to like. While he occasionally used to play a solo, what was lovely about him was his chord work. Also his early tutorial books [the Complete Course in Jazz Guitar series] were wonderful. They showed you how to translate the normal kinds of triads and groups of chords from the popular songs of the day into chords that had more interest and more harmonic tension."

Nor does *The Who Sell Out* disappoint when it comes to more aggressive guitar modes. Penned by Townshend's friend and occasional musical collaborator John "Speedy" Keene, "Armenia City in the Sky" tips the hat to Hendrixian psychedelia and is replete with tape-manipulated "backward" guitar leads and wild stereo panning. And the album's hit single, "I Can See for Miles," is a glorious power chord workout in E that gave listeners a taste of the brute force the Who would marshal nightly in concert. Townshend's solo for the song is a masterpiece of minimalism, just an E note rapidly double-picked for the space of some eight bars. This kind of nimble plectrum work on both electric and acoustic guitars would become another Townshend stylistic hallmark.

Finally, like *A Quick One/Happy Jack*, *The Who Sell Out* concludes with another Townshend mini-opera, "Rael (1 and 2)." Once again, the theme is betrayal, only military rather then sexual this time. Packed with great vocal melodies and evocative instrumental interludes, "Rael" finds Townshend consolidating his command of a unique musical form that he'd single-handedly created. The track is one of several on *The Who Sell Out* that feature Townshend on organ as well as guitar. From here on in, his keyboard work would become an integral part of the Who's music.

Townshend went through quite a bit of personal growth in 1968.

He emerged as a hit producer with "Fire" by the Crazy World of Arthur Brown and recordings by Thunderclap Newman. And on May 20, 1968, Pete married Karen Astley, a dress designer he'd met at art school some years earlier and daughter of British TV and film composer Ted Astley, who was then enjoying great success with chic theme music for *The Saint* and other British espionage series.

Townshend also embarked on the spiritual path at this time in his life, becoming a disciple of the Indian master Meher Baba. Pete's spiritual quest was in part the outcome of a bad STP trip he'd suffered on the return flight from the Monterey Pop Festival. Not long after, he was introduced to

Baba's work by Mike McInnerney, a mutual friend of his and Karen's. Spiritual themes would become a key element in much of Townshend's works in the years to come.

But if '68 was a time of personal growth, it was also a time of disillusionment for Townshend. In interviews he hinted that the Who might be nearing the end of their career. The band certainly seemed a bit lost at the time. Quirky singles like "Dogs" and "Call Me Lightning" failed to connect with the pyschedelicized pop market of '68. Against the Who's wishes, Decca released *Magic Bus: The Who on Tour*, a lackluster compendium of previously released material and outtakes clustered around the titular single.

It might well have been the end of the Who, had Townshend not conceived a grand plan to write a full-blown rock opera. "We were feeling quite out of touch and out of place," he explains, "thinking, 'God, we're not selling singles anymore and neither do we fit into this new psychedelic era. We're not an experimental band like the Pink Floyd. We're not a guitar-based blues band like Cream. We don't have the kind of extreme genius of Hendrix. What do we do? And I started to look at *composition* as a big issue."

From this impulse came *Tommy*, one of Townshend and the Who's best known and loved works. It was born at a time when the idea of the double album was really coming into its own in rock, owing to masterworks like Frank Zappa's *Freak Out*, Bob Dylan's *Blonde on Blonde*, and the Beatles' "White Album." But rather than simply fill up two discs with great songs as his predecessors had done, Townshend decided to use the large double-album canvas to create a long-form musical narrative, a grand extension of what he'd achieved with his character-driven pop singles and mini-operas in the past five or so years. He set himself the near impossible task of writing a new kind of opera free of classical music pretentiousness and which would function from start to finish as great, slamming rock and roll. Amazingly he succeeded.

Tommy possesses essentially three musical elements. There are songs that move the plot forward, but then there are also songs that stand out on their own and can function apart from the work. Killer hit singles like "Pinball Wizard" and "I'm Free" are the pop equivalent of operatic arias—unforgettable tunes that are concert favorites apart from their original dramatic context. Thirdly, *Tommy* contains some of Townshend's best instrumental compositions, a majestic "Overture" that ingeniously links the album's key melodic themes before resolving into a bluesy flat-picked acoustic guitar improvisation, and an "Underture" derived largely from the "storm sequence" in "Rael."

Townshend has never been averse to recycling musical ideas. The lyrical theme "It's a boy, Mrs. Walker," originally appeared in an earlier song called "Glow Girl," only there the line was "It's a girl, Mrs. Walker." Modularity is one great lesson to be derived from Townshend's compositional process. Great songs are made up of parts that can be readily interchangeable.

"I was very, very meticulous about making sure that the composition and the harmonics were very structured and clean," says Townshend of *Tommy*. "It was the first cohesive piece in which I used a lot of piano for the writing. It was the first time that I'd really started to be confident that I could play the piano. I probably would have been voicing guitar to piano chords for the first time in a big way. 'Pinball Wizard' was written on the guitar, but 'Amazing Journey' was written on the piano. 'I'm Free' was written on a Lowery organ and the guitar voiced afterwards. 'Sally Simpson' was written on guitar, but a lot of the stuff was actually written on keyboards, and the guitars came afterwards. So I think a lot of care went into the way I was trying to use a guitar to reinforce what I had on piano."

Tommy usually isn't thought of as much of a guitar album, meaning that it doesn't have a lot of distorted tones and bluesy leads. But it does contain a good amount of exemplary acoustic guitar work and inventive deployment of both acoustic and electric twelve-string guitars: a Harmony Sovereign H1270 acoustic 12 and Fender Electric XII.

"I was working with the twelve-string guitar as a free-composition instrument on *Tommy*," Pete explains. "So on stuff like 'Sparks' and 'Underture' I was using a big Harmony twelve-string, a copy of the old Stella type that Leadbelly played. I'd been tuning it down and getting into a kind of pick-driven ragtime where you play a drone on a D and chords on top. I used that to some extent on 'Welcome' as well, which is quite an interesting song because it was entirely written in free time. It's in 6/8, but there's no strict rhythm, just a gentle, homey kind of style. I got the feeling for that just by sitting and playing the guitar. In that atmosphere, the guitar is very comfortable, as a domestic kind of instrument."

Inviting all walks of humanity to "come to this house" and "be one of us," "Welcome" adumbrates the theme of *Lifehouse*, a work that would occupy Townshend for a good portion of his life. *Tommy* itself is a work that sums up many themes and currents in Pete's life and work. The plot is set in motion by the familiar Townshend motif of infidelity and betrayal. The title character is traumatized after witnessing his father surprising his mother with her lover and then killing the lover. As a result of his trauma, Tommy becomes deaf, dumb, and blind, an extreme manifestation of the conflicted, inarticulate, stuttering mod personae of the early Who singles. He becomes a spiritual guru like Meher Baba, but also a sort of rock star like Pete Townshend. Tommy's abandonment by his followers in the final act reflects Townshend's own ambivalence about his rock star status and his deep-seated anxiety over having somehow let down his fans.

While harboring personal doubts and anxieties, Townshend was concocting what would be one of the major rock events of 1969, and indeed all time. *Tommy* was a huge and instant success. It rescued the Who from debt and it satisfied the need of rock fans at the time for big, epic works, and their expectation that rock could, and should, grow into something extremely important. The Who performed *Tommy* to jubilant audiences on both sides of the Atlantic. In concert *Tommy* took on a life of its own, the hard-pounding ferocity of the Who's performance taking the place of the album's carefully arranged layers of French horns, keyboards, and acoustic guitars.

Perhaps the most influential public performance of *Tommy* was at the Woodstock Festival at Bethel, New York, on August 17, 1969. Ironically Townshend has said that this was his least favorite Who performance of all time. Poor organization made the show a logistical nightmare. There was difficulty over getting paid and Townshend had a soon-to-be-famous altercation with radical leader Abbie Hoffman, famously braining Hoffman with his guitar.

Speaking of which, by this point Townshend had switched to Gibson SG Specials as his main stage guitars. The instrument became as much a part of his late-sixties/early-seventies image as the white boiler suits and heavy workingman's boots he'd taken to wearing onstage. An SG is also the guitar heard on the Who's follow-up to *Tommy*, the iconic concert album, *Live at Leeds*. The disc has been hailed as the greatest live rock album of all time. Entwistle said it was his favorite Who album because it was the one that best captured the power and the glory of the Who in their prime.

"We had *Tommy* out there and we were on the road doing a lot of work," says Townshend.

"And we became a really extraordinary machine. We were a fucking great band. The Who were briefly called the Greatest Rock-and-Roll Band in the World. And we were. There was no question about it. I used to wake up on the stage every night and think, 'Oh my God, I'm riding this horse again!' It used to be so extraordinary. We just got very, very good at what we did."

Live at Leeds referenced the Who's rock-and-roll roots with explosive covers of Eddie Cochran's "Summertime Blues" and Johnny Kidd and the Pirates' "Shakin' All Over." It introduced younger fans to earlier Who classics like "Substitute." And for a guitarist who has always denigrated his ability to play single-note bluesy leads in the Page/Hendrix mode, Townshend does an admirable job of just that on *Live at Leeds*.

For the most part, however, Townshend found his own unique way to satisfy early-seventies rock audiences' hunger for instrumental improvisation. He and Entwistle developed an ability to come up with more thematic improvisations right on the spot, weaving melodies together, segueing between different melodic and chordal segments, some totally spontaneous and others drawn from the Who's broad repertoire of instrumental themes.

"I could play anything and John would follow me," Townshend marvels. "Absolutely anything—even atonal stuff—and he could follow me."

Live at Leeds was a brilliant follow-up to *Tommy* because it presented a completely different side of the Who. Its raw rock-and-roll energy provided the perfect counterbalance to *Tommy*'s loftier artistic ambitions. But still, having produced one conceptual double-album masterwork, the onus fell on Townshend to produce another big studio opus that would match or exceed the scope and success of *Tommy*.

Pete had just the thing in mind. It was to be called *Lifehouse*, a science-fiction work that would be based around an extended live Who concert experience, which in turn would provide the basis for an album and film. Pete began working on the project in 1970, soliciting interest from Universal Pictures for the film component, putting together a budget, and initiating a dialogue with London's Old Vic Theater about serving as the site for the concert component.

Townshend was inspired by a few disparate sources, including the convergence of ancient mystical traditions and modern quantum physics in explaining the phenomenon of sound. He was also fascinated by advances in synthesizer technology at the time, which were revolutionizing the way sound could be generated, shaped, and manipulated. He wanted to apply all of this to the powerful emotional and spiritual link he'd felt with his bandmates and audience at recent Who concerts. Still a Meher Baba devotee, Townshend was particularly enthralled with the writings of Sufi mystic Hazrat Inayat Khan (1882–1927).

"He wrote a work called the *Mysticism of Sound and Music*, and I drafted in a lot of those ideas," Pete explains. "How the spiritual effect of music, the energizing effect can be explained with the modern laws of physics: the way we are affected by vibrations and how the world is made up of vibrations. A lot of primitive early quantum theory was woven in, in a bit of a schoolboyish way, by him, which I drafted in. You know I had scientists working with me who would say, 'Yeah, that's really interesting. That's Schrodinger's Cat Free Lunch Theory stuff.' I was finding a new way to examine ideas about what music was doing, very much inhabiting the world I love the most, which is trying to understand why music is so poetic, why music is so spiritual. Why, at its most violent, its most futile, frail, and nihilistic, rock music was capable of spiritual uplift."

Townshend was also consulting with leaders in electronic music, including composer Karlheinz Stockhausen and Roger Powell, the latter soon to become keyboardist for Todd Rundgren's Utopia but at the time designing synth gear for the pioneering ARP company. Just as he'd done with Jim Marshall and Dave Reeves of Sound City, Townshend was once again working with designers of musical equipment to foster a new paradigm in sound creation.

"I was involved with ARP in the development of the first guitar synthesizer, which was bizarrely called the Avatar [which was also a spiritual title accorded to Meher Baba]," Pete recalls. "They made me an early interface. So when my ARP 2500 studio synthesizer landed in the middle of the recording studio, it came with a guitar interface. It was only a single-string interface, but I was playing with note-tracking and envelope-following synthesizer devices in 1971. And I could work with these things. I was also trying to create crude [computer] programs at the time, looking at ways in which music could be used to very literally and accurately convey statistical information about a human being. So I was right in there, but at the same time I was bangin' away at rock and roll and drinking a lot of brandy."

The live performance component of *Lifehouse* was to involve a series of concerts at the Old Vic, each performed before the same select group of audience members. The goal was to achieve a deeper level of mystical connectedness than what Townshend had experienced with different audiences night after night. New songs would eventually be generated by processing statistical data about audience members through computerized synthesizer gear.

As if that weren't ambitious enough, particularly for the early seventies, the whole thing was to be set in a narrative-framing device, an eerily prophetic, dystopian future scenario in which human beings live in physical isolation from one another, only connected electronically by what we might now call a virtual reality network. (With this, Townshend anticipated the development of the Internet by a good twenty years.) Thus deprived of authentic human experience and connection, the population would be saved by an aging rock and roller/guru figure who remembered and could reignite the redemptive power of rock and roll.

Not surprisingly, the project got too big to be practical. Feeling isolated and abandoned, Townshend suffered a nervous breakdown. After doing so much advance work on *Lifehouse* and lining up so many consultants, advisors, and potential partners, he says, "I then realized that the managers of the Who were using hard drugs." Kit Lambert had been a close confidant to Townshend during the making of *Tommy*, but had now become estranged. Nor did Townshend feel much support from his bandmates for the project.

"The more I tried to explain it," says Townshend, "the more I realized that I was Einstein to their cavemen. They just didn't get it. Nobody was getting it. And in the end I literally had a nervous breakdown."

But the work Townshend had done had generated more than enough material for a new Who album, *Who's Next*, one that would rank among the band's greatest. The disc went quickly to tape at London's Olympic Studios, with longtime Who collaborator Glyn Johns at the console as associate producer.

"By that time," says Townshend, "we were in the studio, we had great music, and we were playing great because we'd actually recorded the album *fifteen times* already! Glyn Johns had a very easy job. He made the record in two weeks. It sounded very fresh somehow. And then he said, 'I think this should be a single album.' I said, 'But we've got twenty-six tracks!' And he said, 'Well, I think it will be better as a single album.' And that's what we got. And it *was* better as a single album—for commercial reasons."

Filled with some of Townshend's greatest material, *Who's Next* can certainly stand on its own merits. But songs like "Getting in Tune" and "The Song Is Over" take on extra poignancy when one knows the *Lifehouse* backstory. Ditto for the opening track, "Baba O'Riley." The title alludes to Meher Baba and minimalist composer Terry Riley. The song's distinctive synthesizer track was created by programming biographical data about Baba into a synth.

But even without the *Lifehouse* context, *Who's Next* resonated deeply with the disaffected mood of youth culture in the post-hippie, post-Woodstock, post-Beatles, post-Altamont zeitgeist of the early seventies. The song—or the dream, as John Lennon put it at around the same time—was indeed over. The closing song on *Who's Next*, "Won't Get Fooled Again," dramatically captured the spirit of a time when flower-child utopianism was giving way to militant radical politics. But the song also stands as one of the great rebel yells of all time.

Lifehouse would continue to haunt Townshend and he would revisit it numerous times in later works. The first of these was his first commercially released solo album, *Who Came First*, in 1972. "On that, I collected together a couple of outtakes, demos from *Lifehouse*," he explains. "It had a kind of *Lifehouse* devotional, spiritual feel about it. I dedicated it to Meher Baba."

The introspective, spiritual, and often acoustic-guitar driven vibe of *Who Came First* doesn't prevent Townshend from rocking out when the occasion demands. Two classic tunes that Townshend's liner notes specifically identify as having come from *Lifehouse* are the relatively up-tempo "Pure and Easy" and "Nothing Is Everything (Let's See Action.)" *Who Came First* afforded the general public its first opportunity to hear Pete Townshend demos, which in time would attract a cult following in their own right. With the exception of guest appearances by fellow Baba devotees and friends, including Faces bassist Ronnie Lane, Townshend played all the instruments, did all the vocals, engineered, and produced the disc at his own studio, Eel Pie Sound. While Daltrey, Moon, and Entwistle were all brilliant interpreters of Townshend's material, each one making a profoundly energetic contribution to the music, solo discs like *Who Came First* clearly demonstrate the great extent to which the heart and soul of the Who's identity had always originated with Townshend.

And while *Lifehouse* was never completed, Townshend would soon create the double-album conceptual masterpiece that rock fans had been hoping for ever since *Tommy*. Released in 1973, *Quadrophenia* contains some of Townshend's most inventive compositions and some of his most compelling guitar playing. Following hard upon the mystical, sci-fi speculations of *Lifehouse*, *Quadrophenia* grounded Townshend in a more realistic setting, and one with which he was intimately familiar: the London mod scene of the mid-sixties.

Quadrophenia charts the emotional and spiritual trauma of a quintessential mod kid, Jimmy, as he faces the harsh realities of adulthood and the realization that the things of youth, including mod

camaraderie and even rock and roll itself, cannot save or protect him from these realities. Through a powerful sequence of angry and plaintive rock songs, Townshend depicts Jimmy's psyche as an amalgam of the personalities of all four Who members. This inspired structural device brings out the best in Townshend. He composed evocative musical themes for each of Jimmy's quadrophenic alter egos, brilliantly interleaving, juxtaposing, and overlapping them throughout the album's two original vinyl discs in ways that make perfect dramatic and musical sense, even managing to weave in quotations from early Who songs. *Quadrophenia* is Townshend's baby from start to finish. There were no songs by Entwistle or any other Who members this time, although all contribute some of the best playing and singing of their careers.

Unlike *Tommy*, *Quadrophenia* makes no attempt to reference operatic form or any genre other than great, slamming rock. And while Tommy isn't much of a powerhouse guitar album, *Quadrophenia* is awash in majestic power chords and incisive leads. In recording the album, Townshend relied on a 1959 Gretsch 6120 that had been given to him by Joe Walsh, a guitar that also played a prominent role on *Who's Next*. In concert during this period, however, Townshend would perform on a series of Les Pauls.

But for all of its artistic triumphs, *Quadrophenia* was born of a sense of failure on Townshend's part. "I actually felt as if I'd lost my original brief as a writer," he says, "through being introduced to stadium rock and being one of the main protagonists of stadium rock. I'd lost the feeling of writing for the Who, writing for Roger's voice within the Who, giving him words to sing to express the feelings of inarticulateness, dislocation, and frustration of the audience that we grew up with. I felt I'd lost that. I'd look out into an audience of 86,000 people and think, 'What do they want me to do? I don't know. There's just too many of them.'

"And so I went back to examine what had happened, and to address the fact that, in a sense, the Who—each member a facet obviously voted onto the stage by an individual, Jimmy in the story—had, like everything else in his life, abandoned him. I tried to work that out. And I think I did reestablish that connection, but then realized that there was no way I could speak to these people anymore. Because I was too rich, too successful, and I'd spent too much time in America and not enough time in the Goldhawk Road Social Club in Shepherds Bush. So it was over for me. It was a bitter pill, to use a cliché, because I sensed through the story of Jimmy that through abandonment we are left with a spiritual question. A spiritual opportunity. And that was very necessary. But I somehow wondered where I fitted in to all that, and where the Who fitted in."

Townshend's anxieties at the time are eloquently summed up in one of *Quadrophenia*'s most poignant, and prophetic, tracks, "The Punk and the Godfather." In the song, Pete envisions every artist's worst nightmare, a direct confrontation with a fan who feels let down, disappointed, betrayed even, by the artist's work, and being intimately familiar with that work, can point out exactly how and where it fails. "You could only repeat what we told you," the estranged fan accuses, to which the artist can only respond with an oddly neutered, mechanical, vocoder-processed repetition of one of his old hits, "My Generation."

In an almost heartbreakingly confessional bridge, Townshend—the voice of a world-weary and hard-won wisdom he half wishes he did not posses—tells the kid, "And yet I've lived your future out, by pounding stages like a clown." Just three short years later, the punk rock movement would rise to challenge the bloated, decadent, and unsatisfying spectacle of stadium rock. Townshend was not indicted among the villains, but rather cited as a hero and inspiration.

Part of his tragedy is that he's never been able to realize this fully.

The difficulties of the tour that followed in the wake of *Quadrophenia*'s release certainly didn't help Townshend's depressed mood at the time. The shows were fraught with technical problems and hobbled by Daltrey's well-meaning but ill-advised attempts to explain and elucidate the *Quadrophenia* plotline in wordy spoken addresses to the audience between songs. In concert, *Quadrophenia* never sprouted the wings that *Tommy* had.

"When [*Quadrophenia*] failed to be a really good piece for the Who on the stage, that was an extra kind of slap on the wrist," Townshend admits. "'Cause I suddenly felt, 'Well, this revisiting mod looks like nostalgia, or going over the same ground again.' It was a good album for the Who. And it was an important album. But you know, the people who love it most in their lives—as a rock piece in the traditional sense that, if I look back on it, I can't imagine not having it in my life—the place where it worked the best was in America, strangely enough, where it wasn't a big success, but the people who latched on to it have found it to be very, very important. Because of the feeling of alienation or abandonment that comes when you're about sixteen, seventeen, or eighteen and somehow all the rugs are pulled out from under you. And you throw yourself down. Then you come up with your spiritual question, you know, 'Love Reign O'er Me,' sitting on the rock, 'What happens now?' I didn't provide any answers, of course."

In *Quadrophenia*'s wake, Townshend fell into a protracted period of depression and heavy drinking—this in a band of notorious soaks. In concert, Entwistle would have two plastic bottles attached to his mike stand, each with a straw protruding from its top. One was filled with water, the other cognac. And Keith Moon would start his day with "mild" libations like the British aperitif Pimm's Cup and work his way up to the harder stuff as the day progressed.

"Roger was the only normal soul, who lived a life in the middle of a bunch of very complicated, substance-dependent individuals," says Townshend.

The strain was clearly evident in the band's next album release, 1975's *The Who by Numbers*. While by no means a bad album, it is merely a decent album, which at the time was perceived as a letdown from a great band like the Who. Critics said it sounded like a suicide note. "Slip Kid" and the minor radio hit "Squeezebox" are among the stronger tracks, but the keynote song might well be Townshend's composition "However Much I Booze."

"I wrote these incredibly personal, difficult songs and Roger sang them so incredibly well," says Townshend, "even though he wasn't in the same place as me at all. I was very disaffected, becoming very alcoholic and very perturbed about Keith using extraordinary drug cocktails, which I knew would get him in the end, and maybe having marriage problems. I don't know; but I was very unhappy in the Who at that time, and that came out in the work. What was extraordinary was the way Roger took that unhappiness into his own work and sang it."

Adding to Townshend's woes in the mid- to late seventies were the problems he was beginning to experience with hearing loss and tinnitus. All his years on the cutting edge of high-wattage amp innovations, synthesizer technology, and recording studio experimentation had begun to take their toll. Townshend was one of the first high-profile casualties of the loud revolution.

"In actual fact, where my hearing was suffering the most was in the recording studio," he says. "I'm pretty sure that it's earphones that created the residual damage I have. And where my vanity was suffering most was in the recording studio, because I couldn't come up with the kind of songs the Who needed."

Townshend was able to collaborate with Ronnie Lane once again on an album titled *Rough Mix*, released in 1977. But that record, and indeed the work of many old-guard rockers, was upstaged in '77 by the punk rock explosion that brought bands like the Sex Pistols, the Clash, the Ramones, the Buzzcocks, and others to the fore. Where other veteran rock stars resented being cast as "dinosaurs," Pete's reaction to punk was, typically for him, more nuanced and complex. He seemed to harbor a self-destructive wish for punk to finish the Who off.

"But punk didn't extinguish the Who, and I was very angry about that," he says. "I thought that, 'Well, this will be convenient. We don't even have to be responsible for our own slow suicide. We will get put out to grass.'"

These feelings culminated in an infamous encounter between Pete and two members of the Sex Pistols, guitarist Steve Jones and drummer Paul Cook, at the Speakeasy Club in London's Soho district in March 1977. The Pistols were then riding high on the strength of their game-changing debut album, *Never Mind the Bollocks*. Townshend had come to the Speakeasy directly from a business meeting at which he'd collected a check for over a million pounds sterling, the outcome of some protracted and difficult legal wrangling with management. But rather than feeling triumphant, Pete was in a foul mood. Then he started drinking.

He was soon violently drunk, smashing glassware and throwing punches. Then he spotted Cook and Jones. On being informed who they were, he accosted them, initially mistaking Cook for Pistols lead singer Johnny Rotten. Townshend's intent was to congratulate them, but he ended up frightening them more than anything else, launching into an alcohol-darkened tirade to the effect that rock was dead and the Who a decadent, meaningless sham.

Cook responded by saying he hoped the Who weren't going to break up, because they were his and Jones's favorite band. Townshend told them he was disappointed in them. When Pete left the club later that evening, he didn't make it farther than a nearby doorway, into which he collapsed, unconscious. Sometime later he was awakened by a policeman. And as every rock fan knows today, the policeman knew his name.

The incident became the basis for Townshend's song "Who Are You," the title track for the 1978 album that would prove to be the Who's last great hurrah. Closing the LP on a defiantly triumphant note, "Who Are You" is epic and anthemic in the best tradition of Who classics like "Won't Get Fooled Again" and "Punk and the Godfather," awash in clashing guitar power cords, laced with a menacing keyboard pulse, and endowed with an introspective middle section that leads to a vicious restatement of the song's main chordal guitar riff. Daltrey even manages to work a bellicose challenge, "Who the fuck are you?" into the chorus out.

More than just another clever play on the group's name, "Who Are You" finds Townshend posing the ultimate philosophical question. At a time when punk rock was drawing lines in the sand, everyone in rock culture was questioning his or her identity. Who were they really in rock's new pecking order? But only Pete Townshend could turn existential angst into banging great rock and roll.

Townshend agonizes over the validity, and aging, of the Who, not to mention the ever-present avenging specter of punk, on other album tracks from *Who Are You*. The confessional "New Song" expresses Pete's fear, or perhaps conviction, at the time that the Who were merely serving up "the same old wine in a different jar." In "Music Must Change," he seems to be struggling to accept, and even love, the inevitability of stylistic evolution in music that can't help but make the old guard obsolete.

Perhaps more than any other Who album, *Who Are You* also finds Townshend exploring a wide variety of musical styles. He turns in some of his bluesiest playing ever on "Music Must Change," and embraces the tropes of the musical theater on the stagey "Guitar and Pen," foreshadowing the theatrical work that lay in his future. It falls more to Entwistle to write the album's more typically Who-ish, power chord–charged tracks like "Trick of the Light."

For the front cover photo for *Who Are You*, the Who posed amid a rubble of PA speaker cabinets, flight cases, and thick cables. Keith Moon, dressed in an equestrian costume, straddled a chair with the words "Not to Be Taken Away" stenciled on the back. It turned out to be one of the most bitterly ironic photos in rock history, because Moon was very soon to be taken away. On September 8, 1978, he died of an accidental overdose of Heminevrin, a drug he was taking to help curb his alcoholism. Townshend's worst fears regarding Moon's "narcotic cocktails" had been confirmed.

The drummer had been in poor shape for quite some time. Excessive alcohol and drug consumption had wrecked his physical and mental health, leaving him a bloated, unstable shadow of his former self both on and off the drum kit. Getting through the *Who Are You* sessions had been a struggle for him, and one reason for the disc's stylistic diversity. Townshend and the Who were forced to find musical idioms less reliant on powerhouse Keith Moon–style drumming. Moon can be seen struggling heroically through his final public performance, the concert sequence at the end of director Jeff Stein's 1979 documentary film, *The Kids Are Alright*.

For better or worse, the Who decided to soldier on without Moon.

"We'd be penniless if we hadn't," Entwistle told me in 1994. Kenny Jones, formerly of the Small Faces and Faces, was drafted to take Moon's place. The Small Faces' identification with the mod movement was as pronounced as the Who's in the mid-sixties, which lent a certain historical resonance to Jones's appointment. He was a close friend of the band and had been with Moon on the night he died. Along with Jones, the Who drafted keyboardist John "Rabbit" Bundrick into their ranks.

And with this, the Who became more of a conventional four-piece rock group with lead singer. Jones's style is nothing like Moon's. He's much more of a traditional time keeper. This, combined with Bundrick's addition to the lineup, freed Townshend to explore more traditional single-note rock lead-guitar playing.

"Putting a new band together enabled me to bring into the Who something I'd always wanted, which was another harmonic element," Pete explains. "I'd discovered John "Rabbit" Bundrick while working with Ronnie Lane on *Rough Mix*. As soon as Rabbit played with me, I realized that he was absolutely unique among keyboard players in understanding guitar voicing. He knew what notes were not being played. My voicing is very, very important. Often there will be two- or three-note chords at most, whether I'm playing all six strings or not. The fingerings are all about trying to cover so that you never get four-note chords. There's an inference of complexity there, often where there was none. And he was so locked in to that. So my guitar playing changed, 'cause I felt liberated, to some extent, by that. I'd play a chord, he'd restate it, and then I could play over it. I think my solo playing improved. I became more expressive. As I practiced, I became slightly faster. It was a good time for me musically. Not a great time for the Who, unfortunately, but a good time for me. Well . . . we made a few good cuts."

But the Jones–Bundrick edition of the Who seemed doomed from the start. At a December 3, 1979, Who concert at Cincinnati's Riverfront Coliseum, eleven fans died in a stampede resulting from the venue's open, or "festival," seating policy. For someone with Townshend's profound moral and aesthetic issues with stadium rock, not to mention his keenly felt sense of obligation to his fans, one can only imagine how devastating this event must have been.

Still the Jones–Bundrick lineup completed two studio albums, 1981's *Face Dances* and '82's *It's Hard*. These discs may not rank up there with the Who's classic sixties and seventies work, but as Townshend indicates, they certainly do contain a few very strong tracks that evidence his continued growth as a songwriter. Among these are "You Better You Bet" and "Another Tricky Day" from *Face Dances* and "Eminence Front" from *It's Hard*.

But Townshend preempted the release of both of these Who albums by rolling out *Empty Glass* in 1980, an album that he's often described as his first proper solo album. And it's true. Unlike previous non-Who Townshend releases, this wasn't a side project, a casual lark with a few friends, a compilation of demos, or a limited-issue recording for a handful of fellow Baba devotees. Rather it's a full-on commercial record production, a serious bid for airplay and the charts, and a serious rival for the work that Townshend was doing with the Who in the early eighties.

"I found it very difficult at that time," Pete says, "when I was doing really good solo work, like my first album *Empty Glass*, to justify being in a band that was obviously directionless and had lost a lot of spiritual focus. And yet was blundering on."

With Moon gone, the distinction between Townshend's solo oeuvre and his work with the Who begins to blur. In fact, Jones and Bundrick perform on *Empty Glass*, and some of the album's songs were first assayed by the Who during sessions for *Who Are You*. But freed from the burden of Who history, with its attendant songwriting legacy of giving voice to the inarticulate emotions of youth, Townshend's solo work cut him loose to focus on the issues of adulthood, *his* issues at the time: alcoholism, addiction, relationships, career anxieties, and the spiritual quest to find some kind of meaning in life.

Empty Glass does carry a pronounced spiritual subtext. The album is dedicated to Meher Baba, and Townshend has commented that the title references a metaphor from the Persian poet Hafiz, about the need to bring an empty vessel or empty glass—i.e., an open heart—to God in order to receive blessings, spiritual realizations, or fulfillment. If the heart is filled with other stuff—worldly longings, material desires, etc.—there will be no room to receive divine love.

Townshend's issue, of course, was that his glass was at the time full of "other stuff," notably booze, and all the dark thoughts its abuse can bring on. *Empty Glass* is also heavy on alcoholic imagery. In the credits, Townshend thanks "Remy Martin Cognac for saving my life by making the bloody stuff

so expensive." The inner-sleeve song list and lyric sheet is adorned with line drawings of cognac, whiskey, and champagne glasses arrayed as if it were some sort of oblique rating code. The album cover art itself seems to put an alcoholic slant on the old saying about the optimist's vs. the pessimist's view of a glass as being either half empty or half full. On the front cover Townshend looks serious and perhaps a bit morose, even though he's flanked by two gorgeous models and has a full bottle of wine in front of him. He also appears to have a halo around his head, like the central figure in a religious icon or triptych. On the back cover the bottle appears to be empty, Townshend looks drunk, but happy, as the girls move in even closer and his head is tilted to one side to reveal that what had seemed a halo on the front cover is more likely a circular barroom lighting fixture.

Townshend's mature work has always mingled the sacred and profane. Unlike other rock stars who embraced the spiritual path in the sixties and seventies, Townshend never became too "airy fairy" about it. In fact, much of his mature work seems grounded in the realization that a spiritual awakening doesn't exempt anyone from life's problems. If anything, it brings those problems into sharper focus. He once described himself as a "Sufi alcoholic." So a song like "Let My Love Open the Door" cuts both ways. It can be seen as dealing with divine love or earthly, romantic love. As such, it belongs to a mystical poetic tradition that runs through many of the world's religions.

Another standout track from *Empty Glass*, the Who-ish, rock-centric "Rough Boys," finds Townshend still agonizing over punk, this time in yet another context. "With 'Rough Boys,'" he says, "I was looking, very unconsciously, at my own physicality, my sexuality. And also trying to work out why I was somehow threatened by what had been going on with punk, in a spiritual sense. And that brought forth a whole tumbling array of ideas. I still do use that technique when I write songs— brainstorming onto the page and trying to make sense of it. But at those times, I wasn't even trying to make sense of it. I was just brainstorming, period, and letting it appear on record. That was something that worked on that record, and so I continued with it."

By the early eighties, Townshend had already made all of his great, innovative contributions to rock guitar playing and electric guitar technology. From here on, he would refine his distinctive guitar style, with its unique chordal sensibility, placing it at the service of his mature songcraft. In 1996, I asked him if the launch of his solo career in the early eighties had liberated him from the "guitar hero" role. "Yeah, it did, I think," he replied. "It's a role I've never been entirely comfortable with."

In fact, the rear cover photo of Townshend's next solo album, 1982's *All the Best Cowboy's Have Chinese Eyes*, depicts Pete's frowning face situated between the two necks of a Gibson EDS-1275, as if imprisoned by the guitar, or perhaps by rock stardom. Pete's addiction issues had certainly become exponentially worse in the time between *Empty Glass* and *Chinese Eyes*. He was freebasing cocaine and had become a heroin addict, a dual dependency exacerbated by a reliance on prescription tranquilizers. But he'd beat his addictions by undergoing NeuroElectric Therapy (NET), the notorious "black box" treatment devised by Dr. Meg Patterson, who had also treated Keith Richards and Townshend's close friend Eric Clapton for their heroin addictions.

All the Best Cowboys Have Chinese Eyes deals in part with Townshend's recovery. Dr. Patterson is referenced in the dedication: "This album is dedicated to Meg and other teenagers in love everywhere," which is accompanied by a photo of Pete and his wife, Karen, in their youth, presumably reflecting a resolve on Townshend's part to heal his troubled marriage. The confessional track "Slit Skirts" addresses the same theme with brutal honesty.

"On a song like 'Slit Skirts' from *Chinese Eyes*, I brainstormed right onto the page," Pete says, "and it was all personal grief, self-pity, self-loathing, a feeling of failure in marriage. And were a lot of people were put off, like, 'We don't want to listen to *that*!' But it wasn't an indulgence. I was given a permission as a solo artist to speak about myself. [Other] people said to me, 'I like it when you do that. I like it when you have an interview and talk about your inner fears, because I can't do that. You say things that I identify with and it makes me feel good that someone who has, in a sense, a kind of protected life still suffers from the same kind of human frailties as I do.' That kind of thing. Particularly in the department of gender identity, sexual identity, failure in relationships . . . everything but politics, in my case!"

Townshend had reached a turning point in his life. It was also in 1982 that he announced that the Who would be calling it quits after one last triumphant tour. "When I left the Who in 1982," he says, "there were certain things going on. One was that I wanted to preserve my hearing, what was left of it. I walked away from the Who in 1982 and expected it to disappear. But it didn't."

It's a rare rock star indeed who possesses the verbal acuity and cultural background to become an editor at a major publishing house. But that's precisely what Townshend did in 1983, accepting a post as acquisitions editor at Faber and Faber in London, the prestigious firm that had published the work of T. S. Eliot, Samuel Beckett, and William Golding, among many others. Townshend edited several rock biographies for the imprint, but also cultivated literary friendships with Golding, best known for his novel *Lord of the Flies*, as well as England's poet laureate Ted Hughes.

Townshend had always had literary aspirations, and his songwriting had always possessed the narrative thrust of fiction, but now he was starting to accumulate real literary cred. In 1983 a book of short stories by Townshend, titled *Horse's Neck*, was published. From here on in, most of Townshend's musical work would also carry a literary component. Released in 1984, *White City: A Novel* is a concept album set in a low-income council housing estate in London. It yielded a single, "White City Fighting," featuring guitar work by David Gilmour, who also co-wrote the song. And in 1989 Townshend collaborated with the aforementioned poet Ted Hughes on a musical adaptation of a children's story by Hughes to create *Iron Man: The Musical by Pete Townshend*. Both Daltrey and Entwistle perform on the album, which included one of Townshend's strongest latter-day compositions, "A Friend Is a Friend."

But Townshend's attention would inevitably, and repeatedly, return to his first, failed multimedia conceptual piece, Lifehouse. He drafted elements of the *Lifehouse* story into an unpublished novella, titled *Ray High and the Glass Household*, which in turn formed the basis for Pete's 1993 album, *Psychoderelict*. Both works introduced the disaffected rock star, Townshend-surrogate character Ray High, who would appear in subsequent Townshend works. Live shows that he did around *Psychoderelict* adventurously combined elements of both theater and rock concert, with both actors and musicians sharing the same stage.

The same year as *Psychoderelict* was released, Townshend collaborated with playwright Des McAnuff on a stage version of *Tommy*, also writing a book about the development of the stage production. The show became a huge success. So while Townshend had struck off on his own in 1982,

his Who legacy remained very much with him. Numerous Who reunions have followed in the wake of the band's official "dissolution" in 1982. The first was as early as a July 1985 appearance at Live Aid, followed a full-on twenty-fifth-anniversary tour in 1998.

Despite his issues with hearing loss, Townshend worked hard to find ways to continue performing. These included in-ear hearing protection and the use of onstage Plexiglas baffles to reduce noise from the drum kit and other instruments. But Townshend also took to employing a separate lead guitar player, confining himself to acoustic guitar and electric rhythm, which enabled him to work at lower volumes than he had in the heyday of rampant feedback and towering Marshall or Hiwatt stacks.

In this new guitar role, Pete has relied heavily on Fender Eric Clapton signature-model Stratocasters, retrofitted with a Fishman Power Bridge transducer and EMG buffer preamp to wrest highly convincing acoustic guitar tones from the Strat. An extra knob, fitted below the bridge, allows Townshend to blend this acoustic setup with the instrument's standard electric-guitar pickup configuration, also making Townshend's Strats easily discernible from stock Clapton Strats. Pete tends to prefer this particular Strat configuration in Fiesta Red, with a maple fingerboard.

On the '89 tour he famously impaled his right hand on wang bar of one of his Strats. So while he's had to work at lower volumes in the latter part of his career, his intensely physical approach to guitar playing hasn't changed all that much—although those big stacks of yesteryear have given way to Fender Vibro-Kings with 2 x 12 extension cabinets. "It's loud, loud, loud," says Townshend of the Vibro-King, "but not so loud that it blew my ears out. I got the sound that I wanted. So that's the sound I've drafted into the Who."

One addiction that Townshend didn't beat back in '82 was his attachment to live performance, even if pursuing it meant further jeopardy to his hearing. "When you're in front of a group of people," he says, "and some guy's screaming out 'Play fookin' "Magic Bus!"' or some beautiful girl down the front is mouthing, 'I love you; you can have me,' it just breaks up the whole process. And you think, 'Oh my God, this isn't what I intended. Everything's out of control!' But that's good. And so I'm drawn back to live performance all the time, really." Offstage, however, life's woes continued to make themselves felt. Pete's efforts to rescue his marriage ultimately failed; he and Karen separated in 1994. The mid-nineties were also when Townshend began to speak, often somewhat obliquely, in interviews of suspicions that he'd suffered sexual abuse as a child. It was in part an examination of his early work that drew him down this road of inquiry. He became particularly obsessed with Uncle Ernie, the pedophile character in *Tommy*. And indeed during songwriting for *Tommy* Townshend had found himself unable to write Uncle Ernie's musical theme, delegating the task to Entwistle. Pete also began to wonder about the figure of Ivar the Engine Driver, the seducer in 1966's "A Quick One While He's Away," as he explained to me in a 1996 interview.

"In my first rock opera, I could never work out where his man Ivar the Engine Driver came from. He's a dirty old bugger, basically. I was talking to my mother about it and she said, 'You know, you used to travel by train down to your grandmother's all the time, in the care of the guard.' We used to have this system in the UK where you could put a young child in care of the railway man. And I used to love it. You could walk up and down the train and you felt like you were part of the whole industry of it. Or you might be back in a car with dogs in a cage and the royal mail. But you know, I was somewhere between four and a half and eleven years old, and anything could have happened. I don't remember that anything did. But I suddenly remembered that. And I know that, at some point, my childhood memory of benign trust of men in uniform changed into an absolute distrust of men in uniform. It's healthy, by the way. It's perfectly healthy, but those things are very interesting when you look back at your early work, thinking maybe the lyrics will tell you things. It's been interesting. No great revelations, but very interesting."

The psychotherapy process can sometimes trigger false memories. But around this time Townshend seemed to become obsessed with the question of child abuse. He began to support children's causes and charities. The concept of childhood innocence coming into sudden and all-too-brutal contact with life's harsh realities seemed to move him profoundly. In that same '96 interview, he spoke of the terrible toll that ethnic cleansing in Bosnia had taken on the area's children.

"Whose fucking fault is it?" he demanded. "Who do you blame? It's men. It's women. It's women not being tough enough with their men. It's the ineffectuality of grandmothers. What is it? It's the Balkans. It's life. It's fucking God! You know, where do you take the anger to?"

But it was entirely another traumatic event that rocked Townshend's life in 2002. On June 27 of that year, on the eve of a Who tour, John Entwistle was found dead in a Las Vegas hotel room, in the company of *femme de joie* Alycen Rowse. His death was attributed to a cocaine-induced heart attack. He was fifty-seven years old at the time of his passing, and there were many media comments to the effect that men his age have usually learned to exercise a little more restraint. Ironically, just two years earlier, Townshend had told me, "John Entwistle just hasn't changed at all. I used to worry about that, but now I find it adorable."

Restraint and prudence were never Entwistle's strong suit. Townshend had also once commented that Entwistle's only real addiction was Harrods, the London department store. The bassist was a compulsive shopper, as evidenced not only by his legendary collection of over 200 vintage guitars and basses but also by closets filled with identical pairs of boots in every conceivable color, expensive real estate filled with antique suits of armor, and a seemingly endless conga line of flashy, gold-digger girlfriends. Entwistle was frequently in debt, and many latter-day Who reunions had been motivated out of a charitable urge on Townshend and Daltrey's part to rescue their old friend and longtime bandmate from financial ruin. Commenting on the success of a 2000 reunion tour commemorated on the '03 *The Who Live at the Royal Albert Hall* CD set, Townshend said, "We've done something between us that was very good, and lucrative, by the gods. Luckily for John Entwistle, who would probably be in jail by now for some kind of mortgage infraction."

Townshend himself came close to landing in jail in 2003, when he was cautioned by the British police for using his credit card to access a website advertising downloadable child pornography. Townshend published an anti–child porn tract, "A Different Kind of Bomb," on his own website (Eelpie.com) in 2002, and said he had accessed the pornographic site for research purposes. And investigation showed that, while Townshend had visited the site, he hadn't downloaded any illegal images, hence the caution rather than a sentence. The British tabloids had a field day with the humiliating incident, and the normally loquacious Townshend has become somewhat press shy in the time since then.

Townshend obliquely referenced an incident in the song, "Man in a Purple Dress," from the Who's 2006 album *Endless Wire*. While Townshend has said the song was inspired by the judgment scene in the Mel Gibson film *The Passion of Christ*, it's hard not to sense something more personal in

KEVIN WINTER/GETTY IMAGES

his indictment of hypocritical judges: "How dare you be the one to asses me in this godforsaken mess? You, a man in a purple dress."

In the years since Entwistle's passing, Daltrey and Townshend seem to have grown closer than ever, the rivalry of their earlier days long behind them. Together they lead what has become a relatively stable latter-day Who lineup, with Zak Starkey (Ringo's son) on drums, Pino Palladino on bass, and Rabbit Bundrick on keyboards. Pete's brother, Simon, also frequently plays a role as auxiliary guitarist and backing vocalist. *Endless Wire* also includes a track, "It's Not Enough," co-written by Townshend and his current musical and life partner, Rachel Fuller, Pete and Karen having finally divorced in 2009.

The centerpiece of *Endless Wire* is the Townshend mini-opera "Wire and Glass." Another revisitation of *Lifehouse*, this work is based on Townshend's novel, *The Boy Who Heard Music*, which he published serially on his website starting in 2005. The character Ray High from *Psychoderelict* appears again in "Wire and Glass." This time his work is taken up by a trio of teenagers who manage to achieve the old *Lifehouse* dream of uniting a vast audience in a sort of mystical communion through music's universal vibration. A triumphant concert opens up a mirror door (echoing the mirror that brings about Tommy's awakening) through which dead musical icons of yesteryear appear—everyone from Howlin' Wolf to Eddie Cochran.

"Punk didn't extinguish the Who, and I was very angry about that."

Like many Townshend denouements, it's all a bit mired in visionary mists, but the symbolism seems clear enough. The idea of a younger generation taking up the work of musical pioneers from days gone by is both poignant and encouraging. And it's certainly relevant to Townshend's own story. Were he not to perform or record another note of music, his legacy would be assured. Townshend's guitar innovations are still an immense part of the modern rock-guitar lexicon, a cornerstone, one might say. And recently the rock opera gauntlet has been taken up by Billie Joe Armstrong of Green Day with his hugely successful concept albums *American Idiot* and *21st Century Breakdown*—works that are rife with Who quotations and Townshend-isms. Billie Joe even followed Pete's lead by taking *American Idiot* onto the Broadway stage.

In the nineties Nirvana's Kurt Cobain smashed his Fender Mustang and became an icon for a generation perhaps only dimly aware of Townshend. Meanwhile, Pete's songwriting legacy lives on in the power-pop movement—a term he coined, and which is still ringing out loud today. The neo-mod movement is still scootering along stylishly as well, a splash of color and panache in the grim opening decade of the twenty-first century, proudly sporting the Who's bull's-eye icon as a tricolor badge of courage.

While Townshend's work has always been firmly rooted in his own place and time—be it Swinging London or hippie utopianism—the underlying emotional truths are as universal as the music itself.

"If you set *Lifehouse* in 1999 or 2999," Townshend asked in '96, "will we still be worrying about, 'Does my partner really love me? Do I really love him or her? Am I going to live forever? Is there another life? Is there God? Do I care? And why can't I get my favorite kind of peanut butter anymore?'"

Billy Gibbons

THE COLORFULLY DETAILED WORLD OF BILLY F GIBBONS

GIBBONS: FRIEND OF ERIC CLAPTON." That inscription graces the business card of ZZ Top guitarist and classic rock legend Billy F Gibbons. There is no mention of Gibbons's profession or the name of his band—items that form the more traditional subject matter of business cards. Just the five words cited above, followed by a suite address on Hollywood's Sunset Strip, phone number, and e-mail address.

But then again, what else does he need? Is there anyone on earth who doesn't know rock music's tall, slim, sharp-dressed man, with his scraggly hillbilly beard dangling in stark contrast to his fastidious, if bizarre, mode of attire? Is there anyone who hasn't heard the burning, bluesy voodoo that Gibbons can wrest from an electric guitar and amplifier—a sound that has remained at the core of ZZ Top, that little ol' band from Texas, for the past five decades?

Gibbons is a hard guy to miss. He turns up on network TV shows, at celebrity jams, photo ops, award ceremonies, wrestling smackdowns, trade shows, rodeos, drag races, and county fairs. He clearly digs the limelight and has an amazing ability to stay current, to morph with the times, without actually changing much at all. This is what has enabled him to keep ZZ Top vital through all the fickle changes and vicissitudes of musical fashion.

"What ZZ Top has always done," he says, "and what we continue to aspire to do, is maintain a sense of mystery. Musically, we're familiar enough to be able to mind-read on a certain level. But there's that joker gene that often pops up, where the music will take an abrupt right turn, be it by mistake—the happy accident—or by design. And off we go. We call that 'going to the Bahamas.' But the presence of the blues has never left ZZ Top's repertoire. That's a function of the fact [that] the blues is all we knew, and all we still know. But it's a good thing, in that we maintain an ongoing aspiration to interpret this great art form."

"What ZZ Top has always done, and what we continue to aspire to do, is maintain a sense of mystery."

Billy Gibbons is a man in perpetual motion. And he moves in mysterious ways. When not on the road with ZZ Top, who tour pretty heavily, Gibbons divides his time among residences in LA, Houston, and assorted other locales. No one fully understands the comings and goings of Billy F Gibbons. That's one of the rules.

He's rarely without the latest high-tech smartphone in hand. And the thing rings constantly. At any given moment, he'll have numerous projects underway: a flashy custom car he's designing with one of his many automotive buddies, a new recording project or show, some wild new custom-shop guitar design, a new acquisition for his extensive collection of African art, another piece of custom silver jewelry to commission, a new friendship to forge or an old one to reinvigorate. He's a supreme detail freak: totally obsessive. As a result, only a small percentage of his many projects actually reach completion. They just keep churning away, undergoing endless fine-tuning and micro-adjustment, generating an unending stream of phone calls, e-mails, text messages, and meetings. Billy seems to have an abhorrence of bringing closure to anything.

And he seems to have set his life up so that he'll never be bored. He's possessed of a highly retentive and wildly associative mind that requires constant stimulation. Like a magpie attracted to shiny objects, Billy scoops up printed matter wherever he goes—magazines, postcards, pamphlets, books—tucking them into the side pockets of the slim black blazers he favors. His houses are clutter central. While work was underway on his home in the Hollywood Hills just above the Sunset Strip a few years back, Billy had camped out in the basement. A mattress, located dead center of the room, was surrounded by a swap-meet array of bric-a-brac, fanning out in every direction and ultimately reaching each of the large room's four walls —books, papers, vinyl records, CDs, DVDs, high-tech computer gear in varying states of repair/disrepair, phone equipment, teddy bears, ketchup bottles, mailing tubes, sundry stationery items, cardboard boxes, boom boxes, items of discarded clothing, jewelry, and, of course, guitars and amps of every description. Rare ones, new ones, the weird and wonderful: a Gretsch Billy-Bo Jupiter based on an ax given to Billy by rock-and-roll originator Bo

Diddley, a brand-new black Fender JD Tele adorned with sparkling jewels, a few pawn shop specials, three different vintage Watkins Dominator amps, and a red-orange Tolex Marshall Bluesbreaker.

The LA house has been in Billy's family for years and once belonged to the guitarist's uncle, the celebrated Hollywood cinematic art director Cedric Gibbons. Billy's dad, Fred, was a soundtrack musician and composer for MGM during the thirties. This film legacy forms a huge part of Billy's makeup. His knowledge of film and television history is encyclopedic. The more obscure the genre, the more obsessive he gets, reeling off biographical trivia and names of long forgotten actors, actresses, directors, cinematographers, lighting designers, and soundtrack composers. His wife, Gilligan, is an actress but also holds an MBA.

"Billy's an interesting guy," says Dusty Hill, ZZ Top's bassist and Gibbons's band mate for the past four decades. "He's got a lot of varied interests. If you're involved in some venture he's into, you really get into it."

There's even more stuff at Billy's house in Houston, the city in which he was born on December 16, 1949. Houston is also the site of ZZ Top's recording studio, Foam Box, and eight warehouses containing the bulk of Billy's world-class African art collection, hundreds of guitars, amps, effects devices, and Lord knows what else. The Houston Billy is the one everybody knows: the deep-talkin' Texan with a passion for barbeque, roadhouses, mudflap gals, and stockcar racetracks. The Texan identity is central to the ZZ Top image, particularly the band's first incarnation, which lasted for most of the seventies. For those who hit adolescence or early adulthood during that decade, ZZ Top remains the ultimate beer-drinkin', hell-raisin', good-timin', ass-kickin' party band. This is the ZZ Top of "Tush," "La Grange," "Whiskey'n Mama," and "Enjoy and Get It On."

But as the eighties dawned and extinction threatened, the legacy of the Hollywood Gibbons came to the fore, as Billy ushered ZZ Top into the MTV era and the glitzy age of MIDI sequencers, synthesizers, and drum machines. This is the ZZ Top of "Legs," "Gimmie All Your Lovin'," "Sharp Dressed Man," and "Cheap Sunglasses," songs that remain the best-known and most enduring of the entire ZZ Top oeuvre. The highly visual, detail-obsessed Gibbons was heavily involved in the creation of a series of music videos that helped define a new visual medium and establish an engaging new persona for ZZ Top. They became a pop culture incarnation of the Biblical three wise men, bearded magi, keepers of the gateway to freedom, fun and excitement for a new age of hedonism, as symbolized by the gleaming ignition keys of a hot-rodded '33 Ford coupe.

Some of that eighties fairy dust clung to ZZ Top's garments in the nineties and beyond as they returned to their roots and emerged as curious curators of the blues legacy. Grizzled barrelhouse gurus, semi-mythical characters, they're here to remind us that rock and roll ain't nothin' but the bastard offspring of blues and hillbilly music. This is the ZZ Top of latter-day albums like *Rhythmeen*, *XXX*, and *Mescalero*.

One common denominator in the whole grand pageant of ZZ Top reincarnations is the tasty tone and distinctive guitar style of Billy F Gibbons. Every note is steeped in the rich American musical heritage that Billy absorbed growing up in Houston in the fifties. Some of his earliest musical memories are of the diverse sounds coming out of the radio, what we now call "roots music."

"The favorite channels on the dial," Billy recalls, "seemed to be the R&B stations KYOK and KCOH that played all the blues you could use and also country and western tracks of the day, back when

Hank Williams reigned king. In those radio offerings, one could hear the crossover elements the led to the birth of rock and roll: the blues meeting country, meeting hillbilly, and even bluegrass. All of this wild, 'non legitimate' music, was a heartfelt, more soulful kind of invention. Radios were still in a rather primitive vacuum-tube state back then, so you could turn them up loud and get beautifully rich distortion."

Billy's dad had moved on from Hollywood's studio orchestras to become a conductor of the Houston Symphony Orchestra and high society band leader. But Billy's musical education continued on an entirely different track at age seven, when a reckless babysitter began to bring young master William and his five-year-old sister out to the local Houston night spots, where the future leader of ZZ Top got his first taste of live blues and R&B music, played in the smoky dives that are the proper environment of these musical idioms. The next major turning point occurred on Christmas morning of 1962.

"I got my first guitar on Christmas day, shortly after I'd turned thirteen," Billy narrates. "It was a single pickup, single cutaway Gibson Melody Maker with a Fender Champ amp. I immediately retired to my room and learned how to play the intro figure from Ray Charles's 'What'd I Say,' and by sundown I had started learning the signature Jimmy Reed rhythm lines."

↔ HANGIN' WITH HENDRIX: ↔ LIFE BEFORE ZZ TOP

Billy played in a variety of junior high and high school rock groups during that golden mid-sixties era when bands were forming in garages and basements across America, knocking together their own rough take on the British Invasion sounds of groups like the Rolling Stones, the Kinks, and the Yardbirds. But BFG's first fully professional band was the Moving Sidewalks, a psychedelic blues outfit patterned after Texas's celebrated 13th Floor Elevators. The late sixties had arrived. Hippiedom was taking hold.

"There was this big house in Houston called the Louisiana house," Billy recollects. "It was this giant, beautiful 1920s mansion. And it became the big hippie house in town. There were little cubicles that became rooms to live in. The Elevators lived there. We moved in. The Red Crayola, another remarkable psychedelic band, lived there too. Those guys were artists of all sorts. Visual artists. The house was a real interesting kind of artistic enclave. It was not restricted to just musicians. There were light show guys, all kinds of people."

Billy himself had considered a career in the visual arts shortly after high school. "I had enrolled in art college and then went up to Austin to go to the University of Texas to study art," he says. "But the music was a stronger call at that time. It was either one or the other, and I chose music, although I kept on with my art fixation, this never-ending quest to figure out how to draw a line from point A to point B."

The art school refugee also found ways to manifest his bizarre visual sensibilities through music gear and the Moving Sidewalks' onstage presentation. Billy's mania for the wild customizing of guitars dates back to the heady days of hippiedom. A lot of guitarists back then, from Eric Clapton and George Harrison right on down to kids in garage bands, were painting their instruments in vivid psychedelic colors. Others, like Syd Barrett and Jimmy Page, affixed mirrors to their guitars, the better to reflect and intensify the trippiness of the strobe lights and morphing color blobs of the era's psychedelic light shows.

The field for experimentation was wide open. And Gibbons, typically, thought outside the box. Instead of looking to Timothy Leary, Aldous Huxley, Peter Max, or the art collective known as the Fool for influence, as everyone else was doing, he went back to a more primordial source: fifties rock and roll star Bo Diddley. An elder statesman of rock and roll eccentricity, Diddley is another one of Gibbons's lifelong obsessions. And on the cover photo for the album *Bo Diddley Is a Lover*, the titular artist is seen posing with a fur-lined guitar. This became the inspiration for a series of instruments that would reach its zenith with the iconic furry guitars of ZZ Top's "Legs" video.

In what would become another lifelong behavior pattern, Gibbons collaborated with a fellow artisan to realize his vision. He put together the first fur-lined guitar with the Moving Sidewalks' bassist, D. F. Summers. "He was quite a talented craftsman in guitar building," says Billy of his former band mate. "Only in those days, it wasn't so much guitar building as guitar aberration. We learned how to ruin quite a few guitars real quick. The first furry guitar was a butchered Fender Telecaster. But Mr. Summers helped bring those early custom-guitar ideas into reality."

Another D.F. innovation from this period was a device that enabled a guitar or bass to spin around like clock hands run amok while still mounted on its strap and worn by the player.

"The Moving Sidewalks were out on the Jimi Hendrix tour back in the late sixties," Billy recalls. "And [Summers] dreamed up this contraption then. The one element that one has to remember when using spinning instruments is 'keep your head out of the way.' As the guitar neck passes by, you don't want to get knocked on the head."

The Sidewalks' four-date Texas tour with Jimi Hendrix left a deep and lasting impression on Billy. He got to spend some time with the psychedelic superstar, who encouraged young Gibbons's artistic proclivities. One night after a gig, the two guitarists remained in the venue. Hendrix requested that their amps remain set up. He had a giant white paper backdrop hung toward the rear of the stage and buckets of fluorescent paint prepared. Both guitarists attached sponges to the headstocks of the their guitars and embarked on a ferocious noise jam while simultaneously creating an action painting with the paint-soaked sponges affixed to their instruments. Guitar necks became giant paintbrushes. The Hendrix encounter provided Gibbons with confirmation that he was heading in the right direction by thinking visually and unconventionally. It also pointed the way forward tonally.

"It was unspoken but quite evident that Hendrix threw caution to the winds," Billy notes, "and he decided to do things to and with a guitar that were not necessarily written in any of the how-to books. For instance, it was considered a no-no to chain two Fuzz-Tones together. But I saw Hendrix chain five of them together! And he'd do this personalized dance, stomping on five different pedals, sometimes playing with all five of them on at once. I think it's fair to give him the award for breaking the rules and starting to do things that no one dared do before. That was part of his genius: a total lack of fear."

∿ THE BIRTH OF ZZ TOP ∿

By the time 1969 rolled around, the reverb drenched, combo organ enhanced, early psychedelic sound of the Moving Sidewalks and similar garage psych outfits had been all but totally eclipsed by the heavier, power trio vibe initiated by groups like the Jimi Hendrix Experience, Cream, and Blue Cheer. Around this time, which coincided with the United States' escalation of the Vietnam War, the

Sidewalks' bassist and organist were drafted into the army. This left Billy free to pursue his dream of forming his own power trio. Never one to let the grass grow under his feet, he was more than ready to leave psychedelia behind and embrace the heavier rock aesthetic that would dominate much of the seventies. But his magpie mind would retain tricks and licks he learned during the sixties. And these would re-emerge, albeit utterly transformed, in the years to come.

And so ZZ Top was born. The original incarnation featured Billy, Moving Sidewalks' drummer Dan Mitchell, and Lanier Greg on bass. This lineup recorded one single, "Salt Lick" (b/w "Miller's Farm"). It was okay, but things didn't really gel until drummer Frank Beard and bassist Dusty Hill fell into place as the ZZ Top rhythm section that would reign supreme for the next four decades. Once again, Gibbons needed the right collaborators to help realize his vision.

Hill and Beard had played together in their own psychedelic blues outfit, American Blues, releasing two albums: *American Blues Do Their Thing* and *American Blues Is Here*. "There were song titles like "Chocolate Ego,'" Hill laughs. "You get the idea. Also I'd played with Freddie King on and off. I played at the Fillmore in San Francisco for two weeks with Freddy. Ike an Tina Turner were on the bill, along with Buddy Guy, Blue Cheer, and Electric Flag [a sixties band featuring guitarist Mike Bloomfield and future Hendrix collaborator Buddy Miles.]"

So Dusty and Frank were a seasoned rhythm section, to say the least, by the time they joined forces with Gibbons. "Billy's band opened for Hendrix," says Dusty. "American Blues opened for the Animals and Herman's Hermits. In fact, we had a little party with Herman's Hermits after the show. You can imagine. It didn't go on all night long. Well, at least nobody hit anybody. I think it broke up just in time."

"I don't think they were the partiers we were," Beard adds.

Beard joined ZZ Top first, and then brought Hill into the picture. Dusty beat out a bunch of other potential bassists. His audition quickly morphed from a tryout to a joyous, hour-long jam on a blues shuffle. It's one of the legendary episodes in ZZ Top lore.

"Dusty and I knew each other's tricks," Beard explains. "So automatically his audition sounded four times better than the other bass players we were auditioning. I really wanted Dusty in the band. So when the other bass players were up there, I made sure it was plenty lame. When Dusty got up there, we knew all these little punches and kicks we could do together at certain points. And it was like, 'Wow! Oh man!'"

While clearly influenced by archetypal power trios like Cream and the Jimi Hendrix Experience, ZZ Top brought their own unique flavor to the idiom. In embracing the blues, British guitar heroes like Clapton, Page, and Beck were essentially taking on a foreign musical genre, albeit with great respect and loving attention to detail. But as Texans, Gibbons and ZZ Top were much closer to the source. The Texas blues tradition—which encompasses everyone from Blind Lemon Jefferson to Lightnin' Hopkins to T-Bone Walker to Freddie King and later Stevie Ray Vaughan—runs deep and has always retained a distinctive identity. Texas blues comes from a different landscape and climate than its Mississippi or Chicago counterparts, with a different set of socioeconomic conditions for its African American population. And, of course, rhythms from south of the border have drifted into the cadences of Texas blues. As true Texans, Gibbons, Hill, and Beard were able to tap into this musical tradition in a very deep way. Meanwhile, the new power trio idiom and big guitar amps that emerged in the late sixties enabled them to take these influences and sources in a new direction.

In spiritual circles, there's an old saying: When the student is ready, the master will appear. Likewise, when the musician is ready to attain stardom, the instrument will appear—the vehicle to take him to the heights of musical glory. For Gibbons, it was the 1959 sunburst Gibson Les Paul known as "Pearly Gates." His quest to own such an instrument began when he saw Eric Clapton playing one in a back-cover photograph from the 1966 LP *Bluesbreakers: John Mayall with Eric Clapton*; also known as the "Beano" album, it was highly influential. Billy tracked down a '59 burst owned by a rancher an hour out of Houston and paid $250 for the guitar.

The name Pearly Gates comes from the source of the funding to buy the instrument. Even back then, Billy was a car nut and co-owned a '39 Packard with some buddies. They mutually decided to lend the automobile to a friend, aspiring actress Renee Thomas so she could drive to LA for a big film audition.

"We didn't think the car would make it past El Paso," says Billy. "But it brought Renee all the way to Hollywood *and* she got the part. We figured the car must have divine connections. So we named it Pearly Gates. Meanwhile, Renee called and said, 'Should I send the car back or sell it?' We said, 'Sell it!' She did, and my portion of the settlement arrived the very day I drove out to see the rancher."

And so the name Pearly Gates, with all its attendant magic, was transferred to the guitar. And as Clapton had provided the inspiration for Gibbons's choice of a guitar, Jeff Beck was not only the influence but also the agent for Billy's acquisition of an amp that would become a definitive part of his early tone. The first 100 Marshall stacks were just beginning to appear in the States, but weren't easy to find. Beck's roadie, however, had an in with Jim Marshall himself and hooked up Gibbons and Hill with a Super Lead 100 each, two of the first "made for the U.S." 110-volt Marshalls anywhere.

"Those amps played a big role in how to solve the trio puzzle: how to make three sound bigger than, or more than, three," says Gibbons. "Those distorted tones interacted to fill the holes. The once skinny sound of three instrumentalists suddenly became real wide, no holds barred and all holes filled. It was great for us because we didn't have to hire sidemen. We kept the band three. It was a lot more affordable. Fewer arguments too."

THE LONDON YEARS, PHASE ONE (1970–1972): MICK DIGS 'EM!

By now, ZZ Top were starting to attract attention. Their manager, Bill Ham, secured them a deal with London Records. The guys were delighted to be on the same record label as the Rolling Stones. They promptly holed up in a small Texas recording facility, Robin Hood Brian Studios, and knocked out their debut disc pretty much live in the studio. Aptly named *ZZ Top's First Album*, it was released in 1970.

"We attempted to create material written by the three of us with no idea of where it would go," Billy comments. "What you hear is what you get. The tone of that record is appealing in that we were merely upstart copyists attempting to present our version of the blues, coupled with what we thought would sound like Keith, Beck, Page, Clapton, Mick Taylor, Peter Green . . . those guys. Growing up, Frank and Dusty had listened to the same radio stations I did: the late night station out

of Nashville, WLAC, and the same Mexican border blasters. So we had a shared experience from the start that was able to be brought forward in the creation of ZZ Top, plus the bonus of having newfound heroes in the British Invasion guys. It was a handy way to start."

Of all Billy F Gibbons's many obsessions, the one that preoccupies him most is guitar tone, and the instruments and gadgetry that go into the making thereof. Shortly after the release of ZZ Top's first album, he began collecting guitars in earnest. His first quest was to find a backup for Pearly Gates, but he never found another guitar with quite the same mojo. "Which is why I now have these closets full of wood," he jokes.

"The favorite channels on the dial seemed to be the R&B stations KYOK and KCOH that played all the blues you could use and also country and western tracks of the day, back when Hank Williams reigned king."

But he also discovered that the single-coil pickup tone of Stratocasters and other Fenders make an ideal complement to the beefy tone of humbucker guitars, adding definition and sparkle. In particular, he acquired a 1956 Strat that came heavily into play on ZZ Top's second album, *Rio Grande Mud*.

"Moving from the first album to the second," Billy notes, "we thought, 'It's not out of our realm to use a few different guitars and amps to get some different sounds.' The music explosion that was taking place at the time was providing a wide range of tonal variances. And we were willing to get inventive."

Rio Grande Mud was also the album where Billy began to experiment with slide guitar overdubs in a variety of tunings. "'Apologies to Pearly,' is an instrumental slide number played in open E," he explains. "Open G [DGDGBD] and open A [EAEAC♯E] are two more favorites."

The proletarian "Southern Man" persona that that grounded ZZ Top's image for most of their first decade started to come into focus on *Rio Grande Mud*. Songs like "Just Got Paid" and "Chevrolet" project a strong blue collar, workin' man identity. But the band's fondness for cowboy hats and Western garb was known to cause confusion back in the early seventies. For instance, the crowd was a mite perplexed when ZZ Top opened for the Rolling Stones in '72.

"We got word that Mick Jagger heard our first album and liked it," Dusty Hill relates. "And he wanted us to open for the Stones in Hawaii. That just blew us away. But the next thing I heard was that Stevie Wonder opened for them here in the States and actually got booed at one show. So I was scared to death. We get onstage in Hawaii with our cowboy hats, boots, and jeans and you could hear a pin drop. Somebody went, 'Oh no, they're a country band.'"

"But we had our Marshall stacks cranked and we were ready to pounce for the kill," Billy adds. "We very quickly had to get grinding to dispel the myth: 'Yeah, we may look like we just fell off a wagon, but we're here to entertain.'"

"We got an encore on all three shows we did," Dusty fondly remembers. "And it was written up in *Rolling Stone* or something like that. It was one of the first big steps for us. And I've got great memories of that, like meeting Charlie Watts down at the bar and having a few."

An act that has toured as hard and lasted as long as ZZ Top is bound to have had encounters with most of the major rock legends. None other than Janis Joplin came to their aid one night in Phoenix.

"We got pulled off the stage by the cops in Phoenix," Billy recalls. "Someone had complained that we were using profanity in one of our songs. But Janis wouldn't have it. She said, 'If they don't get back up and complete their work, I won't be singing tonight.' It was a real mess. But she was adamant and made it very clear: 'Somebody might be mistaken. The PA system ain't that great. No one's really sure what we're saying up here.' So we got back up and finished our set. Janis was just smiling about it. She started laughing, yeah!"

∿ THE LONDON YEARS, PHASE TWO ∿ (1973–1976): SHITKICKERS ON ACID

The album that put ZZ Top on the map was *Tres Hombres*, released in 1973. It was the record that crystallized ZZ Top's sound and early style. Like *Rio Grande Mud*, the title *Tres Hombres* reflects the influence of *La Frontera*, the Mexican border flavor that creeps into Texan culture in general and the ZZ Top aesthetic in particular. And by this point, ZZ Top had become a highly seasoned live band—an inevitable by-product of almost constant touring.

"Not to knock London Records, but they didn't do a great deal for us," says Hill. "We were humping every night. Any gig. Every gig. Opening for whoever we could."

At the same time, with two albums under their ornate Western belt buckles, ZZ Top had become comfortable and highly competent in the recording studio. All of these factors helped to make *Tres Hombres* the band's first platinum album and an enduring catalog item to this day.

"*Tres Hombres* was our first breakthrough and it's still a favorite disc with fans and the band," says Billy. "One of the reasons for that is that it has our first Top-10 Hit, 'La Grange.'"

ZZ Top's tribute to a legendary Texas brothel, "La Grange" is a shuffle boogie in a style initiated by bluesman John Lee Hooker and revived by the late sixties blues band Canned Heat. ZZ Top put their own stamp on the idiom, although Billy's low-pitched lead vocal on the track—soon to be a signature vocal styling—came about somewhat by accident.

"We'd cut the music track and I was working on the vocal," Billy recalls. "But somehow it was not gelling. We worked and worked on it. I remember the session had started early and we'd gotten to the point where everyone was getting fatigued and hungry. So I said, 'Look, take a lunch break.' And I remember I was sitting in a metal folding chair, having stood up in front of the vocal mike for hours. I pulled the microphone down and asked the engineer to give it one more try. But he was having some kind of technical difficulty and said, 'Uh, you'll have to wait a minute until I figure this out.' After a little while he said, 'We're running but I'm not sure if we're taking [i.e., recording] this. You'll probably hear it in your headphones, but don't pay any attention to it.'

"So I heard the music start. And I just started horsing around with this low voice. I got through the first stanza of the two. I happened to glance up through the control room glass and the engineer was looking happy and excited, making gestures that seemed to say, 'Keep going. You've got something here and we're getting it on tape!' And that was the take and the final keeper—the vocal you hear on the record."

The extra-beefy guitar track combines two of Billy's favorite guitars: Pearly Gates and a 1955 maple-necked, hard-tail Stratocaster, both pumped through 100-watt Marshalls. The Strat is heard first, stating the song's main chordal theme. Then the Les Paul comes in when the band enters, doubling the Strat's rhythm pattern and kicking the groove into overdrive.

"That '55 Strat is just one of those great-playing, great-sounding instruments," Billy says. "I still have it. By the time we recorded *Tres Hombres*, we'd entered the era of the overdub."

Billy also used the Strat to play both of the song's memorable solos. The second lead is the first ever on a ZZ Top disc to incorporate pinch harmonics, a technique that would become of signature element of Billy's guitar style. "And that happened quite by accident too," he notes. "I had not studied it or anything. I just really came across it and said, 'Gee this is an odd effect.' At that time it was quite novel. Those harmonics can be highly unpredictable. But the technique is basically the pick followed by flesh from the thumb. My question is how does Dusty do it without a pick? How does Dusty play at all is my question. But he plays very well. He's the best, and very loud."

The Fender Broadcaster/Telecaster/Esquire family of instruments forms another of Billy's six-string obsessions. The *Tres Hombres* track "Jesus Just Left Chicago" features a '52 Broadcaster. But it's Esquires that really seem to have captivated Billy's imagination. He owns hoards of them, both vintage models and bizarre custom-art guitars based on the basic Esquire design.

"I was leaving a gig one evening," Billy recalls. "And I just happened to overhear a couple of guitar enthusiasts make a remark. One says, 'Well, if I had a Les Paul like Pearly Gates, I guess I could sound that way as well.' Which kind of jarred me into realizing that playing this dramatic instrument had turned from asset into liability. It wasn't the playing that was being reviewed, it was referencing the ease of success behind the Les Paul. And I complained to James Harmon, my harp-blowing buddy. He grinned and said, 'That makes sense. Why don't you turn the tables?' I said, 'How might I do that?' He says, 'Play a Fender Esquire. You can't get any more basic than that.' After thinking it through, I tended to agree. One pickup by the bridge. It's got a cutting-edge quality and with a little careful tone dialing, you're right in the pocket. And if you can do it on an Esquire, you can do it on anything. It's about as simple as you could ask for. And then stepping up from the lowly Esquire into Telecaster realms, you do get the added bonus of an extra pickup and some tone expansion."

Like *ZZ Top's First Album* and *Rio Grande Mud* before it, *Tres Hombres* was recorded at Robin Hood Brian Studio in Texas. But it is the first ZZ Top album to be mixed at Memphis's legendary Ardent Recording Studio, one more factor that puts it in a different league than its predecessors. Known, with some justice, as the "home of the blues," Memphis, Tennessee, is one of America's great music cities. B. B. King, Howlin' Wolf, Elvis Presley, Jerry Lee Lewis, Otis Redding . . . they all came out of in Memphis. With Sun Studios, Sam Phillips Recording Service, Stax, and Ardent all in town, Memphis has always been a great recording destination as well.

ZZ Top first came to Memphis to play a blues festival. The promoter had heard their records and assumed they were black. This misunderstanding made them the only white artists on the bill, but everything worked out fine in the end.

"There were a lot of local musicians hanging about," Billy narrates. "We made such a good impression that we had the opportunity to meet them after the show was over. All the local hotshot gunslingers were there. And a couple of them said, 'Gee whiz, you guys make some pretty good records. Why don't you consider recording here in Memphis?' I said, 'We've just completed a series of recordings which we're ready to take to the next level. We call it *Tres Hombres*, in keeping with our Tex-Mex origins.' They said, 'Since you already recorded it, would you consider mixing it here? We have a studio here in Memphis called Ardent and there's some real handy talent on the engineering staff. As a matter of fact, Led Zeppelin have just finished recording their *Led Zeppelin III* album at Ardent.'

"Well, that was big news. After a brief discussion we decided, 'Let's give it a try.' And having mixed our first Top-10 record at Ardent, which was a big deal, we now had a bond with music made in Memphis. And we worked at Ardent recording studio for the next twenty years."

It was a no-brainer for the band to head for Ardent when the time arrived to record the follow-up to *Tres Hombres*. The studio sessions would yield half of what became ZZ Top's second platinum success, *Fandango*. The other half of the album was culled from a hell-raisin' live show in New Orleans. So fans got the best of both worlds, some first-rate ZZ Top studio tracks and a taste of the live sound that had made the band a hot concert draw in the seventies. The album also offered a wider palette of guitar tones than any of its predecessors.

"*Fandango* was when we were starting to show up at the studio bringing truckloads of guitars," Billy says. "This was a real turning point in learning how to experiment with unusual gear. It turns out that the engineers who worked at Ardent—John Hampton, Terry Manning, and Joe Hardy—were all gearheads and had rooms of off-the-wall equipment they had managed to amass. One of the favorite amps on that album was a Silvertone 2 x 12 combo that had belonged to Alex Chilton [Memphis legend of Box Tops/Big Star fame who frequently recorded at Ardent]. Many of the artists who passed through Ardent ended up using it. And there was a 4 x 12 tweed Fender Bassman and a little, top-loading, tweed Fender Harvard with a 10" speaker that had belonged to Steve Cropper."

Billy's distorted tones on *Fandango* tracks like "Nasty Dogs and Funky Kings" hit a new level of graininess—a tough, squared-off, highly clipped tone that would become another signature Gibbons guitar timbre. Billy attributes the tonality in part to the advent of solid-state compressors, mike pre-amps, and other studio gear coming into currency at studios like Ardent in he mid-seventies. Elsewhere on the disc, "Heard It on the X" is a superb slide workout in open G, and "Blue Jean Blues" features some of the most lyrical, minor-key, slow blues playing that Billy has ever done. Played on a maple-necked '59 Strat, the shimmering clean tone has amazing depth and clarity.

"That was another studio experiment," says Billy. "The Strat was plugged directly into the board. Our equipment truck had broken down and we had no amps. But the clock was running and the engineer said, 'Well, if you just want to get something down on tape we can plug your guitar straight into the board.' Of course Fenders are by nature ultra clean and bright, so putting that Strat through the board worked for that particular tune. 'Blue Jean Blues' could be called one of the more haunting slow blues–based numbers that we've managed to get down. The quietness of it all allowed that clean effect to be used to good advantage. It's very different from what we're known for, a kind of rash, hard, distorted tone. But it's still a favorite."

By far the best-known track on *Fandango*, however, is "Tush," a brash up-tempo shuffle that became a major hit for ZZ Top. There are numerous, varied, and highly imaginative interpretations of what the word "Tush," as applied in the song, actually means. But it's clearly the tale of one man's quest for something fine, sung with fearsome upper-register intensity by Dusty Hill.

"We wrote 'Tush' at a soundcheck in Alabama in about six or eight minutes," the bassist recalls. "It was hot as hell, and with the exception of a very few words the song you hear on the record is what we wrote that day. We always tape our soundchecks for that very reason [i.e., songwriting]. Usually, though, it's a little lick or a vocal line or something, not a whole damn song!"

The only thing that could match the intensity of "Tush" is a full-on live set by ZZ Top, which is exactly what five of *Fandango*'s songs deliver.

"For that particular show, we were at a famous New Orleans venue called the Warehouse," Billy recollects. "It's a great room, a turn-of-the-century, wood-and-brick warehouse right on Tchoupitoulas Street in a line of many old warehouses. Not only was it a popular place to go, but the sound inside was fabulous. With that much brick and old wood, it was just this resonant box of tone. It didn't really matter what you brought into there, the room made it sound great. Everybody I've ever talked to who played at the Warehouse has said, 'Yeah, isn't that a great-sounding place to play?'"

The platinum success of *Tres Hombres* and *Fandango* enabled ZZ Top to mount one of the most ambitious and bizarre tours in all of rock history, not to mention one of the first big productions to reveal the full scope of Billy F Gibbons art directorial aspirations in all their demented glory. ZZ Top's Worldwide Texas Tour was billed as "Taking Texas to the People." They meant that literally. The 35,000-square-foot stage was hewn in the shape of Texas and weighed thirty-five tons. It took five massive trucks to transport this mammoth stage and all its attendant rigging, not to mention ranch-hand props that included fences, windmills, live cacti, and livestock. Yes, a live steer and buffalo, along with assorted breeds of buzzard and rattlesnake, all had roles in the big extravaganza. They were attended by fully qualified animal handlers, who also traveled with this rolling rock-and-roll circus. Nonetheless, sometimes the critters got loose, terrorizing concertgoers.

As for Gibbons, Hill, and Beard, they were decked out in elaborately stitched and ornately studded Western suits, designed and handmade by the famous country and western tailor Nudie Cohn. The outfits included big 'ol cowboy hats, naturally. Billy and Dusty played custom Gibson axes with Texas-shaped bodies. By this point, Gibbons had begun to augment his collection of vintage guitars with special commissions of new instruments from custom shops and individual builders. John Bolin of Boise, Idaho, is an enduring favorite of Billy's and has managed to keep pace with the often arduous demands of the guitarist's warped visual imagination.

By way of cultural context, the Worldwide Texas Tour rolled down the highway at a time when musical stars like David Bowie, Alice Cooper, Kiss, and Parliament-Funkadelic were mounting highly elaborate concert tours, bringing larger-than-life guillotine executions, spaceship landings, and other spectacles to rock stages. Seen against the backdrop of these big shows, the Worldwide Texas Tour functioned as both competition and parody.

The mid-seventies were also a time when glam was very much the prominent fashion mode in rock. A lot of bands and their fans were trying to look like androgynous, decadent, urban, ultra-hip space aliens. Meanwhile, ZZ Top were going around like shitkickers on acid—very much the antithesis of glam, although every bit as dressed up and image conscious as the glamsters. The cowboy hats that had been a liability in '72 had been transformed into a high-concept statement, a kind of redneck drag. This wry over-insistence on the band's Texas roots was one of several factors that separated ZZ Top from the herd of "Southern Boogie" bands that had also gained currency in the mid-to late seventies. And like all great concepts, it functioned on several levels. More down-home fans could raise a longhorn Bud in the air and holler "Hell yeah!" While hipsters could feel like they were sharing an inside joke. ZZ Top were following the age-old showbiz maxim: Take whatever it is you've got and exaggerate it.

"We very quickly had to get grinding to dispel the myth: 'Yeah, we may look like we just fell off a wagon, but we're here to entertain.'"

"We had a glaring awareness of our inability to look like fashion models," Billy deadpans. "To this day, one of the band's in-jokes is aimed at our fearless bass player, Dusty Hill, who is known for being immune to fashion. Be it clothing, the favorite guitar of the day, the newest amp, you will not find it in Dusty's closet. In the beginning we didn't have time to design wardrobe. We were touring too hard, busting our ass to get to the next show and going onstage in whatever we happened to be wearing. That in itself became part of the perception of ZZ Top: 'Oh yeah, they're those Texas guys, I've seen them. They wear cowboy hats and cowboy boots a lot.' What started out as everyday clothing to leave the house in over the years became a trademark, whether intentional or not."

Keeping the Longhorn State motif going, ZZ Top decided to name their next album *Tejas*, the Spanish spelling for the territory that had once been part of Mexico. It's another classic, bluesy ZZ Top disc, but a pronounced country influence also creeps into the mix. The album's hit single, "It's Only Love," is not only one of the catchiest things the band has ever done, it also possesses an unmistakable twang. And "She's a Heartbreaker" is as country as it gets.

"Oh, without question," Billy concedes. "Around that time I was driving from Houston down to Austin a lot to hear the Fabulous Thunderbirds, who were just getting started and playing "Blue Monday" nights at a pizza joint in Austin called the Rome Inn. And halfway down, you could start to pick up this great Austin radio station, KOKE-FM. One of the DJs on there decided to turn the playlist upside down and create a format that could go from George Jones to the Rolling Stones, back to back. That certainly had an impact on me.

"And at the time, there was this great wave, a new movement coming out of California: country rock. It had started when Roger McGuinn allowed the Byrds to go in that direction on *Sweetheart of the Rodeo*: the cowboy-ification of rock, with pedal steel guitar showing up on rock records. And coming out of that lineup of the Byrds you had Graham Parsons and his band, the Flying Burrito Brothers. And Graham was of course hanging with the Stones in the era when they were doing things like "Wild Horses," "Dead Flowers," and "Country Honk." Along with that there was Poco, the Eagles . . . just a real fun, 'Let's be cowboys for a day' kind of thing.

"So not wanting to be left behind, we took measures to see if we could stay in step with the trend. Some fans were surprised. But some of them remembered that our second single, 'Shakin' Your Tree,' had pedal steel on it. And one of my all time favorite country-twinged ZZ Top numbers is 'Mexican Blackbird' from *Fandango*, which is definitely a slidester's chewed-up version of rock meets country, inspired by that particular period."

But what's interesting is that there's a bit of Keith Richards in Billy's country playing. The chordal voicings and edgy, clean tones on both "It's Only Love" and "She's a Heartbreaker" owe a lot to Keith's London take on the country idiom.

"Oh, without a doubt," Billy admits. "The Stones have been a benchmark for so many aspiring rock musicians. They're true blue interpreters of American music. They took up the blues and R&B at a time when it was by and large being dismissed at home. And they explored country music in the same way. They were pals with some of those California bands. And yes, I would spend hours upon hours studying Keith's playing style and his chord voicings. It took me a long time to realize he played a five-string Telecaster in open G. Boy, that was a brand-new day when I figured that one out!"

THE LONG HIATUS: ZZ TOP EXPLORE THE GLOBE

Shortly after the release of *Tejas*, ZZ Top decided it was time for a break. They'd been touring hard and heavy since 1970, and the logistical rigors of the Worldwide Texas Tour would have sufficed to kill lesser men. "It started out that we were going to take a ninety-day hiatus from public appearances," Billy says. "That allowed us to enjoy a little getaway. Frank went to Jamaica, Dusty went to Mexico, and I was off to Europe. Well, three months became six months, which became a year, which became two years. We were still in touch, but it was kind of a long-distance love affair."

Asked what brought him to Europe, Billy promptly answers, "The first Fripp and Eno album, *No Pussyfooting*." Gibbons had become intrigued with the European art rock movement of the seventies. Former King Crimson guitarist Robert Fripp and Roxy Music vet Brian Eno had become part of a scene that also included players like Pink Floyd associate Robert Wyatt and guitarists Fred Frith and Kevin Ayers, playing in bands like the Art Bears and Henry Cow. It was all a mighty long way from Texas, but it did involve making noises with guitars. So Billy was down.

"Granted, during the Moving Sidewalks days, we got to know Robert Wyatt from the Soft Machine," Billy says. "Talk about head trip, way out there art rock! And in the seventies there was a lot of that art rock kind of scene going on in England. And if you check out the liner notes to some of those early Fripp and Eno releases, they go to great lengths to reveal their studio system: 'You have to go through an echo unit here, then run the signal through this. . . .' It becomes quite fascinating, not only as an insight to what they're doing, it also stimulates one's own curiosity, 'Wow, if they can do that, I wonder if I can do this.' But some of the most obtuse art rock was coming out of Paris, France. So I spent some time there too."

Billy also got interested in reggae music. The Jamaican musical idiom was at a high point in the seventies and very much a part of the decade's "alternative" musical zeitgeist. Billy got to know both Bob Marley and Peter Tosh, spending some time in Trinidad with Marley.

"Bob was an intense kind of guy," Billy says of the reggae icon. "Very set on doing things his way. He was a great leader for that outfit [the Wailers]. He had an incredible rhythm section behind him: [drummer] Carly and [bassist] Aston 'Family Man' Barrett. Carly Barrett's treatment of the beat was so unique. There isn't a two or a four in early reggae. There was a name given to that beat, the one drop. The reggae sound coming out of Jamaica in that glorious period from 1971 to '77 is to this day considered the real essence of when reggae ruled."

THE WARNER YEARS, PHASE ONE (1979–1981): NEW STYLES IN MUSIC AND FACIAL HAIR

So when ZZ Top finally reconvened in 1979, Billy's musical perspective had been stretched in several new directions. In the interim, ZZ Top had left London Records and signed a deal with Warner Bros. The first ZZ Top album on Warner, 1979's *Degüello*, introduced a new stylistic and sonic approach for Gibbons, Hill, and Beard. There is a greater emphasis on clean chorusy guitar tones than ever before, and an arch sense of postmodern irony creeps into songs like "Cheap Sunglasses" and "Fool for Your Stockings." Gone was the horny working man's yowl of earlier classics like "Tush" and "La Grange." ZZ Top were still libidinous, but in a detached, double-entendre kind of way.

It all very much reflects the impact of New Wave, the post-punk musical style that rubbed shoulders with art rock in the late seventies. (Eno had gone on to produce Devo and the Talking Heads; Fripp had formed the League of Gentlemen with a trio of New Wave musicians.) In true DIY punk/New Wave fashion, the members of ZZ Top even taught themselves to play saxophone in order to add some horn charts to the disc.

To go with their new sound, ZZ re-emerged from their hiatus with a crazy new look. During their time off, Gibbons and Hill had grown long beards, unbeknownst to one another. And this chance occurrence, born of nothing more than a reluctance to wield the razor on a daily basis, became the band's new visual hook. Despite his name, Frank Beard refused to participate, an irony that has often attracted comment. He does, however, sport the occasional moustache and/or goatee. Meanwhile, the fully bearded Gibbons and Hill formed a sufficient two-thirds majority for ZZ Top to become known henceforth, and for all time, as "those guys with the beards."

A long beard is a wonderfully open-ended signifier. The new facial appendages tied in with ZZ Top's earlier, hillbilly/shitkicker image. But down through history all kinds of men have sported long beards: hermits, gurus, anarchists, crazed poets, derelicts, Santa Claus and his elves, the Judeo-Christian deity, the Robert Crumb cartoon character Mr. Natural, the mad Russian monk Rasputin. . . . Whatever the hell those ZZ Top chin warmers were supposed to mean, they were light-years removed from any prevailing rock fashion.

And as the beards grew in, interestingly enough, the cowboy hats were gradually phased out. The new accessory of choice was dark glasses, worn both day and night. In fact, *Degüello*'s "Cheap Sunglasses" became the band's new theme song. The dime store shades resonated with the burgeoning New Wave aesthetic. That little ol' band from Texas had morphed into postmodern hipsters.

"One of the highest compliments at the time," Billy recalls, "came from the late rock critic Lester Bangs, who said that 'Cheap Sunglasses' was chosen as a favorite by someone wearing purple hair who did not realize who they were listening to. Thank you, Lester, thank you, purple hair, thank you, cheap sunglasses, thank you, Ray Charles."

From times immemorial, a long beard has often served as a handy disguise. And so it was for ZZ Top. While the sound-bite-crazed mass media focused on the new whiskers, ZZ Top had radically shifted their entire sound and musical approach—right under the noses, as it were, of fans and critics. The ZZ Top beards are rock's greatest McGuffin. A McGuffin is a cinematic trick invented by the great director Alfred Hitchcock. It's an object that captures the audience's attention (a mysterious box, which may or may not contain a bomb, for instance) while key plot developments are snuck past the viewer in order to prepare a surprise ending. So here ZZ Top had appreciably changed their musical style and signed with a new label, but all anyone could talk about were the f--king beards. Press for the album tended to revolve around beard jokes, beard cartoons, funny fake beards on non-band members. . . . In growing those whiskers, they'd written themselves an unlimited musical license. They could decide to become a classical string trio or a trad jazz outfit and they'd still be "those guys with the beards."

Not that they'd gone all that far. There was plenty on *Degüello* for old-time fans to dig, like the bluesy fave "I'm Bad, I'm Nationwide," with its searing lead tones. The guitar solo in "She Loves My Automobile" quotes the Freddie King blues instrumental classic "The Stumble," later popularized by Peter Green in John Mayall's Bluesbreakers. And the double-entendre lyric to "She Loves My Automobile" is very much in the risqué R&B style of forties great Louis Jordan. ZZ Top had managed to reinvent themselves for a new era while keeping one slyly winking eye on their blues roots. Gibbons had found an elusive common denominator linking the outsider cool of his early blues heroes with the postmodern alienation of the New Wave era.

ZZ Top's next album, *El Loco* (1981) continued in the vein of *Degüello*: clean, chorusy/phasey/ flangey guitar tones and rampant double entendres. You don't have to be a lit major to catch the phallic references in "Tube Snake Boogie" and "It's So Hard." "I Wanna Drive You Home" could be an answer song to "She Loves my Automobile." And "Pearl Necklace" is the band's famous poetic euphemism for fellatio.

All of the pieces, however, hadn't quite fallen into place. If ZZ Top were trying to be New Wave, what was with the "818 area code/mellow hits" guitar sound? The complete and utter transformation of ZZ Top would have to wait until the dawn of the new decade and the arrival of two new technological innovations: MTV and drum machines.

ᕦ THE WARNER YEARS, PHASE TWO ᕤ (1983–1992): MTV'S MOST UNLIKELY IDOLS

Released in 1983, ZZ Top's eighth album, *Eliminator*, has sold over 11 million copies at the time of this writing. The band's most successful album ever, it is also their most controversial recording. Some longtime fans were horrified by the band's embrace of synthesizer and drum machine technology, not to mention their ascendancy on MTV, the then-brand-new medium that had become the domain of image-conscious pop stars like Duran Duran, Michael Jackson, and Madonna. But had ZZ Top not been able to move so deftly with the times, they almost surely would have ended up on the seventies nostalgia playlist, occupying a slot somewhere between Molly Hatchet and the Outlaws and probably playing casinos today.

Instead, they're still rocking arenas and share bills with fellow classic rock legends. And time has more than vindicated *Eliminator*, affording it a place among the all-time great rock albums. It is tempting to view *Eliminator*'s retro-futurist sound and ZZ Top's entire eighties makeover as the result of some grand overarching vision on the part of Billy F Gibbons—some wizard-like insight into the direction in which pop culture currents were shifting. But Billy maintains that it was his gear obsession that sparked the whole thing.

"When we got back into Ardent to make *Eliminator*," he recalls, "the storage vault for gear had increased threefold. The uncharted new rooms had all this weird new stuff: new amps, new outboard gear, synthesizers, drum machines . . . We were fascinated by these new contraptions that we knew nothing about. They drew us in with such vigor that we completely ignored the owners' manuals. There was no reading of manuals. It was just too boring. We wanted hands-on immediacy."

And so ZZ Top had found the potent combination that would bring them into the eighties and their era of greatest commercial triumph: raunchy rock guitar sounds coupled with the pounding drive and unrelenting sex machine rhythmic precision of electronic dance music and synth pop. An Oberheim DMX drum machine and Moog Source synth for bass parts now joined the crew, tastefully interwoven with real-time playing from Frank Beard and Dusty Hill.

"The closer a performance comes to being in perfect time, the more trustworthy it is perceived as being," Billy explains. "And that becomes quite attractive. One is more readily drawn to trustable clock time than something that ebbs and flows and leaves you on the sideline, going, 'Where's the beat?' So we had to unlearn the peculiar muscle memory habits developed from live performing, where things do have a tendency to speed up and slow down, push and pull. In the studio you want to leave that behind. You want to get on the groove and hang in there."

But *Eliminator* wouldn't be *Eliminator* without its killer cache of hooky hits. The big winners, "Gimmie All Your Lovin'," "Legs," and "Sharp Dressed Man" presented themselves at different phases of the recording process.

"*Eliminator* was assembled in three stages," Billy explains. "The first was the obvious: bringing in material that we had written on the road or in rehearsal sessions before going into the studio. The second phase was assembling the bits and pieces that were left over from those rehearsals and the first stage of recording. And the final stretch found us composing and creating while in the studio. That's not unusual. In recording, getting started is the uphill challenge. But once the momentum catches on, the process of completion is an easier bit of business. You're already into it. You've got the sounds. The microphones haven't moved. Everybody has their minds focused on the creative process. In my opinion, it becomes more free flowing. The longer you're in there, the easier it gets."

One of the very first tracks the band recorded was "Legs." Gibbons has a vivid memory of the song's genesis. "We were driving down an avenue in this fancy shopping district of Houston," he narrates. "And an unexpected downpour just opened up. Suddenly there appeared this gorgeous, long-legged gal trying to dodge the raindrops. She took off running. Frank, Dusty, and I immediately agreed, 'We need to save her! Offer her a ride. Get her out of this rain.' We turned the car around, but

in the space of half a block, she was gone. She had vanished. She was so fast. Her legs had gotten her out of the rain. We said, 'Man, where'd she go? She got legs and she knows how to use 'em.' As luck would have it, we were on our way to the rehearsal room. We didn't want to miss the opportunity to have some fun with this unanticipated turn of events. So we went straight in and began hammering out the remainder of the song that became 'Legs.'"

But the song languished in limbo for a while, until the band happened upon the rocket fuel that would propel it to the top of the charts. "We had the structure and the words," Billy notes. "But the last piece to fall into the mix was the staccato synth line. That didn't fall into place until we were closing the sessions. By that time we'd had a chance to dig into the new technology. That synth line was the icing on the cake that really made for an interesting sound for that period."

"Legs" perfectly encapsulates *Eliminator*'s powerful modus operandi. It's an effective combination of wildly disparate elements: a Chuck Berry–ish guitar riff, a disco sequencer pulse that could've come right off a Giorgio Moroder production for Donna Summer, and an old-school R&B chord progression—E, C#m, A, B—that dates back to the fifties, if not earlier. Strange bedfellows indeed, but somehow they make beautiful music together. Billy is particularly proud of the solo chord modulations in "Legs," which take off from the C♯m and move around the circle of fifths to F♯m and then B. In the dance remix of "Legs," the solo section gets extended, looping round and round like a flying saucer before finally resolving.

"The old adage about ZZ Top is that we're the same three guys playing the same three chords that were brought to us by the great art form called the blues," Billy observes. "But 'Legs' has an interesting solo bridge. The chord structure departs far and away from a simple three-chord pattern, finally landing on the V chord [B] to get back into the verse. So that too was an interesting composition musically to go with some juicy lyrics."

The very first single that would be released from *Eliminator* was "Gimmie All Your Lovin'." "That song came in the middle of the recording process," Billy elaborates. "It was one of the bits left over from the first phase. We had basically an outline of an arrangement musically, but we had no words written. And I remember having a brief phone conversation with Mick Jagger. He was engaging in a solo project at the time, and somehow the subject of lyrics and content entered the discussion. I left that brief phone exchange inspired by the Rolling Stones and the way I envisioned their songwriting process. So the music track was already laid down and in one sweeping moment I composed the lyrics in the hotel as I was preparing to leave for the studio. It was one of those moments that come to you in a flash, unexpectedly, but steeped in the rather accelerated frame of mind of having spoken to Jagger and kind of aiming at the Rolling Stones' overview."

Eliminator's third monster hit, "Sharp Dressed Man," emerged from a trip to the movies. "The closing credits rolled by, and we were sitting in the theater waiting to see who the director was and all of that," Billy recalls. "The cast of characters was rolling by and one of them was listed as the Sharp Eyed Man. So I was trying to remember which character in the film was the Sharp Eyed Man. Which later morphed into 'Sharp Dressed Man.'"

Try as he might, Billy can't remember the name of the film that gave rise to this revelation. (There's a good challenge for trivia buffs.) But once again, his instinct for latching on to a great lyrical hook didn't fail him. "Once you've got 'the girls go crazy 'bout a sharp dressed man,' that's all you really need," he says. "Fill in a few items of clothing, clean shirt, new shoes . . . and you've got a song. The essence of *Eliminator* was including so many compositions with memorable lyrical hook lines—either the first line of the verse or the first line of the chorus. When you stop and think about memorable songs, there's really only one or two lines that stand out. When we were working on *Eliminator*, we'd have these songwriter shootouts to see who in the room could actually repeat an entire song word for word. We sang Howlin' Wolf and Muddy Waters songs like 'Rollin' Stone,' or Eric Clapton's 'Cocaine,' which was actually written by J. J. Cale, and even 'Hotel California.' And it basically came down to, 'Well, I know the first line of the chorus. That's all I know!'"

"Sharp Dressed Man" is also graced with a particularly memorable solo section, in which Billy alternates slide playing with conventional fretting. He comes off the slide as the song moves from its tonic chord, C, to the second chord in the progression, which is F. It's a tricky move to nail, especially if you don't realize that Billy is playing in an open tuning.

"I played that solo in open E [EBEG♯BE]," he explains. "We experimented with open G and A, but open E was the favorite. Keep in mind that before *Eliminator*, we recorded a version of Elmore

James's 'Dust My Broom' for *Degüello*, which was also in open E. And the day we went into the studio to record 'Sharp Dressed Man,' we just happened to warm up on 'Dust My Broom.' The engineer said, 'Why don't you play some Elmore James stuff to get you in a bluesy frame of mind.' So we were left with a guitar tuned to open E. Eventually we went and recorded the basic back tracks for 'Sharp Dressed Man.' I played the basic guitar track in standard tuning. But when it came time for overdubbing solos, I grabbed the guitar that was still in open E from our earlier jam on the Elmore James tune. So it was time to do some quick transposition. The challenge was coming off the slide solo and fingering the guitar on the solo in open tuning. But it worked out. It just requires a movement down two frets from where you'd be in standard to find that seventh note, which is really the blue note within most structures."

"The closer a performance comes to being in perfect time, the more trustworthy it is perceived as being."

As always, Billy brought a cadre of interesting guitars into the studio to complement the stalwart tones of Pearly Gates. "There was always a Fender Esquire on hand," he notes. "I've got two favorites, a '51 with a black pick guard and a '56 with a white guard and bigger neck. And we used some oddball stuff. Dean Zelinski sent down a couple of things. Besides that, we had a few Gretsches, a few Nationals. . . ."

A well-worn 1955 Gretsch Roundup provided the beguilingly glassy tone for the low-string figure Billy plays in the breakdown sections of "TV Dinners," another hot single from *Eliminator*. "It was that Gretsch with the toggle-switch selector in the middle position," he elaborates. "So both pickups are on and everything turned up full. Those mid-fifties Gretsch guitars are the only instruments that can capture that sound. You can come close on a Fender Jazzmaster. It has a peculiar sound much like the Gretsch with both pickups on. You get that surf like quality."

Gibbons' amps for *Eliminator* included big bruisers like 100-watt Marshall stacks and solid-state Vox Super Beatles, as well as smaller combo amps both familiar and obscure, such as the 50-watt Legend. Around this time, Billy developed an obsession with vintage 18 W combo amps. He began collecting tweedy old 18 W 2 x 12 Fender Dual Professionals and mid-sixties 18 W Marshall combos, all of which figured in the making of *Eliminator*. "We also had a tweed Fender Deluxe, a tweed Fender Champ," Billy adds. "They all held a promise to deliver something really interesting to listen to. And we said, 'Why restrict it to just one? We may find a combination of these amps that works.'"

Which proved to be a logistical nightmare in terms of miking all these amps in the studio. And so the infamous "amp cabin" came into being. "Instead of lining up ten or fifteen amplifiers with a mike on each one," Billy explains, "or having to move a mike each time we wanted to try a different amp, we built a square of amps all facing inward, with one microphone in the middle. And we put a second stack of amps on top of those, all different ones. The idea was, 'Let's put every type of amp on there.' As for the third row of amps, we didn't want them to get too far from the mike, so they were put on top, aiming down. And somebody said, 'Looks like a little ol' cabin.' So we named it the amp cabin. We took photographs of this crazy construction. We had one of every odd, previously unused amp in this structure, just to see what would happen. This was an extreme example of ZZ Top learning how to experiment with different things."

In another experiment, Billy remembers suspending a microphone over the amp cabin. "The mike had been placed on a pivot," he elaborates. "The wire was being driven by one of the engineers, swinging the microphone to get different phase inversions over this whole contraption. It was a very inventive time, I must say."

Another technological innovation of the eighties was the era's explosion of effects devices, both rack mounted and in stomp-box incarnations. Many of these made their way into Ardent Studios as *Eliminator* was being recorded. Billy employed various MXR devices and one of the first Scholz Rockman headphone pre-amps, one which had been specially modified for Billy by Scholz Electronics main man Tom Scholz of the classic rock band Boston. As with most things, Billy was eager to explore just how far he could push some of these new technologies.

"At one point we figured out a way to chain three harmonizers together using one signal source," he says. "This was pre-MIDI, so any real-time control of parameters had to be manual. Which meant you could play a harmonized solo, and if the engineer knew the chord changes, he could advance between intervals, which would allow you to play in key with the right harmonic intervals between notes. We did one with three changes. We limited it to that."

But Billy wasn't averse to going old-school either. For the yearning solo on *Eliminator*'s slow blues number, "I Need You Tonight," sung by Dusty Hill, Gibbons employed an analog tape–based echo from a vintage quarter-inch tape machine at Ardent, equipped with a variable speed oscillator (VSO) to regulate motor speed, thus putting the echo repeats in time with the song's tempo—which is pretty much the way people had been doing echo since the fifties. Billy's canny ability to blend the vintage with the cutting edge in just the right proportions is one key to *Eliminator*'s power and ZZ Top's longevity.

The profound mass culture impact and enormous commercial success of *Eliminator* is, of course, inextricably linked to the trio of video clips for "Gimmie All Your Lovin'," "Legs," and "Sharp Dressed Man." For any rock fan—or *anyone*, for that matter—who was around in the early eighties, it was impossible to hear even a few bars of any of these songs without having visual images from the clips immediately spring to mind: the flashy *Eliminator* car, a custom hot-rodded 1933 Ford coupe; the trio of hot eighties babes, and the avuncular presence of ZZ Top themselves flashing the signature hand jive mudra formally known as "the presentation."

It was a pivotal moment in rock history. MTV had been launched in 1981, broadcasting nothing but music video clips 24/7. The problem was there was a scarcity of what would now be called content. Most rock and pop artists weren't routinely making promotional video clips back then. So early MTV tended to be dominated by the more fashion conscious and visually literate British synth-pop acts like Depeche Mode, Duran Duran, and Spandau Ballet, and dance-oriented artists like Michael Jackson and Madonna, who were accustomed to a more visual, "song and dance" mode of presentation and were therefore ahead of the curve when it came to video.

Into this stylish arena, in 1983, came three grizzled sidewinders from Texas, unlikely but ultimately welcome guests at this strange new party. "We had a couple of forward-thinking, behind-the-scenes guys," says Billy, "and saw the opportunity for us to engage in this new thing called video."

For art school graduate and pop art aspirant Billy F Gibbons, the music video phenomenon was a dream come true: a chance to move far beyond even the vast visual ambitions of the 1976 Worldwide Texas Tour. An opportunity to create a visual analog to the mojo sound of rock and roll. Gibbons possesses a keen awareness that America's most powerful creative contribution to the world is not its highbrow art but rather its colorful popular culture: big finned Cadillacs and other masterpieces of Detroit mobile sculpture, rock and roll, the blues, Hollywood moves. . . . These are the art forms that fascinated the entire world for much of the twentieth century and continue to be globally influential.

Billy had long been an aficionado of dirt-track hot-rod culture in particular. He'd worked with automotive chop artists Pete Chapouris and Jake Jacobs to create the *Eliminator* car, which became a central trope for both the album and the videos. "*Eliminator*" is a speedway term for a winning vehicle—the one that tops, or eliminates, all competition. Drag-strip artist Tom Hunnicutt created the myth-making graphic illustration of the car for the album's cover. And it was a no-brainer to include the car itself in the promotional clips for the album.

In bringing their unique aesthetic to the video screen, ZZ Top found an ideal ally in director Tim Newman. "This was a period when there was a very small, but select, drawing pool of directors who might be willing to get involved in this video game," Billy recollects. "And Tim Newman's reel arrived. Tim really had a grasp on a totally American pop culture feel. He'd done advertising work for Coca-Cola. He had done so much work that brought in the bright lights and neon signs and pretty girls with cars. He liked what we did. He liked the fact that we had the car and the pretty gals wanted to get on camera. So it was a combination that seemed to work. The first crack out of the box was 'Gimmie All Your Lovin',' followed by 'Sharp Dressed Man' and 'Legs,' creating what we call the ZZ Top Trilogy, our first entry into Videoland. In those days, it was a weekend shoot that started on Friday at six p.m., and you had to quit by Sunday at six a.m.. You had to stay up all night, hanging out with the good lookin' gals, drivin' fast cars. Good combo. Wing it."

As director, Newman faced a unique challenge: how to create an appealing pop music video clip around three guys who, by their own admission, were hardly photogenic, no longer in the full flower of youth, and whose sex appeal would be apparent to only a very small, highly bizarre percentage of the viewing public. The answer was to create narrative, rather than performance-based, video clips in which ZZ Top appear on the sidelines of the main action, yet are still somehow essential to the proceedings: kind of like the chorus in ancient Greek drama.

So each of the clips features the same elements: the *Eliminator* car, a trio of sexy girls tricked out in full eighties hot regalia, and a young, working-class protagonist caught in a dead-end job. In each video ZZ Top appear, quasi magically thanks to a video "dissolve" effect, and deliver the protagonist from his or her mundane existence. In each case the car is, quite literally, the vehicle of deliverance. The symbolically charged moment occurs when Billy, Dusty, and Frank toss the keys to the car, glistening with video enhancement and adorned with the ZZ Top logo, to the protagonist. So the band functions, in essence, as magical benefactors, the three wise men. The car keys become the gift of the magi.

Much of the imagery is based on the mystical connotations of the number three: the holy

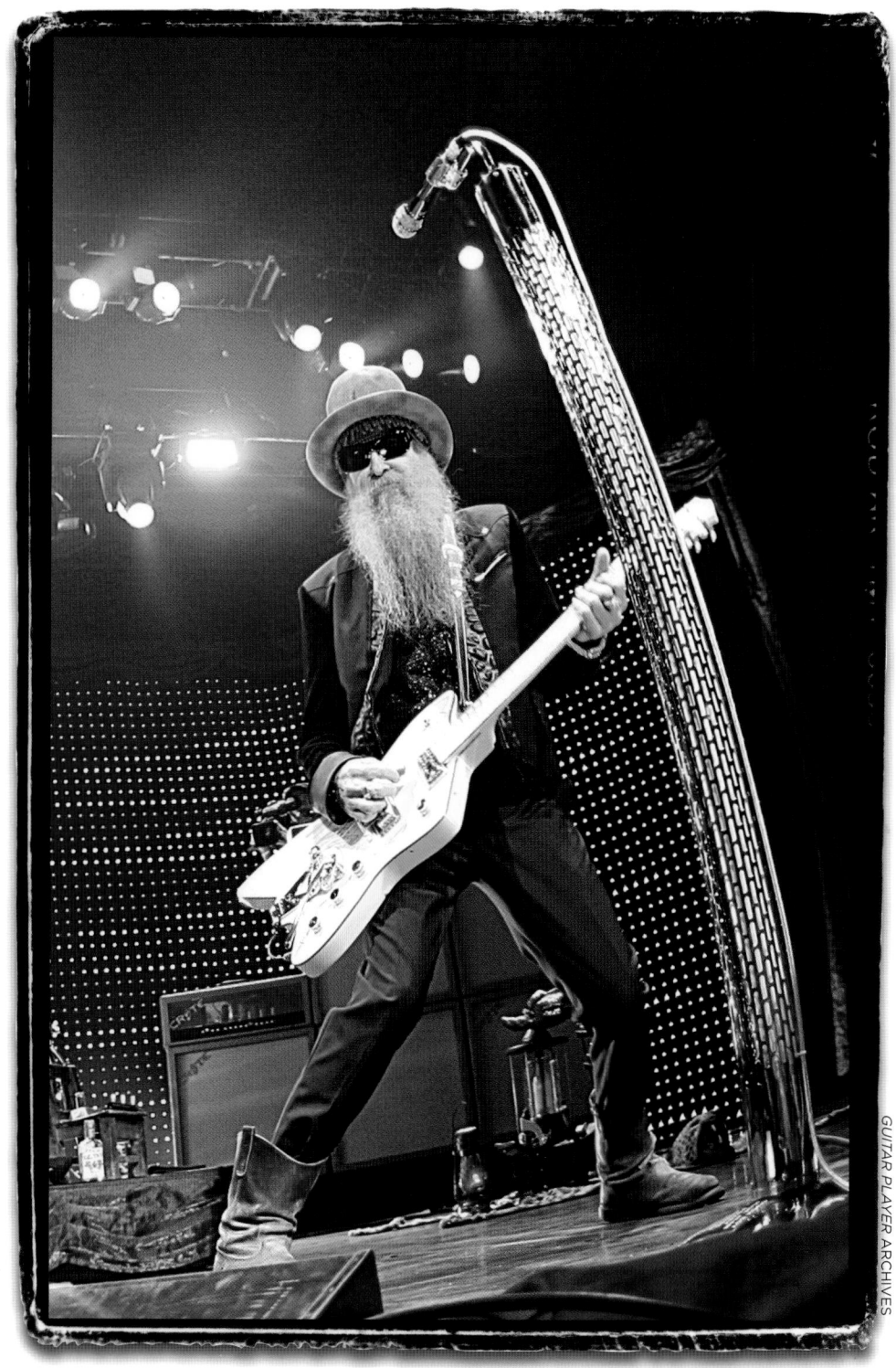

trinity, the three witches in *Macbeth*, the three wishes granted in nearly every culture's folktales. The three girls function as counterparts to the three ZZ Top guys—extensions of the band's power to rescue the protagonist from servitude and drudgery. In the "Gimmie All Your Lovin'" video, the three girls take the car mechanic protagonist for a ride and give him some hot lovin'. (Off camera of course.) In the "Legs" clip, they become agents of feminine empowerment, helping the protagonist, a harassed shoe store clerk, to discover and unleash her own inner babe-hood.

The girls bring the sex. ZZ Top bring the rock and roll. The subtext of all the videos, of course, is the redemptive power of rock and roll itself. The music has long been treasured as a "way out" for working-class people, whether by actually becoming a rock star or just locking yourself in your room and blasting rock music until the pain goes away. With *Eliminator* and its video clips, ZZ Top brought that grand rock-and-roll tradition, not to mention its blues antecedents, into a new medium, a new decade and a whole new pop music paradigm. Needless to say, it did wonders for the band's career. In the seventies, they'd pretty much been a working man's band. But with *Eliminator*, their appeal began to cross gender and class boundaries.

"The video expansiveness and explosion brought the guys and girls together," Billy observes. "They wanted to be part of this ever-promising successful ending to the films. And they started showing up in the audience. There were guys with their girlfriends who could relate to the happy ending. It's what everybody wanted. Still do."

Amid all the eye candy that flashed by in the video trilogy, guitar geeks were quick to pick up on the outlandish instruments wielded by Billy and Dusty. In the "Gimmie All Your Lovin'" and "Sharp Dressed Man" videos, they perform on vintage, yet strangely headless, Fenders (a Strat and P-Bass, respectively), emblazoned with racing pinstripes. What no one knew was that these sharp-looking axes weren't actually playable.

"The headless Fender guitars were the genius brainstorm of our friend Jim Hammond, who was in Fort Worth, Texas, willing to assist in any way he could, knowing that this filmed moment was coming up," says Billy. "Around this time, the first Steinberger instrument appeared, the first headless guitar, which had started to show up in videos. And I remember seeing Andy Summers playing the [Gitler] fishbone skeletal guitar, which was really outside. So the headless guitar seemed to be the order of the day. Well, we had none. So we went to see our buddy Jim in Ft. Worth. He said, 'Well, do you have a couple of guitars?' I said, 'We've got these matching Fenders. They're left over from when we wanted to play surf music: Olympic white with tortoise-shell pick guards.' He said, 'Yeah, I can help you out. Give them to me a second.' Well, he was gone for fifteen or twenty minutes. He went into his back room, where he had a construction shop. He pulled out a big band saw and cut the headstocks off. He got some fishing line and drew it down the back to replace the strings. And that was our headless instrument. We got plenty of questions. 'How did you tune those things?' The good news is you can get away with that on film."

Starting out as emissaries for the all the wild freedom embodied by the great state of Texas, ZZ Top now became worldwide ambassadors for the free spirit of all American culture. The cover art for 1985's *Afterburner*, with its space shuttle imagery, expanded the visual metaphor to embrace the entire universe. But the sound offers the same blend of eighties synth technology and vintage fifties guitar tone as *Eliminator*. Perhaps the band was doing a lot of camping at the time. This was the album that gave the world "Sleeping Bag," "Woke Up with Wood," and "Velcro Fly." It also contained the only power ballad in the ZZ Top canon, "Rough Boy." With cavernous, digitally detuned drums, and layers of velvety synth chording, it was another huge hit for the band: a slow-dance fave, but also somehow believable. How else can a guy who hasn't shaved in eight years seduce a lady than by offering himself up as a "Rough Boy"?

Recycler is the third and last in the series that Billy calls ZZ Top's "-er" albums. The name *Recycler* is perhaps all too apt. Synth pop was dead as a doornail by 1990, when the disc was released, and the *Eliminator* formula, so fresh at first, was starting to sound mighty stale. The band themselves seemed to realize it. *Recycler*'s most successful track, "My Head's in Mississippi," harks back to the bluesy grind of ZZ Top's earlier days while also hinting at what was to come.

❧ THE RCA/BMG YEARS (1992–PRESENT): ❧ REFUGE IN THE HOME OF ELVIS

In 1992, ZZ Top signed a new record deal with RCA for what was reported in the trade press to be a whoppin' great chunk of money, a phenomenal deal even for those wild, crazy, high-flyin', Bill Clinton, dot.com bubble nineties. Right on the brink of the record industry's almost total meltdown and the subsequent global decline of the world's entire economy, the Texan trio had once again landed in the honeypot. A bonus for Dusty Hill was that RCA had been the label of his number-one rock-and-roll hero, Elvis Presley.

The band's first album for their new label was 1993's *Antenna*. It marked the beginning of ZZ Top's third incarnation, one that is almost the direct antithesis of their flush, tricked-out eighties sound and persona. The ZZ Top of the nineties and beyond is a lean and hungry beast. The sound is stark and nasty, like a spiny serpent slithering through a dry, barren desert, intent on survival, yet still somehow lookin' for some tush. The music offers a stripped-down yet triumphant restatement of the core ZZ Top values: gritty blues and the sound of steel strings amplified through vintage tubes. The title of the album paid homage to the lawless Texas radio stations that had inspired Gibbons, Hill, and Beard when they were kids.

Rhythmeen (1996) came next. It too is a raw and bluesy outing, but as always, Billy had a few twists to add to the plot. "During the recording of *Rhythmeen*," he relates, "Rick Rubin [producer of Tom Petty, Slayer, Red Hot Chili Peppers, and others] had turned me on to one of his acts called Bark Market. Wow. Just a scary band. And the guitar players' favorite tuning was down to C♯ and B. So we began experimenting with really low tunings. *Rhythmeen* is probably the best example of ZZ Top's foray into the super-low frequencies. It not only changes the way you play but the way an instrument begins to sound. There's a standard tuning, but who says so? It's whatever you come up with."

Billy's fascination with collecting African artifacts began around the time of *Rhythmeen*. This is roughly when he also began to sport a distinctive piece of headgear, a sort of dark brown beanie fitted with nubs of fabric somewhat resembling dreadlocks just starting to grow out. Billy often describes it as an African hat. Once, when asked to remove it in a bar, he told the barman, "*Es mi pelo*. It's my hair."

The African preoccupation is also reflected on *Rhythmeen*.

Several tracks include African tribal percussion instruments from Billy's collection, including massive log drums. Some of these currently reside in the front yard of the guitarist's Hollywood residence, beautiful lawn sculptures, but like most African *objets d'art*, functional as well.

"When we were in the studio recording the log drums," Billy narrates, "the engineer kept coming on the talkback saying, 'Is something broken in there? I keep hearing this rattle.' We checked the drum kit, the guitars and amps, but finally we realized that sound was coming from the log drums. Inside we found these bits of rubber, shapeless chunks right from a rubber tree. Apparently they'd been put in there deliberately to create this buzz when you hit the drum. So those African tribesmen, they knew about distortion, man!"

ZZ Top celebrated their thirtieth anniversary in 1999 with *XXX*, another fine collection of Delta musings and double entendres, this time with a hip-hop influence thrown into the mix. And the band's latest release is *Mescalero* (2003), a potent distillation of all that is intoxicating about ZZ Top. Against a grainy backdrop of low-down dirty guitars, Billy sings in a sepulchral croak that could peel the paint off of Tom Waits's barn. And there's even a leering, leather-lunged Dusty number, "Piece." The disc brings the boys back to *La Frontera*. There's the occasional dash of marimba, concertina, and lyrics *en Espanol*. The cover art replays the *Eliminator* videos as a Mexican Day of the Dead cartoon. Though drunk and long deceased, the guy gets the girl and roars off down the highway. Off to the roadside, three bony hands flash the victory sign. *Los Tres Hombres* rock on.

ZZ Top albums are further and fewer between than they once were. But Gibbons seems of late to have effortlessly sidestepped (transcended?) a declining music industry. On December 14, 2005, he married the actress Gilligan Stillwater, the couple reluctantly taking the plunge after having known one another for some twenty years. And Billy himself has begun to carve out a career as a television personality, notably playing the role of a rock-and-roll dad who intimidates his son-in-law in the crime drama *Bones*. One senses that even if electricity, the mass media, Internet, and all forms of telecommunication were to disappear tomorrow, Billy F Gibbons would still find a way not only to survive but to draw attention to himself.

At the time of this writing, ZZ Top have once again entered the studio with uber-producer and music biz Svengali Rick Rubin, another gentleman with a copious beard. One of the producer's specialties is reviving the career of veteran musical artists by bringing them back to their roots and core values, a service he's performed for everyone from Johnny Cash to Neil Diamond. It's reported that this is what he's up to in the studio with ZZ Top as well.

"It's an interesting affair," says Gibbons. "Rick is a remarkable fellow. He is not afraid of experimentation. I think it sounds attractive to say, 'we're going back to basics and back to roots.' But I don't think we ever left. We threw in a couple of interesting additives along the way. But it's still three guys playing three chords and trying to uphold the presence of interpreters. Now we're not the originators. All we want to preserve is that sense of interpretation."

Of course, Gibbons has also often said that he's planning a solo album, an EP with his pal Keith Richards, and a disc of ZZ Top classics as performed by the band today.

Will any of these recordings ever see the light of day? With Billy F Gibbons there's no way of telling. That's another one of the rules. But it's nice to know that his hyperactive, uniquely creative brain shows no signs of slowing down.

James Burton

THE SOUL OF A SIDEMAN

THE SOUND AND STYLE of James Burton and his Fender Telecaster guitar are deeply engrained in the fabric of popular music. Our very notion of what an electric guitar sounds like owes more to Burton's playing than many of us realize. The quintessential sideman, he has contributed—often anonymously, but always vitally—to the music of the past sixty years, from Elvis Presley to Elvis Costello, from Merle Haggard to the Monkees, from Johnny Cash to John Denver, from Wanda Jackson to Emmylou Harris, from *Louisiana Hayride* to *Shindig!* Perhaps more than any other guitar player, Burton's career spans all the great entertainment media of the past half century or so: television, film, records, radio, and live performance. He was multimedia before anyone knew that word. That's one factor that has enabled his crisp, clean riffs and snaky melodicism to embed themselves so thoroughly in our collective consciousness.

As a guitar hero, Burton is resolutely against type. When the lead guitar player became a demigod in the sixties and egos loomed larger than towering Marshall stacks, Burton remained content with the sideman's humble role, contributing to the music without having to hog the limelight, conveying more emotional truth in a concise twelve-bar solo than other guitarists put across in a twenty-minute feedback free-for-all.

"It's very interesting to listen to a group of people play and find some way to add something to it," Burton says. "And it's not how fast you play or how much you play. It's what you play and where you place it in the song. That's the most important."

Burton's elegantly understated guitar style is an extension of the man himself—a soft-spoken, plain-dealing, God-fearing country boy born in the small town of Dubberly, Louisiana, on August 21, 1939. "My mother told me that I loved music ever since I was big enough to walk," he recalls. "Every time they'd play the radio, I'd dance to the music they were playing. She knew I had music in me."

> *"It's not how fast you play or how much you play. It's what you play and where you place it in the song. That's the most important."*

When James was around ten, his family moved to Shreveport, Louisiana, an important crucible for American roots music and career launching pad for both Hank Williams and Elvis Presley. Not long after the move, Burton received his first guitar, a simple acoustic. "My dad played a little guitar," he says. "But nothing serious. I'm self-taught. You might say God was my teacher. So I had the best teacher in the world. I trained my ear and learning how to play off of listening to records and earlier guitar players and just music in general. The early guitar heroes that I loved were Chet Atkins, Les Paul, and Merle Travis. I used to love to watch Merle on those early TV shows where he would play [bluegrass standard] 'Nine Pound Hammer' and all those great songs."

At around age thirteen, James graduated to his first electric guitar, a '51 or '52 Fender Telecaster purchased by his parents. At the time, the Tele was a brand-new instrument—a blank canvas, if you will, awaiting some gifted mid-twentieth-century artist to come along and create a new mode of expression around the bright, steely tone of this new kind of solid-body guitar. James Burton became one of the pioneering guitarists who formulated the Telecaster "vocabulary."

"At age thirteen, I was already playing in little talent shows and stuff," he recalls. "I'd win maybe a $100 bond or something like that. Music was my love, and the guitar was the natural instrument for me to play."

When he was fourteen, Burton joined the house band for the seminal country music radio (and later television) program *Louisiana Hayride*, broadcast live out of Shreveport on radio station KWKH. The fledgling guitar player received a first-class education playing alongside legendary country musicians like pianist Floyd Kramer and steel guitar players Felton Pruett, Sonny Trammell, and Jimmy Day. Meanwhile, Burton had already begun to moonlight at the local Shreveport clubs, backing singer Dale Hawkins. It was as a member of Hawkins's band that he created one of his first signature riffs, for the song that would become the rock-and-roll standard "Susie Q."

ARCHIVE PHOTOS/GETTY IMAGES

"I was underage, just fourteen years old, and I had to get a permit from the courts to actually go into the nightclubs and work with Dale Hawkins. I came up with this little guitar lick and this little instrumental that we would play every night. We started to get requests for it. I didn't even have a name for it. They just said, 'Play that instrumental!' And later on, Dale said, 'I need to write some lyrics to this little guitar lick thing.' He did and that became 'Susie Q.'"

The song was recorded at KWKH radio in Shreveport, the same place where *Louisiana Hayride* originated. "It was up on the third or fourth floor in this building downtown," Burton recalls. "We went in there on a weekend and this good friend of ours recorded it in the studio. We had one or two mikes sitting around. And then Dale got this record deal with Chess Records, who put out the song. Man, we started getting all kinds requests for 'Susie Q.' It got a lot of play and became an overnight success."

With that lick and song, Burton says he found his own unique take on electric guitar playing, a potent amalgam of country, blues, and nascent rock and roll. The key is his unique approach to combination picking, a blend of both plectrum and finger-style playing.

"When I wrote 'Suzy Q,' I got into that finger-picking thing, like the Chet Atkins style, only I

did mine completely different," he explains. "Because I didn't use a thumb pick like Chet. I used a flat pick and a finger pick on my second [middle] finger. My style came together doing 'Susie Q,' playing the bass string and rhythm feel along with the lead picking. Very similar to the Chet and Merle Travis style, but I created my own identity out of that."

Burton soon got to take that style all the way to Los Angeles as a guitar player for rockabilly singer Bob Luman. Those heady mid-fifties years witnessed the breakthrough of a brand-new, high-energy, intensely rhythmic mash-up of R&B and country music called rock and roll. Rockabilly was (and is) a wild, outsider rock-and-roll subgenre placing extra emphasis on the country side of the equation. As such, it proved a perfect medium for Burton's emerging guitar style. His gig with Luman had come through *Louisiana Hayride* producer Horace "Hoss" Logan, who also managed Luman. Can't get more country than that.

And so a sixteen-year-old Burton set off for the West Coast as part of Luman's band. "My parents weren't crazy about me leaving home," he admits, "but my career started to skyrocket." For a teenage boy hitting the road as a professional musician, the temptations and pitfalls must have loomed large. Then, as now, drugs and booze were everywhere. But early exposure to this aspect of the traveling musician's life seems to have afforded Burton a perspective that has left him a steady and sober road warrior.

"I saw all that stuff when I was fourteen or fifteen years old," he says. "Seeing all them people pull themselves down. I learned about that at a very early age. And I agreed not to participate and be a part of that. There are lot of people, not just entertainers but people in sports and other fields . . . a whole range of people who seem to have a 'crutch' problem. That's what I call it. If you have to have a drink to get onstage, I call it a crutch. A lot of people gotta have that to do what they feel is their best. But I don't go there. I want to help these people the best way I can. I don't ever downgrade anybody. I just want to help them, pray for them."

An extremely youthful James Burton made his screen debut backing Luman in the 1957 Roger Corman "roxploitation" flick *Carnival Rock*. This slice of rock culture camp would prove the first of many Burton appearances in the visual media. The next step in that career trajectory came when Luman recorded a cover of the Billy Lee Riley rockabilly classic "Red Hot" in LA for Imperial Records.

"We were rehearsing the song at Lew Chudd's office, who was the owner of Imperial Records. And Jimmie Haskell, who was music director on the *Ozzie and Harriet* show and also working for Lew, was there too."

The Adventures of Ozzie and Harriet was one of the archetypal sitcoms of television's early days. An exciting new mid-century medium, television had first become commercially available in the late forties and rose to prominence in the fifties, buoyed by variety shows and sitcoms depicting the relatively harmless trials and tribulations of fictitious middle-class Caucasian families. Typical of the genre were *Father Knows Best*, *The Donna Reed Show*, and the aforementioned *The Adventures of Ozzie and Harriet*, starring big-band leader Ozzie Nelson, his wife, Harriet, and their two sons, David and Ricky. This was the only sitcom where the actors were an actual family. And the younger Nelson sibling, Ricky, was a talented singer and real-life rockabilly devotee of artists like Elvis Presley and Carl Perkins. Ricky had launched a career as a pop/rock-and-roll singer in tandem with his acting role on his family's hugely successful television show. He was signed to Imperial Records, which is how he met Burton on the aforementioned Bob Luman "Red Hot" date.

"We were rehearsing at Imperial with Bob," Burton recalls. "James Kirkland was on bass and Butch White was on drums. Ricky was there on business and he wanted to hear the music. He said, 'Who's in the room playing?' They said, 'That's Bob Luman and his group the Shadows. We had the name the Shadows back then. Ricky came in and stayed for about three hours listening to us play. And the next day he sent a telegram out to the home we had out in the [San Fernando] Valley in Canoga Park. He wanted us to come to General Service Studios, which is where they did the *Ozzie and Harriet* show. And he wanted us to bring our instruments, so we did. We met the whole family and we played a little bit for Ozzie. He said, 'Hey, man, this is great. You guys mind doing something on the TV show?' We said, 'Sure, we'd love to do it.'"

"When I wrote 'Suzy Q,' I got into that finger-picking thing, like the Chet Atkins style, only I did mine completely different."

One thing that set *Ozzie and Harriet* apart from other TV family sitcoms of the era was a concluding segment devoted to a musical performance by Ricky and his band. This brief but hugely influential spot brought rock and roll into American homes that weren't quite ready to accept African American rock and rollers like Little Richard and Chuck Berry, or more edgy white rock-and-roll performers like Elvis Presley and Jerry Lee Lewis. So Burton's guitar work was heard by a wider audience than other rock players enjoyed at the time. The TV appearances were complemented by a string of hit singles that made Ricky Nelson a major pop idol of the late fifties and early sixties. Burton made his debut with Nelson on the 1958 track "Poor Little Fool."

The tune had been written by Eddie Cochran's girlfriend, the songwriter Sharon Sheeley, and originally presented to, but rejected by, Elvis Presley.

"It didn't really fit Ricky either," says Burton. "But I took the song and we rewrote it, redid it, recorded it, and it became a hit."

A string of well-crafted hit recordings followed in its wake, including "Lonesome Town," "Travelin' Man," and "Hello Mary Lou." A versatile performer, Nelson's voice and delivery were equally suited to ballads and up-tempo rockers alike. "Lonesome Town," from 1958, features Burton on acoustic guitar and backing vocals from the Jordanaires, who were Elvis Presley's backup singers—a harbinger of things to come in Burton's eventful career.

The 1961 pop classic "Travelin' Man" was originally written for the legendary Sam Cooke by Burton's friend, the tunesmith Jerry Fuller. The song adheres closely to the harmonic and melodic structure of Cooke hits like "Wonderful World" and "You Send Me." But Cooke's manager nonetheless passed on it. The demo was literally fished out of the manager's trash can by Nelson's bass player at the time, Joe Osborn. It became one of the biggest hits of Nelson's career and indeed the entire era.

One thing that nearly all of Ricky Nelson's hits have in common is a concise, compelling

James Burton guitar solo. These are some of the records that help establish the rock guitar solo as a set piece, a mini-composition in its own right. So it's amazing that they were all improvised on the spot, according to Burton. "I played the solo in one take and off the top of my head on 'Hello Mary Lou' and all those tunes. We worked fast in those days."

In the early part of Burton's tenure with Nelson, he actually lived with the singer's family in what would seem to be a real-life counterpart to the warm, wholesome home environment depicted on the Nelsons' TV program. "They invited me into their home," Burton fondly recalls. "I was like the third son. It was Ricky, David, and James. Ozzy just said, 'I know what it's like being away from home at such a young age. You're a part of our family anyway, so we'd like you to be with us.'"

On breaks from touring and performing on television with Nelson, Burton would return home to visit his family in Louisiana. And it was on one of these vacations back home that he met the love of his life, his wife, Louise. They met at the home of Louise's sister, who was married to one of Burton's musician pals.

"They invited me over to dinner one night and Louise was there. That was quite a night. Louise was a lovely lady and we hit it off. Afterwards I offered to drive her home and we went for a little ride. And of course you like to go to your favorite spots to have a drink and visit with friends. So Louise and I had a pretty interesting night and a great visit. We became real good friends and later on we got married. She was eighteen when we got married and I was twenty-one or twenty-two. I was working with Ricky and she was working for Sears and Roebuck, in the cosmetics department. When we first got married, she stayed in Shreveport for about a year, working her job, and then she came out to California, and that was it."

The couple established their home in Toluca Lake, a leafy LA suburb that was also home to celebrities like Bob Hope, Frank Sinatra and actor William Holden. Traveling and working musicians often find it hard to maintain a relationship and home life, but this has never been a problem for the steady, steadfast Burton.

"You learn to separate your business and your pleasure," he says. "You have to. Louise is a very busy lady. She had her own real estate and mortgage company in Toluca Lake. So we both had our businesses going."

Like many American rock and pop stars of the fifties and early sixties, Ricky Nelson's fame began to fade with the coming of the Beatles and the British Invasion to America in late '63. But Burton didn't miss a beat, transitioning easily from Nelson's band to the Shindogs, who were the house band on America's most popular rock music television show of the mid–sixties, *Shindig!* Produced by English showbiz entrepreneur Jack Good, the ABC-TV program was American television's leading and most influential showcase for British Invasion hit makers like the Beatles, the Rolling Stones, the Who, the Kinks, the Yardbirds, the Hollies, the Zombies, and their compatriots, not to mention the top US pop and rock talent of the mid-sixties.

As the program's house band, the Shindogs backed vocalists ranging from Marianne Faithful to Howlin' Wolf. They also did prerecords for many of the less adept self-contained groups who appeared on the show. The group would then lip-synch to the prerecord before the cameras.

"We did a lot of live stuff, but most of it was prerecorded," says Burton. "We probably ended up recording 90 percent of the show for the artists who came in to do the show. It was just great playing behind people like Jerry Lee Lewis, Ike and Tina Turner, and Howlin' Wolf."

It's difficult today to convey the impact of *Shindig!* on mid-sixties American youth culture. The show was watched religiously by teens and preteens and was far superior to network competitors like *Hullabaloo* and *Shivaree*. In the days long before cable television and the Internet, opportunities to see the great rock-and-roll bands and singers of the day were far and few between. There were only three broadcast networks and two or three local stations in any given area.

Network variety shows like Ed Sullivan's program would feature, at best, one rock band per show, often in a patronizing context. So rock and roll would command only three to five minutes of an hour-long program. Of the network pop programs that did present an all-music format, *Hullabaloo* was lamentably old-school, forcing visibly reluctant British Invasion icons to participate in lame comedy routines and the like. But with Jack Good's understanding of both the US and UK scenes, *Shindig!* was far more tuned in to what the youth culture wanted to see and hear.

"Jack knew what was going on," says Burton. "When we first met, he said, 'James, I love all the solos you played on all those Ricky Nelson records. I want you to be a regular on the show. I want you to be on every week.' I said, 'Well gee, Jack, that's great. What'll we do?' He said, 'We'll put a band together.' I said, 'What are we going to call this group?' He said, 'Oh, you'll be the Shindogs.'"

Along with Burton, many of the top LA-based musicians passed through the ranks of the Shindogs, including Glen Campbell, Billy Preston, Delaney Bramlett, Larry Knechtel, and Leon Russell. Short of Swingin' London itself, the program was the place to be in the mid-sixties.

"*Shindig!* was where I first met my old buddy Keith Richards, and Mick Jagger, Charlie Watts, and all those guys," Burton recalls. "When they came and did the show we just became real good friends. We were all like a family. It was great hanging out together and getting to know each other."

Shindig! also served Burton as a gateway to the top session work going down in LA at the time. "My phone just lit up," he says. "I was doing four or five sessions a day, seven days a week, with all different artists." In this period Burton worked with the Beach Boys, Buffalo Springfield, Buck Owens, Jan and Dean, Dean Martin, Mae West, Nat King Cole, and Nancy Sinatra, among many others. He was one guy who could do it all, a country date, a rock record, or a big orchestral session. He famously—or perhaps infamously—was one of the "stand-in" guitarists for the Monkees, along with Louie Shelton and Gerry McGee. The Monkees were derided at the time for not playing their own instruments on their records. But few people back then realized that one of the surrogate guitarists was also the guy who had "ghosted" the guitars for a good many of the acts on *Shindig!*

"Louie, Gerry, and I did some of the music for the Monkees TV show and then we did the records," says Burton. "We played on 'Last Train to Clarksville,' 'I'm a Believer,' and all that stuff."

One can only marvel at the sheer volume of session work that Burton did in this period. How could he handle all those dates? Does he read music?

"Not enough to hurt my playing," he laughs. "The great thing is that most people who work with me already know my past work and kind of want me just to do what I do. Like when I did a record with Henry Mancini. He came in and he had this music all written out that he came over and put on my music stand. He said, 'James, this is my idea of how the song should be. But don't

pay any attention to that. I want you to do your thing.' That's what most people want, just for me to be creative and be myself. That's the good thing about training your ear so that you can hear things beyond just the basic structure of the song and what the other people are playing. You can figure out where you can fit in."

Burton is almost as famous for the gigs he turned down as he is for all the work he's done. For instance, he passed on a chance to become part of Bob Dylan's touring band and declined the initial offer he received from Elvis Presley.

"They called me to do *Elvis's Comeback Special* [NBC-TV broadcast] in 1968, but I was doing an album with Frank Sinatra. We had a very busy week scheduled, and they didn't want me to take the time off. So I couldn't do it. But I recommended a friend of mine, Tommy Tedesco, and everything was cool. And then in '69 Elvis Presley called me and asked me to put a band together. We talked about everything. In fact, when we were talking on the phone he said, 'You know, I watched the *Ozzie and Harriet* TV show just to see you play the guitar and hear Ricky sing. I said to myself, 'The king of rock and roll watching me on TV?"

Right from that first phone call, Presley and Burton formed a deep bond. "It was like Elvis

and I had known one another all our lives," Burton marvels. "Our background in music was the same: country, gospel, and rhythm and blues. Elvis told me he didn't want to do movies anymore for a while. When he came out of the army [in 1960] he'd done nothing but movies for nine years. But he wanted to go back to his live audience. He really missed being onstage with a live band."

Presley's comeback was a somewhat risky move: 1968 was a long way down the road from his mid-fifties heyday as a sexy, young rock-and-roll icon. He'd put on a few pounds and his records were just barely making the bottom of the charts. The films he appeared in were increasingly dismal and almost universally panned by critics. Presley had also begun a flirtation with prescription drugs that would ultimately prove fatal. Moreover, the whole zeitgeist had shifted by '68. Psychedelia and Flower Power had claimed the fascination of the rock audience and mainstream culture. The day belonged to bearded Indian gurus and earnest young men sporting sandals, caftans, and long, flowing hair. Would anybody still be interested in a hefty country boy in a white leather bell-bottomed jumpsuit?

"It was just great playing behind people like Jerry Lee Lewis, Ike and Tina Turner, and Howlin' Wolf."

Presley's '68 TV special had given the lie to naysayers, turning his career around and putting him back in the limelight. But facing a live audience was a whole other matter. Presley struggled with stage fright on the evening of July 26, 1969, the opening night of a four-week engagement at the International Hotel in Las Vegas. The room was packed with celebrities, including Cary Grant, Sammy Davis Jr., Fats Domino, Ann-Margret, and Tom Jones. But it was James Burton to whom the King turned for solace on the eve of his return from exile.

"Elvis came up to me backstage before the show," Burton recalls. "He said, 'I'm so nervous. I'm climbing the wall, man. I don't know if I can go out there.' And I said, 'Elvis, I guarantee you that everything will be all right. When you walk out there, don't even pay any attention, just do three or four numbers, one right after the other, bam, bam, bam. Just get into it. It'll break the ice and it'll be like playing back home at Graceland. Those folks are gonna love you, man. They're dying to see you. The good Lord is going to bless us all.' We went out there and those people went nuts."

And so Burton became Presley's anchor, invariably standing just to the left of the King onstage. In live performances, Presley often seemed eager to turn the spotlight over to Burton for a mid-song guitar solo, as if handing over a heavy burden to a friend willing and able to bear the weight for a while. There was a hint of weariness and perhaps even desperation in the phrase Presley used night after night to set up a guitar break, "Play the song, James."

Presley could be unpredictable onstage as well. Arrangements were frequently abandoned. "The conductor would be pulling his hair out," Burton recalls. "Like if you have an eight-bar intro to a song with strings and horns. Everybody is playing, and Elvis might decide to come in after four bars instead of eight. Whatever Elvis wanted to do. It was his show. And that's what we'd do."

ROBERT KNIGHT ARCHIVES/REDFERNS/GETTY IMAGES

Set lists were jettisoned as well, or never drawn up in the first place. "We never did the same show twice," says Burton. "You never knew what Elvis was going to do. You couldn't take your eyes off him. You had to watch him every second. He was an incredible showman. When he walked on that stage, he had the people in the palm of his hand. And we had him covered. If he wanted to do "Blue Christmas" in the middle of August with 120-degree weather outside, it didn't matter to us. We were there with him. And he loved it. We were his family. I was very close to Elvis. He knew that I was going to tell him the truth and he loved that. We had great communication both on and offstage."

All of the players in Elvis's band were exceptional, anchored by the rhythm section of Jerry Scheff on bass and Ron Tutt on drums. Another *Shindig!* alumnus, Glen D. Hardin, eventually joined on keyboards. So Burton was in good company.

The affable guitarist also won the acceptance of the so called Memphis Mafia, the circle of buddies with whom Elvis had grown up and who surrounded him most of the time, acting as bodyguards, minders, and assistants, but mainly just keeping Elvis vibed up and jolly. Burton became a regular at Graceland, Presley's Memphis mansion where the King held court, sometimes with his wife, Priscilla, and brand-new daughter, Lisa Marie, also in attendance.

"We even did some recording at Graceland," Burton says. "The only problem was that Elvis would only come down and join us when he wanted to. He'd be up in his bedroom. We might be there eight hours before he decided to come down."

Another Graceland ritual was the dispensation of lavish gifts from Elvis to his loyal retainers. "I have a lot of jewelry and clothing that Elvis gave me," says Burton. "Rings, bracelets, necklaces, and some of those real nice custom shirts that he used to have made up. The ones with the puffy shoulders and band around the arm. Beautiful shirts. Sometimes we'd have a night of giving. He'd clean out his closets. But for some reason I was never around when he was giving out keys to cars. But whoever was there, man. . . . You didn't have to be a friend. If you were standing around, you might get the key to a new Mercedes, Cadillac, or Lincoln Town Car. Elvis would say, 'I want you to take this with you when you leave tonight. I don't ever want to see it again.' He was just so generous. Just a wonderful, gifted, and loving man."

During his tenure with Elvis, Burton added a home in Las Vegas to the one he had back in Toluca Lake. "We worked in Las Vegas so often with Elvis, and I didn't want to say in a hotel," he says. But perhaps Burton's most prized possession from this period of his life and career is a simple gold chain with a pendant in the shape of the letters TCB with a lightning bolt beneath.

"Elvis put that around my neck, and that was the only way you could get that TCB," Burton says. "It means 'Taking Care of Business.' And the lightning bolt is 'As Fast as You Can.' That was his motto."

It was during his time with Presley that Burton also acquired the instrument with which he is perhaps most closely associated today, his '68 Telecaster with paisley body decoration. This too was a gift. "When we opened at the International Hotel in '69, I got a call from a good friend of mine at Fender, Chuck Widener. He said, 'James, I got a guitar here with your name on it.' I said, 'Really? I'm getting ready to go to Vegas and rehearse with Elvis. Can you send the guitar to me?' He said, 'No, I want you to come down. I want to buy you lunch and I want you to check this out.' So I went and met him down in Fullerton, California, where the Fender factory was. I went in his office and the guitar was in a case in the corner. He said, 'There it is. Go check it out.' I went over, opened the case, and said, 'Oh my God. No, Chuck. This is not me.' He said, 'Yes, man. That's you. Take that guitar. I put that aside for you. That's yours.'" Given the cultural context, one can understand Burton's initial reluctance to embrace the instrument. The paisley Teles were developed in 1968 to cater to the burgeoning market for all things psychedelic. The hippie scene was peaking. Swirling paisley patterns were a very popular motif in youthful clothing design, as well as poster and album cover art for psychedelic rock bands. Paisley was thus heavily associated with the whole sixties counterculture package: hallucinogenic drug use, Indian mysticism, sexual liberation. . . . But Burton was as far from psychedelic as a man can get. A devout Christian, steadfast, down-home country picker.

"Whatever Elvis wanted to do. It was his show. And that's what we'd do."

Unlikely combinations, however, often turn out to be magical. Burton took the guitar with him to Vegas. "For the first two weeks of our time at the International Hotel, I played my old Tele—the one my mother and dad bought me. The one I played on all those 'Susie Q' and all those Ricky Nelson records. That guitar's been on thousands of records. But after two weeks, Red West came up to me. He was one of the Memphis Mafia guys who worked with Elvis. "Red said, 'James, play that new guitar tonight.' I said, 'I don't know. . . . It's a little too flashy. I don't know what Elvis might say. He might come down on me onstage. I don't wanna take a chance.' But then I got to thinking, 'What the heck? If he's gonna say something, I might as well get it over with.'

"So I played the paisley guitar on the first show that night. And Elvis didn't say anything onstage. I'm doing 'Johnny B. Goode' and he's standing there acting like he's playing the guitar. I was sure he saw it. Elvis always kept an eye on me for cues and playing licks. But he didn't say anything. So in between shows, we had about an hour off. I was in my dressing room. Red came down and said, 'James, Elvis wants to see you in his dressing room.' I said, 'Oh my God, here we go. . . .' So I went to Elvis's dressing room and he said, 'James, I notice you were playing a different guitar tonight.' I said, 'Yeah, I was a little nervous about bringing it on, Elvis. I thought it might be too flashy or not look good onstage.' He said, 'No, man, it looks great. Sounds great. Play that guitar.' My heart jumped back into place."

While also maintaining his usual busy schedule of session work, Burton remained with Presley right up until the iconic rock singer's passing in 1977. August 16 of '77 is a day that the guitarist will never forget. He was en route to Portland, Maine, with a group of Presley's musicians and backup vocalists. They were slated to commence a new tour there. The plane stopped in Boulder, Colorado, to refuel. Trombone player Marty Harrell went off to make a phone call.

"I figured I'd go call Louise," Burton remembers, "but I never made it to the phone. Marty was on the way back, and as we got close to each other I noticed he had a very strange look on his face. He came up to me and hugged me. He had tears in his eyes and he said, 'Elvis passed away.' Cold chills went all over me. I couldn't believe it. I said, 'Marty, is this a joke?' He said, 'No, it's for real.' So we went back to the plane and told the rest of the cast what happened. Needless to say, it was a long flight from there."

Presley had been found dead of a prescription drug overdose on the floor of one of the bathrooms at Graceland. Burton got the first flight he could book to Memphis and arranged for Louise to meet him at Graceland. "When I arrived, Ann-Margret, James Brown, and a lot of other people were there," Burton remembers. "Priscilla wanted to take me in the room where they had the casket. I told her no. I wanted to wait for my wife to get there. So when Louise came, we went in and saw Elvis. It was tough. James Brown had been in there for hours. I spent some time talking with Ann-Margret. She and Elvis had been real close." A few years earlier, Burton had lost another close friend and musical associate, the country-rock pioneer Gram Parsons, who died of a drug- and alcohol-related death in 1973. Burton had played on all three solo albums by the brilliant but troubled Parsons, who'd run with Keith Richards, but regrettably lacked Keef's miraculous gift for staying alive against all odds to the contrary. During Burton's time with Parsons, did he see any signs that his friend might not be in this life for the long haul?

"No," Burton replies. "You never go there. You don't look that far into the future. You live for today and hope for tomorrow. The main thing is what you're doing today. Gram and I were just loving making music together and being together. We were close, but we didn't hang out much. I had my family in California and Gram and I were at different points in our lives."

It was through Parsons that Burton met Emmylou Harris. The angel-voiced singer had been Parsons's musical partner and sometime girlfriend. And when Harris launched her solo career on Warner Bros. with the 1975 album *Pieces of the Sky*, Burton joined the singer and her producer Brian Ahern to cut the album in a big mid-century modern house in Beverly Hills. Also on the dates were Burton's fellow Elvis bandmates Ron Tutt and Glen D. Hardin. On bass was another *Shindig!* alumnus, Ray Polhman. Burton would record with Harris throughout the seventies and into the eighties and played guitar in the original lineup of her touring group, the aptly named Hot Band.

Country and rock music were merging in a big way in the seventies, with the ascendancy of artists like Harris, the Eagles, and others. And once again, Burton was uniquely qualified to take part, just as he had during the rockabilly fifties. His country roots run as deep as any, having made significant recordings with country icons like Merle Haggard, Hoyt Axton, Johnny Cash, Charlie Rich, Ronnie Milsap, Rodney Crowell, Hank Williams Jr., and others. His nimble Dobro slide-guitar work is as treasured as his crisp Telecaster stylings and serves him particularly well in country contexts.

"I got into Dobro fairly early," he says. "I figured if I could play guitar, I could play that too. So I got into all the different tunings and stuff."

But for all his country cred, Burton can effortlessly shift gears and play on a rock or pop record with equal sincerity and conviction. Artists in every genre have come to rely on him. There's a supreme confidence in his playing that has nothing at all to do with ego. Quite the opposite, it is born of a profound selflessness and humility.

"I'm just letting the good Lord do his job," he says. "He gave me my tools to work with and all the rope for how far I needed to go with it. This life is a blessing, and God wants us to use the talent that he gave us."

After Presley's passing, Burton began an extended musical partnership with John Denver, touring and recording with him over the course of sixteen years and twelve albums, right up until Denver's untimely death in a 1997 aviation accident. Joining him in Denver's band were his longtime comrades Jerry Scheff and Glen D. Hardin. The eighties and nineties also brought collaborations with everyone from Jerry Lee Lewis to Elvis Costello.

"I got to play with both Elvises," Burton laughs. "How about that! I was in my office in Toluca Lake one day and my phone rang. I picked up the phone and this voice said, 'Hello, James, this is Elvis Costello.' I said, 'The real Elvis Costello?' And he said, 'Absolutely.' He invited me to come play on his [1986] album *King of America*, along with Ronnie Tutt and Jerry Scheff. And that's when I met my good buddy T-Bone Burnett. I've done a lot of stuff with T-Bone, like Roy Orbison's [1988] TV special, *A Black and White Night*.

> *"There are so many great guitar players in the world and I've been blessed to have many of them as my buddies—Chet Atkins, Les Paul, Dick Dale, Jeff Beck, Jimmy Page, Pete Townshend, Hank Marvin, Don Rich . . . all of them."*

In recent years, Burton has found particular favor with latter-day classicists like Costello, Burnett, Gillian Welsh, and Jim Lauderdale—artists with a strong sense of musical history, who base their own phenomenal creativity on a solid and deeply nuanced awareness of working within a time-honored tradition. For them, as for us, Burton is a living embodiment of that tradition. A true patriarch, but one who is never content to rest on his laurels and is always pushing his craft to the next plateau.

In 1990 James and Louise left California and returned to live in Shreveport. "My family is here and so is hers," he says. "Her daddy got very ill and she wanted to come back and spend some time and be with him. When we came back for a visit, she found this wonderful place on the lake and talked me into it. So we bought the house and moved back. We just enjoy being here, although of course my work takes me all over the world. I'm in and out of Nashville, New York, LA, and London all the time. I enjoy the travel."

The Burtons maintain close ties with their son, Jeff, and daughter, Melanie. James has even done some recording with Jeff, who is a singer-songwriter. The drummer for that particular project was Darren Osborn, the son of bassist Joe Osborn, whom Burton hired to play in Ricky Nelson's band back in 1959 and who famously retrieved the "Travelin' Man" demo from the trash can.

Another major recent priority for the guitarist has been the James Burton Foundation. The charitable organization raises money to buy instruments to place in schools and children's hospitals,

helping to fill the void left by cutbacks in music education budgets for public schools in recent years. The foundation's big annual fund-raising event is a celebrity concert, the James Burton International Guitar Festival, held in Shreveport on or around Burton's birthday on August 21.

"The first show was in '05 and the artists were Brad Paisley, Steve Wariner, Dr. John, Steve Cropper, Seymour Duncan, and Eric Johnson. It was a great feeling. The guys all donated their time and talent for the children. We raised money to buy instruments and get music back in the schools. The payback is a wonderful thing. These kids are going to take over our legacy after we're gone. We just want to give them the best education and the best in instruments."

Donations can be made via jamesburtonfoundation.wordpress.com or sent to James Burton Foundation, 714 Elvis Presley Avenue, Shreveport, LA 71101. "You can donate money, guitars, or other instruments," says Burton. "We don't make a dime. All the money goes into the benefit fund for the children. So far we've given out over 6,000 guitars."

Burton suffered severe damage to both his ankles in the nineties when he fell from a tree he was trimming. A recent automobile accident has left him with persistent shoulder pain. But even these challenges don't seem to have slowed him down too much. In 2009 he won a Grammy for Best Country Instrumental for his contribution to the instrumental track "Cluster Pluck," on Brad Paisley's *Play* album. Paisley and Burton's co-guitarists on that recording were Vince Gill, Steve Wariner, Redd Volkaert, Albert Lee, John Jorgenson, and Brent Mason. The same year Burton won the Grammy, he was also inducted into the Louisiana Music Hall of Fame, an honor conferred upon him onstage at that year's James Burton International Guitar Festival.

If James Burton has met with great generosity in this life—and indeed he has—it is because his own generous nature has attracted good things and good people to him.

"There are so many great guitar players in the world and I've been blessed to have many of them as my buddies—Chet Atkins, Les Paul, Dick Dale, Jeff Beck, Jimmy Page, Pete Townshend, Hank Marvin, Don Rich . . . all of them. It's been wonderful being able to work with all these great guitar players and great entertainers. To be a part of their lives and have them be a part of my life as well. I'm thankful for the talent God gave me and my family and being able to help the children and newcomers in the business and to do good things. What a great life. I'm truly blessed."

David *Gilmour*

THE QUIET MAN

A DEFINING MOMENT—if not *the* defining moment—in David Gilmour's life came in early 1968, when he was twenty-two years old. He was in a Bentley, en route to a gig in Southampton in England with three members of the band he recently joined. The band was Pink Floyd. The three other musicians in the car were bassist Roger Waters, keyboardist Rick Wright, and drummer Nick Mason. Along the way, they were supposed to pick up the group's fifth member and leader at the time, the brilliant but psychologically unstable Syd Barrett, who had become increasingly troublesome, ruining several live shows and TV appearances with his erratic behavior. One of the Bentley's passengers—Gilmour recalls that it was Waters—said, "Oh, let's not pick up Syd."

"It certainly wasn't me." says Gilmour. "I was the new boy at the time, in the back of the car. And off we went to Southampton. We were playing with the Incredible String Band and Tyrannosaurus Rex that night."

With that offhand, but fateful, tdecision, Syd Barrett was ousted from Pink Floyd and David Gilmour found himself abruptly thrust into the limelight. A quiet, reserved man in the classic British mode, he was in many ways the antithesis of the extremely charismatic, wildly imaginative, and—at the time—hugely popular Barrett. Imagine if Mick Jagger had been booted from the Stones circa 1972 and Charlie Watts put forward to take his place.

Added to the pressure of having to fill Barrett's shoes musically and creatively was the fact that Gilmour had been Barrett's close friend since age fourteen. So it was difficult for him not to feel like a usurper. He played many of the band's early post-Syd gigs with his back to the audience for much of the time.

Yet—also in the characteristic British manner—Gilmour simply got on with the job. Not only did he persevere; he ultimately triumphed.

David Gilmour's plaintive, melodic lead guitar playing and ethereally soaring vocal style became the distinctive sonic signatures of Pink Floyd, a key factor in making the Floyd one of the most successful, enduring, and beloved rock groups of all time. Under Barrett's leadership, they might well have never made it out of the sixties, ending up a psychedelic footnote in rock history, filed somewhere between the Chocolate Watchband and Clear Light. But, due in no small part to Gilmour's unmistakable guitar style, Pink Floyd's music, brand, and name are still going strong today.

In the process, Gilmour has become a bona fide guitar hero. There is in his playing a profoundly natural and effortless quality that accounts for its tremendous appeal, but also tends to mask Gilmour's mastery as a guitarist. Never one to overplay or overemphasize technique, he is one of the most consummately tasteful players in the rock guitar god pantheon.

"I didn't start figuring in guitar-playing polls for a lot of years," he quietly states. "But I think one thing about the fingers and brain I've been given is that the fingers make a distinctive sound. I think I am instantly recognizable. I can hear myself and just know it's me. And other people do too. That may be a benefit. The way my fingers are, which is not very fast, I have to do things a different way. I play melodies that come to my brain. It's connected to things like Hank Marvin and the Shadows—that style of playing where people can recognize a melody with some beef to it."

Effortless as Gilmour's playing may seem, his musical path hasn't always been an easy one. The void left by Pink Floyd's early loss of its original leader, front man, and songwriter often placed Gilmour at odds with Roger Waters over the band's direction and leadership. Waters's approach is very much based on his psychological and socially conscious lyric writing, whereas Gilmour always stressed musicality. The resultant creative tensions made for some memorable combinations of words and music—classic songs like "Money," "Dark Side of the Moon," "Comfortably Numb," and "The Wall"—but also took an emotional toll on both men. Waters left Pink Floyd in 1985, leaving Gilmour to soldier on—once again—with the remaining original band members and some auxiliary players.

But increasingly over the years Gilmour's attention turned to his own solo projects. He reluctantly participated in a Pink Floyd reunion performance at London's Hyde Park in 2005. The historic event fueled eager rumors of a more protracted reunion of the classic Floyd lineup. However, the death of Rick Wright in 2008 precluded that from ever happening.

Which is fine by Gilmour. He's quite comfortable keeping Pink Floyd in a past-tense context. These days he is very much an elder statesman of rock, a tall, generously proportioned man with close-cropped white hair and, on most days, a snow white stubble of facial hair to match. He has a palatial home outside London that he shares with his second wife, Polly, their two children, and one of the world's greatest guitar collections. An avid pilot and plane spotter, he also has a collection of historic aircraft. When he wearies of all this, he can adjourn to his houseboat recording studio moored in an idyllic spot on the river Thames, just downstream from Hampton Palace. Life is good. When Gilmour does emerge for the occasional gig, solo CD, or high-profile guest appearance, he is greeted with the adoration of a dedicated and somewhat obsessive fan base.

"I think one thing about the fingers and brain I've been given is that the fingers make a distinctive sound. I think I am instantly recognizable. I can hear myself and just know it's me."

"Music is in my blood," he says. "It's what I do, although I'm not driven to do it all the time these days," he says. "I'm in my second marriage, I have young children, and I'm determined to enjoy my children growing up and be there for them more than I was with my first set of children. When one is younger and more ambitious, other people's needs tend to get rather ignored in one's quest to do as well as one can. And now my ambition is a little less than it was. But once I get going on a music project and I'm in the mood and my obsessiveness for the project kicks in, I do tend to become rather a perfectionist. And I certainly think the work I'm doing now is as good as anything I've ever done."

The genteel tone of Gilmour's current life by the river Thames is very much a reflection of the academic gentility of his childhood, which took place alongside another English river, the Cam, from which the historic university town of Cambridge takes its name. Born on March 6, 1946, Gilmour is the son of genetics professor Doug Gilmour and his wife, Sylvia, a teacher and filmmaker. This professional, pedagogic Cambridge family background is something that David shared with his two early friends and future Pink Floyd members, Roger "Syd" Barrett and Roger Waters.

The young David Gilmour first took to the guitar at age thirteen, at the tail end of the first great rock-and-roll wave in Britain and amid the early glimmerings of the American folk music boom. He cites folk players like Leadbelly and Pete Seeger as early influences, but also electric guitarist Hank Marvin, the leader of Britain's rock instrumental hit-makers the Shadows. "I learned guitar from Pete Seeger's tutorial album, *Folksinger's Guitar Guide*," Gilmour recalls. "That was the first instruction I had. The first track taught you how to tune it. That was pretty important."

Gilmour was fourteen when he first made the acquaintance of Syd Barrett. "We were friends first, then picked up the guitar," Gilmour recollects. This guitar-playing friendship lasted all through high school and continued as the two young men moved on to Cambridge's College of Arts and Technology. Barrett majored in art and Gilmour in modern languages. By then, rock and roll had entered an exciting new phase with the ascendancy of British bands like the Beatles, the Rolling Stones, the Kinks, and the Yardbirds and their many contemporaries. Soon Gilmour was making is own bid to become a would-be "British Invader."

"I was playing professionally in groups before Syd," says Gilmour. "And there's nothing like playing professionally. You've got to get on a stage and you're being paid for it. So you improve very quickly, because you have to. And Syd, technically speaking, was not as good as me when we were at college. We sat around learning Beatles songs, Rolling Stones songs, R&B and blues songs. I can recall spending some time working on 'Come On,' the first Stones B side or whatever it was. Working all that out, playing harmonicas and stuff. He'd know something and I'd know something and we just swapped, like people do in back rooms everywhere. He then left that college and moved up to an art college in London, which is when Pink Floyd got formed."

Barrett moved to London with another of his Cambridge friends, Roger Waters, both attending Regent Street Polytechnic. It was there that they connected with keyboardist Rick Wright and drummer Nick Mason, forming the Pink Floyd Sound, a name devised by Syd Barrett in honor of two obscure American bluesmen, Pink Anderson and Floyd Council. Of course, the band's name was eventually shortened to Pink Floyd. The group quickly became the toast of London's burgeoning psychedelic music scene, garnering a reputation for freeform, freak-out live performances combining a light show and film projections with passages of wild aleatoric instrumental improvisation. Barrett excelled at employing unconventional playing techniques to coax otherworldly sounds from his Fender Telecaster, the body of which he'd covered in mirrors to reflect and intensify the mind-bending lights and colors hitting the stage.

Yet Barrett could also turn around and craft letter-perfect psychedelic pop singles like the classics "Arnold Layne" and "See Emily Play." The latter track appeared on Pink Floyd's 1967 debut album, *Piper at the Gates of Dawn*, an enduring masterpiece of British psychedelia. Combining a childlike sense of wonder with a trippy, free-associative dream logic, Barrett's lyrics and music reflected the late-sixties mood of flower power innocence and consciousness-expanding experimentation with then-new hallucinogenic drugs like LSD.

Barrett became the darling of Swinging London, the Pied Piper of LSD. But the substance that had provided his magic carpet ride to fame and fortune also proved his undoing. He began to binge excessively on acid, which unraveled what may well have been an already psychologically unstable personality. Syd became abusive to girlfriends and dysfunctional as a performer. He was famously catatonic and mute during a Pink Floyd appearance on television's *American Bandstand* program, during the Floyd's first U.S. tour. Onstage, Barrett would detune his guitar and bang on the open strings randomly, and quite loudly, as the rest of the group attempted to perform songs from *Piper at the Gates of Dawn*.

And so Syd's old friend David Gilmour was called in to fill in on guitar, playing the parts that Barrett was no longer capable of playing, or perhaps simply no longer willing. To the best of Gilmour's recollection, he played about four shows with Barrett before Syd exited Pink Floyd, leaving Gilmour as the group's sole guitar player and new de facto lead singer. It was quite a leap for him, to say the least. While his old mates Barrett and Waters had become psychedelic pop stars in Britain's capital, Gilmour had stayed behind in London Cambridge and pursued a more mundane musical course, playing guitar with local groups the Newcomers and Jokers Wild, which were what we would now call Top 40 cover bands.

"We did Beach Boys, the Four Seasons, Rolling Stones, Beatles . . . the lot," Gilmour recalls.

"It was a very wide selection of songs, as with all bands who do bars and dances. You do all kinds of stuff. It was quite a good training."

Jokers Wild had managed to release a single—their rendition of Sam & Dave's "You Don't Know What I Know," with a cover of Otis Redding's "That's How Strong My Love Is." The disc sank like a stone when UK pirate radio broke the Sam & Dave original. And of course the Rolling Stones 1965 cover of "That's How Strong My Love Is" is the UK version that's best remembered today.

Given this journeyman background, it was a considerable stretch for Gilmour to move into the far more successful, drastically more original, and appreciably weirder Pink Floyd. But he plunged right in with characteristic aplomb: "I was aware of what Pink Floyd were," he says. "I knew them all for quite a long time. So I was expecting it to be strange and avant-garde. I rather enjoyed the process."

"I learned guitar from Pete Seeger's tutorial album, Folksinger's Guitar Guide. *That was the first instruction I had. The first track taught you how to tune it. That was pretty important."*

Gilmour's first recording sessions with Pink Floyd were for *A Saucerful of Secrets*, the band's second album and an attempt to follow up on the success of *Piper at the Gates of Dawn*. Barrett had done some recording for the album at London's fabled Abbey Road Studio before dropping out of the group. One person who was particularly pleased with Barrett's departure was Pink Floyd's producer Norman Smith. A fairly straight-laced Abbey Road staffer, Smith had engineered the Beatles early singles and had very little use for Syd's erratic behavior and lack of studio discipline.

"David Gilmour came in and things really looked up for me," Smith recalled shortly before his passing in 2008. "Because David was a completely different guy than Syd Barrett. Gilmour listened to everything I'd say. He loved learning from me about recording and sound techniques. Music-wise, he was interested in my past as a jazzman. Well, they all were. So I encouraged them and said, 'Let's have a couple of jam sessions then.' And we did. I went over to the piano and started something up. We had several sessions like that with David and they loved it. They were really good 'getting to know you' sessions. And also when David came, the group accepted a bit more of the melodic ideas that I had."

But still, says Gilmour, "once or twice Norman had to sort of swallow and face up to the fact that we weren't going to do it the way he thought." The abstract instrumental title track for *Saucerful of Secrets* was one such instance. The piece grew out of an effort to translate into music a diagram drawn by Roger Waters and Nick Mason, both of whom had studied architecture at Regent Street Polytechnic.

"To be honest, I'd just joined the group sort of a few minutes before that," Gilmour recalls. "So I just joined in and did my bit where appropriate. I remember watching Roger and Nick sitting around drawing weird shapes on a piece of paper. In the middle section of 'Saucerful of Secrets,' most of the time the guitar was lying on the floor. And I took one of the legs unscrewed from a mike stand. . . . You know where you have three legs a foot long—thick sort of steel? I was just whizzing that up and down the guitar neck, not very subtly."

But onstage at the time, Gilmour's role was still to be a Syd surrogate. "We weren't playing any tracks from *Saucerful of Secrets* live," Gilmour explains. "We were playing virtually all Syd's stuff. And they wanted me to sing his songs. Nobody else wanted to sing them, and I got elected. That was my job, to come and play Syd's parts and sing his songs. Initially, anyway. There was a long time when I was singing 'Astronomy Dominie' and all those things from the first album. Because there wasn't anything else to do. We had to do something. It was either that or back to Bo Diddley covers."

Fittingly enough, for his role as a Syd surrogate, Gilmour was equipped with a Fender Telecaster during his earliest days with Pink Floyd, but soon switched to a Stratocaster—the guitar that was to become his signature instrument. "I was twenty-one when I joined Pink Floyd—it was two months before my twenty-second birthday," he recalls. "And for my twenty-first birthday I'd gotten a Telecaster. I'd been in possession of that Telecaster for about ten months by then and that's what I started off on. But when we came over to the States for the first tour I did with Pink Floyd—in the summer of 1968—TWA [Trans World Airlines] lost my guitar in transport. So from Philadelphia I had to take a train to New York and go to Manny's [music store] and buy a new guitar. And I thought, 'Well, I'll get a Stratocaster this time.' So I got a Stratocaster, went back to Philadelphia, and played it that night."

The Strat would of course become an integral part of Gilmour's yearningly melodic guitar contribution to Pink Floyd, its steely tone soaring above Rick Wright's lush, atmospheric keyboard textures and the resolute rhythmic structures forged by Mason's drums and Waters's bass. But all of that was still in fairly scant evidence in 1968, following Syd Barrett's departure from Pink Floyd. Indeed, any prognosis for the group's survival would have looked quite bleak at the time. They'd not only lost their psychedelic heartthrob front man, singer, and guitarist, but also the guy who wrote the hit singles. At that point, no one else in the band had anything like Barrett's songwriting gift.

So there was a gaping void to be filled. But who best to fill it?

As Pink Floyd's new guitarist and best singer, Gilmour seemed the logical candidate to fill Syd's shoes. But he was fresh out of a copy band and hadn't really developed his songwriting skills. Meanwhile, Waters had his eye on the leadership role. He'd contributed to the songwriting and singing from the start. And in many ways, he had more in common with Syd. Both had lost their fathers at an early age, which became the basis of a deep bond between them. And it was Waters and Barrett who had gone off to art school in London together and formed Pink Floyd, leaving Gilmour behind in Cambridge. Waters and Barrett even shared the same first name, Roger.

What would emerge over time was a great—if always tense—songwriting partnership, pairing Gilmour's deeply entrenched musicality with Waters's unique lyrical sensibility. But it took several strange and aimless years for that to develop. Immediately following Barrett's departure, Pink Floyd had little choice but to fall back on the avant-garde improvisational side of their musical portfolio for both their live shows and their recorded output, which included 1969's *Ummagumma*, 1970s *Atom Heart Mother*, and the trippy soundtracks for the films *More* (1969) and *Zabriskie Point* (1970). Sonic experimentation, audio collages of "found" sounds, live retreads of earlier album cuts, and disjointed snippets of journeyman songcraft were the order of the day.

Fortunately for them, hit singles became less of a priority as rock and roll morphed into "album rock" at the dawn of the seventies. In fact, hit singles came to be rather looked down upon as rock music acquired pretensions to fine art seriousness. And Floyd's experiments with noises and randomness happened to slot in very nicely with the European art rock scene that was gaining momentum at the time.

"I don't think the band knew quite what direction they wanted to go in after Syd had left," Gilmour recalls. "And I certainly don't know that I could really understand what their direction was. Because there didn't seem to be one."

But out of the endless space jams and Pink Floyd's ever-increasing arsenal of music gear, a way forward finally did arise. While preparing material for the band's fifth album, 1971's *Meddle*, Gilmour began screwing around with a device called the Binson Echorec. "The Binson was an Italian-made delay unit," he explains. "It had a circular metal disc with [recording and playback] heads touching that. It had some wonderful delay techniques, which they don't have on anything they've ever made since. There was one thing it has where it does lots of repeats and you select the ones that it emphasizes. So it has little repeats and big repeats, and they all feed back into each other."

The device spawned two of *Meddle*'s most memorable tracks, the epic "Echoes" and the infectiously driving "One of These Days (I'm Going to Cut You Into Little Pieces)," the latter song featuring both Gilmour and Waters on bass guitar. "'One of These Days' came about from all the different things I was trying out on the guitar with the delay, to make various effects and sounds, a lot of which were also used on 'Echoes,' in fact," says Gilmour. "Roger one day decided to try it out for himself—this technique that I was developing—on the bass guitar. And he came up with the basic start of a riff, which we all worked on and turned into 'One of These Days.' For some reason, we wanted to do a double track of the bass. I was going to do one and Roger was going to do the other. We were going to play them both together live. You can actually hear it if you listen in stereo. There's one bass on one side and that's me. Then a bar later Roger joins in on the other side. We didn't have a spare set of strings for the spare bass guitar, so the one that follows in is very dull-sounding as compared with the other one. We'd sent the roadie off to buy new strings, but he wandered off to see his girlfriend instead.

"For the middle section," Gilmour continues, "another piece of technology came along, which was an H & H amp with vibrato. I tuned the vibrato to more or less the same tempo as the delay. But the delay was in three-quarter increments of the beat and the vibrato went with the beat. I just played the bass through it and made up that little section, which we then stuck on to a bit of tape and edited it in. We covered the joins with cymbal crashes."

"One of These Days" is spacey yet coherent, combining the sonic adventurousness that had by now become a Floyd trademark with a propulsive bolero-esque beat, rollercoaster dynamics, and dramatic organ stabs. It became a staple of the then-new "album rock" FM-radio format, satisfying a new rock audience's hunger for a deep listening experience, but one that also had a bit of melodic hook to it. The seventies had arrived, and Pink Floyd were to play a huge role in the decade's rock music. FM radio was broadcasting rock music in stereo with lots of deep bass. Concert PA systems and lighting gear were becoming more sophisticated. All of this coincided almost magically with Pink Floyd's discovery of a style and artistic vision that would make their texturally evocative studio

GIJSBERT HANEKROOT/REDFERNS/GETTY IMAGES

recordings and spectacular live shows one of the most ambitious and successful undertakings of the entire classic rock era.

"The *Meddle* album," says Gilmour, "is really where all four of us were finding our feet—the way we wanted to be."

But the album that really put the band on the map, of course, was 1973's *Dark Side of the Moon*. One of the bestselling records of all time, it offers a near perfect balance of Waters's brooding lyrical sensibility and Gilmour's expansive musical vision. It is the first Pink Floyd album to give full voice to Waters's big themes as a songwriter: social injustice, metaphysical angst, and the madness of Syd Barrett.

Waters's lyrical concept for *Dark Side of the Moon* is eloquent in its simplicity. The trials and sufferings of the human life cycle are neatly summed up in four themes, each with its own song: (1) "Time," (2) "Money," (3) War ("Us and Them"), and (4) Madness ("Brain Damage").

On *Dark Side*, Waters imagines himself inside Syd's madness. He appropriates Syd's insanity as the inevitable outcome of his own grim conclusions about life. It's one of the eeriest transferences of identity in all of rock. After struggling for years with the void left by Syd's absence, Roger Waters ultimately becomes Syd—fictively anyway. Like Banquo's ghost, Syd's specter would haunt many of Waters's greatest contributions to the Floyd canon.

At the time, Waters was quite heavily influenced by John Lennon's first solo album, *Plastic Ono Band*, which Lennon had created after undergoing psychologist Arthur Janov's primal scream therapy, in which patients relive emotional traumas from early life in order to release and finally relinquish the pain of those traumas. Through the *Plastic Ono Band* album, Lennon dealt with his feelings of having been abandoned by both his parents and with his conflicting emotions regarding his mother. And through *Dark Side of the Moon*, Roger Waters dealt with the childhood trauma of his father's death in WWII and the pain of losing his friend Syd Barrett to madness.

Waters's words tell the story, but it's Gilmour's plaintive guitar work that brings the emotions to life. *Dark Side* is where the guitarist's distinctive style comes fully to the fore—blues-based, to be sure, but recontextualizing the blues' primordial howl for a generation that had been psychedelicized and subsequently disillusioned. The album's best-known track, "Money," is a sardonic take on advanced-stage capitalist greed set to a twelve-bar structure. The rhythm lopes along in 7/4 time like a machine that's slipped a cog, the banal "ka-ching" of a cash register marking the downbeat. But then the groove pares down to a muscular 4/4 for Gilmour's tripartite guitar solo.

"'Money' was Roger's riff," says Gilmour. "He came in with the verses and the lyrics more or less completed. And we just started making it into a record. We sat and made up the middle sections and guitar solos and that stuff. We invented new riffs. We went back to 4/4 for the guitar solo and made the poor saxophone player [Chris Parry] play in 7/4 for his solo.

Gilmour traces the lineage of these time-signature shifts to both Lennon and Syd Barrett. "That's something Roger and I were both very keen on," he says. "John Lennon used to do that a bit, and Roger's a John Lennon fan. So I think he was keen on doing that because of John Lennon. And Syd was also very strange with time. He would sing a line, and when he finished singing the words he would change the chord. The time to change would be at the end of the lyric—it could be seven and a half beats for all anyone knew or cared. There are moments when it's very nice to get out of the structure of four or eight bars and change in the middle. We did it loads of times."

Extended guitar solos, often over twelve-bar blues structures had come into vogue in the late sixties. It provided a pretext for far too many guitarists to noodle on interminably over chorus after chorus. But Gilmour's extended guitar solo for "Money" does something completely different. Each of the three solo choruses has its own distinct sonic identity and mood, so there's a real sense of almost narrative progression, like a story unfolding.

"I wanted to make a dramatic effect with [the song's] three guitar solos," Gilmour sates. "The first solo is ADTed—artificially double-tracked. And the third one is actually double-tracked. And I remember I wanted the track to break down to dry and empty for the second chorus of the solo. I think I might have gotten that idea from Elton John doing 'Lucy in the Sky with Diamonds.' I have a vague memory of him doing a version of that song where suddenly it goes completely dry and empty. If I remember correctly, the dry bit in 'Money' came out of that."

Gilmour played the first two solos on what would become an iconic instrument for him, his legendary black Strat. A 1969 Fender Stratocaster bearing the serial number 266936, it had been acquired in 1970 under circumstances oddly similar to those surrounding the purchase of his very first Strat in '68. The black Strat was a hasty replacement guitar, plucked from the wall of Manny's Music in New York after Gilmour's guitars vanished in an equipment heist that cleaned out Pink Floyd's entire equipment truck while the band was touring in the States. Despite these modest origins, the black Strat would be Gilmour's guitar for many years to come. Simply a great-sounding Stratocaster, although one of no rare or special vintage, it's an instrument that Gilmour had no qualms about taking on the road with him, or modifying with new necks, pickups, routing, and hardware as part of his ongoing tonal quest.

As for the third solo section of "Money," Gilmour played it on a custom guitar made by luthier Bill Lewis. "He was a guy in Vancouver," Gilmour recalls. "The guitar had two whole octaves on the neck, which meant I could get up to some high notes that I couldn't get on a Stratocaster."

Gilmour remembers using a Fuzz Face and Binson echo unit on 'Money,' but can't recall if he used a Hiwatt or a Fender Twin amp. Both amplifiers were in common use by him at the time. He generally paired his Hiwatt with a WEM 4 x 12 speaker cabinet.

By this time, Gilmour was well on his way toward amassing his now-legendary vintage guitar collection. The mid-seventies were when he acquired perhaps his best-known piece, an off-white 1954 Stratocaster with gold hardware bearing the serial number 0001.

Among many other rare guitars, he also acquired a Lake Placid Blue '57 Strat that once belonged to Homer Haynes of the bluegrass duo Homer and Jethro. Gilmour had also become interested in lap steel and pedal steel guitars. Perhaps most significant among these is a fifties Fender 1000 Twin Neck pedal steel used on "One of These Days" from *Meddle* and "Great Gig in the Sky" from *Dark Side of the Moon*. "I guess I was never particularly confident in my ability as a pure guitar player," he says. "so I would try any trick in the book. I'd always liked lap steels, pedal steels, and things like that. On tour I used to use two cheap Jedson lap steels customized with Fender pickups for the slide parts. The one used for 'One of these Days' is tuned to an open E-minor chord—E B E G B E, from low to high. The other one is basically tuned to a modified open G chord [D B D G B E, low to high] that I used for 'Great Gig in the Sky.'"

A disagreement broke out between Gilmour and Waters over the mixing of *Dark Side of the Moon*. "I wanted it to be big and swampy and wet, with reverbs and things like that," Gilmour recounts. "And Roger was keen on it being a very dry album, because he was influenced a lot by John Lennon's primal scream album [i.e., *Plastic Ono Band*]. All that was very dry, and that's what Roger wanted. We argued so much about that that it was suggested that we get a third opinion. So we got [producer] Chris Thomas in to mix it. Chris's role was essentially to stop the arguments between Roger and me. We were going to leave him to mix it on his own, with Alan Parsons engineering. But of course the first day he went in there, I found out Roger sneaked in there. So the second day I sneaked in there. And of course from then on we were both sitting right at his shoulder, interfering. But luckily, Chris was more sympathetic to my point of view than he was to Roger's."

Creative tensions between Gilmour and Waters would escalate in the years to come. In his emphasis on musicality, Gilmour was often seconded by Rick Wright, who had a background in jazz piano. Whereas Waters in his emphasis on lyrical concepts was often supported by Nick Mason. But remarkably, the arguments, while heated, took place predominantly in a tone of gentlemanly rivalry. Voices were rarely raised and the situation never degenerated to the level of physical violence. "It's threatened to," says Gilmour. "But it's never actually come to that."

The polite reserve of the Pink Floyd camp was something that surprised longtime Gilmour guitar tech Phil Taylor when he first came to work for the band in 1974, shortly after *Dark Side*'s release. The vibe wasn't quite what Taylor was expecting when he reported for duty at what he describes as a small, dingy rehearsal room in King's Cross in London.

"Whereas other bands I'd worked for seemed very much like a bunch of mates, Pink Floyd always seemed more like gentlemen turning up to the office for work. Not that they weren't friendly. But it didn't have the same kind of vibe as other bands."

"Social hours" is how Taylor describes the work schedule as Pink Floyd got down to work at Abbey Road to record the follow-up to *Dark Side*, 1975's *Wish You Were Here*. "Incredibly for those days, I think we worked Monday through Thursday from about 10 a.m. till eight or nine in the evening. Whereas a lot of other bands would work ridiculous hours all through the night, the Floyd had been through all that thing already. So again it felt very . . . well, not quite like an office job. But it almost didn't feel like rock and roll."

The members of Pink Floyd have never lived up to the wild rock star stereotype. Tales of drug excess or groupie debauchery figure very little, if at all, in their story. So Taylor's account of a comfortably staid and well-regulated recording schedule for *Wish You Were Here* is particularly suited to the band's collective profile in general and Gilmour's life situation in particular during the mid-seventies. He was about to settle into his first marriage, with the American painter Virginia "Ginger" Hasenbein. In preparation for the day, the couple had begun selecting draperies, furniture, and other domestic fittings for the townhouse in Notting Hill that was to be their home.

Nonetheless, there were plenty of pressures at the "office." Pink Floyd faced the challenge of following up the phenomenal success of *Dark Side of the Moon*—a daunting prospect for any band. On top of this, the band had signed a lucrative new contract with Columbia Records and were expected to deliver the goods in a major way.

"I think that's what *Wish You Were Here* was about, as far as Roger was concerned," Gilmour states. "It's about that feeling of 'What do you do when you've done everything?' That's what we were left with after *Dark Side*."

There were further complications as well. As Gilmour was just about to enter the estate of holy matrimony, Mason and Waters both were in troubled marriages that would end in divorce. Mason's domestic strife tended to render him listless and depressed in the studio, which undermined his musical performance and thus brought him into conflict with Gilmour. The guitarist had begun venturing out of the Pink Floyd fold and working with other musicians, including the Sutherland Brothers and Quiver (whose drummer Willie Wilson went all the way back to Jokers Wild with Gilmour) and a new singer at the time who was destined for great success, Kate Bush. From the perspective of these outside vantage points, Gilmour had begun to regard the musical capabilities of some of his Pink Floyd bandmates in something of a dim light.

Still the band surmounted all of these challenges. *Wish You Were Here* finally crystallized when

MICHAEL OCHS ARCHIVES/GETTY IMAGES

Waters took one composition, "Shine On You Crazy Diamond," and built a concept around it. Once again the focal point was Syd Barrett. *On Dark Side*, Syd had figured as a kind of martyr to the ugliness and brutality of modern life. *On Wish You Were Here*, Barrett becomes a martyr to the ugliness and brutality of the music biz. Syd's crack-up, during Pink Floyd's first flush of success, was appropriated as a mirror for Waters own growing discomfort with rock stardom.

While mixing down *Wish You Were Here* at Abbey Road on June 5, 1975, Pink Floyd received a surprise visit from the song's subject—none other than Syd Barrett himself. Since leaving the band, Barrett had become a recluse, growing older, fat, and bald in the basement of his mother's home, devoting much of his time to painting. He turned up at the studio—dressed in a trench coat, head shaved bald, and clutching a plastic bag—on the day that had been set aside for a celebration of David and Ginger's wedding at the Abbey Road canteen. Guitar tech Phil Taylor was one witness to this bizarre, and for several band members quite unsettling, encounter.

"Pink Floyd have always generally been pretty good at hiding their emotions," says Taylor. "So at that time, in my memory, none of that was shown. But I do remember sitting down for a cup of tea with David and Syd at one of those small, thirteen-inch square Formica tables in the canteen, with Syd on my left and David on my right. I was a fly on the wall listening to a brief conversation they had, which was quite illogical. I remember sitting there saying, 'What?!?!?'"

Despite all the tensions, challenges, and strange interludes, *Wish You Were Here* proved another triumph for Pink Floyd. "For me, it's the most satisfying album," says Gilmour. "I really love it. I mean, I would rather listen to it than *Dark Side of the Moon*. Because I think we achieved a better balance of music and lyrics on *Wish You Were Here* than we did on *Dark Side of the Moon*. *Dark Side* got a bit too much into the importance of the lyrics and neglected some of the tunes, the vehicles. Some of those vehicles didn't always seem like they could carry the weight. For me, it was always important that the vehicle stood up on its own as a piece of music. Then you put the words and stuff on top of that. To me, one of Roger's failings is that sometimes, in his effort to get the words across, he uses a less-than-perfect vehicle."

Over the course of the next three Pink Floyd albums, the balance would shift increasingly in Waters's direction. *Animals*, released in 1977, marked a few firsts. It was the first album where Rick Wright didn't participate in the songwriting, the start of a marginalization process that would eventually evict Wright from the band. *Animals* is also the first album that Pink Floyd recorded in their own recording studio, Britannia Row, although this turned out to be something of a mixed blessing.

"We'd literally just built it as a studio and it was really not ready for use," says Gilmour. "There were lots of bugs in it and the sound in there was pretty awful. The walls hadn't been properly sound-treated. It really wasn't ready to do records in yet. Very primitive. But you know, when you've got a new toy, you want to use it."

All of these factors contributed to a stripped down, lean and nasty sound on *Animals*—a departure from the usual, floaty Floyd atmospherics, which just happened to chime in with the mood of the punk rock revolution that was then underway, targeting veteran bands like Pink Floyd as redundant, bloated dinosaurs. Roger Waters's Orwellian lyrical concept for the album, also suited the mood of punk rock and the grim economic recession that gripped Britain in the late seventies. *Animals* divides all humankind into three metaphorical classes, pigs (upper class oppressors), sheep (the docile masses who do as they're told), and dogs (the sharpies, hustlers, crooks, insider traders, and others who live outside the law and game the system).

Gilmour and Waters co-wrote the album's side one epic, "Dogs." It grew out of an earlier composition called "Raving and Drooling" and was adapted lyrically by Waters as his concept for the album emerged. "The *Animals* concept didn't come up until the album was about three-quarters finished," says Gilmour. "I don't think Roger had it in his mind before then."

The instrumental high points of "Dogs" are the track's glorious interludes of harmonized guitar leads, which alternate between two- and three-part overdubbed harmonization. The net effect is quite majestic. In Pink Floyd's music, Gilmour's melodicism often offsets Waters's dour lyrical outlook, an effective contrast that is one key to the band's enduring appeal.

"The last line of the first solo is a three-part descending augmented chord," says Gilmour. "Which is quite nice and I was very proud of. Then Roger went and wiped it—by mistake—and I had to re-create it."

Gilmour played these solo sections on a custom Fender Telecaster routed through a Hiwatt amp and a pair of Yamaha rotating speaker cabinets. The latter, says Gilmour, "weren't synchronized in any way. It was just whatever came out. I used to use two of those onstage, as well as the regular amps. It made a big difference in the sound—a slightly Leslie [cabinet] effect."

Pink Floyd's tour for *Animals* featured what is perhaps their best known stage prop, the giant, inflatable pig from the album's cover art that floated above the stage like some unsettling presence. This porcine blimp, of course, came right out of the album's imagery, an apt symbol for the overfed ruling classes. But there's also something slyly referential in the image as well; punk rock doctrine often decried bands like the Floyd as bloated and oppressive.

Pink Floyd's reputation for elaborate stage shows had grown steadily ever since the earliest days of their light-show freak-out psychedelic performances. But putting on more and more extravagant shows with each subsequent tour also put a strain on the group.

"It was actually very difficult," says Gilmour. "We spent years gathering people around us—experts. Just gaining expertise in all the areas we wanted to be good in. It was a lot of work, but we looked forward to playing."

Sometimes, anyway. The *Animals* tour was fraught with tension. The whole ritual of rock performance was starting to get on Waters's nerves. And Gilmour basically thought the band was playing like crap on many occasions.

"The tour finished on not a great note, as has been well documented," he says. "There was a scrappy gig in Montreal in a big stadium in July of '77. That was the one where Roger spat on someone in the front row, the incident that led to Roger's writing *The Wall*. And I'd been so pissed off with the quality of some of the gigs that I'd left the stage at one point and gone back to the mixing desk while the others did a blues jam."

Gilmour is not a man to lose his cool easily. "In all the years I've worked for him, I don't know if he's ever even shouted at me," says Phil Taylor. "He's very laid back, David. Very restrained." So for Gilmour to describe himself as pissed off at the quality of some shows on the *Animals* tour is a

dramatic indicator of the profound and escalating tensions within Pink Floyd during this period. The disastrous tour left more than one band member wondering if it was worth carrying on with Pink Floyd at all.

"After the tour ended, for the rest of '77 and the beginning of '78 nobody in the band had had any particular plans for what we might be embarking on subsequently," says Gilmour. "And I guess I was bored. So I decided I'd go have a bit of fun and make a record with some old pals. I rounded up Rick Wills and Willie Wilson, some old friends who were very encouraging."

The result was Gilmour's first solo album, the aptly titled *David Gilmour*. Perhaps, either consciously or subconsciously, the guitarist was exploring what a post-Floyd career might feel like, or how the general public might respond to a Floyd-less David Gilmour. His wife, Ginger, joined Wills and Wilson in encouraging Dave to go solo. So they packed up the guitars and drums and all headed down to the South of France to record at Superbear Studios, a favorite Floyd haunt at the time.

Gilmour had already begun jamming with his old Jokers Wild drummer, Willie Wilson, sitting in with the latter's band, Quiver. Bassist Rick Wills was with seventies hit makers Foreigner at the time, another seasoned pro. The three musicians made up a compact, muscular power trio, proving an amiable vehicle for Gilmour's songwriting ideas. Different aspects of Gilmour's talents emerge on the disc. The instrumental opening track, "Mihalis," offers an unlikely yet felicitous combination of Hank Marvin and John McLaughlin stylistic influences, and "No Way" showcases Dave's bluesy side. "It's Deafinitely" blends echoes of Jeff Beck riffology with bouts of slide guitar madness. "Short and Sweet" takes a powerhouse Who-ish approach and was co-written by Roy Harper, the folk pop eccentric who had sung the lead vocal on Pink Floyd's "Have a Cigar."

But other tracks on the album illustrate just how much of the overall Pink Floyd sound and style originated with Gilmour. "So Far Away" and the double-time outro to "Cry from the Street" are drenched in the glorious guitar harmonies that adorn so many Floyd tracks. The floaty "There's No Way Out of Here" and "I Can't Breathe Anymore" could almost be tracks from some lost Floyd album. The latter song might even be taken as an answer song to Pink Floyd's "Breathe," and both seem to reflect Gilmour's conflicted feelings about Pink Floyd at the time. To some extent, he may well have felt trapped in the group; and with his creative input circumscribed by Waters's increasing control of the material, Gilmour may well have felt that he couldn't breathe anymore. At any rate, *David Gilmour* certainly proved that Gilmour was able to conjure up some of the old Floyd magic in the absence of the others, and do so in far less time, and with much less hassle, than it took to complete a Pink Floyd opus.

"We knocked it out in two and a half weeks, basically," he says. "It was a refreshing change of speed from the way Floyd went about things. A change of tactics. But in the end, I had to admit to myself that I really am a bit of an obsessive. So I wouldn't always want to record the way I did on *David Gilmour*. But it was that moment. That was just how that particular moment felt."

Gilmour might have gone further in a solo direction had he not found himself on somewhat unstable financial ground by the end of '78. Pink Floyd were on the verge of bankruptcy. A financial advisor named Andrew Oscar Warburg had led the group into some ill-advised business investments, creating tax problems for the band as well.

The only way out was for Gilmour, Waters, Mason, and Wright to put any personal differences aside and come up with another bestselling Pink Floyd album, something on the order of *Dark Side of the Moon*. As always, Waters had a couple of ideas ready to go. One was the concept for what eventually became his first solo album, 1984's *The Pros and Cons of Hitchhiking*. His other idea grew out of the 1977 incident when he'd spat on a concertgoer during a performance in Montreal. Waters was appalled at himself. What could possibly make a sensitive, intelligent, and usually quite reserved musical artist behave like that? Waters came up with a concept for an album that could chronicle a rock star's descent into psychological trauma and catatonic withdrawal from interaction with others. Only this time, Waters wasn't going to use Syd Barrett's insanity as his narrative vehicle. The new work he had in mind was a very thinly veiled autobiography.

This, of course, was the concept that Gilmour, Mason, and Waters elected to make into the next Pink Floyd album. It would become their one of their most successful and best known works, *The Wall*. But it was also the most difficult Pink Floyd album to make, a protracted and painful process that would include Rick Wright's departure from the band, dismissed by Waters for "not pulling his weight," in the bassist's view.

To help bring the album to completion, and act as referee, the band hired rock vet Bob Ezrin to serve as producer. Ezrin was known for his ability to midwife dark, difficult concept albums and to deal with dysfunctionality, having produced several Alice Cooper discs and Lou Reed's bleak opus, *Berlin*. He helped Waters massage his overall concept. And when the band entered the studio, Ezrin helped keep Gilmour and Waters from one another's throats.

"It was, for the most part, a typically polite British enmity that existed between them," Ezrin recalls. "They were obviously close on many levels. And there was an unadmitted mutual respect beneath all the arguing and bickering going on between them. But the tension was always present, because there was a war between two basically dominant personalities. Each one had a need to express himself in his own style, and sometimes those styles were very different. Sometimes they approached the same piece of material from an entirely different point of view. So my job was often to be Henry Kissinger and run back and forth between the two, trying to arrive at a workable middle ground."

Recording for *The Wall* got underway around April 1979 at Britannia Row. But after a few sessions the band was informed by management that, owing to their tax issues, they would have to finish making the album outside of England. As rock-star tax exiles tend to do, they moved operations to the South of France and continued work on *The Wall* at Superbear before completing the album at Producers Workshop in Los Angeles.

Waters had demoed some songs for the album, but others remained to be written. It was difficult for Gilmour to get any of his own compositional ideas onto the disc. But in the end he succeeded in collaborating with Waters on three tunes, "Run Like Hell," "Young Lust," and "Comfortably Numb." The latter song would of course become one of the best known and loved pieces from *The Wall*, and indeed the entire Floyd canon.

"Bob Ezrin's desire was to make *The Wall* a Pink Floyd record rather than Roger's solo record," Gilmour recalls. "Roger wanted it to be all his solo project. He didn't want anyone else to contribute to the writing. But Bob thought there should be other people's writing on the album. So he said to me, 'What have you got?' And I played him my demo for 'Run Like Hell' and what became 'Comfortably Numb.' Bob said, 'Oh, they're really nice. We should include them.' Roger said, 'Well . . . all right.' It was a long, hard process making that record: throwing bits away, tough editing, going to meetings. . . ."

A brilliant evocation of the narcotized, desensitized malaise of life in late-twentieth-century consumerist society, "Comfortably Numb" combines the best of Waters's lyrical incisiveness with some of Gilmour's finest music. It is one of several songs on *The Wall* to employ a lush orchestral arrangement, written by Ezrin and Michael Kamen, which further enhances Gilmour's musical themes. Though few in number, Gilmour's songwriting contributions to *The Wall* impart a welcome element of melodicism. They contrast effectively with Waters's own compositions, many of which are sung in a style that Waters developed especially to portray the work's main character, Pink—a crabbed, stagily strident set of vocal mannerisms a bit reminiscent of the Kurt Weill/Bertolt Brecht operas of twenties Berlin. When "Comfortably Numb" comes along, midway through *The Wall*'s second disc, its effect is not unlike that of an operatic aria—a burst of sublime melody that momentarily lifts the listener out of the creaking mechanics of plot development. The chord progression and some melodic elements for "Comfortably Numb" came from a song idea that Gilmour had developed for his *David Gilmour* solo disc, the guitarist discloses:

"I'd recorded a demo of it when I was at Superbear Studios previously, doing my first solo album. We changed the key of the opening section from E to B, I think. Then we had to add a couple of extra bars so Roger could do the line, 'I have become comfortably numb.' But other than that, it was very simple to write. And it was all done before the orchestration was added."

Gilmour contributed an especially expressive guitar solo on "Comfortably Numb," one of the most famous and iconic solos of his entire career. Once again, Gilmour relied upon his black Strat to deliver the tone he had in mind for the solo. By this time, the instrument had undergone several modifications and now had a DiMarzio DF1 pickup installed in its bridge position and a custom neck fashioned by luthier Grover Jackson, then at Charvel. Although the "Comfortably Numb" solo is beautifully structured, the guitarist says very little forethought, if any, went into it:

"As far as I remember, I just went out into the studio at Superbear, bunged five or six solos down, and then just picked the best bits from each one.

Gilmour vaguely recalls using "a Big Muff [distortion pedal] with an Electric Mistress flanger" to get his distinctive tone for the solo: "all this stuff going through an amp." Bob Ezrin remembers that they used a Yamaha guitar cabinet with a rotating speaker combined with either a Hiwatt or Marshall amp:

"The Yamaha gave it a kind of unearthly quality, which, when added to the basic sound of a distorted, singing Hiwatt, created that beautiful, multitextural guitar sound that you hear at the end of the track. I must say, on that album we probably did every kind of guitar sound known to man, and some that were never done before. One good thing about working with a band like Pink Floyd is their natural inclination toward experimentation. We tried all kinds of new approaches—for that time—to recording. We did a sixteen-track basic reel and then we had a twenty-four-track slave reel. And then we slaved them together with mini mag [a synchronization format that predates SMPTE time code and was quite primitive by comparison]. Which was pretty dicey when you look back on it. Kind of like flying without a cockpit."

Tempers flared during the mixdown of "Comfortably Numb" in Los Angeles. "There were arguments about how it should be mixed and which backing track should be used," says Gilmour. "I think it was more of an ego thing than anything else. Roger and I actually went head to head over which of two different drum tracks to use. If you put them both on a record today, I don't think anyone could tell the difference. But it seemed important at the time, though. So it ended up with us taking a drum fill-out of the one version and putting it into the other version by editing a sixteen-track tape—splitting it down the middle so you have two strips of tape, one-inch wide.'"

"Whereas other bands I'd worked for seemed very much like a bunch of mates, Pink Floyd always seemed more like gentlemen turning up to the office for work."

A particularly heated confrontation between Gilmour and Waters took place over dinner one night at an Italian restaurant in North Hollywood. "There was no screaming, though," says Ezrin. "It was all very English, very direct; 'You're a fuck and you have no reason to live.' That sort of cold, head-on English confrontation. And I was right in the middle of it. I was fighting at that point for the introduction of the orchestra and the expansion of the Pink Floyd sound into something that was more theatrical, more filmic. But Dave really saw 'Comfortably Numb' more as a bare bones track with just bass, drums, and guitar. Roger sided with me on that particular point. What we ended up with is the body of the song being more heavily orchestral, and then the end clears out somewhat and is more rock and roll. So 'Comfortably Numb' is a true collaboration because it's David's music, Roger's lyrics, and my orchestral chart!"

The Wall of course became a massive success for Pink Floyd, propelled by the hit singles "Another Brick in the Wall (Part 2)" and "Comfortably Numb." Waters's conceptual plan for *The Wall* included a feature film—which was ultimately released in 1982, starring Bob Geldof—and a series of big-budget live concerts. Pink Floyd shows had always been elaborate spectacles, but the production for *The Wall* concerts outdid anything that had come before. The main visual conceit was a massive wall that stagehands constructed at the edge of the stage, while the performance was in progress, using massive artificial "bricks." By the end of the show, the band was entirely cut off from the audience's view by the massive wall, a symbol of the isolation that Waters had come to feel performing in massive sports arenas.

The production was too elaborate to tour. So Pink Floyd decided to do extended runs at venues in four major cites: Los Angeles, New York, London, and Dortmund, West Germany. Opening night in Los Angeles, on February 7, 1980, was marked by a little unscripted drama when a stage curtain caught fire early in the performance. Luckily the crew was able to extinguish the flames before they could get out of control and the show went on. The job of coordinating the music with all the elaborate staging elements fell to David Gilmour, who was appointed musical director for the show.

"For me, *The Wall* show was terrific fun," he says. "It was really an achievement for everyone involved, particularly Roger. But I had to take on the role of music director and deal with a lot of musical details onstage so that Roger didn't have to think about that. It was really tough at first. Later on, it got a little easier, once we all got into it. But I had a huge cue sheet up on my amps, because we had all these cues coming up on monitors or onscreen, and there were different DDL [digital delay line] settings, which I had to transmit with very primitive equipment to all the delay lines onstage. Very tricky. Except for the 'Comfortably Numb' solo, there were virtually no moments where I could say, 'Forget everything. Just play.' You know? It was very rigid. Whereas on all the previous tours—*Wish You Were Here* and *Dark Side of the Moon*—there were moments that could be extended longer or made shorter if you liked. *The Wall*, quite reasonably, because it wasn't that kind of project, didn't have that."

Gilmour's dramatic guitar solo turn during "Comfortably Numb" was one of the highlights of the live shows. As in the studio, he used his black Strat to play the monumental solo, only now the bridge pickup had been switched out once again, with a custom Seymour Duncan now in place. But while Gilmour speaks with a certain amount of pride about *The Wall*'s accomplishments and says that he enjoyed the live shows, it clearly isn't his favorite Pink Floyd work.

"My view of what *The Wall* is about is more jaundiced today than it was then," he says. "It now appears to be a catalog of people Roger blames for his own failings in life, a list of 'you fucked me up this way, and you fucked me up that way.'"

While the commercial success of *The Wall* extricated Pink Floyd from their financial difficulties, it exacted a heavy toll in other ways. By the dawn of the eighties Pink Floyd was down to three members: Waters, Gilmour, and Mason—three grown men who had grown apart and begun to pursue outside musical projects and other interests in life. Still they convened to record one last Pink Floyd album together, aptly titled *The Final Cut*. It started with some material left over from *The Wall*. But the project found its lyrical and conceptual center in Waters's outrage over Britain's involvement in the 1982 Falklands War. This led him to re-explore his feelings about WWII and the death of his father in combat, themes that had also figured in *The Wall*. Indeed, the brutal folly of war has always been a prominent theme in his work.

And in many ways, *The Final Cut* was a warm-up for Waters's full-fledged solo recordings. Involvement from Gilmour and Mason was minimal, as Waters became increasingly dictatorial and reliant on a cadre of session musicians he'd assembled during the creation of *The Wall*. When *The Final Cut* was released in 1983, it was politely, though hardly enthusiastically, received. Fan polls regularly nominate it the worst Pink Floyd album of all.

And with this, the second great incarnation of Pink Floyd, the post–Syd Barrett "dream" lineup, came to an end—not with a bang but a whimper. Although still not officially disbanded, all four members threw themselves into solo projects.

Gilmour completed his second solo album, *About Face*, which was released in 1984. The disc stands in stark contrast to '78's *David Gilmour*. Where the guitarist's first solo effort was a casual affair, tossed together on a two-week jaunt down to France, *About Face* is a full-blown bid for eighties pop stardom. The production is steeped in that decade's big-budget slickness—massive gated snare drum sounds and the inevitable Fairlight CMI (Computer Musical Instrument) synthesizer, which cost more than a boat at the time. Gilmour is supported by topflight studio players, including session ace drummer Steve Porcaro from eighties hit makers Toto, and bassist Pino Paladino, who would go on to play with everyone from Jeff Beck to the Who. A triumvirate of great keyboardists contributed to the disc: Steve Winwood, ex–Deep Purple member Jon Lord, and film composer Anne Dudley from the Art of Noise.

From the album's title to the songwriting and production values, everything about *About Face* signals Gilmour's intention to put Pink Floyd behind him, turn himself around, and head off in a fresh new direction. The cover photo depicts Gilmour unshaven and in a road-worn leather jacket, his thumb jerked out horizontally like a man trying to hitch a ride on the next available musical trend. Or maybe it's a signal to his Floyd bandmates, "I'm outta here." Or perhaps one of the album's many jabs at Waters, "Hit the road, Jack!"

Gilmour assays a number of distinctly un-Floydian styles on the album, from the up-tempo dance-funk lead single, "Blue Light," to the British folk feel heard in the intro to the song "Murder." The guitarist also grasps his way forward lyrically on *About Face*. For all his musical talent, lyrics were never a particularly strong suit. This was never much of an issue during his long collaboration with the prolific Roger Waters, but has posed an ongoing problem in his post-Waters career.

And indeed Gilmour takes a page from Waters's thematic book on "Cruise," an ironic political reflection on U.S. president Ronald Reagan's deployment of Pershing II cruise missiles in Britain during the eighties.

Elsewhere on the album, Gilmour got a lyrical assist from none other than Pete Townshend. In many regards, the Who mastermind made an ideal stand-in for Waters. Both are songwriters who plumb the depths of psychology and rock star angst, often in ambitious, long-form concept albums. While there was never any question of forming a band together, Townshend and Gilmour became close friends. The two had first met during sessions for *The Final Cut* at Eel Pie, Townshend's floating barge studio on the Thames.

"I think I went down there to record some grand piano," Gilmour recalls. "I saw Pete there and he said how much he liked my first solo album. Not many people had said that, so I was very pleased. Some time after that, Pete told me that he was having some difficulty writing music. I said, 'Would you ever like to have a crack at writing some lyrics for a couple of my things?' I sent him three songs and he sent back three sets of lyrics. Two of them suited me well. One didn't. He did the two on *About Face* and he did the other one ['White City Fighting'] on his *White City* album."

Townshend's lyric for "Love on the Air" was penned within twenty-four hours of Gilmour's request for lyrical assistance. On *About Face*'s other Townshend collaboration, "All Lovers Are Deranged," Gilmour seems to take more than a poetic cue from Pete. The song features an edgy, angry guitar solo that is distinctly Who-ish.

There is quite a bit of anger on *About Face*, albeit mostly expressed in a polite, reserved

Gilmour-esque vein. Gilmour is trying to work his way out from under the four-hundred-pound gorilla that is Pink Floyd. Yet at the same time, he is the gorilla—or at least one quarter of it. Which makes it especially poignant when majestic Floydian guitar harmonies and leads break out on tracks like "Let's Get Metaphysical." There are even lavish orchestrations by *The Wall* team of Bob Ezrin and Michael Kamen.

And Gilmour takes a few direct lyrical shots at Waters. "You Know I'm Right" is very much in the vein of "How Do You Sleep," John Lennon's musical ambush on Paul McCartney, or "You Don't Move Me," Keith Richards's put-down of Mick Jagger. Only instead of wallowing in acrimony, Gilmour's song seems more steeped in regret and frustration over the insolubility of his differences with Waters.

A similar mood hangs over the closing track, "Near the End." This end-of-disc "farewell for now" also functions as an elegy for Pink Floyd. Gilmour confesses to feeling "disconnected and dry" in the absence of the band that had been his main creative outlet since 1968. His parting line, "Is there a feeling that you've been deceived?" is oddly reminiscent of Johnny Rotten's famous "Ever get the feeling you've been cheated?" eulogy for the Sex Pistols.

Clearly there was no going back. In 1985 Waters served official notice that he was no longer a member of Pink Floyd. Of all the solo projects by Pink Floyd members that came in the wake of *The Final Cut*, Waters's *The Pros and Cons of Hitchhiking* enjoyed the greatest success. Where Gilmour had enlisted heavyweights like Pete Townshend and Steve Winwood on *About Face*, Waters brought in Eric Clapton to play on *Hitchhiking*. It was the start of what would be a protracted and public game of one-upmanship between the two former allies.

The year 1986 was an eventful one for Gilmour, the start of a new chapter in his life, in many regards. His fourth child, Matthew, was born that year. And he acquired his own floating recording studio on the Thames. It's called Astoria and it rides at anchor in an idyllic spot just outside of London, downriver from Hampton Court Palace, moored at a bankside garden that once belonged to the eighteenth-century actor David Garrick. The craft itself is steeped in showbiz history, having been built in 1912 by the English entertainment entrepreneur and casino owner Fred Karno.

"He was the guy who discovered Charlie Chaplin and Stan Laurel and people like that," Gilmour explains. "He wanted to have his own private home place, knocking shop, whatever. It was never built to sail. It's strictly a houseboat. If you want to move it, you get a tug and tow it. My idea was to make as good in here sound-wise as we could, without fucking with the space too much."

Gilmour started to acquire a newfound gravitas in this latter phase of his career. This is when he starts to become the portly, gray patriarch of classic rock. People stopped calling him Dave Gilmour. It became strictly David.

"Oh, he hates being called Dave these days," Phil Taylor confides. "Don't do that because you'll be very unpopular if you do. He admits it after all these years. He says, 'Well, I never liked Dave.' Well, why didn't he tell us before? It's funny to have known him all that time and suddenly it's 'David.' But hey, that's what he likes. It's not a problem for anybody."

Round about '86, Gilmour made another momentous move, laying aside his fabled black Strat in favor of mid-eighties Fender '57 reissue Strats. "They sounded a bit livelier than the black Strat and they felt nice," explains Phil Taylor. And these '57 reissues were the instruments that Gilmour played when he reconvened Pink Floyd in 1986, getting back together with Rick Wright and Nick Mason.

It was an inevitability, in many ways. In their solo endeavors, neither Gilmour, Mason, nor Wright had met with anything like Pink Floyd's level of success. Meanwhile, Pink Floyd's absence from the music scene hadn't done anything to diminish their popularity. Quite the contrary. Their radio airplay and critical status continued to increase throughout the eighties. Pink Floyd had become a "classic" band of almost Beatle-esque standing. And with all members still alive, the market was hungering for new product.

And so Gilmour, Mason, and Wright got together in the tiny tracking room of Gilmour's floating studio. It's more a sitting room than a professional recording space—something that would do nicely for tea with the vicar, possessing a low ceiling adorned with an elegant plaster rosette.

"You can get a really good drum sound in here," says Gilmour. "We started out in Olympic Studios [London's legendary rock studio] trying to get good tracks done there. But we found that when we got here, we were getting a better drum sound than we got in the big Olympic rooms. We had the drums in one corner and me standing around with a guitar, but with an amp stuck in the next bedroom. [Astoria] has a number of small rooms we can use as booths. We can stick a Leslie cabinet in the kitchen. What the rule books say is going to work sometimes doesn't. And vice versa."

Eventually, though, the project grew out of Gilmour's cozy boat. Work continued in a variety of studios, including Britannia Row (Gilmour had long since sold his interest in that facility to Mason), and three top LA recording palaces: A&M, Can-Am, and Village Recorders. A small army of A-list session players and singers also contributed, including Bob Ezrin on keyboards, Tony Levin on bass, Jim Keltner on drums, and Tom Scott on sax.

Released in 1987, *A Momentary Lapse of Reason* is a transitional work—three old bandmates finding their way forward in the absence of a domineering fourth member. A few tracks, including "Learning to Fly" and "One Slip," found their way into the hearts of diehard fans. But the tour that followed was a major success. By the late eighties, Pink Floyd's live shows became more of a focal point for fan interest than the band's studio recordings. They'd taken on the importance that Grateful Dead concerts had, and continue to have, for devoted followers of that band—an opportunity to relive a golden era of rock history, especially for those who weren't even born when the original discs come out. And in keeping with Pink Floyd's reputation, the shows became increasingly elaborate spectacles.

None of this sat very well with Roger Waters, who was also performing Pink Floyd material on his solo tours. He dismissed the Gilmour, Mason, Wright configuration as "the Floyd fraud." And so a debate arose as to who was the rightful guardian of the Floyd legacy. Was it Gilmour, whose voice and guitar made up so much of the distinctive Floyd sound, and who enjoyed the additional cachet of having two other founding band members in his camp? Or was it Waters, whose lyrical vision and ambitious concepts had done so much to shape the band's identity and whose bass playing was also an integral part of the band's sonic fingerprint?

At one point Waters went so far as to file suit to prevent Gilmour, Mason, and Waters from using the giant inflatable pig from *Animals* as a stage prop in their shows, claiming the airborne beast as his intellectual property. Gilmour et al. responded by having gargantuan male genitalia affixed to the band's porcine mascot, thus altering its gender and identity sufficiently to obviate Waters's claim of intellectual ownership.

By the dawn of the nineties, however, Gilmour's private life came to occupy him more than matters pertaining to Pink Floyd. In 1990 his divorce from Ginger Hasenbein, his wife of some fifteen years, was finalized. He was remarried on July 29, 1994, to writer and journalist Polly Samson. The guitarist's new wife became a key collaborator on the next Pink Floyd release, *The Division Bell*. In her Gilmour had found someone to work with as closely as he'd once worked with Waters, and a solution to his long-standing struggle with the task of lyric writing.

"She's no shrinking violet," he says of Samson. "She's a professional writer and a pretty opinionated person. She manages to get under my skin and work out what I'm thinking before I even know what I'm thinking."

Once again Gilmour, Mason, and Wright got together in the tiny main room onboard Astoria and began jamming, this time with Guy Pratt on bass. And this formed the nucleus for the work that

became *The Division Bell*. It's a more organic work than *A Momentary Lapse*, far less reliant on outside session musicians, although a few are involved. The work has an overriding theme as well—the tragic inability of human beings to reconcile their differences and live in accord. The titular *Division Bell* is rung in Parliament to call members to debate. The cover art depicts two massive metal faces, set in stony opposition. The melancholy mood of discord and isolation that hangs over the album is reflective of Gilmour's recent divorce and his long, contentious, and ultimately failed relationship with Waters.

One guitar highlight of the album is the instrumental track, "Marooned," which marks the start of Gilmour's love affair with the DigiTech Whammy pedal.

"Press your foot down and it goes up an octave! I really love it," he laughs. "It gives a whole extra dimension to the guitar sound. It has the flavor of that old album *Songs of the Humpback Whale* from years ago, where they recorded a lot of whale noises—that floating thing. It reminds me of the sea."

The tour behind *Division Bell* was another epic success, combining songs from the new album with a generous selection of Floyd classics, including a complete performance of *Dark Side of the Moon*. It spawned the highly successful double live album *Pulse* and a subsequent concert DVD. By now, Gilmour had begun loading his '57 reissue Strats with active EMG pickups. They afforded a solution to the perennial woes of hum and RF interference inherent in traditional single-coil pickups.

"One of the problems with touring, for many years, was interference," he says. "Especially if you are a sort of bastard, like me, who tended to have a huge pedal board with a number of effects. Those effects pedals really tended to pick up interference from the dimmers on the lighting rigs. And we did have extensive lighting rigs with Pink Floyd, which tended to buzz horribly. When I first heard of and got hold of the EMG pickups, they just stopped that dead. I started using them on Strats live. And they sounded great—a very rich, full tone. They didn't sound quite as 'Stratty' in some ways. There's something in the thinness and the particular range that a Strat has that makes it a Strat. And that has a lot to do with the single-coil pickups. So with EMG pickups, you did lose that a little bit. But what you gained in lack of interference and purity of sound made them definitely worth using."

A period of relative quiescence followed in the wake of *The Division Bell* and *Pulse*, as Gilmour focused on family life, the odd session date, and interests apart from music. But he was lured back into the limelight to do a series of solo concerts at London's Festival Hall in 2001. That got him back into the music game, and soon he was working on what would become his third solo album, the idyllic *On an Island*. His modus operandi was much the same as it was for *A Momentary Lapse* and *The Division Bell*. Once again, he shared songwriting duties with Polly Samson and once again Astoria was his base of operations. Co-producing this time was his old friend and Roxy Music guitarist Phil Manzanera. The two go back to the late sixties together, and Manzanera is a near neighbor. Sessions got underway in earnest in 2004. "Time moves slowly these days," Gilmour laughs.

But midway through the project, Gilmour was distracted by something that came up—a full-scale Pink Floyd reunion *with* Roger Waters. What had once seemed impossible was now about to happen. It took Sir Bob Geldof to do it. The punk rock singer turned philanthropist—who had played the lead role in the film version of *The Wall*—was intent on reuniting Pink Floyd for massive Live 8 concert, slated to be held on July 2, 2005, in London's Hyde Park. Coinciding with the G8 economic summit, the purpose of the show was to raise awareness of world poverty. Geldof had interested the politically engaged Roger Waters in the idea of joining the all-star lineup of rock and pop artists who would be performing that day, a lineup that included Paul McCartney, U2, Madonna, Coldplay, Travis, and Elton John, among others.

Geldof got Mason and Wright on board, but Gilmour was the holdout. "I declined initially because I was in the middle of making *On an Island*," he says. "And I thought—correctly as it turned out—that it would open up a can of worms: Pink Floyd reformation stories. And I knew it would take my concentration off the album I was working on. Although it was just one day of appearing, to get to that one day and then go away from that one day afterwards would take a lot of time. Being knocked right off my course for over a month was inconvenient for me. I selfishly didn't want to be inconvenienced by all the things I knew this would throw up.

"So Bob Geldof tried quite hard to persuade me. I figured he'd get along quite fine without me. Not that I didn't support what he was trying to do. I just though he'd do it just as well without a reformed Pink Floyd as with. It was very selfish of me. But then Bob persuaded Roger to call me and ask me."

The call came as quite a surprise to Gilmour. The two feuding, former bandmates hadn't spoken in quite a while. But the fact that Waters had made the first move, a gesture of reconciliation, made an impression in Gilmour.

"After Roger called, I thought about it and realized I would probably really kick myself afterwards if I didn't do it," he says. "I'd look back on it and say, 'Damn, you should have done that.' There were many good reasons for doing it. The good and proper reason was what the event hopefully did achieve. And also it helped put some of the bad blood between Roger and myself behind us."

And so Gilmour, Waters, Mason, and Wright found themselves facing one another in a rehearsal hall once again, mulling over a set list.

"We had a few arguments about it," says Gilmour. "But in the end it came down to the songs that represented Pink Floyd in their heyday. For instance, 'Breathe' is a great one to open a show with, particularly if you're outdoors. And there were other considerations. 'Money' was a good choice. It was very appropriate to the issues at hand. The main objective of Live 8 was to get the leaders of eight nations to get rid of world debt. So 'Money' seemed quite pertinent. Roger was quite keen to do 'Another Brick in the Wall (Part 2)' but I dissuaded him from that. Because I rather felt that, for people in Africa, hearing a song that says 'We don't need no education' was probably not the most appropriate message to be relaying to them."

The group did three days of rehearsals together. "It was interesting to watch," says Phil Taylor, "because you could just see the smile on Roger's face: suddenly to be back in that environment, playing with David and Rick. He'd done odd bits with Nick. But to be playing with them all again, this great feeling was just emanating from Roger, a feeling of 'Wow, this is what it's about. This is what I've been missing.'"

Another poignant reunion took place on the third day of rehearsals. Gilmour picked up and played his black Strat for the first time in some twenty years. The instrument had been on exhibit at the Rock and Roll Hall of Fame but had recently come back into his possession. "It was so exciting

GUITAR PLAYER ARCHIVES

when David went from his red Strat with EMG pickups to the black Strat," says Taylor. "The difference was a amazing. The single-coil pickups, the sound of that guitar. It was really interesting to watch him and the other people in the room. You could tell the difference immediately. Around the place it was like, 'Whoa, what's happening?' Brilliant!"

With characteristic diligence, Gilmour put in another two weeks or so preparing for the show on his own. "I made a CD of the set and had it at my home studio," he explains. "I'd blast it out through speakers and play guitar and sing along to it three or four times every day for a good couple of weeks. I wanted to be very 'on it.' Because I knew it would be a nerve-racking experience, and I wanted to be able to do it like falling off a log. I wanted to be certain that I knew exactly what I was doing every second. And it was a good thing, because I was on the lead instrument and voice pretty much all of the time."

> *"I have great pride and affection for most of my Pink Floyd career. I had a thoroughly good time. Musically and artistically, it was very satisfying, a lot of it."*

The day itself went down like a charm. Pink Floyd was the only group not to receive a spoken introduction. Instead their set began with the recorded heartbeat that they'd always used to open the *Dark Side of the Moon* shows. Growing louder and louder, the sound sent people flocking to get as near to the stage as they could.

"People were just crying and emotional," Taylor reports. "They couldn't believe it. Many thought they'd never get to see Pink Floyd. Of course, a large majority of those people were too young to have seen the band. But there's such a mystique about Pink Floyd. People were mesmerized. And it sounded fantastic, both onstage and in the park."

Waters, Gilmour, Mason, and Wright's stately, beautifully paced set was a major high point in an afternoon and evening filled with standout performances. A historical moment, for sure. Waters looked particularly blissed out, reveling in the conciliatory vibes and the music itself. Gilmour was all business, as usual.

"I enjoyed what was going on, but I had very little time to look at the audience or anything like that," he recalls. "That was all peripheral to concentrating very hard to make sure I got everything right."

For Gilmour, the concert provided a great sense of closure on both Pink Floyd and his troubled relationship with Waters. "It was great to put some of that bitterness behind us," says Gilmour. "I'm very glad we were able to do that."

But that was it. Amid speculation that the successful show might lead to a more extensive tour or a recording, Gilmour made it clear that he simply wasn't interested. "I just don't think it would work," he said at the time. "I think Roger and I have had too long being horrid little despots. I just don't think it would make me a happier human being. Sorry, I'll pass on it."

Instead the guitarist returned to the bucolic environs of Astoria to complete *On an Island*. Old friends and colleagues, including David Crosby, Graham Nash, Jools Holland, Georgie Fame, and Pink Floyd's own Rick Wright, lent a hand. Released in 2006, the disc is very much a reflection of the place where it was made—serene, unhurried. Gauzy layers of shimmering sound unfold at a stately pace, providing a lavish backdrop for Gilmour's soaring, lyrical lead guitar and plaintive vocal style. There are occasional excursions into the blues and other slightly rougher terrain. But mostly this is a record for gazing peacefully at the river."

I was just letting it flow out as naturally as I can," says Gilmour. "There are quite a lot of those melancholy major seventh chords and 3/4 waltz tempos. That must be the mood I'm in."

Indeed, Gilmour seems to have settled graciously into contented maturity. He can pursue music at his own relaxed pace, emerging for the occasional high-profile gig, such as those documented on the *Live in Gdansk* and *Remember That Night: Live from the Royal Albert Hall* DVDs, or to play guitar on a session of one of his rock star compatriots, such as Paul McCartney, Bryan Ferry, or Paul Rodgers. The 2006 death of Syd Barrett and 2008 passing of Rick Wright seem more than ever to have consigned Pink Floyd to the past tense, the gilt-edged back pages of rock history. And that's fine with Gilmour. Not one to dwell on the past, he's perfectly happy in the present moment.

"I have great pride and affection for most of my Pink Floyd career," he says. "I had a thoroughly good time. Musically and artistically, it was very satisfying, a lot of it. Put against the good times, the moments that were no so great are very short. But I have moved on. I have a different working partnership now, working with another group of people and writing with my wife. And I'm finding that this is what I want to be doing. I am satisfied with that. I don't have too much nostalgia for that old thing. It seems to me it's in the past. Been there, done that."

Keith Richards

THE NINE LIVES OF KEITH RICHARDS

KEITH RICHARDS IS THE LIVING EMBODIMENT of rock and roll. Nobody personifies the music, lifestyle, excess, soul, decadence, exuberance, restless freedom, wisdom, and elegantly wasted, effortless panache of rock and roll more consummately than the man they call Keef. The deep lines on his wizened face were etched by a life lived 100 percent for, and in, rock and roll. Richards's ferocious devotion to the music has carried him safely through five decades of mayhem and madness with the Rolling Stones—through busts, jail, grievous bodily harm, poxed groupies, rampaging bikers, bereavements, marriages, divorces, and other relationships with sundry dangerous blondes, a decade-long entanglement with Dame Heroin, and most every other intoxicant known to modern pharmacology.

But his vital connection to rock and roll cuts deeper than all those things—way down into the music's blues roots and out through the branches of rock's African diaspora cousins: reggae, funk, and soul. More than any other group, the Stones baptized the baby boom generation in the mystical waters of the blues. Through them, white suburban teenagers in the mid-sixties United States, Britain, and all around the world adopted the music of mostly impoverished African Americans from the early and middle years of the twentieth century as their own musical truth. Blues is still very much the lingua franca of contemporary popular music. And Keith Richard's guitar is the sacrificial bridge linking our time to the ancient places where the blues was born. I once asked him how such a thing was possible:

"It's bones," he replied, flashing one of his signature skull rings. "'Cause we all probably come from Africa. Some of us just went north and turned white. But if you cut anybody open, bones is white and blood is red, man. It's kinda deep, you know. And I think maybe it speaks to us in that way. Ancient bone marrow responding to the source. Why else should we recognize it? All it points out is the superficiality of racial differences. Hey, beauty's skin deep."

Richards carries all this music not just in his heart or in his head but in his entire body. It's there in the snaky, stealthy way he walks across a room, loose limbed and youthful even as he approaches seventy. And it's certainly always been there in the way he attacks a guitar, arms flailing, his spinal column whipping to the beat. Keef has always been a very physical guitarist, right from the Rolling Stones' earliest incarnation as a lawless, unwashed alternative to the Beatles. Pete Townshend even copped his theatrical "windmill" strum from Keith Richards.

The chunky drive of Keith Richards's guitar work has propelled the trajectory of rock music from the mid-sixties onward. His influence is everywhere. But the funny thing is that, unlike so many other legendary guitarists, there is no single and unitary Keith Richards style. He's a musical chameleon, infinitely adaptive in his ability to assimilate and reflect the color and texture of any musical setting in which he finds himself. He can rock a stadium with the Stones, then turn around and jam in a small club with Muddy Waters. Who else but Keef could sit in a meditative session with his Rastafari brethren, the Wingless Angels, play bass for John Lennon, hang tough with Peter Tosh, or stand up to his hero Chuck Berry?

"First of all, you have to really want it," he says of these accomplishments. "I knew all those guys' stuff so well. Their styles. So it was 'Just give me a crack at it, man.' For me, to be second guitar to Chuck Berry on *Hail! Hail! Rock 'n' Roll* [in 1987], I looked up and realized, 'Shit, man, when you started out, you'd have died and gone to heaven. This was all you ever wanted.' And to play with Muddy Waters several times, yeah, that was great. When I look back and think, 'Who do I know?' 'Who have I played with?' Shit, I played with those guys. That's enough. I don't want no money. The money is nice. Thanks for the money, because otherwise they wouldn't have known who I was. But to have Muddy Waters say to you, 'Hey, show me that lick you did. . . .' Everybody's a perennial teenager when it comes to shit like that."

And while there is no singular Keith Richards style, there are a few constants that weave all throughout his work. One is an incredibly sinewy, supple rhythm guitar approach that can be heard on everything from "The Last Time" to "Beast of Burden." And the glassy, clean leads that surface on tracks like "Spider and the Fly." Not to mention the guerrilla frenzy of an all-out distressed solo like "Sympathy for the Devil." And the massive majesty of open-G-tuning chordal riffs like "Honky Tonk Women," "Brown Sugar," and "Can't You Hear Me Knockin'."

While guitarists like Clapton, Beck, and Hendrix popularized single-note leads as the gold standard of rock guitar playing, Keith Richards comes out of an earlier, arguably more profound, tradition—one that blurs the distinction between lead and accompaniment, foreground and background. For him, the guitar is not so much a phallic symbol as a magic wand—something with which to cast a spell. You may not be fully aware of all he's doing on any given track, but subtract Keith Richards and the magic disappears.

Dartford, Kent, was not a particularly magical place in 1943, when Keith Richards was born on December 18. The Second World War was on and, like many parts of London, Dartford took its share of hits from German aerial bombers, the damage temporarily halting this working-class suburb's gradual ascent to something like middle-class stability. The first and only child of Bert and Doris Richards, Keith was born in the midst of an air raid. He'd later joke that Hitler had him marked for death.

But early domestic conflict affected him more deeply than world affairs. Childhood conflicts with Bert may well be the root of the guitarist's lifelong problem with authority. However, solace was to be found in Doris's love of music, which was transmitted to the child from the womb onward.

"My mother played me jazz and all the standards," Richards recalls. "That stuff just drips off me. She played me Sarah Vaughan, Billy Eckstine, Ella Fitzgerald, Louis Armstrong, Duke Ellington, Count Basie. It's just that rock and roll came along and totally diverted my attention."

Keith remembers the transformative moment of his first exposure to rock and roll, in the form of Elvis Presley's "Heartbreak Hotel." "That led me in," he says. "You didn't hear a lot of rock before that. I was thirteen or something, listening to the radio under the sheets when I was supposed to be asleep. I remember it was coming from Radio Luxembourg, and in England the signal kept shifting. I remember actually daring to get out from under the blanket and walk around the room trying to get the signal back without waking up the parents."

Before rock and roll put its frenzied spell on British youth in the mid-fifties, young Keith had shown surprising—in retrospect—avocations for Boy Scouting and, at age twelve–thirteen, singing soprano in the Dartford Technical College school choir. Choir practice provided a legitimate excuse for getting out of class, until Keith's voice broke and he was ejected. He has said that the expulsion left him with feelings of disenfranchisement and disentitlement that deepened his distrust and resentment of authority.

In short, he was a prime recruit for the rock-and-roll rebellion when that cataclysm took hold of Britain in the mid-fifties. His destiny was further shaped in 1957, when his maternal grandfather, Gus Dupree, a local socialist community leader, taught him the rudiments of guitar. A third fateful moment occurred in the spring of 1961, when Keith reconnected with Mick Jagger. The two had first met as students at Wentworth Primary School, but now, on the threshold of manhood, they renewed their acquaintance on a railway platform in Dartford. They were both en route to classes, Keith at Sidcup Art College and Mick at the London School of Economics.

"Mick could be classified as middle class," Keef notes. "I come from the projects."

Jagger was carrying two record albums that caught Richards's attention, *The Best of Muddy Waters* and Chuck Berry's *Rockin' at the Hops*. Neither record was commercially available in England at the time. The plucky, ever-resourceful Jagger had acquired them by writing directly to Chess Records in Chicago. Richards was aware of Chuck Berry—obsessed with him, in fact. But he hadn't yet heard Muddy Waters.

Here in the digital era, when virtually any piece of music or scrap of information about a musical artist is immediately accessible via the Internet, it's almost impossible to conceive how monumentally important a rare import album was in the sixties for lovers of musical forms such as the blues and folk music. A whole culture coalesced around the quest for recordings by artists like Muddy Waters, whose name possessed an almost mythological resonance for acolytes of the genre. It fostered a powerful sense of camaraderie.

So in the history of rock and roll, Mick Jagger turning Keith Richards on to Muddy Waters was a revelation on the order of Watson and Crick's 1953 discovery of DNA. The world would never be the same. It was also the start of a lifelong bond between Jagger and Richards that has been, in many ways, more powerful than the bonds of marriage. Over fifty years after its first formation, Mick and Keith's friendship, turbulent love/hate relationship, and creative and business partnership still excites major media interest any time there's a falling out, reconciliation, or announcement that the two will reunite for another Rolling Stones album or tour.

"I'd already started playing with the Stones. And the attractiveness of playing in smoky bars and clubs, which is what I really wanted to do, far outweighed making tea in an advertising agency, which was the preferred and natural course of what somebody should do after they'd studied three years in art school."

One immediate effect of that railway platform encounter in '61 was that Richards joined Little Boy Blue and the Blue Boys, a band that Jagger had formed with Dick Taylor (who would go on to play with the Pretty Things), Bob Beckwith, and Allen Etherington. A primitive recording of this seminal outfit survives.

"It was that period when you're sixteen or seventeen," Richards explains. "When Bob Beckwith's parents happened to be away, we could use his room. 'All right, my mom and dad are going out.' And we'd bring the amps over and the Grundig [tape recorder]. Inevitably, we'd get busted, 'cause we'd still be playing when mom and dad would come home."

In the way of fledgling bands, Beckwith and Etherington soon dropped out. And in the summer of '62, Jagger, Richards, and Taylor joined forces with the Rollin' Stones, a band led by blond blues enthusiast and all-around free spirit Brian Jones, said to be the first person to play blues slide guitar in Britain. Also in the lineup was pianist Ian Stewart and drummer Mick Avory, who would go on to many years on the drum throne for the Kinks.

In the half year or so that followed, what we now think of as the classic Rolling Stones lineup coalesced. Taylor dropped out, soon becoming a Pretty Thing. Bill Wyman joined on bass in December '62. The last, but indispensable, piece of the puzzle fell into place when Charlie Watts joined as the Rolling Stones' drummer for life. At first, it was very much Brian Jones's band. Already a gifted multi-instrumentalist, he had started out on sax before moving over to guitar and getting pretty wicked on blues harmonica as well.

Ian Stewart was another key member of the early lineup, and would become a lifelong kingpin in the Stones operation. A blunt-spoken Scotsman a little older than the others, Stu was also one of Britain's best traditional blues pianists.

"The first rehearsal I went to that ended up being the Rolling Stones was above an old pub in Soho in London," Richards reminisces. "I get there and ask the landlady, 'Rehearsal?' And she sends me upstairs. As I walk up these creaky old stairs, I hear this barrelhouse piano playing and think, 'Man, I'm in Chicago!' I'd never been to Chicago at that point, but that's how it sounded to me. And the only guy there was Ian Stewart. He sort of set the whole thing up, 'You guys, you should play.' And in a way, it's his band still."

By this point, Richards, Jones, and Jagger had taken up residence in a squalid flat at 102 Edith Grove in Kensington. Hard as it is today to imagine anywhere in Kensington as squalid, the trio lived in dramatically straitened circumstances with flatmate James Phelge, legendarily subsisting on a staple diet of boiled potatoes and whatever else they could scrounge. The existence was almost monastic, marked by poverty and austerity, if not chastity. Although, according to Richards biographer Victor Bockris, Keef was not overly interested in the ladies in this period, as least as compared with Jones and Jagger. His focus on the music was absolute and indeed quasi-monastic in its level of devotion and fervor.

Edith Grove is where Jones taught Jagger to play blues harp. And where Jones and Richards formed a profound guitar bond based on an intensive study of blues records, particularly those of Jimmy Reed and Muddy Waters. Both of these bluesmen favored a two-guitar approach, Reed often performing and recording with co-guitarist Johnny Taylor, and Waters working with Jimmy Rogers, Luther Tucker, and Pat Hare, among others.

These pioneering electric bluesmen were tapping into the fluidity and freedom of earlier acoustic blues guitar traditions of the thirties. But acoustic blues, as exemplified by Robert Johnson, was principally a solo performance medium. A singer-guitarist like Johnson accompanied himself, switching effortlessly between rhythmic backing and single-note lead lines. The dual-guitar aesthetic of electric blues introduced a division of labor between lead and rhythm, albeit a very loose and lively division. By studying this style intently, Keef formed an approach to guitar playing solidly based on the principle of teamwork.

"When Brian and I started playing together," he says, "we were listening to Jimmy Reed and Muddy Waters. In both cases, you had two guitars weaving around one another. Brian and I would play those things so much—because that's the way you have to do it—that we knew both parts. So then we got to the point where we got it really flash and we'd suddenly switch. The one doing the lead picks up the rhythm and the one doing the rhythm picks up the lead."

There was an undercurrent of interpersonal drama in Jagger, Richards, and Jones' *ménage à trois* at Edith Grove (*ménage à quatre* if you add Phelge, who would soon lend his surname to the Rolling Stones' music publishing company, Nanker Phelge). Jagger perceived a threat in Jones' tight musical relationship with Richards—although Mick would of course prevail in the end. The situation was exacerbated by a fairly extreme level of poverty. Between university and day jobs, Jagger, Watts, Wyman, and even Jones all had some kind of career alternative should the music thing not pan out. But Richards's only recourse, solace, and chance for survival was the music—a true desperado.

"Brian had a day job working in a department store," Keith recalls. "I was the only one who was unemployed. Mainly because I'd only just left art school. I was in no rush to get a job. And if I learned to how to live on virtually nothing, I could take my time and think about it. I remember leaving art school and I had my folder, my presentation. Because when you leave art school, the normal course is you brought your stuff in a folder around to all these advertising companies in London. They'd look at your stuff and say, 'Can you make a good cup of tea?' Their attitude was, 'Oh, here comes another one. I did a couple of those, and after the third one, I took my folder and stuffed it in the garbage.

"I'd already started playing with the Stones. And the attractiveness of playing in smoky bars and clubs, which is what I really wanted to do, far outweighed making tea in an advertising agency, which was the preferred and natural course of what somebody should do after they'd studied three years in art school. But compare that to playing in a club, where these people would come down to watch us play, and they'd pay me! That was far more attractive. The thing is, in art school, you're taught how to advertise yourself. I kind of knew a bit of that game. So when I had to meet these advertising people, I figured, 'Screw you. You'll end up using my music in your ads,' which they did."

By mid-'63, the fledgling Stones became a fixture on the London blues scene, revolving around clubs like the Ealing Jazz Club, Ken Coyler club, and Thursday night blues *soirees* at the Marquee. They became the house band at the Crawdaddy Club, run by Giorgio Gomelsky, an Eastern European hipster and London scene maker who also took on the Stones' management. Along with groups like Alexis Korner's Blues Incorporated (for whom Watts sometimes drummed) and the Cyril Davies All-Stars, the Rolling Stones became poster boys for what Gomelsky had termed BRB, or British rhythm and blues, playing for an audience of purists and devotees that had morphed out of the earlier trad Jazz scene in Britain.

But with the ascent of the Beatles, something much bigger was brewing in the UK. Beatlemania, with its large, hysterical fan base of screaming teenage and preteen girls, had triggered a worldwide interest in young guitar groups from the UK. While the Stones were coming out of a different city and different set of musical influences, they got pulled into the pop group frenzy when their management was taken over by sharp-dressed, fast-talking former Beatles publicist Andrew Loog Oldham and businessman Elliot Easton. Under this guidance, they recorded their first single, a cover of Chuck Berry's "Come On," on May 10, 1963, at London's Olympic Studios, which would become the site of many of the Rolling Stones' greatest recordings. When "Come On" made it onto the UK charts, the Stones' fate was sealed.

"We were a blues band!" Keef protests. "But we made just one little pop—or semi-pop—record and it became a hit. And suddenly chicks screamed at you and you're not really playing for anybody anymore. You can't be heard over the screaming. You're just wondering how you're going to

MICHAEL OCHS ARCHIVES/GETTY IMAGES

get off this stage and safely to the next town before you get ripped to shreds. The gig became that for several years, really. 'How we gettin' in, and how we gettin' out?' Because you knew the show would last ten or fifteen minutes—if that—before mayhem broke out. Chicks fainting, being carried off. I mean, unbelievable. You'd get chicks flying out of balconies like, 'I love youuuu. . . .' Crash. Broken ribs and worse.

"And all the while you're thinking, 'But I'm a blues player!' But what I realized was, 'Ay, if you want to get into a recording studio and have all the time you want and be able to dictate your own stuff, you gotta be famous, man. Otherwise, you're never gonna get in.' So it's not like I didn't want to be famous. I realized pretty quickly that in order to do what I wanted to do musically, fame had to go along with it. That's the only way you could get unlimited studio time and rule the roost and be able to do what you wanted, instead of somebody telling you what to do. So we figured we might as well be famous for a bit. But nobody expected it to last. We thought, a couple of years. That was the lifespan of everything back then."

From the start, the Stones got positioned as the dark, Dionysian antitheses to the sunny, Apollonian pop appeal of the Beatles. In part, this perception was fostered by shrewd PR work on the part of Andrew Loog Oldham, who knew how to make media events out of episodes like a 1965 fine issued to Jagger, Richards, and Wyman for urinating in public, on the wall of a gas station. Being presented as crude, unwashed, and loutish was a sure way to get the attention of the British public. But, hey, they had to take a leak, it was late at night, and the gas station was closed.

Also, while the Beatles were packaged as a collective phenomenon in their early years— four cheeky lads in matching collarless suits—the Rolling Stones always appeared as five distinctive individuals. While they reluctantly agreed to wear matching checked suits for the July 7, 1963, TV debut on Britain's *Thank Your Lucky Stars*, Jagger, Richards, Jones, Wyman, and Watts generally all dressed differently, each cultivating his own distinctive fashion sensibility.

Not that there wasn't an element of calculated marketing savvy behind their image as well. Oldham had dropped Ian Stewart from the lineup because he didn't possess sufficient teen appeal, relegating him to the role of road manager and studio pianist. Nonetheless, the Stones rough-edged cool tended to resonate more with male fans and the kind of female fans usually described as "bad girls." And no matter what your gender, if you were in your teens or twenties in the sixties, you had to declare yourself as either a Stones or a Beatles person. There was no two ways about it.

The distinction wasn't all marketing either. The Rolling Stones' sound was appreciably more raw than that of the Beatles. Where the Fab Four's recordings were produced by a classically trained musician (George Martin), early Stones sides were produced by a PR/managerial hipster/huckster (Andrew Loog Oldham). The real outsider, alternative, proto-punk appeal of the Rolling Stones lies in that murky, reverby Keith Richards/Brian Jones guitar sound. It had the allure of the forbidden—a dark morass where you weren't quite sure what was going on, or who was playing what, and, hey, isn't one of those guitars a little out of tune?

Early on, Richards played a thinline hollow-body Harmony Meteor guitar while Jones performed on a solid-body Harmony Stratotone. Richards also favored a '61 Epiphone Casino, also a thinline hollow-body electric, before acquiring his now legendary '59 Gibson Les Paul Standard retrofitted with a Bigsby vibrato tailpiece. "That was all out of the early English guitar hustling fellows," he says, "Ivor Mairants and all of those stores. 'Got a noice one 'ere fer you boys. . . .' There were only three or four [guitar] stores in London. There wasn't a big network of guitar freaks in those days. There weren't a lot of great guitars around at that time in England. For people like us, the Beatles, and Eric [Clapton], it would take us a long time to find a really good guitar. A lot of thieving went on, I think. A lot of re-spraying."

Richards remembers that '59 Les Paul as "just the best guitar available at that time. It was my first touch with a really great, classic, rock-and-roll electric guitar. And so I fell in love with them for a while."

Another key distinction between the Beatles and the Stones is that the Beatles wrote their own material from pretty much day one, whereas all of the early Rolling Stones hits—"Come On," "Not Fade Away," "Time Is on My Side," "It's All Over Now," "Tell Me," "Little Red Rooster"—were all covers drawn from R&B, blues, and early rock-and-roll repertoire. The more mature perspective of many of these R&B songs, particularly the ballads, made the Rolling Stones seem a little more adult than the Beatles, which was another key element of their appeal. Although one of their biggest early hits, "I Wanna Be Your Man," was a song that Lennon and McCartney wrote for the Stones at Oldham's request.

But if Richards and Jagger weren't a born songwriting team like Lennon and McCartney, they were essentially forced to become one by Oldham. Not that they needed much prodding. They penned a hit, "That Girl Belongs to Yesterday," for Gene Pitney, and another, "As Tears Go By," for Marianne Faithfull. The latter song would later become a hit for the Stones as well, and Faithfull would become Jagger's girlfriend.

Jagger and Richards's ascendancy as hit-making tunesmiths shifted the balance of power within the Stones in their favor, eclipsing Brian Jones, who was a gifted multi-instrumentalist but had little or no apparent aptitude for songwriting. The Stones had been his band in the blues club days; he'd even come up with the name, the Rollin' Stones, adapting it from a song by Muddy Waters. But all that came to a halt when Mick and Keith learned to put words and music together in a catchy way. They would go on to become a songwriting team of tremendous range and poignancy, equally adept at raunchy rockers, tender ballads, arch social commentary . . . you name it.

The first great Jagger-Richards-written Stones hit was "Satisfaction," released in mid-1965. This all-time rock classic typifies many of the patterns of Mick and Keith's modus operandi as songwriters. Richards will often come up with the basic song idea, signature guitar riff, or lyrical hook line, leaving Jagger to draft a full set of lyrics and memorable vocal melodies. The idea for "Satisfaction" famously came to Keef in a Miami hotel room while the Stones were on tour. Legend has it that he woke up in the middle of the night, hummed the main riff into a portable cassette recorder—a new, high-tech device at the time—and went back to sleep. When he discovered the recording the next morning, he had no recollection of having made it during the night.

Along with Richards and Jagger, another key contributor to "Satisfaction" was the Gibson Maestro fuzz tone, a brand-new piece of technology at the time and one of the first guitar-effects pedals. It provided the perfect tone for Richards' brilliantly minimalist three-note guitar hook when the Stones came to record "Satisfaction" at RCA Studios in Hollywood.

"When I wrote the song, I didn't think of that particular riff as being the big guitar riff. That all fell into place when Gibson dumped on me one of those first foot-pedal boxes—the fuzz tone. I actually thought of that line more as a horn riff. The way Otis Redding ended up doing 'Satisfaction' is probably closer to my original conception for the song. It's an obvious horn riff. But when this new toy arrived in the studio from the local dealership or something, I said, 'Oh, this is good. It's got a bit of sustain, so I can use it to sketch out the horn line.' So we left the track and went back out on the road. And two weeks later, I hear it on the radio. I said, 'No, that was just a demo!' The answer was, 'No, it's a hit.' At least Otis got it right. Our version was a demo for Otis."

The Stones would do a lot of recording in the States, particularly at RCA, during the mid-sixties. Their first trip to the land of their musical heroes in 1964 was like a pilgrimage to Mecca. One of their first stops had been Chess Recording Studios at 2120 Michigan Avenue in Chicago, where their icons Muddy Waters, Chuck Berry, and Howlin' Wolf had all recorded. The Stones had their first meetings with all three on their first visit to Chess. They also cut some tracks of their own while there.

"We got there and said, 'Wow, these are what we call studios!'" says Keith. "After what we'd been used to in England—a little hutch with egg boxes on the wall."

The material abundance of America, particularly as compared with postwar Britain, also gave Richards an opportunity to expand his guitar collection and palette of guitar tones. Fender amps caught his ear—both the earlier tweed models and the blackface Fenders that were current at the time.

"When I got to America," he says, "I was in the land of the free . . . and Fenders! There was something about the little herringbone [tweed] box. I fell in love with Fender amps real quick. I think the first one I got was a Twin. Bought me a Twin and my first Fender Telecaster. The Strat I didn't work on until a bit later. But there was something about James Burton's stuff on the Telecaster that was so beautiful. Brian Jones had a deal with Vox and used AC30s, which are a damn good amp. But you don't want two guitar players in a band playing out of the same amp. It's too much the same sound."

The first few years of the Stones' career were one prolonged endurance test, marked by endless touring, often in less than ideal conditions. And once the hits started coming, there was considerable pressure to keep them coming. The group had to sandwich writing sessions and recording dates in between live engagements.

"At the time, the long-playing record album was a very small market," Keith explains. "Top of the line, very expensive. So you had to make a hit 45-rpm single every two or three months. That was draining, man! You had to write and record an A side and a B side every twelve weeks. You've just got "Satisfaction" to number one and you're going 'whew.' Then suddenly there's a knock on the door, 'Where's the new one?' And Mick and I were like, 'Hey, this is like Tin Pan Alley. This is the Brill Building. Here we are in a cubicle, just made number one, and we've still got the hounds on our tail saying, 'Where's the follow-up?' Shit, man. It was nonstop."

While the media painted the Stones and the Beatles as rivals, the two groups actually enjoyed a cordial relationship, to the point of coordinating the release times of their singles so as not to cut into one another's sales. "The Beatles would say to us, 'Hey, how's your new one coming?'" Keith recalls. "'Well, we're still overdubbing; it's gonna take a while.' 'Okay, so we'll put ours out. Is that Okay?' 'Cause we never wanted to clash. There was a deal between us, almost."

Despite the challenges of the mid-sixties pop game, the Rolling Stones acquitted themselves beautifully. Their brilliant string of mid-sixties singles—"Satisfaction," "Get Off My Cloud," "The Last Time," "19th Nervous Breakdown," "Paint It Black," "Mother's Little Helper," "Have You Seen Your Mother, Baby, Standing in the Shadow"—are one of the best studies of two-guitar rock-and-roll interplay available anywhere. And indeed many of these tracks became standard garage-band repertoire, shaping the sound, style, and aesthetic of many post-Stones guitarists.

"I realized pretty quickly that in order to do what I wanted to do musically, fame had to go along with it."

The intense woodshedding that Richards and Jones had done back in Edith Grove finds its fruition in these glorious rock singles. The juicy parts were doled out more or less equally. Jones takes the lead line on "The Last Time," for example, while Keith plays the main riff on "19th Nervous Breakdown." While Keith tended to stick with his Les Pauls and Epiphones in this period, Jones was notorious for switching guitars. At various points, he was closely identified with the teardrop-shaped Vox Phantom and with the Gibson Firebird, among others.

"He was always searching for another sound," says Richards. "Sometimes it was, 'Oh, make up your mind what sound you're going to have, Brian!' 'Cause he'd keep changing guitars."

But Richards wasn't exactly averse to experimenting with odd axes. Take "Mother's Little Helper," for instance.

"The main riff is a twelve-string with a slide on it," he explains. "It's played slightly Oriental-ish. This was even before sitars [became popular]. It just needed something to make it twang. Because otherwise the song was quite vaudeville in a way. And it was just one of those things where somebody walked in and . . . 'Look, It's an electric twelve-string!' It was just some gashed-up job. God knows where it came from or where it went. But I put it together with a bottleneck and we had a riff that tied the whole song together. There's probably some gypsy in there somewhere."

Increasingly, Brian Jones's restless imagination shifted away from the guitar as he began experimenting with a colorful panoply of other musical instruments. He is one of the pioneers of what would later be called world music, embracing sounds from Morocco, India, and various other exotic locales. Meanwhile, salt-of-the-earth Keef took on more and more of the core guitar work. And, of course, he and Mick had the songwriting thing locked down. In a way, acting as the Stones' instrumental colorist was one of the few roles left available to Jones.

"Brian got into the sitar and used it on a few things, like 'Paint It Black,'" Richards recalls. "I found it an interesting instrument—the idea of the sympathetic strings underneath that resonate to the one [sic] string on top. But as far as actually playing it, leave that to the Indians. There's just something about the strings—they were too thin. But Brian loved to dodge around and play dulcimers, mandolins, and things like that. As a musician, he was very versatile. He'd be just as happy playing the marimbas or bells as he was the guitar."

Perhaps more than any other Stone, the blond-haired Jones—with his peacock fashion sensibility, blissfully stoned demeanor, and dandy-ish, dilettante proclivity for picking up exotic new instruments and putting them down just as quickly—came to personify the Swinging London years of 1966–'67. But all the Stones were drawn into that glittering, wide-open social scene wherein pop stars were key members of a new elite, mingling with painters, poets, models, theater folk, gangsters, and aristocrats. Richards's circle of close friends grew to include the influential art dealer Robert Fraser and trendsetting aristo Prince Stanislas "Stash" Klossowski de Rola. It was a time of free experimentation not only with music, but also with drugs, sexuality, Eastern mysticism, and the pursuit of freedom and innovation in all aspects of life and art. Socially, if not geographically, Keef was a long way from Dartford.

"To me, it was no big deal," he says. "There was no real class consciousness, especially at that particular time. England was really shrugging off World War II, at last, by the end of the fifties and early sixties. Everybody was quite willing to change the playing field socially. I certainly had no aspirations in that particular area at all—society or anything like that. But it all happens quite naturally when those people want to know you. We found we were attracting a lot of artists and people like that. I don't know if it was just the novelty or whatever. I have a feeling that there were certain people among the higher strata of English society who felt they were being left behind. And suddenly they wanted to go slumming. Or at least their kids did. Some, God bless them, came from very good families—although I wouldn't have known it. They wanted to be like us. In a way, it was kind of a reverse society. Who do we let in? Rather than us trying to get into their society."

Where Jagger has always been something of a social climber, Richards has always been resolutely egalitarian. It's a key element of his charm.

"Within a short while, especially if you're on the road as a musician, you learn to take people as they come," he says. "It doesn't matter where they come from or anything like that. Because you're always in and out, always traveling. And you learn to size up people really quickly, without even realizing it. You fall into the knack of doing that. Because there's always a barrage of people around, and you're here today, gone tomorrow. So you become pretty astute at sizing up who's who and what's what. If you don't, you get into trouble! The rest of it doesn't matter. You don't have time to go into people's backgrounds. And then two weeks later somebody says, 'Oh, when you spent the night with Princess So and So . . .' And I'd say, 'Who? What do you mean?' 'You know, that chick Lucy.' 'Oh, is she a *princess*? She didn't act like it."

Keith's flat in South Kensington's Cheyne Walk, not too far from Edith Grove actually, became a favorite haunt of London's beautiful people. Some who have stayed there insist that it actually is haunted—by ghosts, that is. Although Keith denies this.

"It's an old house and it creaks a lot. Old houses do that. A lot of people were really stoned there. No doubt they had heightened imaginations. But quite honestly, in the time I lived there, that never occurred to me. If it was haunted by anything, it was haunted by the cops!"

Years later, in 2002, I asked Richards if he'd ever seen a ghost. "Only my own, pal," he replied.

The '66–'67 period also is when the groupie scene began to attract media attention, becoming something of a professional institution within rock. "I'm sure there's been groupies for two thousand years, at least, if not longer," Keef ventures. "But '66–'67 is when you started to see the little teams of chicks who would set themselves up as professional groupies, the Butter Queens and the Plaster Casters. The Butter Queens, yeah. They did loads of wonderful things with butter, apparently. But they didn't butter me up. I used to avoid them like the plague. Anything that smacked of professionalism. 'We've got a plaster cast of Robert Plant's cock. Would you like to add yours to the collection?' No thanks. I never wanted to be part of any collection. But mind, there were some great individual operators out there. There's always wonderful ladies out there. At the end of the day, that's the payback."

But while Richards could take Swinging London's embodiment of *la dolce vita* in stride, all that freedom had a debilitating effect on Brian Jones, who fell deeper and deeper into a kind of perpetual, drug and alcohol induced, walking coma. His decline may have been exacerbated by his romantic involvement with the Italian-German actress and model Anita Pallenberg, whom he had met in Munich in 1965. Blond and beautiful, Pallenberg had a penchant for fast living and black magic. Her relationship with Jones is said to have been mutually abusive. Pallenberg would soon end up with Richards, a turn of events that had a further devastating effect on Jones.

Following the Stones' early blues period, Jones had a second creative flowering during the '66–'67 era with albums like *Aftermath*, *Between the Buttons*, and the Stones' stab at psychedelia, *Their Satanic Majesties Request*. The wistful recorder on "Ruby Tuesday," the courtly dulcimer on "Lady Jane," or the folkloric "comic relief" deployment of the very same instrument on "Cool, Calm & Collected"—these are among Jones's finest, and final, contributions to the Stones. Shortly after these works were recorded, he declined quickly, leaving more and more of the Stones' musical leadership to Richards.

"Brian was an impressive musician," Keef says. "Very promising. He was a sax player to start with. He was dedicated to playing in the early days. I'll tell you, what screwed Brian up was fame. Something snapped in him the minute that came. That was always the strange thing for the rest of us in the band too. But the rest of us tried our best not to get carried away. Like, 'Hey, come on, this might not last long, baby.'"

But the Swinging London lifestyle exacted a toll on Jagger and Richards as well. On February 12, 1967, the police raided a small party at Redlands, Keith's home in Sussex, which resulted in drug possession charges for Mick and Keith. The bust was a tabloid sensation. Marianne Faithfull was discovered by police wearing nothing but a fur rug. Meanwhile, Jones was the target of a separate drug bust.

To escape the pressure of their impending court dates, Richards, Jones, and Pallenberg embarked on a motor trip to Morocco. This proved to be more disastrous in many ways than the drug charges. Pallenberg began the journey as Jones's girlfriend. But by the time it was over, she was Keith's. The turning point was narrated by Richards in what has become the most infamous and frequently quoted passage of his 2010 autobiography, *Life*:

"In the back of the Bentley, somewhere between Barcelona and Valencia, Anita and I looked at each other, and the tension was so high in the backseat, the next thing I know she's giving me a blow job. The tension broke then. Phew."

Richards had embarked on what would be one of the key romantic relationships in his life. But in the process, he effectively put an end to one of the greatest guitar partnerships in the history of rock music. Friction had been developing between Richards and Jones for quite some time. And now there was no way to repair the damage.

"Of course the thing with Anita—then it became personal," Richards says. "I suppose that was the irrevocable break. But shit happens, you know? Yeah, I stole his girlfriend. But only because he was trying to beat her up. I tired to stop it because he was coming off worse. He had two broken ribs and a broken wrist, and Anita just had a black eye. Anita and I fell in with each other. By then, Brian had become pretty unbearable to live with. Which is probably why I ended up with Anita."

Richards traces the origins of his rift with Jones to a situation that had developed months earlier. "Toward the end of '66, I started to get this impression that Brian thought it was his band. He started to get ideas. I think he wanted to be Mick Jagger and couldn't understand why he wasn't. Given the pressure of work at the time, nobody had time to think about it. We just said, 'Oh, Brian, piss off.' Which I think he probably took more personally than it was meant. Alienation started to set in. This grew more intense in the period of *Between the Buttons*, when we had time off and everybody suddenly wasn't on everybody else's back. As I say, we figured, 'It's just pressure. Brian will get over it.' But he kind of separated himself from the rest of the band in a way. It was only a slight nuance at the time. But it grew more intense over the next couple of years."

In the summer of '67, Jagger and Richards were jailed briefly before being acquitted of drug possession charges stemming from the Redlands bust earlier in the year. Jones was also acquitted of his drug charges, on grounds of mental instability. A little less than a year later, the Rolling Stones released a single that seemed to encapsulate all the turbulence they'd passed through, the "crossfire hurricane" of drug busts and busted relationships.

With "Jumpin' Jack Flash," released in May 1968, the Stones kicked free of their psychedelic phase and intruded a lean, mean, bluesy new sound that adumbrated the tonalities of their late-sixties, early seventies golden period. The tough sound of the music and violent imagery of Jagger's lyrics also caught the militant mood of the times, as youth culture's hippie idealism gave way to radical politics and activism. The tune is another sterling example of Jagger and Richards's inspired mode of songwriting collaboration:

"'Jumpin' Jack Flash' comes from this guy, Jack Dyer, who was my gardener: and old English yokel," Keith recalls. "Mick and I were in my house down in the south of England. We'd been up all night. The sky was just beginning to go gray. It was pissing down raining, if I remember rightly. Mick and I were sitting there. And suddenly Mick starts up. He hears these great footsteps, these great rubber boots—slosh, slosh, slosh—going by the window. He said, 'What's that?' And I said, 'Oh, that's Jack. That's jumpin' Jack.' We had the open tuning on my guitar. I started to fool around with that. [singing] 'Jumpin' Jack . . .' And Mick says, 'Flash.' He'd just woken up. And suddenly we had this wonderful alliterative phrase. So he woke up and we knocked it together."

Richards had started to experiment with open guitar tunings during the 1966–'67 period.

"After three or four years constantly on the road, I took a little time off and started to listen to some blues again," he says. "I started listening to Blind Blake. By then, a whole lot of stuff had come out that you couldn't get in England in '61 or '62. So there was a lot to catch up on. I started really listening to stuff I'd gathered here and there. Because we'd go straight to record stores and rifle them whenever we came to America. But I never had a real chance to go through everything. So now I started studying and reading the cover notes and listening to the cats play. So I discovered, 'The guy plays in open tuning, ah!' I started to fiddle around in open D and E tunings to start with."

"Jumpin' Jack Flash" is Keef's first notable use of an open tuning on disc. "On the record I played a Gibson Hummingbird [acoustic guitar] tuned to either open E or open D with a capo," he says. "And then I added another [acoustic] guitar over the top but tuned to Nashville tuning. I learned that from somebody in George Jones's band, in San Antonio in '63. We happened to be playing the World Teen Fair together. This guy in a Stetson and cowboy boots showed me how to do it, with the different strings, to get that high ring. I was picking up tips."

To achieve a compressed distortion effect on the high-strung acoustic, Keith processed it through a Philips cassette recorder, a fairly new device at the time. The device's built-in, lo-fi compression circuitry provided a unique tonality that Richards would also employ on "Street Fighting Man:"

"At that time I was into really compressing the acoustic guitar by running through the early Philips and Norelco cassette recorders, really overloading them," he says. "They came with a little plastic mike and I'd slam that right down into the acoustic guitar. What I was after was to get the drive and dryness of an acoustic guitar, but still distort it."

As if the powerful and inventive guitar on "Jumpin' Jack Flash" weren't enough, Richards also played the booming, zooming bass track. It would prove to be just one of many great bass lines that Keef would lay down for the Rolling Stones.

In many ways, "Jumpin' Jack Flash" was the warm-up for the Stones' next album, the absolute classic *Beggars Banquet*. Eloquently announcing the band's return to their bluesy roots, the album marked a new phase in the Rolling Stones' career in many ways. It was their first collaboration with producer Jimmy Miller, who would work with the Stones on their next few discs—a series of albums generally regarded as their best work ever, consisting of *Beggars Banquet*, *Let It Bleed*, *Sticky Fingers*, and *Exile on Main Street*. On the managerial side, Andrew Loog Oldham was out of picture and New York businessman Allen Klein was in.

By the time of *Beggars Banquet*, the Stones had begun to settle into a new way of working in the studio. Gone were the hurried sessions of the mid-sixties. The album had eclipsed the 45-rpm single as rock music's primary mode of expression. And in the wake of pioneering recordings like *Freak Out*, *Sgt. Pepper's Lonely Hearts Club Band*, and *Tommy*, the rock album had come to be regarded as an art form, a carefully conceived conceptual statement on the part of the recording artist(s). This had led to a much more studied, reflective approach to recording throughout the rock scene.

Where the Stones had once taken hours to knock out a complete track, they now could spend months on a single song, trying different rhythms, approaches, and arrangements. Some band members, like Bill Wyman, tired of the long hours and endless hanging out and left the studio. So they weren't around when the crucial take went down to tape. Which is how Richards ended up playing bass on so many Stones songs. Even when Wyman was present, Keef would sometimes end up on bass.

"Sometimes I'd say, 'Bill, it goes like this,'" Richards recalls. "And he'd say, 'Why show me? You got it down. Let's make it simple. You do it.' There were never any hassles in that respect. And there's some songs where Bill plays keyboards."

The idea of working on albums for months on end also suited the lifestyle into which Keef was settling—if settling is the right word. A fiercely independent character, he's never had much patience for living by anyone's schedule, not even one of his own devising. He'd stay awake for days on end and then crash. He's a man with small regard, if not outright disdain, for the clock or calendar. He sleeps when he's tired and eats when he's hungry. He says that the notions of "three square meals a day" and "eight hours of sleep per night" came in with the Industrial Revolution as a way of making workers conform to factory schedules. Keef would have none of that. Working on music isn't labor for him, not in the exploitative sense. It's honest work and hard work. But more like a labor of love, a creative act. And how could that be regulated by a schedule? Fortunately, the Stones could now afford to book ample studio time.

A dramatic example of the band's new, expansive way of working is the powerhouse opening track for *Beggars Banquet*, "Sympathy for the Devil." A signature song for the Stones, this studio epic finds Jagger assuming the persona of Lucifer himself, taking the listener on a Devil's-eye-view tour of history, buoyed by a propulsive tribal beat. The arrangement went through numerous permutations before arriving at the conga-driven version everyone knows today:

"Mick brought that to the studio as a very Bob Dylanish kind of folk guitar song," Keith says of "Sympathy," "and it ended up as a damned samba. I think that's the strength of the Stones, or any good band. Give them a song half raw and they'll cook it."

Filmmaker Jean Luc Goddard documented the making of "Sympathy for the Devil" at Olympic Studios in London, for his 1968 feature *One Plus One*. The footage captures a dynamic Keith Richards in his newfound role as studio auteur—conducting the backing vocalists, laying down the song's unforgettable bass line, and throwing off one of the greatest rock guitar solos of all time on a Fender Telecaster. Meanwhile, a befuddled Brian Jones strums an inaudible acoustic guitar, unaware that the guitar mike isn't even plugged in.

While revisionist guitar histories invariably cite Jimi Hendrix and Jimmy Page as classic rock's masters of layering and orchestrating studio guitar tracks, Keith Richards is the often overlooked equal of both Hendrix and Page in this essential aspect of rock recording. Another standout track from *Beggars Banquet* clearly illustrates the point:

"When we went in the studio to record 'Street Fighting Man,' we just couldn't reproduce the sound of the original demo I did on cassette. So we played the cassette through an extension speaker so I could play on top of that—shove a microphone into an acoustic and overdub to that. Then we put it on a four track, played it back, and at the same time the guitar was going on, I had [session keyboard great] Nicky Hopkins playing a bit of piano, and Charlie just shuffling in the background. Then we put drums on it and added another guitar while he was doing that. And we just kept layering it.

GRAHAM WILTSHIRE/REDFERNS/GETTY IMAGES

"On 'Street Fighting Man,' there's one six-string open-tuned acoustic and one five-string open. They're both open tunings, but then there's a lot of capo work. There are lots of layers of guitars on 'Street Fighting Man.' There's lots of guitars you don't even hear. They're just shadowing. So it's difficult to say what you're hearing on there. 'Cause I tried eight different guitars. And which ones were used in the final version, I couldn't say."

The Rolling Stones seem to thrive on chaos and cataclysm. And there was plenty of it following the release of *Beggars Banquet*. On June 7, 1969, Keith and Anita—then seven month's pregnant—were involved in a car crash in Sussex. Pallenberg suffered a broken collarbone. The very next day, Brian Jones was dismissed from the Rolling Stones.

"Brian was just cantankerous—even to himself," says Richards. "I just don't think he liked being comfortable really. He wanted to be uncomfortable, to the point of death. It had become so unbearable that Mick and I had to go down and actually fire him. Which was a rotten task to do, especially with him not being in good condition. He was out of it. He got really bad about it. But at the same time, we had a band to keep together."

Jagger and Richards enlisted the help of Charlie Watts for the unpleasant scene with Jones.

"Charlie was the backup," Keith says. "We told Brian, 'If you don't pull your weight, you're not in, man. If you're not there when we're working, and you're so deliberately fucked up . . . if it's gonna be like that, we can't work, you know?' And he said, 'Oh, I've got my own plans and project, you know.' And nobody expected that in a few months he'd be dead."

But that is exactly what happened. On July 3, 1969, Brian Jones was found dead in the swimming pool at his home in Hatfield Sussex, following a night of heavy drinking. Mick Taylor, formerly with John Mayall's Bluesbreakers, was named his successor. He made his live debut with the Rolling Stones at a memorial concert for Jones in London's Hyde Park on July 5, 1969.

Five days later, Keith Richards was among those in attendance at Brian Jones's funeral. The deep bond that had been forged over hours of guitar practice at Edith Grove was now, at least as far as this mortal plane is concerned, finally dissolved. In an odd instance of cosmic symmetry, Keith's first child, his son Marlon, was born one month to the day after Jones's funeral. Keef's life was to be filled with dramatic exits and entrances—both well and ill timed—of people close to him.

"I had a lot of good times with Brian," he recalls. "He was a great player, a good guy to play with. Virtuosity is fine, but my thing has always been what two guitar players can get going together. If you get the right guy to play with, you can sound like an orchestra, if you do it right. You can cover so much ground. When you've got that down with somebody, it's always a pain in the heart when they go somewhere else. You kind of say, 'It's not possible. We do this. We *know* how to do this.' Suddenly the other one is not there."

Any doubts about the future of the Rolling Stones in Brian Jones's absence were quickly dispelled by the band's triumphant next single. Jones had not yet been laid to his final rest when "Honky Tonk Women" was released, with "You Can't Always Get What You Want" as the B side. The A-side track marked Taylor's record debut with the Stones. But, in many ways, the real star of the show was Keith Richard's electric guitar, which he'd placed in a five-string open-G tuning that would become one of his most signature tonalities. Following a cowbell and drum intro by Watts, Keef's five-string comes strutting onto the scene like one of the song's titular loose ladies, brashly stating the rhythm before breaking into a limber intro riff that sets up Jagger's vocal entry.

Jagger and Richards had originally written "Honky Tonk Women" on acoustic guitars as a country number, and would eventually perform it that way on the *Sticky Fingers* album. But it was the full-band electric version that went to the top of the charts in '69:

"Mick and I wrote it as a country song, mainly because we were in the middle of Brazil when we wrote it and only had two acoustic guitars. It was only when we got back I started realizing, 'This might go with the five-string thing.' And I got a great sound on that. Everyone's still trying to recapture that one."

Many Rolling Stones songs are impossible to play accurately or authentically without this simple tuning. You take the low-E string off your guitar. The remaining strings are tuned as follows: G, D, G, B, D. This is another tuning that Richards had discovered during that '66–'67 period when he'd begun to explore alternate tunings:

"I came across the five-string G tuning on slide guitar records first. Then we did a session with Ry Cooder and he turned me on to all these other cats, slide players. I played around with it a bit and realized you could do chordal stuff with these slide tunings. Nobody else had really done that. It was a really effective slide vehicle, but I'd never heard anyone using it from a rhythm point of view.

"Because the five-string tuning is basically three notes [G, B, and D in various octaves] you had to put your fingers in new places to play minor chords and different discords and suspensions. I started working things out in five-string tuning and that got me back into studying and transferring ideas to and from six-string tuning. With one six-string and one five-string playing, there were just interesting tonalities that happened, just because of the sympathetic ringing off the instruments."

The final piece of the puzzle fell into place when Richards discovered that Fender Telecasters were the ideal instrument for his rhythmic application of the tuning. "I realized that the Telecaster lent itself especially well to a really dry rhythm, five-string drone thing. It was so crisp and beautifully consistent. Then I realized that Leo Fender's genius was matching the amp to the guitar. If you really want a nice sound out of a Fender amp you have to use a Fender guitar with it. It's a beautiful electronic marriage. Oh, dear me, well done, Leo! That's why you made the big bucks. A matching pair. That was what really impressed me about it."

"When I got to America, I was in the land of the free . . . and Fenders! There was something about the little herringbone [tweed] box. I fell in love with Fender amps real quick."

The sonic identity and creative momentum that *Beggars Banquet* had established continued to coalesce and gain strength on the Rolling Stones' next album, late 1969's *Let It Bleed*. This is all the more remarkable for the fact that *Let It Bleed* is something of a transitional album for the Stones. It contains Brian Jones's final, if minimal, studio performances with the band, on autoharp and percussion. At the time *Let It Bleed* was recorded, however, Mick Taylor hadn't fully been integrated into the group. Consequently he appears on only two tracks.

But Keef had been carrying the full guitar weight of the Rolling Stones on his own lanky shoulders for quite some time by this point. On *Let It Bleed*, though, he really outdoes himself, stepping to the fore on his composition "You Got the Silver," and finding just the right guitar textures to accentuate the dark, death-haunted mood of keystone tracks like "Gimme Shelter" and "Midnight Rambler."

One of his principle guitars for both seminal songs was an archtop Maton, an Australian instrument that came into his possession. This guitar is responsible for the apocalyptic tremolo guitar menace that informs "Gimme Shelter." And, fittingly enough, it self-destructed right at the conclusion of the definitive take:

"It looked like a copy of the Gibson model that Chuck Berry used," says Keef of the Maton. "The thing had all been revarnished and painted out, but it just sounded great. Some guy crashed out at my pad for a couple of days, then suddenly split in a hurry and left that guitar behind. Like, 'Take care of this for me.' I certainly did. At the very last note of the take, the whole neck fell off. You can hear it on the original track. That guitar had just that one little quality for that specific thing. In a way, it was quite poetic that it died at the end of the track."

The Stones embarked on a landmark US tour in 1969 to promote *Let It Bleed*. Live rock performance had come a long way since the mid-sixties days of package tours and sliding down laundry chutes to escape being mobbed by hysterical teenage girls. The '69 tour was one of the most well produced of its time, with well-designed lighting effects and a fully professional PA. Richards has remarked that it was an adjustment for the band to get used to being able to hear themselves through onstage monitors.

The '69 tour, which would provide the basis for the definitive live Stones album, *Get Yer Ya Ya's Out*, was Mick Taylor's first American outing with the band. It was also the first time the Rolling Stones had played in the States since '66. They'd been banned in the Land of the Free before that, owing to the usual issues with drug use and "lewdness." For all these reasons, a very high level of excitement attended the entire jaunt. Concerts invariably sold out. Some markets even instituted a lottery system whereby the lucky winners got a chance to purchase highly coveted tickets to the Stones' show.

The band had put together an endorsement deal with Ampeg for the tour, so they had a backline of Ampeg amps for the dates. The arrangement also placed one of the then-brand-new Ampeg/Dan Armstrong clear Plexiglas guitars into the hands of Keith Richards. An incredibly flash instrument, with interchangeable pickups, it was a favorite of Keef's on the tour:

"The first one that Dan Armstrong ever made me was a gem," he says. "It was a beauty. It was one of the first prototypes, or first pre-production models, and you could plug those pickups in. I used it onstage quite a bit, although I don't know if anything I did on it ended up on a [studio] record. And then that guitar disappeared. They gave me two or three other ones, production models, that were like a shadow of that particular one. And then I gave up on them. I know what Dan Armstrong had going there, but I guess they probably had to cut some corners on full-scale production."

Working live for the first time with decent audio quality and a slightly less hysterically shrill—if no less enthusiastic—audience, Richards could focus on his guitar tone to a greater degree than had previously been possible. Along with the Dan Armstrong, he relied heavily on a Gibson 335 for the tour, as well as a Les Paul Jr. Both guitars would become go-to instruments throughout his career. Soon he would be carrying as many as fifteen or twenty guitars on tour. At least one from each major guitar "food group."

For the most part, the '69 tour was a triumph. But the ominous mood of *Let It Bleed* would soon prove all too prophetic. On December 6, 1969, the Rolling Stones headlined a free outdoor concert at Altamont Speedway near San Francisco, topping a bill that also included Bay Area rock bands the Jefferson Airplane, Grateful Dead, and Santana. What was meant to be a joyous gathering of the counterculture tribes became a tragedy when audience member Meredith Hunter was beaten and stabbed to death by members of the Hell's Angels motorcycle gang, who had been hired as security guards for the event.

"The Grateful Dead set that up," Richards says in the Stones' defense. "We said, 'You set the show up. It's your area. You done this before. We ain't.' So they did it through their setup, which was their alliance with the Hell's Angels. Which got a little bit too big for everybody, that one. Including the Angels."

Born of the foolishly naive hippie conviction that all outsiders are brothers and sisters—compounded, perhaps, by Bob Dylan's lyrical pronouncement that "to live outside the law you must be honest"—the decision to hire the Hell's Angels as security guards proved to be one of the most ill-advised moves in all of rock history. The biker gang had been a source of tension and trouble throughout the day. Prior to Hunter's murder, a member of the Angels had punched Jefferson Airplane lead singer Marty Balin in the face during a scuffle that ensued after the vocalist had jumped into the crowd to prevent another audience member from being roughed up by the day's security force. Altamont furnished a bitter ending for what had hitherto been a benchmark tour for the Stones. Coming right at the end of the decade, the event was, and is, largely viewed as marking the death of the late'-sixties dream of peace and love. Altamont will long be remembered as Woodstock's demonic doppelganger.

"It was a very strange time" is Richard's eulogy for the sixties. "Very volatile too. The Vietnam War. I first came to the States in '64, '65, playing for these young kids. And a few years later, you got a letter from them from Saigon and their whole world had changed. One moment they're little incipient rock and rollers. A year later they're slogging through the jungle with the Viet Cong, up to their necks in muck and bullets. And we'd get letters from them saying, 'Hey, still remember you guys.' Poor bastards. Shit. So that really wound it up in [America]. Which is why you had things like Altamont. All of the cops were in the army. There was no law. In some places in the country, the Hell's Angels were the ruling force for several years."

The Stones had escaped Altamont with their own lives intact; and it is said that what doesn't kill you makes you stronger. The band was certainly in top form when sessions got underway in the summer of 1970 for their next disc, the third installment of the Stones' golden years tetralogy, *Sticky Fingers*. Continuing a practice that had begun with *Let It Bleed*, the Stones let some of their high-profile friends into the creative process, sometimes credited for their work, sometimes not. Organ great Billy Preston, who'd also recorded with the Beatles, participated in the sessions. Richards had struck up a close friendship with American country rock pioneer Gram Parsons, whose presence is felt on the wistful hit ballad "Wild Horses," although he doesn't play on the recording. Some say Parsons had a hand in writing the song, although he isn't credited. Later on, Marianne Faithfull would successfully claim co-writing credit on another *Sticky Fingers* classic, "Sister Morphine."

By the time *Sticky Fingers* was recorded, Mick Taylor had settled into the group more thoroughly. His contribution to the album's guitar work was substantial. "Mick Taylor and I really worked well together," says Keith. "He was different to work with than Brian. I really had to refocus things. But Mick Taylor is a brilliant guitar player. Some lovely energy. Very sweetly sophisticated playing. Way beyond his years. Very crafted stuff. Lovely sense of melody."

The sessions also cemented what would become one of Keef's most enduring friendships, with sax player Bobby Keys, who'd blasted out the solo on *Let It Bleed* 's "Live with Me" and contributes significantly to the extended outro jam on *Sticky Fingers*' tour de force "Can't You Hear Me Knocking." The track also features one of Richards's most imaginative deployment of his five-string open-G tuning on the song's signature riff. The tuning serves him well on the aforementioned outro jam as well:

"My fingers just landed in the right place and I found out a few more things about that tuning than I'd been aware of before," he says. "I think I realized that even as I was cutting the track. And then that jam at the end—we didn't even know they were still taping. We thought we'd finished. We were just rambling and they kept the thing rolling. I figured we'd just fade it off. It was only when we heard the playback we realized. 'Oh, they kept it going. Okay, fade it out there. . . . No, wait, a little bit more, a bit more. . . .' Basically we realized we had two bits of music. There's the jam and there's the song."

Before *Sticky Fingers* was even released, the Rolling Stones had left England and gone into tax exile. Britain's graduated tax laws at the time required big earners like the Stones to fork over some 90 percent of their income. An onerous tax burden, combined with frequent drug busts and general police harassment, pretty much forced them out of England. The Stones had cut some tracks for a follow-up album to *Sticky Fingers* at Olympic and at Jagger's home studio. But they decided to decamp to France and complete the album there. The result would be the band's sprawling epic double album, *Exile on Main Street*. The album would be often hailed as the Stones' greatest work, and one of the greatest rock albums of all time.

"We all decided we were going to move out of England, due to great pressure from Her Majesty's government," says Richards. "So we said, 'Let's keep going. We'll do [the album] somewhere else.' And we figured, 'Oh, the south of France sounds good.' I mean, what's wrong with that?"

The early seventies were a time of heavy change for the Stones in many regards. They'd moved away from the management of Allen Klein and launched their own label, Rolling Stones Records. Mick Jagger married Nicaraguan beauty Bianca Perez Morena de Macias and settled down to a life of quiet domesticity in France, with the other Stones all living relatively nearby.

Keith and Anita had never felt the need to sanctify their union via anything as bourgeois as marriage. Their son, Marlon, was about a year and a half when they settled into Villa Nellcote, a grand French *maison* with stately neoclassical columns, capacious salons, and a killer view of the Bay of Villefranche. Built in 1899, Nellcote had been inhabited by a succession of financiers and diplomats before becoming the domicile of Keith Richards and his bizarre *ménage*.

"Anita and I went looking at a couple of places, but Nellcote kind of chose us immediately," he says. "It was just an incredible joint. It was like a mini Versailles, and it didn't cost a lot."

While the other Stones lived fairly quiet lives at home, Nellcote quickly became party central, with an endless stream of friends, friends of friends, drug dealers, celebrities, and gangsters passing through the villa's grand portals. Guitars, amps, record sleeves, stereo gear, empty bottles, books and papers, discarded foodstuffs, dogs, a tortoise, rabbit, and assorted other pets were soon all over the floors and furnishings beneath Nellcote's magnificent crystal chandeliers.

The basement at Nellcote became the Stones' recording studio by default. The original plan was to find a commercial facility nearby.

"We figured there's gotta be some decent studios in Cannes or Nice or somewhere around there, even if it was Marseilles," says Richards. "But we checked them all out and it was pathetic. This was 1971. No doubt they've got great joints there now. But then, no. It was, like, forget about it. So then it became, 'Let's rent a house and see if we can do it there.' Which is where the idea of bringing our mobile truck came in."

Now commonplace, mobile recording facilities were in their infancy in the early seventies. But the Stones, always innovators, had put their own recording truck together, initially more as an income source than for their own use.

"The truck had been doing outside broadcast TV and BBC and stuff like that," Keef narrates. "But suddenly it was like, 'We got a truck, man!' In other words, a mobile control room. Suddenly we all looked at one another and said, 'Do you think we can get away with it?' Then we couldn't find a house. So guess what? It's my basement. Talk about basement tapes . . . sorry, Bob [Dylan]."

Below Nellcote's ground floor lay three levels of basement, subdivided into chambers of various sizes and shapes. Together with Ian Stewart, Richards set about hanging microphones and carpets to control acoustic reflections. Home recording was virtually unheard of in '71. The equipment was bulky, prohibitively expensive, and thus, strictly the provenance of rock royalty like the Beatles and Stones. People didn't really know much about recording in spaces that weren't acoustically designed for that purpose. So the Stones were really moving into uncharted territory when they ventured below stairs at Nellcote.

"There were all these little subdivisions in the basement, almost like booths," Richards recalls. "So what would happen was that, for a certain sound, we'd schlep an amp from one space to another until we found one that had the right sound. Sometimes the guitar cord wasn't long enough! That was in the beginning, anyway. Because once we started to work there, my little cubicle became my cubicle. We didn't change places much. But at first, it was just a matter of exploring this enormous basement, saying, 'What other sound is hiding 'round the corner?' 'Cause you'd have weird echoes going on. 'Can you live with it?' And all that. Sometimes we wouldn't be able to see each other even. Which is very rare for us. We usually like to eyeball one another when we're recording."

Summer had come to the French Riviera as sessions got underway, which made the basement at Nellcote extremely hot and humid so that keeping guitars in tune was sometimes a challenge. The environment no doubt inspired the working title of the album under construction: *Tropical Disease*. But it's the dust that Keef recalls most vividly:

"It was a dirt floor. People walked by and there were little clouds of dust. You could see somebody had walked by even after they disappeared 'round the corner. There'd be a residue of dust in the air. It was a pretty thick atmosphere. But we weren't worried about that. Maybe that had something to do with the sound, though. A thick layer of dust over the microphone."

Despite the challenging environment, the songs came fairly quickly. Keith remembers the acoustic-driven country number "Sweet Virginia" as one of the first they worked on:

"I can't remember if that was the actual first. That would be beyond even my phenomenal memory. But I recall that Mick had 'Sweet Virginia' prepared and ready to go. I have a feeling that we'd been playing around with that one on the previous sessions. Maybe *Sticky Fingers*, or whatever. So it was a work in progress."

Another work in progress was a song initially called "Good Time Women," which soon became *Exile*'s one big single, "Tumbling Dice."

"I know we did that one fairly early on in France, because I remember the weather," Richards says. "The basic idea was already there. But it took a while for it to turn into 'Tumbling Dice.' We were stuck for a good lyrical hook to go with this really great riff. So we left it in abeyance for a bit. And then I think Mick came up with the title 'Tumbling Dice,' although he may have got it from someone else, ha!"

The evolution of "Tumbling Dice" is a classic example of the Jagger–Richards songwriting partnership at work. It also exemplifies the way the Stones will often allow a track to develop over time, recording and re-recording it repeatedly and often in many different locales. "You know if you chase a song far enough, you're gonna corner it—like a rat!" Richards laughs.

But the pace was generally brisk down in the basement at Nellcote. "Sometimes we'd get two tracks in a night down there," Keith says. "And then there'd be other times when we'd be three days on one song."

The work schedule was fairly regular, the guitarist recalls. "Charlie Watts was living a long way away, a six- or seven-hour drive, for some reason. But then drummers are quirky, you know. So we'd generally work for four days a week. Five at a push. But the weekends would be off. So it was bank or factory time."

Various Stones would sleep over at Nellcote from time to time. But occasionally inspiration struck when there was less than a full band complement around the place. Which is how Richards's signature track "Happy" came into being.

"It was pretty early in the afternoon," Keith recalls. "Jimmy Miller was there checking on the previous night's session tapes. I said, 'Oh shit, I've got an idea, Jimmy.' He said, 'Well, just lay it down with the guitar.' So I start laying it down and suddenly Jimmy's behind me playing the drums. He came down from the truck and I hadn't even noticed. I'm just hammering away, figuring this thing out. Suddenly I hear these great drums behind me and now it's starting to rock. It's one of these 'three feet off the ground' feelings. And then, suddenly, I hear this baritone sax and there's Bobby Keys honking away. Suddenly it's becoming very happy."

Even the song's lyrics sprang from that initial inspiration. "Most of 'em anyway, in some garbled form," Keith clarifies. "The whole idea was there. 'I never kept a dollar past sunset . . .' That was all there."

The preeminence of "Happy," at the top of the album's third side, coupled with the preponderance of great Keef guitar hooks on *Exile* have led some observers to describe the disc as "Keith's album." But the guitarist is having none of that:

"I don't really get that," he says. "Mick was incredibly involved. Look how many songs there are, and he wrote the bulk of the lyrics. He was very involved. I don't think I was putting in more than anybody else. Charlie was amazing. Everybody was in great form."

Exile does contain some of the most sympathetic guitar teamwork between Richards and Mick Taylor ever committed to disc. They mesh seamlessly, almost telepathically, on track after track. With the exception of "Happy" and possibly "Ventilator Blues," Richards left the bulk of the slide guitar work to Taylor.

But where Taylor's leads can stand out a little too assertively on some earlier Stones recordings—particularly the live *Get Yer Ya-Ya's Out*—here he's dug in deep, roiling along with Keef and fully integrated into the guitar juggernaut. Perhaps this is a factor of the album's ad hoc recording circumstances, combined with the fact that Taylor had been a Stone for about two years at this point and was settling in. Maybe by living close by and actually sleeping over at Nellcote on many occasions, Taylor had fallen into sync with Richards on some elemental level—in much the same way that women living under the same roof will start to menstruate at the same time.

"I also think it was because we were writing songs on the spot," Richards says. "So I automatically fell into doing the chording and figuring out the whole thing. Which gave Mick Taylor a freedom. How does it go? Nobody knows. Mick just came up with line after beautiful line. What a player, man."

Exile is also awash in great guitar hooks based around Richards's signature five-string open-G tuning. It is the secret weapon behind riff-mad classics like "Rocks Off," "Tumbling Dice," and "Happy."

"In a way, with a lot of the five-string stuff on *Exile*, I'd just found that space," Keef says. "You're listening to me in school!"

For a few magic months at Nellcote, everything seemed to fall into place. With sax player Bobby Keys and trumpeter Jim Price right on the premises, the horn charts on *Exile* are a deeply organic part of the music, rather than an overdubbed afterthought, as horn parts all too often tend to be.

"I think that's another one of the beauties of the album," says Keef. "The fact that the horns are actually playing with the band. There is something to be said for having it all in one room. Bobby and Jim were amazing, 'cause they had to make up their parts virtually on the spot. The songs were coming out two or three a night. Sometimes I'd lay an idea for a song on them at the end of a session, early in the morning, so they'd have it in their heads by the time they got back the next day. There were only two of them, a sax and a trumpet. But Jimmy played great trombone as well, so we'd double them up till they became a section."

With so many extraordinary musicians passing through Nellcote, the list of those who were there but *didn't* play on Exile is as amazing as the roster of gifted players on the disc. John Lennon stopped by at one point, drank a bottle of red wine, and vomited. Gram Parsons and his girlfriend, Gretchen, were long-term house guests. In many ways it's surprising that Parsons never made it onto a Stones recording, as far as anyone knows, given that he and Richards were so close. But Keef puts this down in part to feelings of rivalry and jealousy on Mick Jagger's part, the same phenomenon that had left Brian Jones out in the cold:

"If I have a friend, and Gram was my friend, Mick sometimes gives off a vibe, you know," says Richards. "Like, 'You can't be my friend if you're his. It could be a bit to do with that.'"

While a party atmosphere reigned supreme at Nellcote, the basement recordings were a somewhat separate world from the 'round-the-clock debauch taking place upstairs and in a small adjacent guesthouse where the roadies were residing. "Upstairs was a continual ball, if you know what I mean," says Richards. "Unfortunately the Stones were rarely involved, 'cause we were busy working."

But every party has its price and painful morning-after hangover. And on October 1, 1971, burglars got into Nellcote and made off with somewhere between eleven and seventeen guitars (accounts vary), purportedly in retribution for money not paid to dope dealers who had been supplying guests at the villa. This is one memory of Nellcote that's less than happy for Richards, who lost several of his most prized instruments:

"My favorite stolen guitar was a 1964 Telecaster," he says. "It had a lovely sound. I just got used to that one, you know? To me, I can play almost any Telecaster, but the more you play just the one, the more it becomes attached to you. I almost went into a blank after the guitars were stolen. I didn't want to think about it. But I slowly started to build up a new collection since then. I haven't lost one since. I learned my lesson. Don't leave them hanging around on a Saturday night!"

But the loss of these guitars brought others to the fore. Richards had recently acquired a 1953 Telecaster while on tour in the American Midwest. An avid reader of history and literature, he named this guitar Micawber, after an irascible character in Charles Dickens's novel *David Copperfield*. Generally set up for five-string open-G tuning, this instrument would become one of Keef's most iconic guitars, perhaps the best known of them all. But he's also very fond of a '54 Tele he calls Malcolm and also keeps in five-string open-G tuning.

"They always start with M," he laughs. "One is like a feather. The other one, you sink into the ground when you pick it up. I think the heavy one is Micawber."

Just about every notable rock-and-roll junkie has a tale of guitars going missing, and Richards is no exception. It's well known that he and Pallenberg were heavily into heroin during their tenure at Nellcote. In one famous incident, the couple were so out of it that they accidentally set fire to their bed. Observers have marveled at Richards's ability to be as creative and prolific as he was during the making of *Exile* while seriously strung out on dope.

"I found that [heroin] didn't inhibit whatever it was I wanted to do," he says. "If I thought it was diminishing me or that I wasn't putting my fair share into the music, then I'd have been off the stuff right away. And that's a fact. I'm a funny kind of guy. I've got a metabolism you wouldn't believe."

Still, as the glorious Mediterranean summer gave way to winter's chill, the idyll at Nellcote was clearly drawing to a close. The local police were starting to get ugly and the Stones' phenomenal creative streak was wending toward a natural conclusion. Richards remembers "Casino Boogie" as one of the last *Exile* songs to fall into place:

"I think when we got to 'Casino Boogie,' Mick and I looked at each other and just couldn't think of another lyrical concept or idea for the song." At that point Richards recalled another great junkie artist, the novelist William Burroughs:

"I said to Mick, 'You know how Bill Burroughs did that cut-up thing—where he would randomly chop words out of a book or newspaper and then try to sort them up?' That's how we did the lyrics for 'Casino Boogie,' and that was Bill Burroughs's biggest influence on the Rolling Stones."

At the end of November, barely one step ahead of the police, the Stones decamped for Los Angeles. Working at the historic Sunset Sound studio, they began laying overdubs onto the tracks they'd cut at Nellcote. Billy Preston lent his formidable piano and organ talents to "Shine a Light." Pedal steel ace Al Perkins imparted a tearful country lilt to "Torn and Frayed." Upright bass player Bill Plummer left his mark on no fewer than four tracks: "Rip This Joint," "Turd on the Run," "Just Wanna See His Face," and "All Down the Line." A phalanx of backing vocalists added loads of soul and gospel grandeur. Among their ranks, on "Let It Loose" was none other than Mac Rebennack, better known as the celebrated New Orleans pianist and singer Dr. John:

"He just walked in," Richards recalls. "Mac Rebennack's like that. If there's music going on, in one way or another, he's gonna get his ass in there. I love the guy."

By the time overdubs were completed, there were too many tracks in the can to do a single album. And so the Rolling Stones joined the Beatles, the Who, Jimi Hendrix, and other classic rockers who have left the world with a monumental double-album statement.

"The fact that the Beatles had done it probably gave us a sense of, 'Oh, there is a precedent,'" says Richards. "But our point was that we'd put down this body of work and when it came to chopping it down to one album, nobody could agree on which songs to cut. After a while, Mick and I looked at each other and said, 'This is impossible. How about a double? This is all one piece. It's gonna be unique just because of where it was recorded and the way it was recorded.' We sort of nodded at one another and said, 'Let's got for it.' Which gave us hell from the record company. 'Aw, the public hates double albums.' And all of that. But we insisted."

Richards adds that mixing the album was daunting, "Only from the point of view that there was so much of it. Mixing a double album was different than mixing a single album. So we were going into uncharted territory. Mick and I would look at one another and say, 'How many more songs to go?' Mopping our brow, so to speak. But I can't remember it being that difficult, actually. I think we were so intimate with the tracks by then that listening to the overdubs and mixing it just put the icing on the cake. I remember it as being a very joyous couple of weeks. We were all on top of it. Jimmy Miller . . . all of us, we all knew what we were doing. It was just a matter of watching it fall into place. It was one of those rare things, a perfect mixing session."

Sequencing the album, however, was more of a chore. As mentioned previously, much of *Exile*'s magic lies in the way the songs flow from one to the next. But that magic didn't just happen spontaneously.

"Trying to get the track order down was murder, actually," Richards laughs. "I'd be sending cassettes to Mick in the middle of the night—putting my version of what the order should be under his door. I'd come back to my room and there'd already be a cassette under my door with his version of what it should be. 'Hey, Mick, that's pretty good, but you've got four songs in a row in the same key. We can't do that!' You'd come across all these weird little problems that you never thought of. It was like making a jigsaw puzzle. By the time I got the final version, I didn't give a shit anymore!"

While the music on *Exile* is a product of that summer in the south of France, LA's late-seventies aura of faded Hollywood decadence provided a lot of the inspiration for the album's packaging and conceptual framework. The "Main Street" referenced in the title was a seedy thoroughfare in downtown Los Angeles, which harbored a Chinese restaurant that the Stones liked to frequent at the time. The black-and-white front cover images—a bizarre and vaguely disquieting assortment of showbiz freaks and geeks from days gone by—were snapped from the walls of a LA tattoo parlor by photographer Robert Frank. All these elements contributed to a wistful *fin de siècle* mood that permeates the album package.

"I suppose at that particular period, the early seventies, everything else had run out of steam—the Beatles and whatever," related Richards. But at the same time, what was picking up slowly then was stuff like Zeppelin. A whole new energy came in from another generation. There was a lot going on. As I think about it, the Stones were on a roll. So we just followed it."

But no roll can go on for ever—not even rock and roll, and not even when it's the Stones doing the rolling. Despite Richards's protestations of being able to handle any intoxicant, heroin would have a significantly negative impact on his life and creativity as the seventies wore on. People often wonder how he managed to live through this period of heavy heroin use. Most junkies don't survive. Richards attributes his survival to the careful regulating of his dosages of the drug. He says he resisted the classic addict's temptation to take "just a little more" for a bit of an extra high. But still one wonders how carefully one can regulate doses of street dope. Keef's wealth and fame generally gave him access to the purest, highest quality junk available, but not always.

"When I was doing smack, it was actually very rarely on the road," he says. "I would clean up to go on the road. I just didn't want to have that hassle of looking for stuff in strange towns. Which kind of fooled me in a way because I thought, 'Oh, I can stop any time I want.' But of course the minute the tour ended—boom—I'd say, 'Oh, it's time to *relax*.' And I'd go straight back in."

In '72, Keith and his family moved into a hotel in Lake Geneva, Switzerland, while Anita checked into a Montreux clinic and gave birth to the couple's second child, Dandelion Angela Richards, who in later life would adopt her middle name as her given name. Controversy surrounded the birth. Was Keith or Mick the actual father? Dandelion Angela was entrusted to Keith's mom, Doris, who raised her. Her birth mother was heavily addicted at the time and in no fit state to fulfill the full range of maternal duties, particularly given the peripatetic nature of the Richards household during the early seventies. Increasingly as time went on, the necessity of staying one step ahead of the law became a key motivation for frequent changes of location.

In November '72, the gloriously dysfunctional Richards family arrived in Kingston, Jamaica, for sessions at Byron Lee's Dynamic Sound Studios that would result in the Stones' next album, *Goat's Head Soup*. This was the first visit to the island for Keith, who became fascinated with a then-new form of Jamaican music called reggae.

"I lived there just as it was kicking off," he says, "just as *The Harder They Come* was showing in every movie house in Jamaica and [Bob Marley's seminal album] *Catch a Fire* came out. I mean, I was into ska and rock steady before that. But I just happened to be there when there was the big reggae explosion. There was a lot of energy behind it. A lot of cats working, a lot of fun down at Studio One and Dynamic Sounds in those days. So much great stuff—Delroy Wilson, Gregory Isaacs, all those guys."

Upon landing in Jamaica, Richards and his family had checked into the Terra Nova Hotel. But Keith would soon pay $147,000 for Point of View, a mountaintop estate overlooking Cutlass Bay near Ocho Rios. From then on, a part of his heart would always belong to Jamaica. He formed close friendships among the island's musicians and Rastafari brethren, a link that would lead to his participation in a 1997 recording of traditional Rastafarian Nyabinghi chants by a group of his friends, including the reggae star Justin Hinds, he dubbed the Wingless Angels. A second volume of recordings followed in 2010.

At first glance, Keith Richards and Rastafarianism might seem an odd pairing. Rastas, for the

most part, are deeply religious people whose sole drug is marijuana, which they view as a sacrament. Alcohol and harder drugs like heroin and cocaine are frowned upon. Richards, on the other hand, is a free spirit who never met a drug or a drink he didn't like. But he seems to feel a kind of outsider kinship with his Rasta brethren. And there is a rarely glimpsed spiritual dimension to Keef that emerges through his Rasta connection. In 2002, I asked Richards if he is a religious man:

"Spiritual," he quickly responded, "but not religious. And it's a very nebulous spirituality. I wouldn't care to put a name on it. I don't want to place any bets. [American game show host accent] 'Oh, you picked the wrong god. So sorry, it's Allah!' No, I'll take the larger point of view. Hey, give thanks and praises, whoever you are, wherever you are, whatever you are. I never got a postcard from anybody that left this life. Maybe they don't sell stamps up there. I don't know."

Goat's Head Soup was released in 1973. Following the astonishing succession of *Beggars Banquet*, *Let It Bleed*, *Sticky Fingers*, and *Exile on Main Street*, *Goat's Head Soup* seemed a disappointment, despite the success of the singles "Angie" and "Doo Doo Doo Doo Doo (Heartbreaker)." The Stones were entering a period that seemed in some ways a return to the early-sixties era when albums would contain a few hit singles, fleshed out with a selection of lackluster filler tracks.

There was a general sense at the time that they'd lost their edge. They were no longer as young as they once were and suddenly seemed a little less dangerous. Critics accused them of settling into a kind of middle-aged complacency. While much of their work would continue to be superb, and they would continue to command a massive and devoted fan base, the overall cultural impact would never be quite the same.

On December 12, 1974, Mick Taylor announced his departure from the Rolling Stones, a decision that felt like a betrayal to Richards. "I never understood why he left. He's always been a bit restless and a little uneasy inside his skin. But I enjoyed playing with him. I learned a lot from him. We learned a lot about guitar playing from each other. His tone and touch and his melodic ideas wow me. When he left, I just hoped he'd go on to bigger and better things than he did. I thought it was an impetuous move, an ill-considered decision. I had no desire to see him go. We were lucky after losing Brian to get another guy. Mick and I were working real tight, and then it was, 'Oh no, not again.'"

The Stones commenced auditions for Taylor's successor but, behind the scenes, that guitarist had in fact been all but chosen. In April '74, Richards had begun hanging out with former Faces guitarist and Jeff Beck Group bass player Ron Wood, staying at Wood's home to work on the latter's solo album and sitting in with Wood's band for a few London dates in mid-July. Jagger began courting Wood as well, another manifestation of the sense of jealousy and competitiveness that sets in whenever anybody gets too close to Keith. In a songwriting session, Jagger and Wood came up with the Stones' anthem "It's Only Rock 'n Roll (But I Like It)," a bold declaration of the band's core values, which would appear on their *It's Only Rock 'n Roll* album.

But Wood's full acceptance into the Stones would be a gradual process, starting with denials of rumors that he was the band's new guitarist, progressing to announcements that he'd be filling in on guitar for the Rolling Stones' 1975 tour of the United States, followed—at last—by full acknowledgment, in February 1976, that Ronnie Wood was indeed a full-time member of the Rolling Stones.

In Wood, Richards had found a friend, musical partner, and guitar counterpart comparable to—if not quite the same as—Brian Jones. "Woody" was also a much more suitable party partner for Keef than the reticent Mick Taylor. Also unlike Taylor, and more like Jones, Wood had never been particularly invested in single-note blues-guitar leads. In many ways, Woody was equally as adaptable as Keef, capable of putting down the guitar entirely and picking up the bass guitar in the service of Jeff Beck on the latter's seminal *Truth* album, and acquitting himself admirably in that role. Richards would often describe his and Wood's easygoing lead-rhythm interplay as "an ancient form of weaving."

"Oh, he's a lovely guy," says Richards of Wood. "I'm impressed by everything he does. He's a great guy to play with, and a great guy to hang with. You get two guitars and Ronnie Wood in a room and the rest of the world will go by."

Not long after Wood's formal acceptance into the Stones, Anita Pallenberg gave birth to her and Keith's third child, Tara Jo Jo Gunne Richards. Tara is the name of a Tibetan Buddhist long-life deity, but also the name of Brian Jones's friend Tara Browne, who had died in 1966. The protracted middle name, Jo Jo Gunne, was taken from the title of a Chuck Berry tune. Tragically, the nomenclatorial link with Jones's departed friend proved all too prophetic. The child died some two months later, the victim of a mysterious crib death. Keith was on the road at the time, one of the deepest regrets of his entire life.

Ron Wood made his album debut with the Stones on their 1976 disc, *Black and Blue*, a record that initiated a series of dance-oriented recordings by the Stones. This artistic direction was precipitated by two factors: the mid- to late'-seventies ascendancy of disco as a predominant pop music genre, and the parallel ascendancy of Mick Jagger as uncontested leader of the Rolling Stones during Richards's period of severe drug dependency and personal crisis. One of the world's greatest dancers, Jagger was a regular habitué of dance clubs like New York's Studio 54.

The Stones' disco period reached its height with the single "Miss You" from the band's seminal latter-day album *Some Girls*. Not surprisingly, the song does not rank high among Keith Richards's favorite Rolling Stones tracks:

"That was basically Mick's song," Keef dismissively asserts. "Mick said, 'Let's try this disco shit out.' I think he'd been to too many night clubs, actually. The guitar riff basically just suggested itself from the melody Mick was singing. I just shadowed that and ran it behind the voice. It's just a piece of fun, that song. It can get really funky if you get the right tempo and slam it in. Basically you're sitting on Charlie on that."

But while "Miss You" and *Some Girls* ruled the charts, Richards's life was spinning more and more out of control. On February 27, 1977, he'd been charged with possession of heroin for the purpose of trafficking in Canada. In that country, the offense carried a potential life sentence. Keef had been busted many times on drug-related and other charges, but this was serious shit.

It was the start of a two-year ordeal. Richards was placed on probation, in return for which he performed a series of benefit concerts in Canada, featuring the Rolling Stones and Keef's side band with Ron Wood, the New Barbarians. He also underwent addiction therapy, the "black box" treatment that had helped Eric Clapton, Pete Townshend, and others overcome heroin addiction. Kicking heroin while also worrying whether or not he would spend the rest of his days in jail can't have been easy.

Keef would eventually walk free from the Canadian charges, but he would undergo several pivotal life changes in the process. As the eighties dawned, he began to distance himself from the Stones and explore creative life apart from the band that had brought him fame and sustained him in great wealth for many years. Along with a side band with Wood called the New Barbarians, the move away from Stones solidarity was further consolidated with the February 1979 release of Keef's first solo single, a cover of Chuck Berry's "Run Rudolph Run."

Furthermore, Richards long and tumultuous relationship with Anita Pallenberg was coming to an end. In '79, a seventeen-year-old boy fatally shot himself in Anita's bed in the Westchester, New York, home she shared with Keith. The couple had long engaged in side relationships—Keef with a string of gorgeous Nordic models—and Anita was eventually cleared of having any part in the young man's death. But the incident seemed the breaking point. That same year Keith began a relationship that continues to this day, with the American model Patti Hansen—also blond and beautiful. They married in 1983, Keef's fortieth birthday, and have two daughters, now fully grown, Theodora and Alexandra.

By Richards's own admission, quitting heroin in the late seventies was no easy task. "Once you're on it, it's really difficult to kick," he says. "But it ain't impossible. And it's not like getting your leg blown off."

But for a fiercely independent personality like Richards, the idea of being dependent on anything, or anyone, is odious. He's stated that his surrogate high when he first came off heroin was watching the disappointment in the faces of those who offered him the drug as they realized that he had the strength to refuse. Nor was the prospect of facing a live audience without the support of heroin particularly daunting for him, as it has been for other musician addicts.

"I'd faced them before," he says. "I think it was the crowds backstage, the crowds in the rest of my life, that I didn't want to face. But not the audience. I love them always. It was just the pressure of the other thing—being a star and all of that."

Richards's life began to come back into focus as the eighties dawned. The Stones scored another massive hit in 1981 with "Start Me Up," the lead track from their album *Tattoo You*. One more masterful deployment of Keef's five-string open-G tuning, the track had been floating around for years as a demo. It sat idle, buried in the archives, for years, until Jagger had the prescience to exhume it.

"I was convinced that was a reggae song," says Richards of the song that would become one of the eighties quintessential swaggering rock tracks. "Everybody else was convinced of that too. 'It's reggae, man.' We did forty-five takes like that. But then on a break I just played that guitar riff, not even really thinking much about it. We did a take rocking away and then went back to work and did another fifteen reggae takes. Five years later, Mick discovered that one rock take in the middle of the tape and realized how good it was. The fact that I missed 'Start Me Up' for five years is one of my disappointments. It just went straight over my head. But you can't catch everything."

Still, things were not what they once had been in the Rolling Stones camp. Bill Wyman left the group in 1982, on the occasion of the band's fortieth anniversary. As had been the case with Mick Taylor's departure years earlier, Richards struggled with feelings of betrayal and abandonment.

"I was pissed at the beginning," he admits, "like, 'Nobody leaves this band except in a coffin.' That's usually my attitude. I generally get over it. But, to me, to disrupt a rhythm section of such longevity and fame, and one that was such a delight to play with, is a hard one to take. I miss Bill's not being there. I enjoyed playing with Bill very much. But at the same time, you gotta respect his decision. He said, 'Hey, I just don't want to play anymore.' He'd love to be in the Stones, I'm sure, but he's an old man now! He's at least five years older than me. So he's relaxing. Hey, enjoy it, Bill. Good luck, pal!"

Richards's remark about leaving the Stones in a coffin was sadly fulfilled with Ian Steward died of a heart attack in December 1985. Another core member of the Stones team had left the fold.

"If you really want a nice sound out of a Fender amp you have to use a Fender guitar with it. It's a beautiful electronic marriage."

"But in a way, he's still with us," says Richards. "Every time we cut a track, we look up and say, 'Well, what do you think?' And we imagine his answer: 'Bloody load of rubbish.' His idea of winding you up was to put you down. 'Not bad.' That was an A+ from him. You never got better than that. Usually it was, 'Not bad for a bunch of white pricks.'"

Richards is generally a gentle, consummately hip guy. But he can get tough when the occasion calls for it. In a famous 1981 incident, he faced down reggae legend Peter Tosh, who'd threatened him with a gun. Tosh, then signed to Rolling Stones records, had taken up residence in Keith's Jamaican home while the Stones guitarist was away. He refused to leave when Keith returned to the island, saying, "If yuh come anywhere near here, I'll shoot yuh," when Richards phoned from the airport. To which Keef replied, "You better make sure you know how to use that gun, and you better make sure you got the magazine in right way round, 'cause I'm gonna be there in half an hour." Tosh, author of menacing tracks like "I'm the Toughest" and "Steppin' Razor," vacated the premises.

Keef seems to respect and even enjoy receiving "tough love" from others, certainly far more than he values flattery or obsequiousness. His ongoing relationship with rock-and-roll originator Chuck Berry is another prime case in point. Berry is one of Richards's greatest guitar heroes, if not his greatest hero, and the Stones have probably covered more of Berry's songs than those of any other artist. But Keith has certainly taken his fair share of abuse from his idol. He made the mistake of approaching Berry from behind after an 1981 show and got punched in the face for it.

Richards nonetheless came right back and agreed to be music director, bandleader, and rhythm guitarist for two concerts held in honor of Berry's sixtieth birthday in 1986. The shows, and their difficult rehearsals, were captured on film and formed the basis for the 1987 feature *Hail! Hail! Rock 'n' Roll*. In volunteering to anchor Berry's backing band, Keef had set himself up for quite a bit of verbal abuse from the volatile rock-and-roll legend, although no physical assault this time. Few musicians besides Richards could stand up to this kind of punishment—in front of cameras, no less—without cracking.

"Well, Chuck's difficult," Keef allows. "Still a gent. He's just a loner and he doesn't have many friends. That's why he has a little chip on his shoulder. But if you get him going, he's an absolute prize. Energy and knowledge. Just a lot of mood swings. He's hard to handle at times, which is why he's never kept a band together since he got rid of his original one, and never made a record that sounds as good either. He's a little cheap too, that way. That's why he plays with the worst band in town whenever he turns up. But at that same time, he's a sweet guy. Just more fragile than people like Muddy Waters or Willie Dixon."

Increasingly, all members of the Rolling Stones would engage in solo albums, side projects, and sundry other extracurricular activities. In 1987 Keith released an album, *Talk Is Cheap*, with the X-Pensive Winos, a side band he'd formed with Bobby Keys, guitarist Waddy Wachtel, bassist Charley Drayton, and Ivan Neville of New Orleans's first family of greasy, Caribbean-inflected funk, the Neville Brothers. The second Winos album, *Main Offender*, followed in 1992. Jagger has also been highly active as a solo artist with several albums to his credit, including *She's the Boss*, *Wandering Spirit*, and *Goddess in the Doorway* (which Richards refers to as *Dogshit in the Doorway*) as well as recording duets with everyone from David Bowie to Michael Jackson.

But at the end of the day, no individual band member could come close to equaling, let alone topping, the phenomenal success of the Rolling Stones. Richards's solo material tends to come off as great guitar hooks and grooves in desperate search of a melody and memorable lyrics. By the same token, Jagger's solo work tends to come across as great songs, or potentially great songs, in search of the right producer and arranger to bring them to life. Sales of their solo records tended to reflect this all too clearly. Which made a mid-eighties Jagger–Richards rapprochement more or less inevitable.

"I'd been on dope throughout most of the seventies, and I had let Mick take over quite a lot of the day-to-day stuff about the Stones," says Richards. "Over that period, Mick fell into that same syndrome as Brian, of thinking that he'd run the show. When I got off the dope, I said to Mick, 'I'm willing to take on some of the stuff again. Let me shoulder some of your burden.' And I realized that wasn't taken as it was meant. It was taken that I wanted to reassert power, or take power away from Mick. He'd gotten used to running things and didn't want to relinquish that. So I went through a very tough thing in the early eighties with Mick about shots being called without anybody being asked. And certain deals being made without anybody knowing. So you got songs like 'All About You,' to name just one. There's more on some of the Winos records.

"That whole period culminated in 1985 at the end of the *Dirty Work* album, which was our World War III. He'd become so high-handed with everybody that it was just unacceptable to me. So, okay, let's take a break and see what we can do on our own then. I think, apart from Mick, everybody's learned the lesson that Mick Jagger's really good when he's with the Rolling Stones. But when he ain't, I don't think anybody gives a fuckin' toss—whether he gets the message or not.

"It's one of those things, though. In a working relationship with somebody, there's bound to be some of that. One of the reasons Mick and I work so well together is that we're so opposite. I can work with him because I know what's good for him. And what's bad for him too. And I'd rather have him close to me. Because every time he goes off on his own, he screws up royally. It's best to keep him on a short leash."

With the release of 1989's *Steel Wheels*, the Stones entered a new and vital career phase rarely, if ever, granted rock bands of their vintage. A return to the tough, elemental rock sound reminiscent of the Stones' heyday, the album is a glowing testimony to the staying power of the Jagger–Richards juggernaut, not the mention the sustaining, primordial groove of Charlie Watts's drumming. It was also the start of a new phase of live performance for the Stones—an era of extravagant, top-grossing, over-the-top arena spectacles, replete with big-screen projections, fireworks, and a capable cast of supporting musicians, including keyboardist Chuck Leavell, bassist Daryl Jones, and the incomparable Bobby Keys on sax.

"The nineties were interesting," Keef pronounces. "There's almost five years between *Dirty Work* and *Steel Wheels*. It was a very tentative restart in a way. It was almost another chapter. *Steel Wheels* was a damned good beginning, and *Voodoo Lounge* [1994] came up from there. But things were changing in the latter half of the eighties and the nineties. Suddenly you're in that new era of MTV and synthesizers. To me, this is all starting to lose real touch with what we're all about and what basically any band is really all about. We love making records, but basically we're a live band. And the tours have been just great."

The most recent Rolling Stones album at the time of this writing is *A Bigger Bang*, released in 2005. Typically for the Stones, the album was born of difficult and unusual circumstances. Ron Wood had fallen into a wicked crack-cocaine addiction and had to go into rehab. Charlie Watts had been diagnosed with throat cancer and underwent surgery. The treatment would ultimately be successful, and Watts would eventually perform on all of the album's tracks.

"Charlie came back like a ball of fire," Richards reports. "Amazing. I guess he wanted to prove that was still alive and kicking."

I'm just doing what I do, man. You know? . . . It was only when I woke up the next day and read about it in the paper that I realized someone wanted to make a big deal out of it."

But for a few grim months, there loomed large the almost unthinkable possibility that the Stones—and the world—would lose the mighty heartbeat of Charlie Watts's drumming. These thoughts were certainly in the air when Richards and Jagger got together at the latter's home in France to write material and do pre-production for the album that would become *A Bigger Bang*. As crises tend to do, the situation with Charlie seemed to strengthen and reinvigorate the age-old bond between Mick and Keith.

"We sort of eyeballed one another," Richards recounts, "and said, 'Jesus, no buffers this time. It's just you and me, pal! Okay, you're on drums and I'll double on bass. Luckily it didn't come to that, but it was a reality check."

Richards and Jagger both played guitars for the songwriting sessions. Keith brought his black 1957 Les Paul, a '52 Telecaster for five-string, a '79 black Tele Custom, a black 335, and a 1931 Martin 000-45. The latter instrument has become one of Keef's favorites over the years. It's his living-room guitar, and he usually takes it with him when he travels—much to the alarm of vintage guitar freaks. A prewar Martin is an irresistible temptation for would-be thieves. For scratch bass parts, he used a six-string short-scale Silhouette bass that Music Man had custom-made for him.

No stranger to good guitars, Jagger played Taylor and Gibson Hummingbird acoustics, a black '65 Strat reissue from 1980, a red Silvertone, and a French Damico Tele with Barden pickups. In addition to Richards's longtime favorite tweed Fender Champ amps, both men also played through vintage Oahu amps, also small low-wattage models, originally made for Hawaiian guitars. Jagger has had a guitar role in the Stones since about 1966, notably playing rhythm on "Sway" from *Sticky Fingers*. Richards grudgingly rates Jagger "a good rhythm player, man. Especially acoustically. A little problem electrically. He doesn't quite know how to control that. But, hey, Bob Dylan's the same. But Mick's damn good. Keeps getting better."

Giving credit where credit is due, Keef adds that "Mick's a pretty good drummer too, you know. He's got a wicked backbeat, and luckily he doesn't have a lot of flash. So he just sticks to the beat."

A stripped-down, back-to-basics disc, *A Bigger Bang* is a strong entry from the Stones, fully loaded with all the band's core virtues—killer twelve-bar blues, raw rock, and well-wrought ballads. But the epic Big Bang Tour tended to upstage the disc. As Keef says, it's more about the touring these days.

And Richards is the Rolling Stone who seems to relish touring the most. Each mega-million-dollar Stones tour is preceded by media speculation as to whether Keef can persuade Mick to go out on the road again. Much of this is no doubt shrewd PR, very much in the tradition of Andrew Loog Oldham's mid-sixties media machinations. But still, Richards seems to genuinely crave the road more than others. At the end of the day, music—particularly the experience of playing music live—is Keith Richards's most tenacious addiction.

But in 2006 he suffered a setback that may well have compromised his fitness for touring and may even be a factor in the Stones' decision to postpone touring for the band's fiftieth anniversary in 2012. On vacation in Fiji, Richards accidentally hit his head hard on a tree branch while climbing down from the tree. What seemed a minor injury at first ended up requiring emergency brain surgery in New Zealand, which entailed sawing off the top of Richards's skull and later reattaching it with titanium pins. The procedure was successful and performed just in the nick of time. Any later and Keith Richards would have died. He was 63 years of age at the time—a period of life when one doesn't bounce back from serious injuries as readily as one does in one's youth.

There were reports that Keith quit cocaine in 2006. Others said that he'd gone completely straight. This he vehemently denied when I spoke with him in 2010. "Let me put it this way, the rumors of my sobriety are greatly exaggerated. Hey, I cut down a little."

The media tended to play the Fiji accident for laughs, reporting that Keef had "fallen out of a tree." Not entirely unlikely for a man who did set fire to himself on at least two known occasions during his time as a junkie. But in recent years, the legendary larger-than-life character named Keith Richards has tended to upstage the flesh-and-blood man and—perhaps more sadly—the innovative musician who dramatically shaped the nature of popular music in the twentieth century. At times Richards seems to relish, encourage, and even actively participate in this reduction of his complex personality to a media caricature, although he denies this.

"No, I never thought of that. I'm just doing what I do, man. You know? I've always had the opportunity to do it. And I never really thought it was anything unusual. It was only when I woke up the next day and read about it in the paper that I realized someone wanted to make a big deal out of it."

The swaggering "Keef" stereotype became even more firmly implanted in the zeitgeist when actor Johnny Depp based his portrayal of the character Captain Jack Sparrow heavily on Richards's mannerisms and speech patterns in the 2007 film *Pirates of the Caribbean*. "Johnny called me up before the movie came out," Keith says, "'cause I think he was doing the PR for it. And he said, 'Before you see it, you should know. . . . Okay, I admit it, I copied you.' He was in front of the game with me. I've known Johnny for years. Basically, he's a friend of my son, Marlon, and I met him that way. He has a lovely guitar collection by the way."

Richards even agreed to portray Captain Jack's father in *Pirates of the Caribbean* sequels. "Shit, I'll do anything," he said at the time. "How difficult is it for me to play a pirate? Just stick a hat on me, and a beard. Put a patch on it and we're away. Arrggghh."

A more comprehensive and realistic portrait of Keith Richards can be gleaned from his 2011 autobiography, *Life*, co-written with journalist and author James Fox. "He really put me down memory lane," Keith says of Fox. "It's weird, man. Trying to remember everything. And then going through it as the memory comes back, 'Oh God, gotta live through this thing twice.'"

But yet who—particularly among guitar players—wouldn't mind swapping lives with Keith Richards? In 1997, I asked him how many guitars he owned. His answer was typically offhand:

"I have no idea, really. If you told me three hundred, I'd believe you. If you told me nine hundred, I wouldn't doubt it either. Pierre [du Beauport, Keith's longtime guitar tech] has the whole list."

While he's slapdash about the number of them that he owns, however, Keith Richards has always been dead serious about the guitar. His deep love for the instrument is abundantly manifest in his playing, which has been a continual source of inspiration over past half century. His work has taken in vast stylistic vistas over the years, yet he's never strayed from the essential truth of the blues, R&B, and rock and roll music that he fell in love with as a teenager. Keith has often said that the best epitaph any musician can have is simply, "He passed it on." The man has certainly done that.

"The ludicrousness of a seventeen- or eighteen-year-old white kid from London saying he's a blues player, which I used to do, is like, 'Oh, get out of here.'" he reflects. "You have to go through a bit of life, I think. That's why most blues players are not that young. You gotta be able to have a few stories to tell. 'Cause it's a very strict format basically. It's twelve-bars and three chords. You can throw in a few extra, but it's such a malleable form of music that you'll never learn it all. There are so many different ways that you can angle it. It's almost a way of passing along information. It's fascinating. There's so much music out there. I love jazz, classical, and all of that. But I'm still finding out how to work my way through those twelve-bar blues. Although, yeah, I think I've lived a little more now then, when I should have kept my trap shut all those years ago."

ACKNOWLEDGMENTS

First and foremost, I am indebted to Hal Leonard's John Cerullo and Brad Smith—both for initiating this project and for the huge amount of patience and understanding they manifested as the collapse of what we once called "music journalism" and "the music business" delayed completion of this book by several years. Gratitude is also due to Richard McDonald and Mark Van Vleet of Fender Musical Instruments for their support in the early stages of development of this project and for being a class act throughout. Matt Cerullo and Rusty Cutchin of Hal Leonard and Rose Bishop of Fender also offered vital assistance, and patience, during the beginnings of this work.

Immense thanks to my beloved wife, Robin, for her invaluable advice, research assistance, copyediting, and computer expertise and for making a writer of me in the first place. Hal Leonard Associate Editor Bernadette Malavarca played a key role in bringing this work to completion, contributing eagle-eyed editing and superb suggestions throughout the endgame. Thanks to my longtime friend and colleague, *Guitar World* editor-in-chief Brad Tolinski, for keeping my career afloat all these years. This book would be nothing but empty pages were it not for the interviews graciously granted to me over the years by the many superb musicians quoted here, not to mention their peers, managers, friends, and lovers.

Finally, we all owe an ocean of gratitude to the nine guitar masters profiled in this book for so abundantly enriching our musical heritage and our lives.

—Alan di Perna, 2012